MANAGEMENT TODAY

W9-CXL-107

i

Wiley Series in Management

MANAGEMENT TODAY

SECOND EDITION

JAMES A. BELASCO
San Diego State University

DAVID R. HAMPTON
San Diego State University

KARL F. PRICE
Temple University

JOHN WILEY & SONS,
NEW YORK • CHICHESTER • BRISBANE • TORONTO

Copyright © 1975, 1981, by John Wiley & Sons, Inc.

All rights reserved. Published simultaneously in Canada.

Reproduction or translation of any part of
this work beyond that permitted by Sections
107 and 108 of the 1976 United States Copyright
Act without the permission of the copyright
owner is unlawful. Requests for permission
or further information should be addressed to
the Permissions Department, John Wiley & Sons.

Library of Congress Cataloging in Publication Data:

Belasco, James A
  Management today.

  (Wiley series in management ISSN 0271-6046)
  Includes bibliographical references and index.
  1. Management. 2. Management—Case studies.
I. Hampton, David R., joint author. II. Price, Karl F.,
joint author. III. Title.

HD31.B377 1981   658   80-28981
ISBN 0-471-08579-0

Printed in the United States of America

10 9 8 7 6 5 4 3 2 1

PREFACE

As you can see, this book is different. It is designed to allow you, the student, to participate actively in the process of learning about the major concepts of management. This book will serve as a useful learning tool because it will require you to become actively involved in the learning process.

We know that this approach will work because it has been developed and tested in the first edition. The present book is the result of what we have learned. We have added or significantly revised the chapters on Planning; Control; Staffing; Power, Influence and Conflict; and Division of Labor and Job Design. We have also added new cases, and in most instances have replaced the Management Examples with newer, more up-to-date material. In a few instances, we found that the old examples are still relevant, so we did not replace them, a case of "oldies but goodies." What we have not changed is our belief that the experiential approach to learning about management is exciting.

In a lecture course, all that you have to do is sit there and listen to the professor tell you what is important and then prepare for his tests. Following the approach used in this book, an *experiential approach,* you will have to do a large part of the work yourself. You will experience the concepts and problems of management. Then, once you have had the experience, you will be in a better position to understand what the text material is all about. You will be an active participant in your own learning process, and as a result, you may not learn exactly the same things that the person sitting next to you learns, but what you will learn will be relevant to you.

To accomplish this end, the chapters of the book are laid out as follows: First, we'll tell you *where we are going* in the chapter. Then there will be an exercise for you to participate in. Some of these exercises will have you work alone and others will have you working as a member of a group. In some you may be a leader, and in others a follower. In short, you will be able to experience the workings of management from a variety of different perspectives. The exercises are followed by some questions to help you focus on the major learning aspects of the exercises and to aid in the classroom discussion of your experiences. The questions are then followed by a body of text material in which we, the authors, state our opinions on the concepts under consideration and try to integrate your experiences with the general body of management literature. In most chapters, this is followed by a short article, usually from a business periodical like THE WALL STREET JOURNAL or BUSINESS WEEK which shows how the concept under study really fits into the business world. The last major portion of the chapter is a case. The object of the case is to allow you to test your knowledge and understanding on a situation that is as lifelike as we can make it in a book.

In short, the book is designed to take you from an experience to an understanding of that experience to the point where you can apply the lessons from that experience to other situations in the world around you. The book is designed to make learning a meaningful experience, and also an enjoyable one.

Learn and enjoy!

James A. Belasco
David R. Hampton
Karl F. Price

TO THE INSTRUCTOR

Books are used by both students and instructors. Since this textbook is written for the student, we'd like to take this space to talk to our colleagues, who will use this book in the often perilous but always challenging task of education.

This book is designed to help you, the instructor, teach management in an enriching and lively way. It's been our experience, and that of many other users of the first edition, that the variety of activities, management examples, and cases offers many educational opportunities. For the present edition, we have designed a complete instructional support package to help you choose and use the particular activity, management example, or case that will maximize the educational clout in your classroom. Included in the accompanying Instructor's Manual are:

1. Complete lecture outline.
2. Step-by-step instructions in setting up and administering activities.
3. Detailed information on alternative ways to use management examples and cases.
4. Supplemental student activities and projects.

The *Instructor's Manual* helps to carry through our central theme: people learn best by doing. The combination of our text and the *Manual* will help you to design exciting things for your classroom, which will best help your students to learn about management. That's the essential mission for us all.

Welcome to the world of *Management Today.*

ACKNOWLEDGMENTS

Chapter 1

"Mastering Management in Creative Industries," *Business Week,* May 29, 1978. Copyright © 1978 by McGraw-Hill, Inc.

Chapter 2

"The Brewmasters: Colorado's Coors Family Has Built an Empire on One Brand of Beer," *The Wall Street Journal* (October 26, 1973). Reprinted by permission of *The Wall Street Journal,* copyright © Dow Jones & Company, Inc., 1973. *All rights reserved.*

"Management by Results." From *Incidents for Studying Management and Organization* by Richard N. Farmer, Barry M. Richman, and William G. Ryan. Copyright © 1970 by Wadsworth Publishing Company, Inc., Belmont, Calif. 94002. Reprinted by permission of the authors.

Chapter 3

"An 'Old Girl Network' is Born," *Business Week,* November 20, 1978. Copyright © 1978 by McGraw-Hill, Inc.

C. B. Richards and H. F. Dobyns. "Typography and Culture: The Case of the Changing Cage," Reproduced by permission of The Society for Applied Anthropology from *Human Organization,* Vol. 16, No. 1, Spring 1957.

Chapter 4

"Work in the 21st Century: A New Way," by Jonathan Wolman. Reprinted from *The San Diego Union,* October 29, 1978. Copyright © 1978, The Associated Press. *All rights reserved.*

Chapter 5

"One Way/Two Way Communication" is adapted from *A Handbook of Structured Experiences for Human Relations Training,* Volume II, J. William Pfeiffer and John E. Jones, editors, San Diego, Calif.: University Associates Publishers, Inc., 1974.

"U.S. Firms Worried by Productivity Lag, Copy Japan in Seeking Employees' Advice." *The Wall Street Journal* (February 21, 1980). Reprinted by permission of *The Wall Street Journal,* Copyright © Dow Jones & Company, Inc., 1980. *All rights reserved.*

"The Early Work Schedule." From *Human Behavior at Work* by Keith Davis. Copyright © 1972 by McGraw-Hill, Inc. Used with permission of McGraw-Hill Book Company.

Chapter 6

"Factory Blends U.S., Japanese Styles," by David Smollar. Copyright © 1978, *Los Angeles Times*. Reprinted by permission.

Chapter 7

"Intergroup Negotiations" is adapted from *A Handbook of Structured Experiences for Human Relations Training,* Volume III, J. William Pfeiffer and John F. Jones, editors, San Diego, Calif.: University Associates Publishers, Inc., 1974.

"Teaching How to Cope with Workplace Conflicts." *Business Week,* February 18, 1980. Copyright © 1980 by McGraw-Hill, Inc.

Chapter 8

"Lost in the Desert," Copyright © Human Synergistics, 1970. Used by permission.

Chapter 9

"Waldenbooks: Countering B. Dalton by Aping its Computer Operations," *Business Week,* October 8, 1979. Copyright © 1979 by McGraw-Hill, Inc.

"Golden Transit Company" from Henry L. Sisk, *Principles of Management: A Systems Approach to the Management Process,* 1969. Reproduced by special permission of South-Western Publishing Company, 5101 Madison Road, Cincinnati, Ohio 45227.

Chapter 10

"Hospital Was Ready for Them," by Sara Schwieder. Reprinted with permission from *The Philadelphia Inquirer,* October 17, 1979.

"Long Range Planning." From *Incidents for Studying Management and Organization* by Richard N. Farmer, Barry M. Richman, and William G. Ryan. Copyright © 1970 by Wadsworth Publishing Company, Inc., Belmont, Calif. 94002. Reprinted by permission of the authors.

Chapter 11

"Greeting Cards, Incorporated," is adapted from Zoll, *Dynamic Management Education,* 2nd Ed. Copyright © 1968, Addison-Wesley Publishing Company, Inc., pages 73–80 and 216–232. Reprinted with permission.

"The Organizational Upheaval," from *Future Shock* by Alvin Toffler. Copyright © 1970 by Alvin Toffler. Reprinted by permission of Random House, Inc.

Chapter 12

"Planners and Operators" is adapted from *A Handbook of Structured Experiences for Human Relations Training,* Volume II, J. William Pfeiffer and John F. Jones, editors, San Diego, Calif.: University Associates Publishers, Inc., 1974.

"The Brand Manager: No Longer King," *Business Week,* June 9, 1973. Copyright © 1973 by McGraw-Hill, Inc.

Chapter 13

"Personnel Manager's In-Basket" from *Personnel: An Open Systems Approach,* by Charles J. Coleman. Copyright © 1979. Reprinted by permission of Winthrop Publishing Company, Inc., Cambridge, Mass.

"Employee Relations and Union Organizing Campaigns," by James H. Hopkins and Robert D. Binderup. Reprinted from the March 1980 issue of *Personnel Administrator,* copyright © 1980, The American Society for Personnel Administration, 30 Park Drive, Berea, Ohio 44017, $26 per year.

"Fiery Provocation." Reprinted from *Critical Incidents in Management,* 4th Ed., by John M. Champion and John H. Jones. Copyright © Richard D. Irwin, Inc., 1980.

Chapter 14

"False Reports." Reprinted from *Critical Incidents in Management,* 4th Ed., by John M. Champion and John H. Jones. Copyright © Richard D. Irwin, Inc., 1980.

"Morality or Ethics? Two Approaches to Organizational Control," by David K. Berlo. Reprinted from the April, 1975 issue of *Personnel Administrator,* copyright © 1975, The American Society for Personnel Administration, 30 Park Drive, Berea, Ohio 44017, $26 per year.

"Quality Control." From *Incidents for Studying Management and Organization* by Richard N. Farmer, Barry M. Richman, and William G. Ryan. Copyright © 1970 by Wadsworth Publishing Company, Inc., Belmont, Calif. 94002. Reprinted by permission of the authors.

Chapter 15

"Capitalizing on Social Change," *Business Week,* October 29, 1979. Copyright © 1979 by McGraw-Hill, Inc.

"21st Century Electronics." From *Incidents for Studying Management and Organization* by Richard N. Farmer, Barry M. Richman and William G. Ryan. Copyright © 1970 by Wadsworth Publishing Company, Inc., Belmont, Calif. 94002. Reprinted by permission of the authors.

CONTENTS

I.
INTRODUCTION

Management is a field with many approaches and few arrivals. That is, there is plenty of theory and advice on how to manage, yet skillful managers are scarce. Either all those approaches aren't so hot or there is a breakdown in learning and skill-building.

We think there is merit in such current ways of thinking about management as the systems approach, the contingency approach, the behavioral approach, and so on. We think there is merit in such current ways of studying management as the case method approach and the experiential approach. But we think that exclusive reliance on any single one of these approaches to thinking about and studying management is a mistake.

We are more interested in the arrival than the approach. And, to help you arrive at useful ways of thinking and acting like managers, we will use all the approaches and anything else we can get our hands on. But, beyond these introductory comments, we won't be talking about the approaches; we will be talking about managing.

LEARNING MANAGEMENT

People learn management in many different ways, but it is usually through a combination of work experience and some amount of study. Each of the authors of this book, for example, blended many years of business industrial experience with various combinations of full-time study, years of night courses and, eventually, completion of Ph.D.'s in Ivy League Universities. We have worked and managed in steel, aerospace, atomic energy, retail, automotive, chemical, drug, food, opera, education, and other companies. But then we turned out to be professors and, by comparison with most managers, overdid the education a bit.

However, the specific mix of studying and experiencing is probably not so important as is the use of both modes of learning. As modern scholars of the psychology of consciousness point out, the human brain's cerebral cortex has two hemispheres, each of which has a distinctive mode of experiencing reality. The left hemisphere involves the rational, analytical, intellectual, verbal, information-processing modes. The right involves the intuitive, impressionistic, whole-sensing, relational, and feeling mode.

The hallmark of traditional means of learning management in courses has been reliance on the orderly, rational mode. The pattern has been to "cover the subject." This emphasis has two problems. First, it may help people to impose order on a disturbingly confusing reality, pass tests, and so on, but it isn't clear that it helps people operate skillfully as managers. Second, it isn't all that much fun.

You can't learn swimming by sitting on the edge of the pool and committing to memory the principles of swimming. Similarly, you won't learn managing by sitting in class committing to memory the principles of managing. Of course, we can't give you a company or department to jump into and manage. But, we can arrange for you to plunge into situations and try out some managerial strokes. Just as the sudden splash of cold water, and the gulp of water instead of air can shock you with many impressions, so can various class simulations of management experience. And just as the splash and gulp in the pool can teach, so can the management action exercises.

You can see that this book is different from most textbooks. This difference in appearance reflects its design to take advantage of both modes of learning, both hemispheres of the cerebral cortex. It does so by using both text discussion, research, principles, cases, and other materials, the more familiar "rational" textbook contents, and by something quite different: experiential exercises. These will have you stand in the shoes of production worker, boss, staff or line employee, negotiator, giver and receiver of money, and decision maker under pressure. Each situation will cause feelings and impressions. Those feelings and impressions can help you learn too, especially when you have a chance to combine them with rational analysis. This book is meant to help you put it all together.

PLAN OF THE BOOK

The first thing we plan to have you do in each chapter is to jump into the pool of experiencing. Then we plan to have you climb out, and, with your fellow students and instructor, look back at what happened and consider what you can learn from it. This will take the form of a 30-minute structured exercise at the beginning of each chapter followed by discussion.

The only thing that precedes the exercise is a preview of chapter contents called, Learning Objectives. You should read it and the Instructions for each exercise before coming to class when exercises are scheduled. Reading the instructions can help prepare for the productive use of class time. And we guarantee that class time can be lively and rewarding.

So much for the first part of each chapter. A total chapter outline will typically look like this:

Learning Objectives
Activity

The Text
Management Example
A Case
Summary and Principles

The text follows the activity as you can see. It will refer to the activity, but its main contribution is to discuss, selectively, current ideas and practices. For example, Chapter 11, Organization Structure, will present several alternative types of organization structure, indicate the distinctive features of each, and describe a logical means of deciding which ones seem useful in various circumstances.

Following the text there is a management example. It might be an excerpt from *The Wall Street Journal* or *Business Week* that describes the practices of a particular company or a current problem. In Chapter 11 the example happens to be an excerpt from Alvin Toffler's book, *Future Shock,* describing the rapidity of reorganization and its effects on people. Discussion questions follow each example.

After each example, we have presented a case. It too has discussion questions to guide your analysis.

Finally, each chapter closes with a summary and principles. It reviews and summarizes the chapter contents. It also concludes with a few principles. They are not the sort of principles meant to allow you to close your mind and seal it with dogma. They are, rather, meant as observations that have value for deciding upon management practices.

CHAPTER ONE THE HOW AND WHY OF MANAGEMENT

LEARNING OBJECTIVES

At the conclusion of this chapter you should be able to:

1. Explain the reasons for the existence of organizations.
2. Describe the major characteristics of organizations.
3. Differentiate between task and social organizations.
4. Describe the basic reasons for the existence of managers.
5. List the five functions of the manager.

ORGANIZATION SIMULATION

I. Purpose
   A. To allow the students of the class to form a purposeful organization.
   B. To demonstrate the dynamic nature of organizations.
   C. To create a situation in which the students can experience some of the important aspects of organizational life.
   D. To create on-going organizations in which the students can practice some of the skills that will be presented in later chapters.

II. Premeeting Preparation
   A. None.

III. Instructions
   A. During the first week of class, when your instructor makes the time available, you should form into groups of approximately five people.
   B. Your group should then form an organization to accomplish some purpose. The purpose may be to make or sell a product or service, to engage in a charitable or educational activity, or anything else that is reasonable (and legal).
   C. Within the next two weeks (by the date your instructor specifies), your group must submit a written proposal to your instructor. Your proposal must include your goals, plans, an organization structure, and how you intend to control the organization (a form for submitting your proposal follows these instructions). Everyone in your group must sign the proposal indicating his or her agreement with the project. There is a place for your instructor to sign agreeing that if the goals are reached within the time frame specified, the group members will be qualified to pass the course. (This does not mean that they will pass the course. That will depend on the quality of whatever other work is required.)
   D. Over the remainder of the semester, work to achieve the goals that your group agreed to in the proposal.

PROJECT PROPOSAL

We the undersigned, with the approval of our instructor

_____

intend to initiate the following project that will qualify us to pass this course.

NAME OF ORGANIZATION:

GOALS OF ORGANIZATION:

DESCRIPTION OF ORGANIZATION:

PLANS:

TIME FRAMEWORK:

SIGNED:

_____   _____

_____   _____

_____   _____

_____   _____

APPROVED: DATE:

_____   _____

THE TEXT

Shared Goals What do General Motors, the Green Bay Packers, your local bank, and the United States government have in common? Quite simply, they are organizations. They are conglomerations of people who share similar beliefs about the goals of the organization and how those goals should be reached. Obviously, from the examples given and others that you can readily bring to mind, organizations come in all sizes and shapes. But no matter how large or *Division of Labor* small they are, they all have one thing in common. In order to complete the complex tasks facing them, it is necessary for the individuals in those organizations to pool their talents and to divide the work required to accomplish the goals of the organization. It is this division of labor that is basic to all organizations created to accomplish specific tasks.

Cooperation The earliest organizations were probably formed when people began to realize that they needed help in coping with their complex environment. They learned that several people cooperating were much more effective at hunting than those same people hunting individually. This was particularly true when large animals were being hunted. These first hunting groups were probably not organizations in the true sense of the word, since they were more like packs that formed only for the duration of the hunt, and there was no real division of labor within the group.

ORGANIZATION DEVELOPS

Different Skills As time passed, some of these hunters might have realized that some of the individuals in the group had different skills. Some could run fast, whereas others might be good spear throwers. Similarly, it might have been discovered that one member of the group who was a poor hunter made the best spears in the tribe. When the hunting parties began to split into groups, one to chase the game into a trap set by the other group, the simplest form of the division of labor was accomplished. These organizations became more complex as people began to specialize in spear making, cave painting, berry gathering, and any number of tasks facing prehistoric people.

Organizational As the environment in which people lived became more and more complex, *Society* the need for organizations grew. Governments formed, armies were created to conquer and defend, and business organizations began to develop, all to satisfy human needs. We now live in a society in which organizations, both business and social, play a most important part in our lives. Our society is a conglomeration of organizations that provide goods, services, and social benefits to its members.

Hagar the Horrible by Dik Browne © 1974 King Features Syndicate.

THE ONE-PERSON OPERATION

But what about the person who makes and sells leather belts or pottery or candles on the campus? Is that person an organization? The answer is NO, because there is no division of labor. There is no need for it. The craftsman is capable of buying the leather, cutting it into strips, dyeing it and tooling it, putting on the buckles, and finally selling the finished belts. He or she does all of the aspects of the job and does not take advantage of increased productivity through specialization of labor, and by the same token, does not have any problems coordinating the efforts of a number of people working on diverse but interrelated tasks.

DIVISION OF LABOR

Increased Efficiency Why don't we just do everything like the craftsman, and not worry about forming organizations? The reason, which should be most obvious to us at this point, is that in our highly industrialized society, the division of labor allows us to produce complex products more efficiently. For example, the earliest automobiles were custom built by Henry Ford and other men like him. These men could only produce a limited number of cars, and the price of these vehicles was well beyond the reach of most people. The demand for motor cars existed, but there was no way that a few people building cars by hand could satisfy that demand. As a result, the price of automobiles remained quite high.

Lack of Trained Manpower In situations where there is unsatisfied demand coupled with high prices, new producers usually enter the field. The problem faced by any aspiring auto manufacturer was that there just were not enough people around who had all of the skills necessary to build an automobile "from scratch." Not only were trained people not available, but training people in all of the needed skills would be practically impossible on a large scale. It was much

Cost Savings more reasonable to split the work among a number of individuals and train them only in that aspect of the work for which they were responsible. By splitting the work in this manner, less highly skilled workers could be employed, with a resultant savings in labor costs. These workers, after training, would become more and more efficient at their assigned tasks as they became experts in that task. Also, these highly specialized employees were *Specialization* more efficient because they did not have to continually shift from job to job, with the resultant lost time in picking up new tools and deciding just what had to be done next. As a result, the division of labor brought about increased productivity.

Increased As the newly trained workers began to bring about the expected productiv-*Productivity* ity increases, the cost of producing automobiles began to drop. This drop in costs could be reflected in increased profits for the manufacturer, or it could be passed on to the customers in the form of lower prices. The latter approach was Henry Ford's philosophy, as all productivity increases were passed on to the customer, and the price of the Ford car dropped year by year. Strange as it may sound, this actually increased the profits of the Ford Motor Company, because as the price of cars dropped, more and more people were able to afford them. The profit margin may have remained the same per car, but as more and more cars were sold, total profits increased. Increased division of labor leading to lower costs, which stimulate higher demand for the product, which in turn requires increased employment, is a fact of life in any industrialized society.

PRESSURES OF COMPLEXITY AND TIME

Another basic reason for the formation of organizations is that there are some jobs that are either too complex or take too long for any one person working alone to accomplish. Here the issue may not be increased productivity, but the accomplishment of the goal. These jobs require organization too.

Complexity There are many tasks in our society that are too complex for any one person to accomplish alone. The development of atomic energy, the building of today's modern computers, and putting a person on the moon are all tasks that were highly complex and beyond the abilities of any one person.

Let's look at the space program as an example. It took three astronauts working together just to handle the spacecraft that took them to the moon and back. The controls, even with the aid of computers, were too complex for one man to handle. And the astronauts who flew to the moon certainly didn't build the spacecraft or the rocket that launched it. The crew didn't design the hardware or the launch facilities, just as the individuals who designed the facilities didn't make the flight. The success of the project was attributable to the fact that thousands of individual specialists were organized to carry out a project that simply dwarfs the abilities of any one person.

Complexity alone is not the only factor that necessitates the formation of organizations. Often it is imperative that an undertaking be completed by *Time Pressures* some deadline, either real or imagined. If the time pressure is too intense, even the simplest of jobs may be impossible for one person to complete. If this is the case, division of labor and organization is again needed.

There are many situations of this type in all aspects of our lives. For example, a firm of architects working to complete the design of a major office building could have one person working on the design. But, if the drawings had to be completed on a deadline that made it impossible for the one architect alone to complete them, it would be necessary to split the work among a number of architects. The task was complex, but given enough time, it could have been completed by one architect working alone. The time pressure made this impossible. As you think about this point, you will probably realize that job complexity and the time needed for completion are often related. Either reason may force the need for an organization, but it is usually a combination of the two.

UNCERTAIN ENVIRONMENT

Shared Risk Together with growing complexity, humans are faced with uncertainty in their environment, and have always searched for ways of reducing this uncertainty. Our cavemen formed into hunting groups partly to reduce the uncertainty of the hunt. One individual hunting alone might not be successful, and the lack of success would be quickly translated into hunger, and if continued, into starvation. But a group of people hunting together, and sharing the results, would have a much better chance of catching something that they could share. Just because one individual did not catch anything would not necessarily mean hunger. When successful, the group would share the catch so that the unsuccessful as well as the successful hunter would have food to eat.

Modern insurance is just an extension of this concept. A group of people share the risks that no one person could accept alone. If a house burns down and the owner is not insured, that person would have to bear the brunt of the loss alone. But if tens of thousands of people share the loss, each accepting a small portion of it, no one person faces financial disaster. Insurance is just one example of how we organize to reduce the uncertainty in our environment.

TASK VERSUS SOCIAL ORGANIZATIONS

Task Organizations Until now we have concentrated our attention on organizations that were formed for the purpose of accomplishing specific tasks. General Motors exists to build automobiles, whereas the Green Bay Packers are in the business of winning football games. Of course, both are in business to return a profit to their stockholders, but nonprofit organizations can also be task organizations. Instead of producing products, most nonprofit organizations provide social services such as education, protection, and social welfare.

Social Organizations   There are, on the other hand, organizations that exist only to satisfy some of the needs of the members of that organization. Those organizations are social organizations. A bridge club usually exists to allow its members to satisfy their needs. Playing bridge is not a task to be accomplished; it is merely a way for people to get together and engage in an intellectually challenging activity.

Purpose   The way to tell whether an organization is task oriented or socially oriented is to examine the purpose of the organization. Both types of organizations come in a variety of sizes and many different forms, so purpose is the key. This is important because we do find social organizations engaging in activities that are clearly directed toward accomplishing a task. We might find a social club raising money to support a hospital or the Lion's Club collecting eyeglasses for people who cannot afford new glasses, so the determination of the type of organization depends on the basic purpose of that organization. In these cases, if the organization exists for the charitable purpose, it is a task organization, but if the charitable activity is only a vehicle for allowing the organization's members to meet and satisfy their personal needs, it is a social organization.

THE NEED FOR MANAGEMENT

Organizations form for many reasons, but the point that we should now be able to see is that they exist to serve human needs. Organizations allow people to do things, to overcome obstacles, to control their environment in ways that no one individual alone could hope to do. Through specialization of labor, coordination of effort, unity of direction, and the intelligent use of resources, organizations can accomplish what no one individual could accomplish alone.

Problems   But organizations create problems that an individual alone does not have to worry about. The first, and most obvious problem, is that as tasks are divided and individuals begin to become specialists on parts of jobs, rather than in the entire job, problems of coordination develop. The manager must split the job up into small parts and then coordinate the individuals doing the parts in order to achieve the desired outcome.

Of course, once the work is divided the manager must ensure that the tasks are accomplished in the proper order and at the proper time. One person working alone, our beltmaker for example, does not face the problem of coordinating the efforts of several people, each working on some portion of the beltmaking process. The beltmaker does not have to make sure that everyone understands exactly what has to be done, why it has to be done, and for whom it has to be done. In short, that person is not a manager, because coordinating the work of others is one of the major functions of the manager.

FUNCTIONS OF THE MANAGER

Although there is some disagreement among writers on management of exactly what the functions of the manager are, five functions seem to be more or less universally accepted. Some authors may add some others, but the key functions are (1) planning, (2) organizing, (3) directing, (4) coordinating, and (5) controlling. (See Figure 1.1.)

Planning   Planning involves decisions concerning how the organization is to accomplish its goals. This includes deciding what is to be done, how it is to be done, when it is to be done, and by whom it is to be done. Without planning, any organization will just drift along and will probably soon disappear.

Organizing   Organizing involves the preparations necessary for implementing the plans. The manager must determine who reports to whom in the organization. With jobs divided, it will be important for some individuals to be in charge of coordinating the efforts of the members of the organization, and those people must be identified and the relationships among them clearly defined. Organizing also requires that the manager define the paths by which communications will flow within the organization.

Directing   Directing involves leading and motivating the members of the organization in such a way that the overall goals of the organization can be achieved. In addition to achieving the organization's immediate goals, the manager, through leadership abilities and the ability to motivate subordinates, must satisfy the needs of the employees so that the organization can continue to exist in the future.

Coordinating   Coordinating involves ensuring that the diverse but interrelated activities in the organization are directed toward the accomplishment of the organizational goals. If the activities of the members of the organization are not coordinated, people will be working at cross-purposes, and in some cases against each other. Obviously, the larger the organization, the more complex the job of coordination.

Controlling   Controlling involves guiding the organization in the direction that it should be going in order to accomplish its goals. This involves monitoring the activities of the organization and comparing them with the organizational plans. If there is disagreement between the plans and the actual performance of the organization, it is the manager's job to make the changes needed to bring the performance in line with the plans. The alternative is to modify the plans.

Decision Making   You may have noticed, and wondered why, decision making has not been

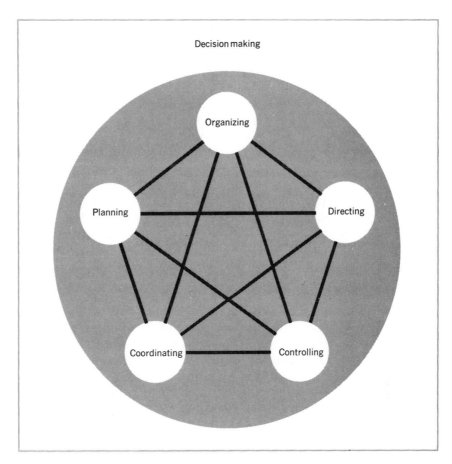

Figure 1.1   Functions of the manager.

included as one of the functions of the manager. Well, making decisions is an important part of all of the management functions, and in fact it underlies everything that the manager does. When making plans, decisions must be made about alternatives. When organizing, the manager must decide what type of organizational structure will best suit the needs of the organization. When directing, appropriate leadership styles and motivation must be decided upon. In coordination, decisions need to be made about what parts of the organization require additional help in integrating their activities with other units in the organization. When they are controlling, managers must decide if the differences between what was planned and what actually took place are important enough to worry about. The manager is always making decisions; it is more a characteristic of a manager than a function of the manager.

If our beltmaker expanded operations to the point where five people were employed; one person spending full time purchasing the raw material, another cutting the leather into strips, a third dyeing the leather, another tooling the belts, still another attaching the buckles, our beltmaker would become a manager. As such, that individual would have to plan the operations of the organization, organize the people to ensure efficiency, lead and motivate the organization members, coordinate the efforts of the five people, and control the overall activities of the organization.

Manager as Decision Maker Within the framework of the goals of the organization, profit-making or nonprofit, the manager is called upon to make innumerable decisions concerning the operations of that organization. If the organization is a profit-oriented business, the manager must consider the impact of decisions on the profitability, and ultimate survival, of the firm. If nonprofit, the organization is faced with another set of constraints: it must demonstrate its value to society. It must show that its output, in whatever form it takes, is worth what it costs to keep the organization running. Otherwise, it faces extinction.

What this means is that the manager must understand the environment in which the organization is embedded (Figure 1.2) and use the knowledge of the environment to temper organizational decisions. For the sake of clarity, we have shown the organizational environment as being composed of four sectors: physical, economic, political, and social.

Optimizing Decisions The organization that ignores its environment (in its broadest sense, not just the physical environment) is likely to be making less than optimal decisions.

Each of the areas of the environment—economic, social, political, and physical—makes demands upon the organization on a variety of matters. A

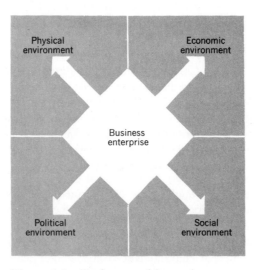

Figure 1.2 Business and its environment.

significant part of the manager's task in decision making is to read the environments, and determine how much weight should be placed on the demands from each area.

To Whom Should the Manager Listen?

Listen to whom? Well, we now have the manager listening to inputs from all of the areas of the external environment, but there are other groups to whom the manager must also be responsive.

The manager must satisfy the customers, stockholders, creditors, and employees, to mention a few. So, to whom should the manager listen? To all interested parties, and the manager must decide how much weight to give to each group's desires in making decisions that affect them.

The manager must make the firm profitable to satisfy the stockholders and to have enough money to pay creditors and employees. A reasonable product must be produced at a reasonable price to satisfy customers, the government is satisfied by the firm obeying the law and paying taxes, and society is satisfied if the organization is a "good citizen."

The role of the manager then is to steer a course for the organization that on the one hand produces a net good for society (products, profits, taxes, jobs), whereas on the other hand causes the least damage to society (depletion of resources, pollution).

Cost of In all organizations the functions of management require great effort and
Management expense. Expense in terms of money, certainly, but also in terms of time and skill. But without this outlay for managerial talent, the organization would be little more than a mob. Quite clearly then, one of the major tasks of the management of any organization is to provide the skills in carrying out the managerial functions needed to keep that organization functioning smoothly.

In the chapters that follow, we shall examine how the manager's job is translated into the everyday operations of the organization. We shall analyze the problems faced by managers, both within their organizations and in the environment in which their firms must operate. We shall accomplish this by allowing you to experience some of the problems faced by managers and to act like a manager. We shall provide text material that should assist you in integrating your experiences with what is known about managerial skills, and we shall look at the problems faced by managers in different types of organizations and at different levels of those organizations.

POSTSCRIPT

THE DEVELOPMENT OF MANAGEMENT THOUGHT

It may be true that there is nothing new under the sun, and this is certainly true about most of the material in this book. We, the authors, have not developed this book in a vacuum. Most of the material is not new, and in fact, much of it is probably centuries old. We stand at the end of centuries of thought and contemplation about organizations and what makes them tick, and we also stand at the starting point of future centuries of management thought. It seems that at this point it might be useful for you, as students of management, to see how we have arrived at this point in our understanding of organizations and management.

Prior to the beginning of the twentieth century there was little systematic development of a body of knowledge concerning management and organizations. It is true that people have long thought about these topics, and pieces of knowledge about management and organizations have appeared from time to time. But systematic study of organizations really didn't take place because there were few organizations large enough or permanent enough to study. There were some exceptions, mainly armies or religious organizations, which could have been studied, but in those the authority relationships were so clearly defined and power so absolute that little thought was given to improving the management of those organizations.

Toward the end of the nineteenth century and into the beginning of the twentieth, things began to change. The Industrial Revolution had swept through Europe and the United States, and as a result large manufacturing organizations replaced the farm as the major influence in most Western nations. This shift caused people to begin to study organizations seriously in an attempt to improve their efficiency, to improve their ability to survive, and to make them a better environment in which human needs could be satisfied.

In general, there have been four major movements, or schools of management thought in the past 100 years: Scientific Management, Human Relations, Administrative Theory, and the Behavioral schools of management thought.

Scientific Management

This major school of management thought spanned the period roughly from 1880 to 1930 and focused its attention on improving productivity through careful study of the worker, the task, and the workplace. The most famous proponent of this school was Frederick W. Taylor, often called the father of "Scientific Management." Taylor and his contemporaries, the best known of whom were Frank and Lillian Gilbreth, Henry Gantt, and Harrington Emerson, were continually striving to apply scientific principles to industry in an effort to improve efficiency and reduce waste. They assumed that individual workers could be taught the best ways to do their jobs and then motivated to do as they were told by paying them for their increased production. Taylor and his followers felt that the workers would see that it was in their best interest to be as productive as possible to maximize their earnings. In short, the goals of management and the workers would be the same, maximum production. Taylor believed that only when there was a mental revolution in which both management and the workers realized that they had to work together for their common good, could industry realize its true potential.

Human Relations

Growing out of the Scientific Management school was the "Human Relations" school of management thought. This school is generally considered to span the period from about 1930 to 1950. The major thrust of the Human Relations school came from Elton Mayo and the now famous "Hawthorne experiments." In the best tradition of the Scientific Management school, Western Electric Company carried out a series of experiments in their Hawthorne plant to determine if changing the working conditions in the plant would increase productivity. When they discovered that any change in working conditions, good or bad, applied to the experimental group produced increased productivity, the company officials turned to Professor Mayo of Harvard University to explain what was happening. Mayo's explanation was that people were not economically motivated robots, they also responded to their co-workers. Beside the need for money, people also have a need to feel that they are accepted, that they belong. Mayo and his followers believed that if management could reduce conflict in the organization, the increased harmony would increase worker satisfaction and ultimately lead to increased productivity.

Behavioral School

Growing out of the interest of the Human Relations school in the behavior of individuals within the work group, the Behavioral school developed in the early 1950s. While the Scientific Management school concentrated on the task, assuming that people were motivated by economic considerations, and the Human Relations school assumed that people were motivated by their need to feel accepted, the Behavioral school assumes that the individual is motivated by a complex variety of needs. There are many individuals associated with the Behavioral school, but probably the best known are Douglas McGregor, Abraham Maslow, Rensis Lickert, Chris Argyris, Frederick Herzberg, and David McClelland. Basically, most of these authors feel that modern organizations in their attempt to be efficient tend to break jobs down to the point where the individual has to act only in the simplest of ways. In these situations people are unable to exercise either their abilities or their intellect. They urge management to enlarge and enrich jobs to make them more suitable for worker's abilities and so that they will provide an environment in which individuals can satisfy their complex needs.

Clearly this is only a capsule sketch of these three schools of thought, and by no means did one school die when the next began to develop. There has been a continual development of the earlier schools as the later ones developed, even though the emphasis of study shifted from tasks to groups to individuals.

Administrative Theory

The one school of management thought that has spanned the entire period from 1900 to date is the Administrative Theory school. This group concentrated its study on organizations and top and middle management. Probably the best known member of this school was Henri Fayol, a French industrialist. Fayol focused on the task of management in his 1916 book, *General and Industrial Management*. He proposed 14 principles of administration as well as five elements of administration: planning, organizing, commanding, coordinating, and controlling, which you can see are the same as our five functions of the manager. In general, the members of the Administrative Theory school have concentrated their efforts on the areas of the division of labor, how authority is distributed within organizations, line-staff relationships, and the span of control of managers, or how many subordinates a manager can effectively control. As opposed to the other schools of management thought, some of the major contributors of this school were top executives in business or the military.

MASTERING MANAGEMENT IN CREATIVE INDUSTRIES

In Gulf & Western Industries Inc.'s modern New York City offices, Martin S. Davis, a conservatively clad executive vice-president, rides up in an elevator with a man wearing jeans, a sweater, and a big political button. Davis, pointedly, says nothing. "He was a Paramount Pictures executive," Davis explains. Would he have commented about the strange attire if the man had been, say, a corporate financial officer? "Probably," Davis says.

Managing people in the so-called creative industries—moviemaking, recording, mass-market publishing, and the like—simply calls for different rules, not the least of which is making people in the creative end of the business feel that Big Brother is not watching. These are industries where computerized market research does little good, where an idea session in someone's living room takes the place of a research and development laboratory, and where long-term growth and sales projections are often little better than a shot in the dark. Whether the company is an independent, free-wheeling studio or part of a giant conglomerate such as G&W or Transamerica Corp., B-school training simply falls short of what is needed. Some prerequisites for the successful manager:

- The courage to act on gut feeling and a nebulous sense of the public's tastes when assigning top dollar to film production or book promotion.
- The ability to stroke people whose egos are outsized, and whose work habits are peculiar at best.
- A willingness to bury any latent Napoleonic instincts and persuade, rather than order, creative staffers and artists to follow a profitable path.
- A strong business sense that can attend to details such as keeping warehousing costs down,

Source. Business Week, May 29, 1978.

improving distribution, and holding budgets in line without interfering with the creative process.

The odds against success are sobering. Hundreds of books are published for every one that hits the best-seller list, only one of five movies ever turns a profit, and probably less than 5% of all single records and only 20% or so of all record albums ever break even. Unfortunately, there is no surefire formula or discernible pattern. *The Godfather* pulled in $129 million on an initial cost of $6.8 million for Paramount, while *The Great Gatsby,* an $8 million endeavor for which the movie company had similarly high hopes, netted only $24 million.

Even in hindsight, most of the more truthful heads of creative companies admit that many of their biggest successes were surprises to them. "Who could have really predicted that *Bubbles* [Beverly Sills' autobiography] would sell 130,000 copies?" asks Stanley Sills, who, in addition to being Beverly's brother, is group general manager of ITT Publishing, an International Telephone & Telegraph Corp. group that includes Bobbs-Merrill Co. among its holdings. "I told my sister that if she sold 25,000 copies, she'd be an institution."

Keeping Protected

Sills recalls that about the same time Bobbs-Merrill put out *Bubbles,* it also published a book by Aleksandr Solzhenitsyn's wife, giving an inside view of what the world-famous Russian author was really like. "This was something we felt certain that people would want to read," Sills says. "I think we sold all of 8,000 copies, and we would have had to sell at least 15,000 just to break even. I guess to some extent, this business is a gamble in which you throw the dice and hope."

Of course, most of these companies have found ways to hedge their bets, at least partially. Publishing houses have sizable backlists of books that bring in respectable incomes each year—

how-to books, textbooks, and the like. Film studios have lucrative incomes from their film libraries, which bring a pretty penny from television networks, as well as from their made-for-TV series and movies. And in the case of those companies that are part of conglomerates, a corporate financial cushion helps them keep at least the semblance of an even keel. "This is a cyclical industry where you can't predict your upsides, and having a company like G&W behind you lets you protect your rear end in case of a downside," explains Barry Diller, chairman of Paramount Pictures Corp.

Diller's comment might surprise anyone who caught the full-page advertisement that ran in *Variety* magazine earlier this year condemning conglomerates as the ruination of all things creative. The ad ran shortly after the much-publicized defection of five high-level executives at Transamerica's United Artists subsidiary. Although neither Transamerica nor UA would discuss that debacle with BUSINESS WEEK, Diller and other G&W creative executives quickly came forward to cry foul for the record.

"There is zero corporate participation in deciding which books we buy," notes Richard E. Snyder, the flamboyant and feisty head of G&W's Simon & Schuster Inc. publishing subsidiary, who adds that the editorial board at S&S serves to make sure that individual editors do not get carried away on bad acquisition decisions. "I retain 99.9% of decision-making authority," Snyder says.

Diller claims an equal degree of freedom at Paramount. "We'll tell G&W we expect to put, say, $60 million on the line for film production and plan to distribute maybe 16 films this year, but we aren't expected to get more specific than that," he explains.

Turning Around

As long as their creative instincts are left unfettered, such executives seem to welcome corporate "meddling" into their businesses. Prior to G&W's purchase of Simon & Schuster in 1975, "we didn't even have a purchasing department," Snyder recalls. "We had inefficient warehousing and dingy little offices all over the city," he says. Now G&W has moved S&S into plush offices in New York's Rockefeller Center, where it is paying less total rent than it did three years ago and has slashed its accounts payable tally for supplies.

G&W gave similar help to Paramount, recalls Davis, who was with the foundering movie studio for eight years prior to its purchase by G&W in 1966. He claims that the conglomerate modernized the film distribution system, systematized methods for deciding how many prints of each movie were needed, and formed a huge and efficient foreign distribution network as a joint effort with MCA Inc. the consistently profitable entertainment conglomerate that recently made it big with *Jaws*.

Possibly most important, G&W had the foresight to cut Paramount's excess staff and take a $29 million early write-off on money-losing films. It was also G&W's influence that got the film company into the lucrative television business, helping it acquire Desilu Studios. "We had one red year, in 1969—a bad year for the entire industry. But we've been in the black ever since," Davis claims.

The Talent Search

Still, even Paramount's Diller concedes that "financial controls are not going to make our picture choices any better." So the quest for managers who feel equally at home with creative decisions and with balance sheets continues fast and furious in these industries. Most of these managers grew up in the business. "I'd never buy bringing a guy from a lumber company into the entertainment business," notes Sidney S. Sheinberg, president and chief operating officer of MCA. Although an attorney by education, Sheinberg points to his work as a radio announcer in his youth, his marriage to actress Lorraine Gray, and his 19-year tenure with MCA as proof that he has paid his dues as far as sensitivity to the creative process goes. Similarly, most heads of record companies have been in the music industry since they were teenagers, and most chief editors in book and magazine companies rose through the editorial ranks.

Companies have been putting out fewer movies and books over the last few years, however, and the supply of potential managers may be slowly drying up. Raiding among rival companies for top people is increasingly common. "The musical chairs in the movie industry are incredible," notes G&W's Davis. "In the days of second features you could build up a stable of talent, but now we just don't have a training ground." Adds Simon & Schuster's Snyder: "I spend at least 30% of my time looking for people to bring into S&S who are disciplined, almost compulsive workers and who can deal with intangibles."

Not surprisingly, money is a prime motivator for keeping top managers. Two of the three best-paid executives in the U.S. last year were with American Broadcasting Cos., with both of them grossing more than $1 million in total compensation. And industry scuttlebutt has it that the defecting United Artists executives left as much because of discontent over compensation as they did over disagreements with parent Transamerica on UA's artistic freedom.

Art for Money's Sake

But nowhere is the importance of money more apparent than with the salaries and advances paid to big names in these industries. "Creative artists" may be nonconformist, but apparently they are as interested in their own bottom line as any businessman. "I used to think artists signed contracts based on personal relationships they have with the company, but I've concluded that it almost always comes down to money," notes Arthur Mogull, president of United Artists Records Co. Companies are willing to pay top dollar because it usually comes back in higher profits, Snyder at S&S explains. "Our safest bet is the book that we pay a $1 million advance for, because the author has a brand-name image and we can be pretty sure he'll sell."

But money, while definitely necessary, is nonetheless not sufficient. All of the industry executives BUSINESS WEEK spoke with say they spend inordinate amounts of time coddling, nurturing, and otherwise "managing" creative people. "Employees may be out until 2 a.m. and not make it to work until 11, but you just have to accept certain eccentricities," notes UA's Mogull, who adds that as much as 90% of his time goes to personnel relations. "When someone hits a writing block, you have to be almost like a therapist to get him out of it," notes the manager of a five-person department of magazing writers. "You simply cannot separate being sensitive to the people from being sensitive to their work."

Artists' Relations

Handholding and persuasion are important in bringing together the artist's conception of his own best interest and the executive's gut feel for what the public wants. Dee Anthony, whose Bandana Enterprises Inc. manages such rock stars as Peter Frampton, notes that he deliberately shied from talk about record sales when he persuaded one of his singers to team up with a new band recently. "I had to convince him that there would be a chemistry that could work," he says. Anthony notes that many recording companies are beefing up artists-relations departments to shape subtly performers' careers toward salable records.

The recording companies seem to have the mix of good business sense and good personal relations down pat. Superficially, they are as informal as the offices of an underground newspaper. At RSO Records Inc., for example, the blue-jean-clad receptionist yells questions to executives in neighboring offices, a vice-president interrupts a meeting to look for a pen that turns up in his own pocket, and Albert E. Coury, the slender 43-year-old president, who sports frayed blue jeans, a football jersey, and scruffy suede cowboy boots, looks more like a disc jockey than the head of a company that projects sales of $130 million to $150 million this year. Yet he obviously knows what he is doing: RSO, with a relatively small stable of 14 acts under contract, boasts 4 of the top 10 single record hits in the country as well as 4 of the top 50 albums. "I help the artists pick their songs, but I'm aware of their temperaments, so I don't offend them," Coury says. "They like to feel like they're the only act on the label."

Even the staunchest supporters of the "business is business" theory of managing creative industries admit that flexibility and a bit of psychology are absolute necessities. "It is very important for creative types to be as informed as possible about business, and vice versa," says MCA's Scheinberg. "But you'd better not try to run by a set of hard and fast rules, because by definition you would squeeze out the very elements of creativity that make it work." And Dennis C. Stanfill, chairman and president of Twentieth Century-Fox Film Corp. but also a veteran of such "noncreative" posts as corporate finance specialist with Lehman Bros., adds that even he will let a film go over budget when artistic demands are justified. "We have strict financial controls but administer them with a degree of flexibility," he says. "You have to give quality creative people your confidence.

A Delicate Balance

That does not necessarily mean letting them run the show, of course. RSO's Coury recalls a time when he was with Capitol Records Inc. and had to persuade Paul McCartney of Beatles fame to change the song mix on a new album. "He accepted my argument," Coury says. Result, according to Coury: The album took off in the U.S., but in Britain, where it went with McCartney's original choices, sales were substantially lower.

Similarly, studio chiefs adhere to common-sense rules of thumb—holding off release of a potential big hit until Christmas or Easter, or until a current blockbuster has peaked. Still, they will grant directors and other creators consultation privileges on ad campaigns and distribution decisions, if for no other reason than to assuage insecure artistic egos. "The narcissus factor is much bigger than in other businesses," sums up Samuel Z. Arkoff, chairman and president of American International Pictures Inc., a small independent studio known both for its willingness to take chances on new talents and for Arkoff's somewhat autocratic managerial style. "Committee decisions haven't worked in this field, and I'm not particularly renowned as a handholder," he says. "But even I have to be more tolerant than if I were in some other business."

Discussion Questions

1. In what ways are companies in the "creative industries" the same as other companies?
2. In what ways are companies in the "creative industries" different from other companies?
3. What unique managerial talent is required for success in the "creative industries"?

STONEHENGE

On the Salisbury Plain in southern England stands Stonehenge, a massive monument to prehistoric man (Figure 1.3). Constructed over a period of time from 1800 to 1400 B.C., Stonehenge was constructed in three distinct stages. In the first phase, beginning about 1800 B.C., a circular ditch and bank of earth 320 feet in diameter was dug. The ditch seems to have been about 7 feet deep. Inside this circular ditch a series of 56 (?) holes were dug and then filled with chalk. These holes, called Aubery holes, may have been used for astronomical predictions, such as predicting eclipses of the sun and moon. A large stone called the Heelstone was erected outside the ditch. This stone is 20 feet high and weighs 35 tons. Standing in the center of Stonehenge on the longest day of the year, one can see the sun rise directly over the tip of the Heelstone. This is true today just as it was 3500 years ago.

The second phase, started about 100 years after the first ended, saw the setting of the Bluestones. These stones, 82 in number, were set in two concentric circles. The stones, each weighing 5 tons, were brought to Stonehenge from a quarry in Wales approximately 240 miles away. Two hundred and fifteen miles of this distance could be covered by water, but at least 25 miles of overland transportation of these stones was necessary. This in 1700 B.C.!

In the third and last phase of the construction, the Bluestone circles were partially disassembled and the largest of the stones at Stonehenge were brought to the construction site. These huge stones, called Sarsen stones, weighed up to 50 tons and were quarried from a location about 20 miles away. The Sarsen stones were used in two ways. First, there is a horseshoe-shaped construction of stones set in the center of the monument. The open end of the horseshoe faces out toward the Heelstone. The horseshoe is made up of five sets of three stones each. These sets of three stones are called Trilithons. Two of the stones stand upright while the third rests on the top as a crosspiece. These stone crosspieces weigh about 7 tons and are placed on the top of the upright stones, making them about 20 feet above the ground. The second use of the Sarsen stones was to make a circle of 30 stones that encircle the entire monument. These stones each weigh about 25 tons. It all adds up to an impressive tonnage of stones, and is even more amazing when you realize that all of the work was done with stone and bone tools.

What was Stonehenge? Was it a temple, a monument, or a tribute to the dead? No one really knows, but Gerald Hawkins in his book *Stonehenge Decoded* presents the theory that Stonehenge was really a giant astronomical computer that would allow the priests of the time to predict all manner of phenomena such as the longest and shortest days of the year, the beginning of the seasons, and even eclipses of the sun and moon, probably frightening

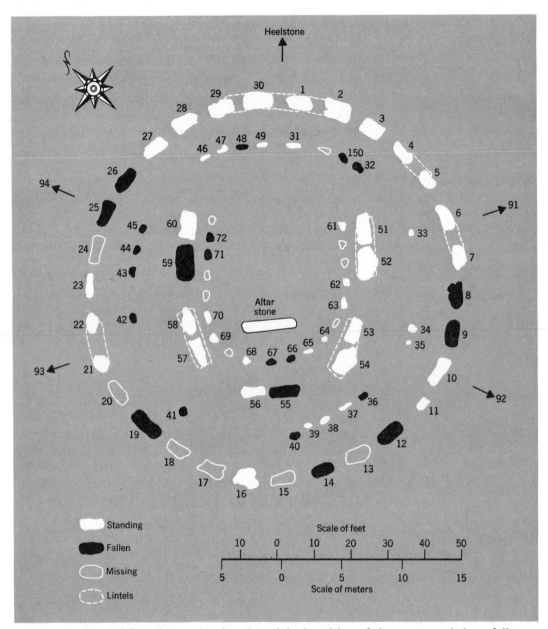

Figure 1.3   Plan of Stonehenge showing the original position of the stones and those fallen or missing. The code is as follows. Stones: 1–3, Sarsen Circle; 31–49, Bluestones; 51–60, Sarsen Trilithons; 61–72, Bluestones.

British Crown Copyright, Reproduced with the Permission of the Controller of Her Britannic Majesty's Stationery Office.

experiences for people 3500 years ago. Whatever its use, Stonehenge must have been important because it is estimated that 1,500,000 days of physical labor were required to construct this amazing monument to our prehistoric ancestors.

Discussion Questions

1. How advanced would English management have had to be to build a monument this complex?
2. How do you think the English organized their people to accomplish this feat?

SUMMARY AND PRINCIPLES

Organizations exist to serve human needs, and management exists to make those organizations work. In general, organizations allow people to complete tasks that are either too complicated for them to complete on their own, or tasks that would take too much time to do by themselves. The complexity of our society, partly the result of organizations, would be impossible to deal with without the existence of organizations. We simply couldn't satisfy the needs of people without the existence of organizations. Even in the simplest kind of living, opted for by those who "drop out" of society, organizations exist, as exemplified by the food co-op.

One of the most important characteristics of organizations is the division of labor, but this also means that they must be cooperative systems. The division of labor allows an individual to become expert at the task being worked on, and reduces the overall cost of the product being produced. In this way we are able to make automobiles that everyone can afford and at the same time have the time and energy left to do other things.

The need for cooperation creates the need for managers. The role of the manager includes planning, organizing, directing, coordinating, and controlling the different activities required to accomplish the goals of the organization. The manager must plan the work, coordinate the efforts of other members of the organization, assign responsibilities, attract and keep good people, set goals, and solve problems. In short, it is management's job to ensure that all of the ingredients are available to keep the organization operating smoothly and efficiently.

Here are some principles:

1. Organizations develop in response to the needs of people.

2. Organizations require the division of labor and cooperation on the part of organization members.

3. Division of labor leads to more efficient production as the individual members of the organization become more and more expert in their jobs.

4. Organizations cannot operate efficiently without someone acting in the capacity of a manager.

5. The five basic functions of the manager are (1) planning, (2) organizing, (3) directing, (4) coordinating, and (5) controlling.

II.
INDIVIDUAL AND GROUP

We have had a brief introduction to the nature of organizations and management. In this part of the book we will take a closer look at the human side of management.

Chapter Two, The Individual in the Organization, explores the relationship between people and the organizations in which they work. We shall bring to light some aspects of management that are critical to organizational effectiveness and personal fulfillment, but that are often not considered in any systematic way.

Chapter Three considers the unofficial realities of group processes, their advantages and disadvantages, and the contributions that group life makes to humanizing organizations.

Chapter Four, Motivation, presents a theory of human needs and develops its implications for management. It contrasts alternative management styles, revealing their effects on motivation.

Chapter Five, Communication, reveals the consequences of different patterns of communication, discusses obstacles to effective communication, and suggests means for improvement.

Chapter Six, Leadership, considers specific activities that leaders perform. The contributions of leadership to human satisfaction and organizational achievement are discussed as are alternative leadership styles and means of improving leadership.

Chapter Seven examines the way managers get and use power to accomplish their objectives. This chapter also explores the origins of interpersonal conflict in the organization and means for managing conflict.

CHAPTER TWO # THE INDIVIDUAL IN THE ORGANIZATION

LEARNING OBJECTIVES

At the conclusion of this chapter you should be able to:

1. Describe the person/organization contract.
2. Describe and illustrate the zones of acceptance and rejection for employees and employers.
3. Discuss four sources of tension between individuals and organizations.
4. Recognize and discuss three ways individuals adjust to organizations.
5. Recognize and discuss two basic ways that organizations influence individuals.
6. Discuss techniques for creating and maintaining the Person/Organization contract.

THE PERSON/ORGANIZATION CONTRACT

I. Objectives
   A. To identify and voice individual learning preferences and expectations for this course.
   B. To hear and understand the instructor's preferences, plans, and expectations for this course.
   C. To discuss and clarify these mutual preferences and expectations.
   D. To confront any differences or problems and explore means of dealing with them.

II. Premeeting Preparation
   A. Read the instructions.
   B. Use page 35 to jot down any of your own preferences or questions you wish to ask the instructor and bring these notes to class for use in discussion.

III. Instructions
   A. For this exercise the class will divide into groups of five to seven persons. Each group should appoint someone to record the group's comments and later use them in discussion with the instructor. The group should develop comments and questions on two main topics.
      1. Student preferences and expectations for the course:
         What do you hope to learn in this course (your expectations and preferences)? How is the learning you hope for to be of use to you? What can the instructor do to help you learn what you want to learn? What can you do to learn what you want to learn?
      2. The instructor's preferences and expectations for the course:
         You can ask the instructor any questions you believe relevant to effective learning in this course. For example, you might want to know such things as: the instructor's views of how people learn, how evaluation should be conducted, what part the instructor plays and believes you should play in the class, what needs to be learned, how it is related to your future jobs, and so on.

   > Time for Step A: 15 minutes

   B. The instructor will then meet with all of the spokespeople together to discuss the comments and questions students have prepared. (Students who are not spokespeople should observe this meeting. If possible, the spokespeople and instructor should draw up their chairs to form an inner circle. The rest of the class should arrange itself around them in an outer circle):
      1. The instructor's first job is to listen to and understand what you are saying about your preferences and expectations.

2. Second, student spokespersons should question the instructor's expectations and preferences.
3. Third, the instructor and student spokespersons should explore any apparent differences or problems. They should commit themselves to the agreed upon contributions by both parties.

> *Time for Step B: 15 minutes*

IV. Discussion

Your instructor will help you explore what happened in the exercise and its meaning for management.

> *Time for discussion: 10 minutes*

WORKSHEET

Student/Instructor Preferences and Expectations

Before and during the class discussion called for in the Person/ Organization Contract Exercise, you should jot down your thoughts on the topics to be discussed.

I. What do you hope to obtain from this course? Why are you here?

II. What do you plan to do to obtain what you want? What would you like the instructor to contribute to the course?

THE TEXT

The exercise you have just completed provided an opportunity to describe and share the preferences and expectations that students and the instructor hold concerning this class. Chances are the experience was a new one for you. It may have aroused feelings and questions that leave you a little uncomfortable.

After all, what usually happens when you enroll in a course is that the instructor tells you what he or she requires. Period. You are not asked to recognize your own ideas and feelings and describe them for the instructor.

You might well wonder why you were asked to participate in this mutual effort at recognizing and discussing views about the course. You might also wonder just what on earth the exercise has to do with management. The text that follows will respond to these concerns and share with you some of the lessons that follow from being aware that the relationship of person and organization involves a web of mutual expectations and preferences that can be thought of as a contract.

THE PERSON/ORGANIZATION CONTRACT

Organizational Society Our society is a society of organizations. We are born in organizations, educated in them, governed by them. We get our food from them, our clothes from them, our health care from them, our justice from them. We get our money by working in organizations. In the end we are buried by organizations.

Network of Agreements While we remain alive however, and, particularly as we function in organizations as employees, students, managers, or instructors, we are involved in a continuous flow of transactions with organizations or with people on behalf of organizations, and we make judgments about the fairness or adequacy of those transactions. Some of these transactions are economic and visible. You pay me so many dollars and I work so much for you. You give me a good grade if I do so much work of a certain quality. But this visible part is only a portion of the total person/organization contract.

The rest of it is often neither stated nor actually recognized and agreed to by both parties. We call it a contract, though, because it involves give and take. The contract is a mix of preferences, expectations, and demands the parties impose or try to impose upon one another.

Recognizing Needs The purpose of the exercise you just completed was to give you practice in seeing and expressing some of the terms of a person/organization contract to which you are a party. How good a contract is depends upon how well it meets the needs of the parties involved. So a first step for each party is to identify his or her own needs.

One quality of psychologically healthy persons is that they have a reasonably clear sense of their own feelings and ideas. They let these feelings and ideas guide them in responsibly living their lives. They tend to put it all together, as the saying goes.

Healthy organizations and the managers who represent them, for the most part, also have a clear sense of their goals. These goals guide them in defining their expectations for employees. In their own way, they have it all together too.

Unfortunately, neither individuals nor organizations are as effective in fully experiencing and seeing their true feelings and legitimate requirements as they might be, nor consequently are they as effective as they might be in entering into soundly based person/organization contracts. Many persons have great difficulty responding to the opportunity posed by the Person/Organization Contract Exercise. Used to having no say during most or all of a long history as students, they sometimes are suspicious or puzzled when asked to state their preferences or expectations for learning in this course. As one student put it, sadly, "I don't know what I am supposed to prefer." For their part, instructors who are more accustomed to announcing their expectations than to hearing those of students also find it a real challenge to listen carefully to the preferences and expectations for learning of their students.

But when the discussion gets going less inhibited students sometimes say things like this:

All I want is a grade so I can get a degree so I can get a job. How should I know what I want to learn? I don't know anything about management. You are supposed to know best. You have more information. You are paid to organize the course and teach it. You tell me what you want. What do I have to read? Will there be tests? What sort? When?

Other students say things like this:

I want to learn some principles so I can know what to do when I am a manager. I want to be able to know how to approach a problem and come up with a good solution. You can help me by pointing out the main ideas and arranging what we do so it will help me know how to manage.

Dependency Needs The instructor who listens carefully usually notices that students are, in effect, saying that they depend upon the instructor for quite a bit of help in structuring the activities of the course so that the time and effort spent will help them meet their preferences. In the preceding examples one student expresses no interest in the subject and no notion that it could help later on the job. That student is willing, however, to do what is necessary to pass. The other student wants to learn how to think like a manager. The instructor, who is in the position of something like a manager of this learning organization, can anticipate then that these expectations and preferences are going to affect what happens during the course.

Commitment Some instructors respond with views like this:

I agree that I should plan activities and ask you to do things that, according to my judgment, will help you learn useful ways of acting as a manager. I should also give you information on my ideas about how and when I plan to measure your performance so you can plan your time and focus your efforts. I do think you can count on me for those things. We might have differences of opinion along the way, but I hope you will feel able to confront me when you think something is amiss.

Hidden Clauses   Of course, merely expressing some of the intentions they recognize at the outset of a relationship does not assure that agreements will be kept or that most of the important terms of the contract have even been identified. Who knows, maybe the instructor now feels hostile toward that student who said all he wants is a grade. Maybe that hostility will lead to subtle discrimination against that student.

Maybe that student resents being in the course and feels he must be there to qualify for the job, but the whole thing is boring. Maybe these feelings will lead that student to feel no commitment to learning in class. Maybe resentment and lack of interest will lead to absenteeism and poor performance. Maybe this will set the stage for receiving a poor grade.

Many Contracts   Finally, it needs to be recognized that there is not one contract between a person and an organization; there are several. There are person-to-person psychological contracts, between fellow workers, superiors and subordinates, employees of the company and customers, clients, suppliers, and others. In this class there will be psychological contracts not just between students and the instructor, but between students and students, and between students and project or exercise groups in which they have brief or long-lasting membership. There will be expectations and preferences in these relationships too. They will define the zones of acceptance of the parties to each contract.

ZONES OF ACCEPTANCE

Student to   The zone of acceptance of a party to a contract marks the boundaries of
Student Pressure   acceptable behavior. If you don't pull your weight in a group of students working on a project, you may expect to find out that you had better contribute your share. If you try to take over the group, you may be accepted or you may be rejected and told not to be so pushy. People are always giving and receiving messages about the acceptability of their actions.

At work, employees have zones of acceptance that define how much authority their managers have. When a request, instruction, or directive from a superior or some other source within the organization concerning the job falls within this zone, the employee accepts it and acts upon it. If the attempt to influence the employee falls outside of that individual's zone of acceptance, it is rejected.

Contract Violation   For example, a recent graduate of an M.S. program in chemical engineering was hired by a large corporation in its research division. She understood that the position would be in basic research studies. But, after 11 months, she quit. In explaining the reasons for resigning, the engineer explained that she had been repeatedly assigned to help various product development groups solve their problems. This had disrupted her thought processes and interrupted work on her own project so that almost no progress had been made. She felt pressured to help these groups every time they asked because her superior believed that everyone should help out on the development projects. Besides, it would seem uncooperative if she didn't help out. But these disruptions had been extremely irritating, and she finally resigned because an important clause of the psychological contract had been violated.

Managers, too, have zones of acceptance that define the limits of employee behavior. The same thing that happened to the chemical engineer happens to managers in their dealings with subordinates. The employee's behavior or evident attitude can fall within or outside of the superior's zone of acceptance. If the subordinate is seen as insubordinate (doesn't follow directions), incompetent (can't do the work), or otherwise not acting within the limits of the superior's zone of acceptance, the superior rejects the subordinate in some way.

For example, in the late 1960s and early 1970s, many colleges and universities fired radical economists, sociologists, political scientists, and other faculty members. Administrators complained that although they had hired a faculty member to teach, say, the Principles of Economics, that wasn't what was taught. Instead, the professor actually conducted the course emphasizing third-world economics, or why socialism was superior to capitalism, or in some other way used the class to express a particular (and minority) point of view. Whatever the merits of any of the positions taken in these episodes, the situations illustrate employee conduct outside the employer's zone of acceptance.

SOURCES OF TENSION

When developments fall outside the zone of acceptance of either the individual or the organization, tension results. There are four major reasons why the zone of acceptance is violated, thus producing tension between people and organizations (Figure 2.1).

First, organizations are broken down into roles for people to perform. Managers think that roles or jobs as designed to get tasks done. The roles, consisting of distinctive sets of job duties, are planned and organized. There is the role of receptionist, clerk, foreman, accountant, employment interviewer, design engineer, cook, machinist, and so on.

Roles and People   After designing the paper organization, managers then hire people to carry out the roles. But, lo and behold, the people are human beings with

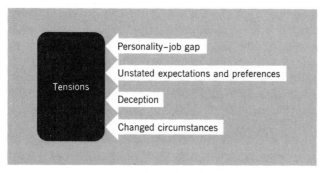

Figure 2.1 Sources of the tension between persons and organizations.

ideas, needs, and styles of their own. They may be bigger or smaller than their roles, but their humanity makes them something more than robots carrying out the programmed roles.

The people are simply different from the roles. Hence, the manager who thought he was hiring a secretary discovers he has a would-be executive who interferes with subordinates. The manager who thought she was hiring a salesperson finds that she has someone who concentrates on the paperwork in the office rather than getting out and meeting customers. In each case, the difference between human beings and planned roles accounts for some tension between the person and the organization.

Expectations Second, expectations and preferences are sometimes unstated, but later brought to bear in judging performance. The college senior is hired by a public accounting firm and nothing is said about the length of his hair. Later, not-so-gentle hints are made that it would be better if his hair were not so long.

The young employee complains that nothing was ever said about hair and that, in any case, he can't see the connection between hair and accounting work. His boss is apt to regard him as immature. Angered and disappointed, the young man might quit and his boss feel lucky to be rid of him.

Honesty Third, not presenting matters honestly can lead to strains between individuals and organizations. In an eagerness to recruit engineers, aerospace corporations for many years stressed the creative challenge to be found in the work they had to offer. In many instances, those engineers who were hired found their tasks trivial and unrewarding. The inflated expectations made their disappointment sharper.

People looking for jobs sometimes hide their preferences and claim to be interested in what they think the employer wants them to be interested in. Later, when behavior on the job shows the real preferences of these employees, the conflict of interest becomes visible.

Changing Circumstances Fourth, circumstances can change so much that new expectations and preferences become more important than the terms of the original psychological contract. A job that once stressed careful workmanship might be changed to make quantity of output more important than quality. The pride and satisfaction the employee felt in the work might then be swept away. The individual might feel cheated and deprived.

Similarly, individuals grow and change. What they once valued on the job may have been a good fit with the employer's needs. But new interests can make the secretary try to be an administrative assistant when the boss still wants a secretary.

PATTERNS OF ADJUSTMENT

Because zones of acceptance can change over time and new sources of tension between individuals and organizations can come into play, the adjustment a person makes to the organization is not fixed but changing. By looking at the patterns of behavior of a great many persons in a great many organizations, it is possible to find at least a half-dozen modes of adjustment. These include: the Obedient, the Defiant, the Climber, the Apathetic, the Lover-Hater, the Creative Individual. Each has its recognizable qualities and likely results. As you read the following descriptions of each, we suggest you consider your own mode of adjustment to organizations within your own experience, including schools you have attended or are attending.

The Obedient

"My organization, right or wrong" is the catchword of the obedient individual. This person accepts the authority of the organization wholly. Anything the organization asks that person to do falls within the zone of acceptance of the obedient individual.

Experiments have been conducted that show that this style is much more common than most people think. Americans think Germans are like that. But experiments show that Americans would give painful, even fatal electric shocks to other persons merely because they are told to do so by an authority who calls himself a research scientist.

Underlying the pronounced willingness to accept authority is a mixture of feelings and ideas. There is the old notion that all established authorities reflect the will of God. They know best, have more information, and so on. There is the sense that moral responsibility is taken over by the authority, and one is thereby freed of that burden. There is a sense that power is on the side of authority. There is also the escape from the stressful freedom of choice. The boss or the instructor says this is what we shall do now, so we do it. Often obedience is the path to acceptance and reward.

The Defiant

The defiant individual stays in the organization but fights it all the way. Visit a class in an elementary school and you can usually spot a child or two whose main energies seem devoted to derailing the teacher's efforts. The same mode of adjustments can be found in high school and even in university classes.

A film of the late 1960s, *Cool Hand Luke,* starring Paul Newman, tells the story of a defiant prisoner in a southern chain gang. Luke's unyielding individualism in the face of brutal regimentation led to his death. In a typical business organization, zero accommodation to the requirements of the organization is more likely to lead to being fired.

The Apathetic

The apathetic individual is neither actively obedient nor actively defiant. The apathetic is simply drowsy. School makes this individual drowsy; the job makes this individual drowsy, but nonetheless, the apathetic stays around.

Boredom   The apathetic individual's place in the organization calls forth no lively involvement or commitment. Daydreams rather than concentration fill this person's mind. As a result, the apathetic tends to be a lackluster performer who obtains lackluster rewards. The apathetic mode has many names, such as "spring fever," and "the blue-collar blues." Just how common this mode is is not certain. It visits almost everyone sometimes, but seems to stay almost permanently with some persons.

The Climber

The climber aims to move up the organization. In the Horatio Alger stories so popular in America around the turn of the century, the hero was such a person, working to move up the economic ladder. The climber succeeded by luck and by pluck. Because pluck was the thing an individual could influence, everyone was urged to do so.

Pluck   Pluck takes the form of hard work to get the job done and more. Many extremely productive people have said that perspiration accounts for 90 percent of their success, inspiration for only 10 percent. Those who climb to the top of organization structures often succeed because they concentrate intense desire and strenuous effort on that goal. They may, however, risk the anger of superiors, colleagues, and subordinates while pushing their way upward.

The Lover-Hater

The lover-hater has the worst of both worlds. Neither pure unquestioning obedience or climbing, nor pure defiance of apathy characterizes this individual. The lover-hater has mixed emotions, running hot and cold about the organization.

Ambivalent   The boss and the company can be the greatest one week and the absolute worst the next. While hot the lover-hater obeys and shows more pluck than most people. While cold, the same individual hates with equal vigor. This type of individual finds the organization is not as consistently congenial as the climber or obedient finds it, nor is it consistently uninteresting as the apathetic finds it.

The lover-hater often has strong ambitions and personal goals, and finds sources of tension in what may seem to most people obvious and necessary exercises in coordination, control, and traditional authority in the organization. The lover-hater hopes for special recognition and status, but doesn't know how to climb and usually overestimates his or her own gifts or talents.

In short, the lover-hater has a neurotic work life. Unable to deal with reality in a rewarding way like a healthy personality, not to blot it out like a psychotic, this type of individual is intensely disturbed by it. Worse, the lover-hater can't quiet the tensions because this personality type has no stable, effective way of coping with organizational requirements.

DOONESBURY

The Creative Individual

The creative individual has the best of both worlds. Individual needs have not been denied in a total acceptance of the organization's needs. There isn't the status anxiety of the climber, who is never sure of success. Nor is there the misfit or sleepy mode of the defiant or apathetic, nor the unstable mode of the lover-hater.

When it comes to doing what the organizational role requires, the creative individual finds it easy to perform effectively. This individual does well, and in the process gets personal satisfaction and organizational support.

When it comes to any capricious or inappropriate attempts by the organization to influence behavior or attitudes that are not instrumental to carrying out the job, the creative individual is his or her own person. Where others might imitate the mannerisms of superiors in a "magical" attempt to gain favor, the creative individual follows his or her own preferences. Neither meek nor rebellious, the creative individual is matter-of-fact in doing what the work calls for.

In summary, there are several ways that individuals adjust to organizations. And the way any individual adjusts may change over time. The problem faced by each person who will work in an organization (and that includes most of us) is to realize accommodations that are truly satisfying. If we do not, we face 40 years of alienation or aggravated work life in the organization.

Copyright © 1973 by G. B. Trudeau. Distributed by Universal Press Syndicate.

PATTERNS OF INFLUENCE

Just as individuals adjust to organizations, so organizations seek to adjust or influence individuals. The individual's style impinges on the organization, but the organization is not passive. It uses two major methods to get people to do what it wants: reward and punishment. Each method tends to produce a different kind of involvement for individuals in the organization.

Involvement can range from a condition of alienation (being in the organization but personally estranged from it) to a condition of commitment (being in the organization and personally absorbed in or attracted to it and to its purposes). Punishment-centered influence, which relies on threat and fear, tends to foster alienated adjustments such as apathy and defiance. Reward-centered influence tends to foster committed adjustments such as obedience and climbing. Figure 2.2 depicts the scale of involvement and methods of influence associated with types of involvement.

Figure 2.2   The scale of involvement.

Reward

Rewards can be either material or symbolic. Pay, promotion, and fringe benefits are the common material rewards organizations use to induce people to contribute their efforts to accomplish organizational purposes. Unless these are sufficient, an organization cannot hire or retain employees.

Paradoxically, however, these same material rewards often seem able to do little more than induce a person to enter and stay in the organization. An individual may belong, but not produce. In other words, there may be involvement, but only in an alienated way.

Identifying with
Authority
Other rewards, symbolic ones, some of which are intangible, count for much in fostering more committed involvement. These rewards include all kinds of positive inducements. For example, a chance to identify or feel pride in associating with a company, superior, or a work group can encourage a person to perform well. A feeling that a superior or associate has expert knowledge, or that his or her position is correct and legitimate, can encourage a person to agree with that person's request or directions. A feeling of satisfaction in doing challenging and useful work can also encourage performance.

Organizations use all of these rewards to influence employees to enter the organization and carry out work. In doing so, they trade in hopes and promises. But there is a negative method of influence. It trades in fear and threat.

Punishment

Punishment takes various forms, some easy to recognize, some subtle and unofficial. Discharge, demotion, layoffs, and fines are clear. Often, however, punishment is not announced or even admitted. Here are a few examples of subtle punishment. A boss might use pale words to describe a subordinate's work on a performance evaluation form or assign uninteresting work that *The Cold Shoulder* does not lead to advancement. Someone might be left out when a luncheon is planned. Often the punished individuals must figure out for themselves that they are being punished. Then, the problem is to discover why.

You may be surprised to learn that in organizations you are more likely to experience the subtle variety of punishment than the direct, easily recognized kind. Subtle or direct, however, punishment is meant to make unwanted behavior too costly to continue.

Psychologists have learned that punishment is a less efficient form of influence than reward because it contains serious side effects. Punished people have reason to be fearful or hostile toward the source of punishment. They may quit, be overly careful, or become defiant or apathetic. None of these behaviors helps get the job done where cooperation, effort, and creativity are needed. Rewards tend to be free of these problems. But rewards are effective in bringing about good performance only if employees see that they must perform well to get the rewards. If rewards are available just for belonging to the organization, they don't reinforce doing a good job.

Managers must emphasize rewards, both for being in the organization and for doing a good job within it. This is the path to developing committed involvement. A negative, punishing emphasis brings forth alienated involvement at best.

CREATING AND MAINTAINING THE PERSON/ORGANIZATION CONTRACT

A manager must try to achieve and maintain committed involvement on the part of subordinates. Then, the manager must try to create a working relationship in which the individual's and the organization's zones of acceptance are not violated. None of these goals is easy to reach. But the person/organization contract provides a way of attempting to reach them. There are useful steps that a manager can take to make the deal rewarding for both the individual and the organization (Figure 2.3).

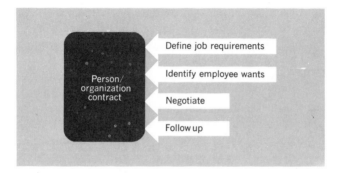

Figure 2.3 Steps in creating and maintaining the
Person/Organization contract.

Legitimate   First, the manager can find out what behavior and attitudes are really
Requirements needed for effective job performance and insist upon them. If the sales job
calls for friendly readiness to help dozens of customers every day, grouches
are out. If the labor negotiating job calls for firmness and ability to with-
stand hostile, aggressive treatment, maybe grouches are in. The real job
requirements must be identified and used as a yardstick to measure applicants and the performance of people already on the job.

Equally important, the manager should not insist upon behaviors and attitudes which he or she likes but that are not truly called for by the job.
Managers must try to overcome their own biases if they find themselves
favoring white or black persons, Christians or Jews, young or old, male or
female, or long- or short-haired people; such qualities are usually irrelevant
or even illegal as a basis for selecting employees. The manager must not
insist that employees refrain from partying at home since that is not a legitimate concern. The right to bargain for the person/organization contract's
terms is keyed to the legitimate working needs of the organization.

Consider an example from business history. In the early days of the Ford
Motor Company, Henry Ford just couldn't keep from interfering in the
personal lives of his employees. For example, if as a Ford employee you
smoked, drank, or danced (unless it was square dancing, which Henry Ford
approved), you asked for trouble. Those restrictions not only applied at work;
they applied at home. And there was a "Sociology Department" headed by
Harry Bennett, who always carried a gun to see that things went along
smoothly. In this atmosphere, employee discontents festered, eventually leading to the bloodiest union-management confrontations in the auto industry.
With 20-20 hindsight it is easy to see that Ford seemed confused about what
his company actually needed from its workers.

But Ford was not unique. Many organizations have seemed confused and,
like Ford, have changed with the times, trying to require a more sensible, less
arbitrary conformity from its employees. Consider the U.S. Navy, for exam-

ple. One of the authors walked by a Navy recruiting office and noticed a new poster in the window. The poster showed three young black men; one was combing his Afro hairstyle and seemed to be scowling. The caption said: "The Navy has changed so you don't have to."

Even though the author might better be described as a middle-aged white man rather than a young black man, the message was not lost on him. The Navy wished to communicate that it was now more willing to accept a wider range of individual preferences and styles than it traditionally has been willing to accept. To wit: "You can be black, have long hair, scowl, and still be a member of our organization."

The Navy may be overstating the changes in order to get more young men to join. Some sailors report pressure to wear their hair shorter, and black sailors rioted against alleged discrimination on aircraft carriers in 1972. Even so, there may be real changes, not just in the Navy but in typical business and government organizations as well, when it comes to the old problem of establishing suitable managerial expectations and preferences.

Second, the manager can find out what employees want. Most managers feel they know this, but when the manager's list of employee wants is compared with a list provided by the employees, the order of preferences doesn't often match. Although thinking that fringe benefits are most important, the manager may be astonished to learn that employees gripe most about their jobs being designed so that they can't do high-quality work.

Discover Employee Desires   A manager can simply ask employees what their preferences and expectations are. The list should then be repeated back to the employees to ensure that the information has been correctly received. The manager must be careful not to mislead people into the false hope that something will be done to meet every employee wish. The purpose of obtaining the list is to learn what employees see as rewards. The manager can't define the rewards; the employees do. If the manager wants to build committed involvement through rewards, it must be through an understanding of what employees prefer and value.

Negotiate   Third, once preferences and expectations for both sides are identified, the manager needs to negotiate reasonable contracts with employees. In the process the manager must voice organizational expectations and requirements and hear employee expectations and requirements. The differences must be faced and not hidden under the rug. The bargain should be struck with the understanding that it is to be reviewed and changed as circumstances dictate, by getting together and facing the new issue.

Follow-up   Fourth, the manager must check to make sure the contracts made are not violated. The behavior of supervisors reporting to the manager must be watched. The manager must see to it that the organization's policies, procedures, practices, and jobs square with standing person/organization contracts.

Suppose that the corporate president agrees that promotions are to be based only on specific items of job performance. If supervisors use other items to decide promotions, the president must spot this. If the contract isn't enforced, it will become a wry joke.

On the other hand, if managers and employees, instructors and students try influencing one another in a planned and open way, perhaps they will learn to violate one another's zone of acceptance less often. There is no assurance that this will happen. But it is likely that some violations of the contract come from ignorance and misunderstanding between individuals and organizations. A method of facing one another's preferences and expectations may reduce those sources of tension.

SUMMARY

The pattern of people/organization expectations, said or unsaid, is a key sector of the manager's territory. Unless the manager learns this part of the territory well, he or she will never be able to tap the full power of the human organization. The manager can, however, start right now by becoming attuned to the zones of acceptance, sources of tension, patterns of adjustment, and patterns of influence that operate in the present relationships.

THE BREWMASTERS:
COLORADO'S COORS FAMILY HAS BUILT AN EMPIRE ON ONE BRAND OF BEER

Golden, Colo.—Like many other companies, Adolph Coors Co. thinks athletic recreation is important for its employees. Consequently, the family-owned brewer, located in this small central-Colorado community 15 miles west of Denver, sends executives and workers to rugged, outdoor-survival schools. It subsidizes golf so that employees can play 20 rounds a summer for $5. It underwrites ski trips.

Coors employes, as might be expected, are delighted by this attention to their well-being. But the brewing company has more in mind than the therapeutic benefits of fresh air and has therefore attached some strings to its sports package: It insists that every employe who participates in its program must compete—even in such normally noncompetitive pastimes as skiing.

"If you can't fight competition, you don't need to survive," asserts William K. Coors, the company's athletic, 56-year-old chairman and president.

Indeed, no single trait so dominates this feisty company as its obvious delight in coming to grips with its competition. And in so doing, it has battled its way to the position of the nation's fourth largest brewer. "I take a lot of satisfaction in opposing all the forces that would like to put us out of business," Bill Coors says.

And such forces abound, Mr. Coors contends. Among them: the three giants of the brewing industry, who together hold 45% of the national market; numerous labor unions; civil-rights groups; antialcohol individuals, or "drys," who remain a potent force in much of the company's marketing area; and, most recently, the Federal Trade Commission, which last August ordered Coors to stop fixing prices and to alter certain practices relating to its distribution.

Source. William M. Bulkeley, Staff Reporter, *The Wall Street Journal,* October 26, 1973.

A Best Seller

To date, at least, such factors haven't been much of a deterrent to Coors's growth. Although distributed in only 11 Southwestern states, Coors Banquet Beer—the company's only brand—is the best-selling beer in 10 of them. In California, it has 41% of the market, compared with only 18% for industry leader Anheuser-Busch. A phenomenal 68% of the beer sold in Oklahoma is Coors. And although Coors will churn out 11 million barrels of beer this year, up from 9.8 million last year, demand so outstrips supply that the company rations its product among distributors. (The tight-lipped company declines to reveal its profits; however, last year, when it was under investigation for fixing prices, it disclosed that its volume in 1971 totaled $350 million.)

Coors's obvious success is all the more surprising considering that certain of its operating procedures are considered highly unorthodox in brewing circles. Its advertising expenses, Bill Coors says, are currently less than $1 a barrel and have averaged one-quarter of those of major competitors. While many brewers have logically built their breweries close to major population centers to cut shipping costs, all Coors beer is brewed here in the world's largest single brewery, and the average barrel travels over 900 miles. And despite a volume growth rate of 12% compounded annually Adolph Coors Co. has steadfastly refused to go to the bank for a loan since the first Adolph Coors set up a little brewery in this mountain valley a century ago.

What, then, is the secret of Coors's success? Product quality, the company says, boasting that Coors "is the most expensively brewed beer in the world." (It sells at retail in the "popular-price" range.) A plant geneticist works full-time to develop improved strains of barley for malting, and most hops are imported from Germany. Unlike most beers, chemical additives aren't used anywhere in the process, even as preservatives or to hasten aging. And the beer is aged, packaged, shipped and stored cold to prevent the deterioration that might otherwise occur, since Coors contains no preservatives and isn't pasteurized like most other beers.

No Help Wanted

Other breweries, of course, have other boasts; and more than the nature of its product, however expensive or tasty, sets Adolph Coors Co. apart from others in its field. Another distinguishing company characteristic, for example, is a scorn for outside expertise. "We don't bring in many outside specialists," Bill Coors says. "We'd rather make our own mistakes."

Consequently, what advertising and promotion that the company undertakes are handled by an in-house staff. Construction at the brewery is done by Coors's own construction crew. The company's engineers designed the machinery for the can plant. And Coors executives rest secure in the knowledge that the company turns its back on outside managerial talent, preferring instead to promote longtime employes through the ranks.

"The company encourages you to rise as high as your abilities let you," says Everett L. Barnhardt, a vice president and director who started as an office boy in 1931. Or, he might add, as high as possible without bumping into a Coors. For the Coors family is very much in evidence in company's key slots, including Bill in the chairmanship and presidency, his brother, Joseph, executive vice president and president of Coors Porcelain Co., a subsidiary; Joseph's two sons, Jeffrey (director of research and development), and Peter (in the management training program); and Adolph Coors IV, Bill and Joseph's nephew, who is also in the management training program.

Coors has been very much family-dominated since it was founded in 1873 by the first Adolph Coors, a German orphan who stowed away on a U.S.-bound ship to avoid conscription into the German army. Golden in those early days of the Coors brewery was a brawling mining town, and the new beer company was modestly successful throughout the closing decades of the nineteenth century, going so far as to diversify into the making of glass bottles for use as containers.

In the 1890s, Coors converted its bottle plant into an operation producing a variety of porcelain products, a venture that paid off when prohibition came to Colorado in 1914 and the company was forced to get out of the beer business.

In 1917, Coors began producing malted milk, and between then and 1956, when the company dropped out of the field, it produced about 20 million pounds of the product, mostly for Mars Inc., the candy maker. "If it hadn't been for malted milk, the beer business wouldn't be here today," Bill Coors has said.

By the time prohibition was repealed in 1933, the leadership of Coors had passed to Adolph II, son of the founder. (Adolph I died in 1929.) Once again, the company was back in the beer business; and throughout the remainder of the 1930s, the '40s and '50s, Coors continued to prosper.

In 1960, the company's fortunes were overshadowed by a family tragedy: the kidnapping and murder of Adolph Coors III, who, at the time of his death, was chairman of Coors's board. (The kidnapping motive was ransom.) The victim's father, Adolph II, had been sharing leadership responsibilities with his son; after the murder, he remained the real boss of Coors, even though his official title was treasurer, until his death in 1970 at the age of 86. He was succeeded by his son, Bill, the current chairman and president.

Spartan Quarters

Bill Coors runs his empire from a spartan cinder-block office in the brewery. Private offices are frowned upon at Coors, and even the president's working space holds a desk for his brother. Cramped, ill-ventilated conference rooms are in constant use, and nobody has a secretary for himself. Lush financial fringe benefits, such as bonuses and stock-option plans, are nonexistent.

But despite these factors—and despite the strong hold by members of the Coors family on top jobs—management employes appear almost fanatically loyal to the company. For one thing, sources in the company say, salaries are high. Then, too, the area is considered a desirable place to work and live. And finally, management men say, the company is simply a nice place to pursue a career and the Coorses are highly respected as managers.

This cozy atmosphere, however, doesn't permeate all levels of the Coors operation. The company's relationship with its blue-collar unions, for example, is notoriously bad. A case in point: In 1968, 13 construction crews struck Coors; but the company refused to budge on contract offers, and many of the construction workers subsequently resigned from the union and returned to work.

The construction unions are still officially on strike, but Coors doesn't seem unduly concerned—perhaps with good reason. In 1959, the company successfully weathered a 118-day strike by Brewery Workers International Union Local 366, which has represented Coors brewery workers since 1933. Coors, unruffled, continued production with college students and supervisors. "After that," says James Silverthorn, president of the local, "this was practically a dead union."

Environmental Protection Agency; the company recycles almost all of its waste, and that which can't be recycled is burned in an incinerator that is nearly pollution-free.

Despite its ultramodern equipment, most of the company's business philosophy dates back to the first Adolph Coors. Indeed, allegiance to the founders' guiding principles—particularly the idea of fiscal conservatism—has led the company to reject some seemingly attractive possibilities. For example, Coors Container Co., the company's can-manufacturing subsidiary, helped develop the technical process for making a two-piece aluminum can; Coors, however, sold the process to container industry giants like Continental Can Co. and American Can Co. "We could have dominated the industry," says Robert L. Mornin, president of Coors Container. "But we would have had to borrow from the banks, and Coors doesn't do that."

Grounds for Dismissal

Highlighting Mr. Silverthorn's observation is the current brewery-workers' contract: It specifically requires workers to cross other unions' picket lines around the brewery, thus drastically weakening the brewery union's bargaining power. It also contains 21 grounds for dismissal, one of which is criticism by workers of the company or its products, and the last of which is "any other act of dishonesty, gross misconduct or neglect not listed above."

In view of such labor-relations difficulties it might be asked why the workers don't go elsewhere. The answer, Mr. Silverthorn says, is that Coors is "a pretty fair employer." He adds: "We couldn't live under a contract like that if they weren't."

Among workers' benefits, the local's president says, are wages that are high for the Denver area and that are comparable to those paid by brewers elsewhere. Other amenities include the free beer served in the company cafeteria (there is no rule at Coors against drinking on the job) and the fact that work is performed in a spacious, stainless-steel setting with computerized control of ingredients, shipments and distributors' supplies. Coors's plant has won an award from the

Family of Conservatives

The Coors family is also known for its conservatism in political matters. Adolph II, for example, is remembered as a noted backer of right-wing causes. And Joseph Coors, whom a Denver lawyer describes as "slightly to the right of Commodore Vanderbilt," aroused liberal ire with his successful campaign in the late 1960s to drive the radical Students for a Democratic Society off the University of Colorado campus when he was a regent.

Liberal groups have also directed considerable ire toward the company for alleged discriminatory hiring practices. Major complainants are Mexican-American groups, who perennially boycott the company based on charges that it violates equal-employment-opportunity laws. None of the charges have been upheld by the court, however; and Bill Coors is philosophical about the Chicano boycotts. "We still can't brew enough beer to meet demand," he says.

Mr. Coors is more concerned, however, about recent criticism from the Federal Trade Commission, which last month ordered the company to halt such practices as suggesting beer prices to its distributors and trying to prevent retailers of Coors draft beer from selling competing draft beer. The company argues that it needs control of its distributors to assure a strong retail operation and to make certain that its beer is kept cold to maintain quality, and it is therefore vigorously opposing the ruling.

"If we have to," Bill Coors asserts, "We'll take over distribution ourselves, and Coors will become the biggest beer distributor in the world."

Discussion Question

1. List and discuss the terms of Coors's contract with its employees.

Update

Although there have been many changes at Coors since the 1973 article appeared, much of the person-organization contract remains the same. An article in *Business Week,* September 29, 1980, reports that a new generation of Coors is heading the company in many different directions. Jeffrey Coors, 35, and his brother, Peter Coors, 33 (the first M.B.A. in the Coors family) introduced Coors Light Beer, the company's first new brand, and a super-premium beer (to compete with Michelob and Lowenbrau), Herman Josephs. They are also planning to build a second brewery on the east coast, to supplement their Golden, Colorado facility. To push these new products, they spent $46 million in advertising in 1979, an unthinkably high expenditure just seven years ago.

Despite these changes, conditions have changed very little for Coors employees since 1973. Coors' tough anti-union stand led to a strike in 1977, which ended when the employees returned to work and voted out the union. Chicanos and other minority groups have filed employment discrimination charges and instituted boycotts against Coors, but with seemingly little success. The strong competitive drives also remain. Coors' vice-president of sales, Fred A. Vierra, said, "We're wiser. We're tougher and better prepared. We can leap tall buildings at a single bound."

MANAGEMENT BY RESULTS

Joseph Caramatta, the founder, owner, and president of Wholesale Electronics, was an avid student of modern business practices. He had recently completed a management seminar and had been especially impressed by a lecture entitled "Management by Objectives; Appraisal by Results." For Joseph, the theme of the lecture was that only results count, that one reason managers are not required to punch a time clock is that they are judged by results rather than time spent at a desk. After class, Joseph asked the instructor, Professor Jack Hugh, if the concept might not be applied to most workers as well. In a rather offhand manner, Professor Hugh said that it probably could be so applied.

Several weeks later, Joseph called all his employees together and informed them that each employee would be given certain objectives to attain. Normally, he would not be required to work any particular number of hours so long as he attained his required results. There were certain exceptions to this policy; such employees as the receptionist and the warehouseman were required to be present whenever the firm was open.

Together with his office manager, Joseph worked out the objectives for each of the ten employees to which the policy applied. A week after his announcement, the new system was started. As far as Joseph could determine, everything was generally going well. Sales and profits were slightly higher than in previous periods.

Joseph felt that there was one problem area. Miss Snyder, who had been in charge of answering certain inquiries, was arriving for work at 10 o'clock and leaving at 2 o'clock. Since no one else worked for so short a period, Joseph decided to discuss the matter with Miss Snyder. One day as she was leaving the building, he called her into the office and asked her how things were going.

"Is there any problem, Mr. Caramatta? Have I forgotten to answer any letters?"

"No, nothing like that, but I think that the rest of the office resents the hours you keep."

"But Mr. Caramatta, we agreed that my objective was to have every inquiry answered within 24 hours. And I have always done that."

"Yes, I know. But we had been receiving an average of 40 inquiries each work day. And it takes an average of 12 minutes to answer each. If you are really doing your work, you should be spending eight hours on your job."

Source. Richard N. Farmer, Barry M. Richman, and William G. Ryan, *Incidents for Studying Management and Organization* (Belmont, Calif.: Wadsworth Publishing Company, 1970), pp. 111–112.

"Oh, that was before you adopted your policy of management by results. I had been analyzing the correspondence for months. All but 5 percent of the letters can be answered by some combination of 50 paragraphs. I put those 50 paragraphs on tape for the new computer-controlled typewriter. Now I can have 95 percent of the letters answered in five minutes each. Since we get the mail at 10 o'clock, I can have all the programmed letters ready by 11. By 1 o'clock I have answered the hard ones, and by 1:30 the automatically prepared letters are ready for me to sign. Why should I stay?"

Discussion Questions
1. What caused this tension between Mr. Caramatta and Miss Snyder?
2. Describe the terms, stated or implied, of the person/organization contract,
   (a) as Miss Snyder sees it;
   (b) as Mr. Caramatta sees it.
3. What should Mr. Caramatta do now?

Whether either side is aware of it or not, the relations between persons and organizations involve a psychological contract. Each side has preferences and expectations that stake out a zone of acceptance. When the behavior or apparent attitude of either the individual or the organization conflicts with the other side's expectations and preferences, that zone is violated.

These violations produce tension between the individual and the organization. Organizations want actors for roles, but people are more complicated than their roles. Organizations and individuals sometimes fail to voice their expectations. Worse, they misrepresent them. As if these were not enough sources of tension, circumstances change and demand new arrangements.

Individuals do find ways of living their work lives in organizations. These adjustments include a range of possibilities: obedience, defiance, apathy, climbing, loving and hating, and creative individualism.

At the same time, organizations find ways of influencing individuals. These include rewards and punishments, and the relative dominance of either can affect the patterns of individual adjustment and involvement. Punishment fosters alienation. Rewards foster commitment.

Finally, as a means of managing the relations between individuals and organizations, it is possible to get the person/organization contract out into the open and consciously and mutually shape its terms. To do this managers can identify organizational requirements, learn of employee requirements, explore areas of agreement and disagreement, settle upon some agreement, and then monitor and update the person/organization contract as necessary. While the complex and enduring differences between individuals and organizations assure an endless supply of tensions, consciously facing them can offer some hope for individuals amd organizations to manage those differences in mutually satisfying ways.

Here are some principles:

1. The expectations and preferences that people and organizations have for one another affect the performance and satisfaction of both parties.

2. Many of these expectations can be stated and examined. Both parties can affirm their commitment to activities meant to satisfy mutual requirements.

3. Person/organization contracts need to be reviewed and maintained.

4. Persons should examine their own mode of adjustment to their organizational role. They should examine the origins of their adjustment and assess its profitability to themselves.

5. Managers should examine the patterns of influence they apply to em-

ployees. They should learn what patterns of employee adjustment are associated with existing influence practices and assess the value of existing influence practices.

6. Managers should purge inappropriate expectations and illegitimate requirements whenever they creep into their contracts with employees.

CHAPTER THREE

GROUPS IN ORGANIZATIONS

LEARNING OBJECTIVES ─────────────────────────────────────

At the end of the chapter, you should be able to:

1. Define a group and the four stages of group formation.
2. Describe the common structural and interactional elements of groups.
3. Illustrate four ways in which groups contribute to organizational effectiveness.
4. Discuss four ways that groups can interfere with effective organizational performance.
5. Define three ways managers can more effectively manage groups.

LONG-TERM LOVE PARTNERS

I. Objectives
   A. To experience a group activity
   B. To identify group processes
II. Premeeting Preparation
   A. Read the instructions, including the Ranking Form (Figure 3.1) and the Group Observation Sheet (Figure 3.2).
III. Instructions
   A. Select the teams.
      1. For this exercise, form as many groups of 8 to 10 Discussants and 2 to 3 Observers. Each 8 to 10 person Discussant group should be matched with a 2 to 3 person Observer group.
      2. The observing team once chosen, should leave the room to be briefed by the professor. Observers are to follow the Group Observation Sheet in noting specific behaviors that occur during the discussion period. Observers may be provided an opportunity during the review period to feed back their observations to the group as a whole.
      3. During this period, the Discussants are to individually complete the Ranking Form (Figure 3.1), rank ordering from 1 (most important) to 10 (least important) those traits which they consider important in a spouse or long-term love partner.

      Time for Step A: 5 minutes

   B. Discussion of the rankings to reach consensus decision
      1. Discussants will meet and reach a consensus decision concerning a single set of rankings for their group. The Discussants in each group should be arranged in a circle, as nearly as possible, and far enough removed from other Discussant groups to prevent interference with the ongoing talks. The Observers will sit and/or stand around the Discussant group during the discussion period.

      Time for Step B: 15 minutes

   C. The Discussants and Observers shall individually complete the Group Observation Sheet (Figure 3.2).

      Time for Step C: 10 minutes

IV. Discussion

Your instructor will help you to explore what happened in the exercise and its meaning for management.

Time for Discussion: 15 minutes

Figure 3.1   Ranking Form

In the space provided below, list the 10 traits you would consider to be most important in your choice of a spouse or a long-term love partner. First, list the 10 most important characteristics, then rank order these characteristics from 1 (most important) to 10 (least important).

Important Characteristics for Spouse or Long-Term Love Partner

Ranking from 1 (Most Important) to 10 (Least Important)

_____   _____

_____   _____

_____   _____

_____   _____

_____   _____

_____   _____

_____   _____

_____   _____

_____   _____

_____   _____

Figure 3.2   Group Observation Sheet

Please analyze the group activity in which you have just participated or observed by completing the following form. Please be specific in citing who, what, when, where, and how.

1. Norms
Did everyone speak, or only a few; was there listening to everyone or were certain people interrupted; was the task taken seriously, or was there a general feeling "it doesn't matter"?

_____

_____

_____

2. Goals
Were the goals to get done as soon as possible, to hear everybody out, to just have fun without taking the task seriously?

_____

_____

_____

3. Leaders
Was there a relatively permanent leader, or did leadership switch from person to person; was leadership clearly established or were there many struggles over who would be the leader; did the leader (or leaders) concentrate mostly on getting the task done, or was there lots of joking, etc; was the leadership democratic or autocratic?

_____

_____

_____

4. Interactions
Did everyone participate or did only a few people participate?

_____

_____

_____

5. Activities

Who wrote in the group, who summarized, who went to the board?

_____

_____

_____

6. Sentiments

Who was involved in the group, and not involved; who was positive about the group activities and who was negative; who was irritated with the group activities and who was eager to participate?

_____

_____

_____

7. State of Group Development

Was the group in the "forming," "storming," "norming," or "performing" phase of group development?

_____

_____

_____

People in organizations are not robots; they are humans cast together who interact in groups. People cast together in work groups sooner or later develop common ideas about how to act, what is good, and what is bad. They also develop means of enforcing these unofficial or informal requirements.

For example, a group of salespeople in a department store decided to ignore the formal individualistic commission scheme. They agreed to take turns waiting on customers and to register sales in each other's names to equalize commissions. They developed this plan and enforced it by applying pressure to anyone who began to accumulate more sales than the others.

In another case, a work group in a gypsum mine developed a system of assigning the dirtiest jobs to the newest man. This system was enforced by mentioning what needed to be done by the new man. Then everyone just looked at him.

The exercise you just experienced can be looked upon as a kind of laboratory demonstration of these same processes of developing group norms and applying them. The exercise brought together various personalities and cast them together in a situation requiring discussion, decision, and interaction.

Like most exercises, this presented a partly ambiguous situation to groups who interpreted it their own ways. It was a little like a page in a coloring book set before the group and the group colored it in with its own behavior. Essentially, this is the same process that occurs when work groups fill in the gaps and breathe life and depth into the formal work requirements and relationships. This always happens as individuals cast together in a situation form a group. In the following chapter, we will examine the process of group formation and the role groups play in organizations.

DEFINITION

Groups Are People First, what is a group? A group is not just a random collection of people. All
Who Need Each those who live in the same apartment house need not be a group, as all
Other To Americans are likely not part of the same group. Although groups exist
Accomplish a everywhere, not everyone belongs to every group. A group exists when people
Common Purpose need each other in order to accomplish some common goal. This mutual interdependence leads to interactions and communications, and a feeling of belonging together, in the pursuit of common goals. For example, a gathering of people in a gas line is not a group until they act together to repel a crasher seeking to cut into the line. Their joint actions in pursuit of a common goal are what make them a group.

GROUP FORMATION

Groups Come Together by Forming, Storming, Norming, and Performing

Groups usually go through four distinct steps in their formation. It often takes some time for a collection of people to become a full-fledged group. The first stage is "forming." During this period, group members test the expectations and establish the ground rules for both task behaviors and people-to-people relationships. Second, "storming" takes place as the individuals express their individuality in rejecting each other and the leader. Some people who decide not to participate further may even leave the group. Third, "norming" takes place; in-group feelings, group cohesiveness, standards, and roles emerge. Lastly, with the expectations clear and personal relationships settled, "performing" takes place. In this final stage, the group devotes its energies to task accomplishments. Virtually all groups go through these stages. The further away the group is from the performing stage, the less effective the group will be in accomplishing its task. Professional sport teams go through these stages every season. Those teams that get through the first three steps before the season begins usually finish higher in the standing.

PROPERTIES OF GROUPS

Each group is unique. This is due not only to the uniqueness of each individual member, but also to the structure of the group. Although groups differ in specific structure, all groups share similar structural properties.

Norms

First, all groups generate and enforce standards of behavior and performance, called norms. When their standards are below those required by the formal organization, they are called output restrictions, or goldbricking. When they exceed formal standards, they are sometimes called rate busting. These ideas cover how to act, what is good or bad, and what certain people should do. Group members develop ways to enforce these standards and expectations. These norms help the group maintain predictability and encourage cooperation.

Goals

Second, groups develop goals of their own. Group standards, rules, and even output quotas are only the means to reach an unstated goal, such as making the workplace less tense and competitive, spreading out the work to maintain employment, and achieving a just distribution of both benefits and dirty work. Such goals are not often stated, but can only be inferred from informal practices.

Leaders

Third, groups have leaders. Although the formal organization chart may show who is in charge of the department, the person who can really get things done may be someone of lesser rank. The most popular and influential member of the group often personifies the group's preferences, which may not be the same as those of the official leader. Leaders perform activities that help the group accomplish its mission (task accomplishment), and keep itself together (social-group maintenance). Task-directed activities include planning, directing, securing resources, and distributing the group's "goodies." Social maintenance activities include smoothing relationships between members, telling jokes to relieve tension, and arranging for fun times.

Status Systems All groups develop an internal pecking order in which some people are rated higher than others. Sometimes this ranking takes place on the basis of personal characteristics, such as athletic skill, joke-telling, age, sex, height, or education. Other times, job factors such as job title, salary, work schedule, or work location will be the basis for differentiation. Status is a ranking based on personal factors (such as age, education, and sex), and/or job factors (such as job title and salary). All groups have status systems that differentiate one member from the other.

Cohesiveness Some groups stick together more than others. This sticking together is called cohesiveness. Generally, more cohesive groups are more effective. A cohesive group is more likely to accomplish its goals, because all group members will work hard toward their common end. Of course, not all cohesive groups have pro-organization objectives. A cohesive group with a low productivity goal also will be effective in accomplishing its antiorganizational objectives. Cohesiveness is facilitated by members who are similar in age, sex, ethnic, or occupational backgrounds; the opportunity for frequent communication among members; a high group status; outside pressure; and a few numbers of people in the group. Varying amounts of cohesiveness are found in all groups, and will influence the group's effectiveness.

Interactions, Activities and Sentiments In addition to these elements of how the group is organized (its norms, leaders, status systems, etc.), all groups have three basic internal elements: interactions, activities, and sentiments. Interaction consists of who communicates with whom about what and in what manner. It includes both verbal and nonverbal communications. Activities cover what people do in a group: the walking, sitting, assembling, computing, and so on. Sentiments are those feelings, attitudes, and emotions that are inferred from the group member's behavior. All of these internal elements interact with each other. Activity affects interactions which affects sentiment which, in turn affects activities. All of these factors are both causes and effects of each other, and are the building blocks and lifeblood of any group.

All groups have a similar structure in that all groups have norms, goals, leaders, status systems, and cohesiveness. Similarly, all groups have interactions, activities, and sentiments coursing through their veins. Although all groups look alike structurally and interactionally, each group is different and unique.

ADVANTAGES OF GROUPS

Groups contribute to effective performance of the formal organization and individual satisfaction in several ways. The formal job descriptions, organization charts, and policies and regulations never anticipate everything that needs to be done if the organization is to function effectively. Spontaneous *Spontaneous* cooperation is needed to fill in the actions that the formal organization fails *Cooperation* to require.

Work groups improvise and innovate to meet special situations. Often the formal organization is too slow and clumsy to respond to quick changes in circumstances confronting the organization. Informal procedures and actions are devised by the work group on the spot.

For example, an aircraft manufacturer was unable to accomplish production work promptly and according to official specifications. The specifications prohibited the use of a device, the tap, used to align sections of the wing where existing holes did not align correctly. Although use of the tap was officially prohibited because it could weaken the structure, workers, supervisors, and inspectors conspired informally to allow the use of the tap when necessary. Excessive or careless use was criticized, but workers were issued taps from the tool crib and supervisors looked the other way when they were used. Had the tap not been used production would have been much slower and probably impossible.

In another case, an aircraft maintenance and modification facility, work officially flowed through a series of functional departments in assembly line fashion. Strict adherence to this procedure sometimes caused a group further down the line to wait a long time to receive an aircraft delayed at some earlier phase of the line because of a lack of parts or some other problem. Supervisors and workers developed an unofficial practice of informing one another of such delays and arranging for work crews further down the line to come and complete their work while the aircraft waited. This practice reduced the amount of slack time in the maintenance and modification processes.

Discipline Groups also provide effective discipline. In the case of the tap, any nonessential use of the tap brought severe criticism from fellow employees. The problem was to use the tap, but in a carefully controlled way. Those workers who had difficulty performing the necessary doublethink to use what was forbidden, but used it only when absolutely necessary, were threatened by peers and inspectors until they learned the proper limits of the use of the tap. Officially, of course, the formal organization did not even permit the use of the tap.

Belonging Work groups also contribute to effective performance in an indirect way. By building ties of friendship through working together, work groups can help bind the individual to the organization and provide a measure of social satisfaction. Work groups make personal involvement possible in large, impersonal organizations. Thus, by keeping individuals attracted to the organization and by keeping them committed to performing up to the group's standards, the informal organization aids performance.

Protection/   Groups also help to provide protection and predictability to the individual.
Predictability When caught in the big impersonal organization, belonging to a group helps people to know what to do and what other people expect. Also, in adverse times, the group offers protection to individual members against threats from outsiders. Unions, for example, offer protection from arbitrary management actions, and a way to predict work expectations.

DISADVANTAGES OF GROUPS

Groups can interfere with effective performance, just as they can aid performance. Sometimes groups develop standards and subgoals that are at odds with the standards and goals of the formal system. The result is that success for the work group is failure for the formal organization.

Conflicting Goals   A classic case of a clash between informal and formal organizational goals is exemplified by the problem of narcotics use in the county jail of a large western city. For a long time drugs had been finding their way into the jail, and occasionally there were obvious signs of their use. The sheriff decided to crack down because his re-election was coming up and the newspapers had picked up word of the use of drugs in jail. His plan was to put all inmates arrested on narcotics charges or with records of narcotics use into a common tank and assign them green uniforms. This contrasted with the previous method of handling these inmates. Before, they had intermingled with other prisoners. The result: The narcotics inmates conspired more effectively than ever before and drugs were increasingly used in the jail.

Despite the obvious differences between inmates of a jail and employees of a business firm, the same conflict of goals between the informal and the formal systems can exist. For example, a group of workers wiring telephone equipment set productivity quotas lower than those management hoped to encourage through its incentive pay plan. The law of the group proved stronger than the law of the management.

Refusal To   It is also true that just as the informal organization can encourage cooper-
Cooperate ation, it can also block it. In many factories operating two or three shifts a day, the outgoing shift foists off its unresolved work problems on the incoming shift. It is not uncommon, in fact, for rework to be left an entire day until the shift that produced the defective parts returned. This can slow down production and cause major accounting headaches.

Resistance   The informal organization can also provide powerful resistance to change, particularly when the group is located in a strategic position in the production line. Tire builders in the rubber tire industry and doffing crews in the spinning rooms of textile plants have, at various times, resisted the introduction of new equipment and methods through the use of wildcat strikes. Other work groups have been more subtle and use such tactics as "malicious compliance." This amounts to following the new method so precisely that it fails and looks absurd. Customs inspectors or police officers have been particularly successful with this strategy.

Discourage Sometimes group norms can become so powerful that they discourage
Creativity individuals from trying new ideas. This is "group think," which has produced such notorious political fiascos as President Kennedy's Bay of Pigs invasion, and President Nixon's Watergate conspiracy. Every day there are thousands of unreported, less spectacular management fiascos traceable to the same group pressure problem. Very homogeneous and cohesive groups are so attractive to their members that they discourage dissent and creativity.

In short, groups are a "given" in an organization. They are neither good nor bad—they just are. As a constant part of the organization's reality, a manager must learn how to manage groups effectively.

THE SUCCESSFUL MANAGEMENT OF GROUPS

Encourage Equity There are several techniques managers can use to get groups to work for the organization and not against it. At the onset, it is important that the group feel that it has been equitably treated by the organization. This feeling of equity comes from a sense of distributive justice. Distributive justice is a feeling that the group's balance of inputs and rewards are equal to those of other groups. Thus, if one group works hard, but receives the same rewards (pay, status, recognition) as another group that doesn't, the sense of distributive justice has been violated, and antiorganization norms are likely to emerge. It is important that the manager prevent the group from feeling underpaid, overworked, and underappreciated. Usually, participation in dividing the pie is one way to encourage feelings of equity and fair play. In this way the manager can encourage pro-organization norms in the group.

Increase The manager needs to encourage the pro-organization group to become
Cohesiveness cohesive, so it can effectively accomplish its pro-organization objectives. The manager can do this by limiting the size of the group, placing group members close together, selecting new members who are similar to current ones, and putting them under some time pressure. All of this will encourage cohesiveness. Cohesive groups, particularly if they have pro-organization norms, are likely to work for the organization.

Recognize Hidden All group activity occurs on two levels. At the same time that individuals
Agendas deal at the cognitive level with issues, they are also dealing at the emotional level. Thus, a discussion of production problems may also be a search for recognition on the part of several individuals, and a defense of their ego on the part of others. Both "what" and the "why" of interactions in a group are

vital to the final outcome. Listening to both can help the manager deal more effectively with the "real" issues being discussed in a group.

In short, it is possible to improve the effectiveness of the many groups with which a manager deals. Establishing equity can improve the probability of the group having pro-organization goals. Increasing cohesiveness can help translate these positive organization norms into effective performance. And, listening for the hidden agendas can help the manager deal with the real issues in a group. In these ways, managers can improve the effectiveness of the ubiquitous groups that populate the organization.

CORPORATE WOMAN

An 'Old Girl Network' Is Born

Three years ago, Nancy Korman, a partner in a Newton (Mass.) public relations and graphics firm called 760 Associates, made a sales pitch to a Boston construction executive, only to be told that his business always went to a fellow member of an all-male breakfast club. "While he was making business deals, I was doling out snap, crackle, and pop," says Korman.

Today, Korman still dishes up breakfast cereal for her husband and two children, but she is no longer excluded from the buddy system. She has founded her own, the Women's Lunch Group, made up of some 60 Boston business and professional women who meet monthly at the Harvard Club. "Members are not allowed to talk about their kids, their husbands, or their emotional crises," says Korman firmly. "We don't want people who are finding themselves or searching out new lifestyles. We are interested in people who can contribute to each other in the marketplace."

Making Contacts

Korman's problem is not unique, and, fortunately for the women who share it, neither is her solution. All across the country, women are organizing their own exclusive luncheon or dinner groups, and inevitably they are called—whatever their official names—old girl networks. Huddled over quiche and white wine, they are making the same contacts their male counterparts have made for years over cigars and brandy in their clubs.

"We saw we needed to make the buddy system work for women the way it works for men," says Patricia B. Wyskocil, a founder of Women in Business Inc. in Los Angeles. "We didn't need help for 'emerging' women. We needed help for women at the middle or near the top."

Costly Lunches

The new networks have more in common with businessmen's clubs than with feminist groups. They are determinedly business-oriented, exclusive, and frequently expensive. In Denver, founders of the two-year-old Women's Forum set a $75 annual fee in order to hire a part-time executive director so that members need not volunteer for clerical work. Lunches cost as much as $10, which is high for Denver. Philadelphia's Forum for Executive Women charges a $50 membership fee. Most members report that their companies foot the bill, just as they do for members of male business clubs.

Typically, the clubs take no political or even feminist positions (apart from supporting the Equal Rights Amendment) but are quick to act in what they regard as their own sphere. The Women's Forum switched its luncheons from Denver's University Club when it learned that the club bars women from full membership. And when H. J. Heinz II, chairman of H. J. Heinz Co., explained that the company had no women on its board because it could find no qualified women, the Executive Women's Council of Greater Pittsburgh sent him a roster of its membership.

No Secretaries

The clubs are a phenomenon of the past two or three years, and most were formed as women moved into middle and upper management posts and realized that they lacked necessary contacts. In almost all cases, the founders rapidly discovered that there were more potential members than they had expected. Almost all of them have had to turn away applicants.

When the Denver group set its entrance requirements—past accomplishments, leadership traits, and a position of influence—the founders feared that they would "end up with a bunch of old women," says President Elizabeth Wright Ingraham, a Colorado Springs architect. Instead, most of the members are in their 30s and 40s, including organizers of Denver's newly opened Women's Bank; the Democratic candidate for lieutenant-governor of Colorado, Nancy Dick; and Judge Zita L. Weinshienk. The forum recently changed its bylaws to allow membership to exceed 100. Other groups have tightened membership requirements to keep out executive secretaries and young women seeking their first business jobs.

Groups in larger cities tend to restrict their membership more severely than does Denver's forum. In Philadelphia, for instance, members must have management jobs paying at least $25,000 a year—or jobs that, in the club's view, should be paying $25,000 a year—and established members resent the emphasis on job-hunting by younger members. They say that the group's value to them is that it facilitates communication. "I just wanted to be able to pick up the telephone and talk to a woman who had some of the problems I had, but I didn't know anyone," says one of the founders of Pittsburgh's Executive Women's Council.

For others, the clubs clearly play an important psychological role. Associating with members of the network "has removed an invisible ceiling I had created over my head," says Wyskocil, who has moved from administrative assistant to the president to vice-president of the First Los Angeles Bank since the formation of Women in Business. "The group has provided me with a low-risk, high-trust environment."

Another Los Angeles member, Virginia C. Oaxaca, discussed a job offer as senior vice-president of Gibraltar Savings & Loan Assn. with her network cronies because she was unsure whether she could handle it. "We talked about the pros and cons, about career paths. The group alleviated a lot of my concern," says Oaxaca, who took the job.

Getting Help
In Philadelphia, the women discuss business-related social situations that would probably draw uncomprehending stares from men. One recent topic, for example, was how to handle dinner party talk when the woman of one couple and the man of the other are business associates. The women also call on club members for help in situations where they feel they could not ask a man. Judith von Seldeneck, a partner in an executive search firm, says, "If I have a job to fill and don't understand exactly what that job entails, I can call a forum member at a management consulting firm to fill me in."

But, like the members of a men's club ripping up Howard Cosell, the businesswomen also debate the merits of Jane Pauley and Barbara Walters. At a recent meeting, they talked about the advantages and disadvantages of having children.

The old girl networks are too new to have generated any charges of reverse discrimination, but that could come. Meanwhile, some clubs have moved toward including men in functions. November is "Bring a Man to Dinner Month" at Pittsburgh's Executive Council. And early next year, the Philadelphia forum plans a joint meeting with its male counterpart group, the First Monday Club. The men suggested the meeting.

Discussion Questions
1. How would you describe the structural (norms, goals, leaders, status system) and interactional (activities, interactions, and sentiments) characteristics of the "Old Girls Network"?
2. How might this "network" contribute to or interfere with the effectiveness of the organization to which these "Old Girls" belong?
3. If one of your employees joined this "network," how might you get the "network" group to work for your organization's goals?

A CASE

THE CASE OF THE CHANGING CAGE

Part I

The voucher-check filing unit was a work unit in the home office of the Atlantic Insurance Company. The assigned task of the unit was to file checks and vouchers written by the company as they were cashed and returned. This filing was the necessary foundation for the main function of the unit: locating any particular check for examination upon demand. There were usually eight to ten requests for specific checks from as many different departments during the day. One of the most frequent reasons checks were requested from the unit was to determine whether checks in payment of claims against the company had been cashed. Thus efficiency in the unit directly affected customer satisfaction with the company. Complaints or inquiries about payments could not be answered with the accuracy and speed conducive to client satisfaction unless the unit could supply the necessary document immediately.

Toward the end of 1952, nine workers manned this unit. There was an assistant (a position equivalent to a foreman in a factory) named Miss Dunn, five other full-time employees, and three part-time workers.

The work area of the unit was well defined. Walls bounded the unit on three sides. The one exterior wall was pierced by light-admitting north windows. The west interior partition was blank. A door opening into a corridor pierced the south interior partition. The east side of the work area was enclosed by a steel mesh reaching from wall to wall and floor to ceiling. This open metal barrier gave rise to the customary name of the unit—"The Voucher Cage." A sliding door through this mesh gave access from the unit's territory to the work area of the rest of the company's agency audit division, of which it was a part, located on the same floor.

The unit's territory was kept inviolate by locks on both doors, fastened at all times. No one not working within the cage was permitted inside unless his name appeared on a special list in the custody of Miss Dunn. The door through the steel mesh was used generally for departmental business. Messengers and runners from other departments usually came to the corridor door and pressed a buzzer for service.

The steel mesh front was reinforced by a bank of metal filing cases where checks were filed. Lined up just inside the barrier, they hid the unit's workers from the view of workers outside their territory, including the section head responsible for over-all supervision of this unit according to the company's formal plan of operation.

Source. Reproduced by permission of the Society for Applied Anthropology from *Human Organization,* vol. 16, no. 1 (Spring, 1957).

Part II

On top of the cabinets which were backed against the steel mesh, one of the male employees in the unit neatly stacked pasteboard boxes in which checks were transported to the cage. They were later reused to hold older checks sent into storage. His intention was less getting these boxes out of the way than increasing the effective height of the sight barrier so the section head could not see into the cage "even when he stood up."

The girls stood at the door of the cage which led into the corridor and talked to the messenger boys. Out this door also the workers slipped unnoticed to bring in their customary afternoon snack. Inside the cage, the workers sometimes engaged in a good-natured game of rubber band "sniping."

Workers in the cage possessed good capacity to work together consistently and workers outside the cage often expressed envy of those in it because of the "nice people" and friendly atmosphere there. The unit had no apparent difficulty keeping up with its work load.

Part III

For some time prior to 1952 the controller's department of the company had not been able to meet its own standards of efficient service to clients. Company officials felt the primary cause to be spatial. Various divisions of the controller's department were scattered over the entire 22-story company building. Communication between them required phone calls, messengers, or personal visits, all costing time. The spatial separation had not seemed very important when the company's business volume was smaller prior to World War II. But business had grown tremendously since then and spatial separation appeared increasingly inefficient.

Finally in November of 1952 company officials began to consolidate the controller's department by relocating two divisions together on one floor. One was the agency audit division, which included the voucher-check filing unit. As soon as the decision to move was made, lower level supervisors were called in to help with planning. Line workers were not consulted, but were kept informed by the assistants of planning progress. Company officials were concerned about the problem of transporting many tons of equipment and some 200 workers from two locations to another single location without disrupting work flow. So the move was planned to occur over a single week end, using the most efficient resources available. Assistants were kept busy planning positions for files and desks in the new location.

Desks, files, chairs, and even wastebaskets were numbered prior to the move, and relocated according to a master chart checked on the spot by the assistant. Employees were briefed as to where the new location was and which elevators they should take to reach it. The company successfully transported the paraphernalia of the voucher-check filing unit from one floor to another over one week end. Workers in the cage quit Friday afternoon at the old stand, reported back Monday at the new.

The exterior boundaries of the new cage were still three building walls and the steel mesh, but the new cage possessed only one door—the sliding door through the steel mesh into the work area of the rest of the agency audit division. The territory of the cage had also been reduced in size. An entire bank of filing cabinets had to be left behind in the old location to be taken over by the unit moving there. The new cage was arranged so that there was no longer a row of metal filing cabinets lined up inside the steel mesh obstructing the view into the cage.

Part IV

When the workers in the cage inquired about the removal of the filing cabinets from along the steel mesh fencing, they found that Mr. Burke had insisted that these cabinets be rearranged so his view into the cage would not be obstructed by them. Miss Dunn had tried to retain the cabinets in their prior position, but her efforts had been overridden.

Mr. Burke disapproved of conversation. Since he could see workers conversing in the new cage, he "requested" Miss Dunn to put a stop to all unnecessary talk. Attempts by female clerks to talk to messenger boys brought the wrath of her superior down on Miss Dunn, who was then forced to reprimand the girls.

Mr. Burke also disapproved of an untidy working area, and any boxes or papers which were in sight were a source of annoyance to him. He did not exert supervision directly, but would "request" Miss Dunn to "do something about those boxes." In the new cage, desks had to be completely cleared at the end of the day, in contrast to the work-in-progress piles left out in the old cage. Boxes could not accumulate on top of filing cases.

The custom of afternoon snacking also ran into trouble. Lacking a corridor door, the food bringers had to venture forth and pack back their snack tray through the work area of the rest of their section, bringing this hitherto unique custom to the attention of workers outside the cage. The latter promptly recognized the desirability of afternoon snacks and began agitation for the same privilege. This annoyed the section head, who forbade workers in the cage from continuing this custom.

Part V

Mr. Burke later made a rule which permitted one worker to leave the new cage at a set time every afternoon to bring up food for the rest. This rigidity irked cage personnel, accustomed to a snack when the mood struck, or none at all. Having made his concession to the cage force, Mr. Burke was unable to prevent workers outside the cage from doing the same thing. What had once been unique to the workers in the cage was now common practice in the section.

Although Miss Dunn never outwardly expressed anything but compliance and approval of superior directives, she exhibited definite signs of anxiety. All the cage workers reacted against Burke's increased domination. When he imposed his decisions upon the voucher-check filing unit, he became "Old Grandma" to its personnel. The cage workers sneered at him and ridiculed him behind his back. Workers who formerly had obeyed company policy as a matter of course began to find reasons for loafing and obstructing work in the new cage. One of the changes that took place in the behavior of the workers had to do with their game of rubber band sniping. All knew Mr. Burke would disapprove of this game. It became highly clandestine and fraught with dangers. Yet shooting rubber bands *increased*.

Newly arrived checks were put out of sight as soon as possible, filed or not. Workers hid unfiled checks, generally stuffing them into desk drawers or unused file drawers. Since boxes were forbidden, there were fewer unused file drawers than there had been in the old cage. So the day's work was sometimes undone when several clerks hastily shoved vouchers and checks indiscriminately into the same file drawer at the end of the day.

Before a worker in the cage filed incoming checks, she measured with her ruler the thickness in inches of each bundle she filed. At the end of each day she totaled her input and reported it to Miss Dunn. All incoming checks were measured upon arrival. Thus Miss Dunn had a rough estimate of unit intake compared with file input. Theoretically she was able to tell at any time how much unfiled material she had on hand and how well the unit was keeping up with its task. Despite this running check, when the annual inventory of unfiled checks on hand in the cage was taken at the beginning of the calendar year 1953, a seriously large backlog of unfiled checks was found. To the surprise and dismay of Miss Dunn, the inventory showed the unit to be far behind schedule, filing much more slowly than before the relocation of the cage.

Discussion Questions

1. It appears that as management increased its control over the Voucher Cage, it destroyed or at least damaged an informal organization that had definite advantages.
   Discuss.

2. Assuming that the move had to take place, how would you have acted if you had:
   (a) Mr. Burke's job,
   (b) Miss Dunn's job?

Groups emerge out of the mixture of the formal requirements placed upon people at work and the individual personality characteristics of those people.

Groups are an ever-present part of the organization's scene. All of us are members of many groups. All of these groups have similar structures—goals, norms, leaders, status systems, and varying degrees of cohesion. Inside, all groups have interactions (what people say), activities (what people do), and sentiments (what people feel). Although all groups have similar structural and interactional elements, each group arranges these elements to generate a unique personality.

In their formation, groups go through the distinct stages of forming, storming, norming, and finally, performing. All groups go through these stages, although some take so long in the first three stages that too little time is left over for effectively doing the group's work. Groups contribute in several ways to the formal organization. Work groups provide cooperation and improvisation to meet operating requirements not envisaged in the formal organization design. They also exercise discipline over their members. They help to satisfy individual member social needs and provide for important protection and predictability. Groups can work to the disadvantage of the formal system as well. Groups within the system can develop their own goals, which may clash with those of the formal organization. The work group may pursue its own goals to the detriment of official goals. The work group loyalties may block intergroup cooperation, or block innovation when the group sees either as contrary to its special interest.

Managers can improve the effectiveness of groups by establishing a sense of equity, encouraging cohesiveness and listening for the hidden agendas in member's conversation. In all, the manager must recognize that groups are an organizational fact of life. The manager needs to manage groups to work for, not against, the organization.

Here are some principles:

1. Because the shape of the formal organization and work technology affect the pattern that groups formation will take, managers should consider the human and social consequences of organizational design, plant layout, and workflows.

2. Groups have similar structural elements of goals, norms, leaders, a status system, and varying levels of cohesiveness. Internally, groups have interactions, activities, and sentiments.

3. Groups develop through four stages: forming, storming, norming, and performing.

4. Groups contribute to organizational effectiveness by providing spontaneous cooperation, discipline, protection, predictability, and to individual members a sense of belonging.

5. Groups can block organizational effectiveness by developing conflicting goals, refusals to cooperate, resistance to change, and group think.

6. Managers can more effectively manage groups by encouraging a sense of equity, developing group cohesiveness, and hearing the hidden agendas of individual members.

CHAPTER FOUR **MOTIVATION**

At the conclusion of this chapter you should be able to:

1. Distinguish three levels of human needs.
2. Describe how shifts occur in the motivational power of needs at different levels.
3. Describe how work can satisfy needs.
4. Describe and illustrate how management actions affect motivation.
5. Describe several steps managers can take to increase motivation.
6. Discuss some problems in the management of motivation.

ACTIVITY ─────────────────────────────

THE MONEY GAME

I. Objectives
   A. To experience giving and receiving.
   B. To explore the feelings and ideas associated with these activities.
II. Premeeting Preparation
   A. Read the instructions.
   B. Bring some coins to class.
III. Instructions
   A. For this exercise the class will divide into groups of 8 to 10 persons.
   B. Each group should gather around a table or desk or form a circle on the floor.
   C. Group members should put all their change on the table, desk, or floor area in front of them.
   D. No one may talk, whisper, gesture, or otherwise communicate to anyone. No one may cover up his or her money during the exercise.
   E. Three activity periods will follow. The instructor will tell you when to stop and start each one. Here's what to do in each period.
      1. Each group member may *give* change from his or her fund to whomever in the group he or she wishes.

      > Time for period 1: 5 minutes

      2. Each group member may *take* change from anyone else in the group.

      > Time for period 2: 5 minutes

      3. Each group member may *give* to or *take* from anyone else in the group.

      > Time for period 3: 2 minutes

   F. At the end of the exercise each group member keeps whatever he or she has.
IV. Discussion
   Your instructor will help you explore what happened in the exercise and its meaning for management.

   > Time for discussion: 20 minutes

THE TEXT

Many researchers have contributed to our understanding of what motivates individuals and affects their expectations. Probably the best known motivation theorist is Abraham Maslow, who structured a hierarchy of needs as the scheme for his theory of motivation. The following discussion of needs is drawn from Maslow's work.

Every individual is unique. But all individuals have some things in common. For example, we all have certain physical, social, and growth needs. The strength of these needs varies from person to person and from time to time within the same person. And the needs express themselves in different ways in different cultures and in different situations within one culture. But these common needs lie behind human behavior, and to know about them is to know an important part of the story of why people do what they do.

MASLOW'S HIERARCHY OF NEEDS

Physical Needs

The most basic human needs are the physical ones. They include such drives as hunger and thirst. The reason the physical needs are described as basic is because life itself depends upon their being satisfied.

Deprived of food, a person's mind can become wholly occupied with getting food. The person becomes moved or motivated to act out of the need for food. The actions that occur will be intended to reduce the need for food.

Basic and Security Needs An apparently similar case is the drug addict. Addicts can acquire a new physical need—drugs. The lives of heroin addicts are grim testimony to the enslavement of people to their need. Such needs lie behind the industry of a portion of the criminals and prostitutes of many cities who must pay $100 or more a day to support their habits.

Above the physical needs, but closely linked to them, is the need for safety or security. People not only crave food and drink, but they crave assurance that it and other things necessary to well-being are forthcoming reliably. People need to feel safe from arbitrary denial of their necessities.

Recent reports from drug addicts, for example, reveal the frequent experience of being "ripped off" by dealers whose drugs are diluted beyond customary limits. Even worse than the fear of getting nothing for something is the fear of dying from impurities in the drugs.

Social Needs

Once the basic needs are relatively satisfied, another set of needs begins to shape human action. These are the social needs. They include the need to love and be loved, the need to belong, to feel accepted by other people and, in general, the need for the warmth and support of human companionship.

When you played the "Money Game" you may have found yourself regulating how much you gave and how much you took out of a desire to preserve good relations with other people in your group. In some cases, people give more to some individuals as a way of expressing particular approval or of hoping to gain approval. In one group, an especially beautiful girl received all the change belonging to the other members of the group (who were all male), plus an offer from one to lie, steal, or kill on her behalf.

Relatedness Needs People do crave the company of others. Unless an individual learns to navigate the social seas, he or she will often feel the pain of unsatisfied social needs. Acceptance, affection, the trust and esteem of others—all these feelings come only to people whose behavior makes them the natural response of others. Those who never learn how to behave in ways that lead to these social satisfactions become isolates. And isolates are among the most troubled and, occasionally, troublesome people in a society. They more frequently become depressed and commit suicide than do other people. They also—in the fashion of Lee Harvey Oswald and other assassins of public figures—have been known to turn their discontents to violence.

Social needs are not restricted to the wish to belong, however. For some individuals the strongest need that affects their interpersonal relations is the urge to influence others. Some people, no matter what situation they are in, seem to wish to exert the most power. They need to win arguments. They wish to lead and influence. In short, they have a stronger need for power than for mere companionship.

Whether through exerting influence or being less dominant, social interaction is the source of important human satisfactions.

Growth Needs

When the social needs are relatively satisfied, still another set of needs begins to govern behavior. These are the growth needs. These include needs to be effective or competent, and to achieve results in whatever one is doing.

In many activities, you may have felt the urge to do it right, to get the job done successfully, to win a competition. You may have set quotas for yourself and tried hard to meet them. In any event, these feelings and actions illustrate the workings of the growth needs. They focus feelings and actions on the task, not on interpersonal relations or on physical needs.

Development Needs People in whom the urge to achieve is extremely strong are rare, but we all have some need to achieve and feel competent. This need is unusual in that success in achieving does not reduce the urge to achieve; it only strengthens it. People can have their fill of food and drink, but people who set goals and work hard to reach them and who taste the reward of meeting their goals do not quit. Instead, they continue to set goals, more challenging ones, and plug away at them. In a sense, the satisfactions obtained from growth in competence and achievement lead not to feeling full, but to feeling hungry for more of the same.

THE NEED TO ACHIEVE

Professor David McClelland has conducted research for many years on what he has called a special "mental virus," the need to achieve. Only about one person in 10 has a very high need to achieve, but those who have high levels of achievement motivation tend to behave as follows:

1. They enjoy taking personal responsibility for solving problems.
2. They set goals that are neither impossible nor easy to meet.
3. They take calculated risks in order to reach their goals.
4. They want and use feedback on their performance.

People high in need for achievement are more often found in business than in other areas. And within business, they are often found in sales jobs. There they have a rich field for problem-solving and getting feedback and they seem to thrive on it.

McClelland believes cultures tend to encourage or inhibit achievement motivation in people through such means as literature. In nations where achievement motivation is higher, on the average, economic development also tends to be higher according to McClelland. Thus, this special mental virus, the need to achieve, might be considered an important resource.

McClelland has also conducted research which suggests that achievement motivation can be aroused and increased by training. Others have suggested that the way the organization designs its jobs and carries out its planning and control activities can also arouse or depress achievement motivation. What is needed to arouse it is a climate which provides problems to solve, encourages goal-setting, and provides support for risk-taking and feedback on performance.

The pleasures of achievement and competence, whether they come from learning to swim, to read, to fight, to sing, or to do anything else, are the pleasures of growing feelings of mastery, of self-esteem, and, often, of the esteem of others. They are the satisfactions of growth and development. And when the physical and social needs are no longer the main shapers of behavior, the growth needs can become powerful. People can hunger for doing things well and feeling good about it with a strength equal to hunger for food or love.

Finally, the pinnacle of the growth needs is the urge to express the special, the unique nature of one's self. What comes into play here are not the achievements and competencies that other people value, but those ways of behaving and feeling that you yourself sense are you being yourself in the best and most satisfying image you hold of yourself. This is the need for self-fulfillment.

SHIFTS IN NEEDS

There is a quality about the way all of these needs work and are arranged that we have implied, but not yet explained; that is, that the three types of needs exist in a definite order. To get an idea of this order, think of a pyramid comprised of three huge layers. The bottom one consists of the physical needs. The middle one is the social needs. The top one is the growth needs. (See Figure 4.1.)

Dynamic Shifts   Movement up the pyramid occurs because satisfied needs do not motivate behavior. As we have already said, social needs don't shape behavior until physical needs are met, and growth needs don't shape behavior until social needs are met. It is only after the need for food and drink is satisfied that one can think about enjoying friends. It is only after some degree of social satisfaction is obtained that one shifts to emphasize the satisfactions of growth and development.

The process also works in reverse. The history of the Donner Party, a band of pioneers whose journey ended in freezing and starvation in the Sierras, illustrates this all too well. When the party began its westward journey, the members talked of high ideals, of the fulfillment of a vision of a better life. The hard traveling and the final lack of food bore down upon the group. The members were driven down the pyramid of needs to the point where no thoughts were left but those of filling empty bellies. The diary of one member of the party reveals that before the trip was ended, the strong practiced cannibalism upon the weak.

Although most shifts in needs are not so dramatic, the basic point is valid.

Figure 4.1   The Pyramid of Needs.

Needs are never fixed at one level on the pyramid. Higher needs replace lower ones when satisfactions reduce the power of lower needs to move people. Similarly, when lower needs don't stay satisfied, they can regain control of behavior. The pleasure of performing a task especially well is not important when one has had nothing to eat for days.

Individual and Situational Differences But we would do well to remember that individuals continue to be unique. One person can be moved by an exceptionally powerful need for security. Another can give little thought to security. This would be possible even if the two were twins and held nearly identical jobs in the same company.

Similarly, needs can vary in their force within the same person over time. Even though someone's job duties, pay, family, neighborhood, and other conditions may remain relatively stable, the desire for one kind of satisfaction can gain in strength while another fades. Mid-career changes are not uncommon, and they are not uncommonly accounted for by shifts in needs. Relatively mild needs for growth can become stronger and lead one to seek new challenges that promise to yield feelings of competence and self-esteem.

Despite these individual differences and changes in needs, the general outline of the pyramid of needs roughly describes the situation for all of us. We are all in the same boat, in that we have physical, social, and growth needs and that the unmet needs have the power to motivate behavior.

WORK AND HUMAN NEEDS

We are all in the same boat in still another sense: most of us need to work for a living. And most of us will find jobs in organizations. Having a job in an organization is a condition that modern life interposes between human needs and opportunities for satisfying them (Figure 4.2).

The result is that work has an important impact on motivation: it is a path

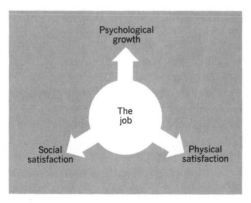

Figure 4.2   The Job and Human Needs.

we all travel in seeking to meet our needs. It's easy to see the connection between work and needs: work earns the money we have to pay for the necessities of survival. For most people during most of history since Adam and Eve were expelled from the Garden of Eden, work of some sort has been the means of gaining food and shelter. In fact, minimal satisfaction of physical needs has been all that most of humanity could hope to gain from working.

Work and Physical Needs   In the early days of industrial development in nineteenth-century Britain, there were strikes in which the only demand of the workers was enough pay so that they could keep alive to continue work. Modern aspirations and demands for fringe benefits, security provisions, coffee breaks, pleasant working conditions, and jobs that satisfy growth needs would have been unimaginable then. But times have changed.

Times have changed for the better in that in many societies, the people who work are sufficiently satisfied in their physical needs, and even in their safety or security needs, so that new wants have opened up. Most early twentieth-century management thought on the subject of motivation was summed up by an oft-quoted remark of Henry Ford's: "You just set the work before the men and have them do it." However, Ford paid $5.00 a day—an extremely high wage at the time. The assumption was that paying well takes care of motivation.

Work and Social Needs   In the 1920s and 1930s, however, some disturbing research findings began to emerge. According to a study at Western Electric, workers were not responding in a predictable way to pay incentives. It seems that there was a chemistry of sorts that occurred among groups of workers. Among other things, this group chemistry could lead members to join together to produce more or less independently of pay, but depending on their feelings toward one another and toward the company.

It finally became clear that work was not simply a direct link between pay and physical needs. Work had an important bearing on social needs, too. Some jobs cast people in the role of isolates, as a study of textile workers showed. And these isolates were absent more often, quit more often, and had more ailments and complaints than people whose jobs cast them in groups. Where the path to productivity was the same path that led to satisfying social needs, productivity was likely to occur. Where the paths differed, productivity suffered.

These were very disturbing findings, indeed. But they merely revealed what had always been true, but unrecognized. Work is a path to feelings of friendly affection, of belonging. At work people can cooperate, they can help one another, and they can derive the positive satisfactions that come of shared activities.

Where pay and security had loosened the grip of physical needs upon motivation, social needs had to be met through work, if work was to motivate. However, jobs were seldom designed to tap the energy behind social needs. So work remained a path to eight hours of near isolation for some people. However, for millions, having jobs in organizations, like belonging to families, unions, or clubs, brought increased satisfaction of social needs.

Work and *Growth Needs* Of course, as we have seen, the satisfaction of physical and social needs does not bring an end to want. It merely opens up a new, higher class of wants: the growth needs. Beyond subsistence and companionship lies the prospect of work that pays off in feelings of achievement, of competence, of self-esteem, and even of self-fulfillment.

Today, despite ups and downs in the job market, more people feel free from lower level needs and want meaningful work. The so called "blue-collar blues" are a result of workers' inability to satisfy their growth needs on the job. They are alienated from work that requires them to behave more like robots than people.

Fortunately, many jobs provide opportunities for growth. A great many people, perhaps the majority, find some opportunities in the course of doing their work to experience a sense of accomplishment and skillfulness. This is possible in jobs that require the use of uniquely human abilities for problem solving, moderate risk taking, regulating one's own performance by setting goals, and using feedback to adjust one's efforts as necessary. These are jobs that call for a committed involvement. In a sense, the job has the person as much as the person has the job.

If the discovery of the importance of social needs at work was disturbing to old-fashioned managers' ideas about how to motivate people, the discovery of growth needs and their role on the job has been revolutionary. Perhaps the hardest lesson of all was the one that followed from the inability of satisfied needs to motivate behavior: managers must make work the path to meeting unsatisfied needs if they would motivate people to perform their jobs.

MOTIVATION-HYGIENE THEORY

Professor Frederick Herzberg of the University of Utah and his associates have conducted a great many studies which show that the factors that satisfy people at work are different from the factors that dissatisfy them. Sources of satisfaction (which he calls "motivators" because they appear necessary for substantial improvements in work performance) are found in the doing of work. These include achievement, recognition, work itself, responsibility, and advancement. Sources of dissatisfaction (which he calls "hygiene" factors because they form the environment of work and keeping them in good order is necessary to avoid a drop in performance below a normal "healthy" day's work) are found surrounding the work. These include company policy and administration, supervision, salary, interpersonal relations, and working conditions.

TUMBLEWEEDS
by Tom K. Ryan

According to Herzberg, maintaining a good "hygienic" work environment doesn't improve motivation any more than sewage disposal or water purification improves health. Just as sewage disposal and water purification help to avoid ill health, however, a good work environment helps avoid dissatisfaction and the loss of productivity it can cause. To improve performance, managers must provide work that is intrinsically motivating. This means job enrichment is a powerful means of arousing motivation.

There are two policy implications of Herzberg's research. Managers must act to maintain hygiene or else dissatisfactions can arise and drop performance below acceptable levels. Managers must provide jobs rich in achievement opportunities if they are to support achievement-oriented behavior capable of producing better than acceptable performance.

MANAGEMENT AND MOTIVATION

As we indicated earlier, to know about human needs is to know an important part of the story of why people do what they do. But it is not to know the whole story. We still must learn how to manage intelligently in light of our understanding of motivation. We will turn now to the rest of the story of motivation and explore the prospects of managing it.

Perceptions and Expectancies To begin with, needs alone do not explain behavior. Several additional factors are involved. Chiefly, they lie in the situation in which the person finds himself, in what the person sees or perceives, and in the mental connections he makes between the situation and that person's needs. A person may feel thirsty, but the action of going to the faucet and getting a drink of water occurs only because of the expectation that the effort will result in the reward of diminished thirst.

One must believe that a given action in a given situation will satisfy what is currently an unmet need. Otherwise there would be no reason to act. Thirst might be powerful, but if no link was known between it and faucets, only chance might lead one to the faucet.

EXPECTANCY THEORY

Professor John Atkinson of the University of Michigan, Professor Victor Vroom of Yale University, Professor Lyman Porter of the University of California, Irvine, and Professor Edward Lawler of the University of Michigan have contributed to the development of a theory of motivation called expectancy theory. Although the theory is formulated in several different ways, it has certain central ideas. These central ideas are as follows:

1. Needs alone do not explain behavior. It is also necessary that the individual expect two things:

a. If he tries he can really do what he is trying to do.

b. If he does it, he will really be rewarded for having done it.

2. Since actions tend to produce multiple results, he must calculate that the rewards will be greater than the costs, however difficult it is to calculate either, thus leaving him with a profit.

3. The implication for management is that it must be possible for individuals to see that effective performance is rewarded if motivation is to be aroused.

Work Instrumental to Satisfying Needs   These conditions, simple and obvious though they may seem, provide the keys to the managerial use of motivation. Work can be a path to the satisfaction of needs. When good performance of the job is seen by an employee to be a path to meeting physical, social, and growth needs, the chances of good performance are increased. What managers must do to manage motivation is arrange conditions so that employees will see the connection between their efforts, their performance, and the satisfaction of their needs.

Job Impoverishment   Psychologists have learned that where people are unable to behave in adultlike ways on the job, unable to use their abilities to think, plan, organize, and be responsible for accomplishing meaningful work, they are unable to satisfy their higher level growth needs. Performance of uninteresting work pays no psychic rewards. No feelings of esteem, of achievement, of exercising one's highest abilities, and certainly no sense of being all one is capable of being can come from such work. All too often, this is the kind of work organizations present to adults. This is especially true in large, highly systematized organizations.

THEORY X AND THEORY Y

The late Professor Douglas McGregor of M.I.T. described two contrasting sets of assumptions about people that supported markedly differing approaches to managing people. The first he called Theory X and, like Brand X in numerous commercial advertisements, it compared unfavorably. Theory X consisted of assumptions such as the following:

1. People are born lazy.
2. They aren't very bright, either.
3. Therefore, if they are to be motivated, people must be directed, controlled, and coerced.

Theory Y consisted of assumptions such as these:

1. People are born with a natural tendency to be active.
2. Intelligence is widely distributed throughout the population.

3. People can be largely self-directing and self-controlling and will work hard to achieve goals they have helped to set.

Theory Y is based on behavioral science research. Theory X is based upon ignorance and traditional false explanations. Moreover, the management practices, for example, tight control and close supervision, which are logically derived from Theory X, are likely to produce the behaviors they are meant to prevent. The management practices logically derived from Theory Y, for example, participative leadership, job enrichment, and self-control, are likely to produce the behaviors the theory regards as natural. In other words, each theory leads to practices that seem to confirm the theory.

Because work in a "nothing" job appears not to be a path to satisfying unmet growth needs, work loses its power to motivate. People see that they must keep their jobs to receive their paychecks, but the work inspires no committed involvement. The result is that for many people the job is a sort of partial retirement in which energy is withdrawn from work. They come to work each day, but they work only halfheartedly.

Managers untrained in the nature of motivation see this result and interpret it as laziness. They complain that people are born lazy. They don't seem very bright or conscientious either. Nor are they grateful. Pay them good wages and benefits, provide good working conditions, and what do you get? Minimal performance, grumbling, and resignations if somebody else offers them a nickel more an hour.

Given the reality of halfhearted workers and this explanation of their behavior, the manager finds only one solution. Crack down. Direct the employees more precisely. Install controls to make sure they obey. Specialize tasks to be sure these louts don't muck up anything important.

What is the result? Not improvement, but even less commitment. Why? Because the job has been stripped even more completely of ways to satisfy growth needs.

The Cost of Misunderstanding Motivation This story may seem too depressing to be true, but it is true. It depicts most of the history of management ignorant of the nature of motivation. However, the bottom line of the story need not be so gloomy. If it is possible to provide conditions that demotivate people at work, it is also possible to provide conditions that motivate them. Fortunately, a great deal has been learned about how to manage to produce conditions better calculated to make work a path to satisfying growth needs.

INCREASING MOTIVATION

Before managers can cope effectively with motivation, they need to recognize that such administrative actions as planning, controlling, leading, and organizing work are also human actions. Controls, for example, don't merely provide neutral data. They also communicate to employees what is apparently important to managers. A manager might simply ask for the two-week budget and expense information when she formerly wanted only a monthly report. Such innocent information-seeking could send scores of clerks and others scurrying to make certain that those figures look the way they suppose the boss wants them to look.

Job Enrichment   The way the flow of work in a plant or office is organized can provide some workers with jobs full of challenge which call forth high levels of commitment and competence. Responsibilities can be built into jobs or taken out of them. Instead of soldering six connections, the electrical assembly worker can put an entire unit together. Instead of keypunching whatever comes along, the keypunch operator can "contract" to do the payroll keypunching for an entire department. The same keypunch operator can handle all the contacts with the department for which he prepares the payroll, resolving any problems himself.

PERSONALITY AND JOB ENRICHMENT

Professor Victor Vroom of Yale University studied the impact of job enrichment upon workers in a large parcel delivery corporation. He observed that job enrichment, through increased participation in decision making, did not improve either performance or satisfaction for workers whose personalities were characterized by low needs for independence and by authoritarianism. According to Vroom's findings, managers cannot expect everyone to respond in the same way to enriched jobs. Some people are more content being closely directed and not having to work on their own.

Wise managers examine alternative approaches to management not just for their technical suitability but for their motivational consequences as well. Consider, for example, the following options.

1. Planning
    (a) Goals set by superior and communicated downward.
    (b) Goals jointly set by superiors and subordinates.
2. Controlling
    (a) Performance measured and evaluated by superior.
    (b) Performance measured and evaluated jointly by superior and subordinates.
3. Leading
    (a) Direction provided by superior.
    (b) Direction provided jointly by superior and subordinates.
4. Organizing
    (a) Jobs specialized and simplified as much as possible.
    (b) Jobs containing problem-solving and goal-meeting responsibilities.

Every Employee In every instance, alternative (b) would seem to make the subordinate's
a Manager job larger. It may not make him more contented, but it would likely make
him more involved by making it possible for the job to yield feelings of
achievement, competence, and other growth satisfactions. Where committed
involvement is a path to better performance and to increased satisfaction, the
management strategy that fosters it becomes attractive (Figure 4.3).

In many instances, greater involvement does lead to better performance,
and better performance leads to effective organizations and satisfied employees. As a result, such practices as participative management and job enrichment have become popular. But there is no universal psychological answer to
be plugged into every situation. Instead, effective management of motivation
calls for a continuing and painstaking analysis of particular situations. It
calls for reasoning backwards—from job requirements to desired behavior,
to making such behavior more likely to occur by making it evident to employees that they can satisfy their needs through effective performance.

SOME PROBLEMS

Perhaps we have made the task of increasing motivation through management seem simpler than it is. There are a number of complications and they,
too, are a part of the story of why people do what they do and why managers
have not made organizations uniformly satisfying places to work.

Personality First, not everyone reacts to goal-setting, self-control, participative leader-
Differences ship, job enrichment, and other motivation-increasing strategies in the same
way. Some people are made overly anxious by increased responsibility and
complexity in their work. Greater involvement can be an agony as well as
an ecstasy.

Work is not central to everyone's life. Many people prefer a job that
permits them to think about other things. They don't look for the job to
fulfill their social or their growth needs. The result of complicated jobs for
these people may be decreased satisfaction and decreased performance.

Second, managers may recognize that if the jobs were redesigned, they
might be more rewarding to people who perform them and even more pro-

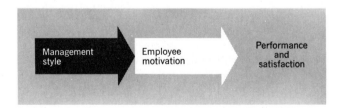

Figure 4.3

Some Limits ductive for the company. But managers have limited authority and power. In many cases they are unable to change the contents of jobs. They are also not readily able to abandon long-established ways of leading subordinates.

Third, there are situations in which one management function or another, leading, for example, just doesn't account for much difference in productivity. The very best leader might only make a slight impact on productivity because productivity depends on other factors, technology, for example. The leader may be very good or very bad whereas motivation and performance remain about the same.

Mixed Results Fourth, even if managers are successful in increasing employee motivation and involvement, the results are sometimes sour as well as sweet. A toy manufacturer, for example, managed to achieve high levels of motivation and productivity in a painting operation in the middle of its production sequence. The result: pressure on preceding work preparation operations to produce more, pressure from succeeding packing and shipping operations to produce less, conflict over new wage inequities resulting from changed bonus earnings, assembly line imbalance, and more. An employment office managed to increase interviewers' motivation to refer and place more job applicants. The result: cheating, secretiveness, neglect of routine counseling duties, and more.

The problem with increasing motivation is that it often results in an ambitious effort, but an effort often flawed by tunnel vision. Note that this effect is not necessary or unavoidable, but it is common especially when there is a narrow, concrete measure of success and appealing rewards for reaching it or worrisome penalties for not reaching it.

But to face these problems is not to miss the more important point: there are tremendous opportunities in a wide range of situations for making work a path to need satisfactions. The manager who knows why people do what they do usually has some chance of arranging the conditions of work so people can see it as a path they wish to travel.

SUMMARY

Economists have means of measuring the degree to which an industrial plant uses its full capacity to produce. But what is missing from these calculations is a measure of the degree to which each employee uses his or her full capacity. Without assuming that everyone ought to be operating at full steam all of the time, it is possible to assume that organizations probably are not arranging conditions of work so that they elicit the levels of motivation and performance they could arouse if a knowledge of motivation were applied.

A careful reading of the law of human nature that says only unmet needs motivate human behavior is the starting point. Next, comes a look at the existing patterns of need satisfaction. Finally, the wise manager blends this information with other economic and technical considerations and designs work well calculated to suit the human and material realities of his situation.

WORK IN THE 21ST CENTURY: A NEW WAY

Labor Participation In Job Decisions Gaining In U.S.

JONATHAN WOLMAN, ASSOCIATED WRITER

The "Quality of Work Life" movement, a worldwide effort to expand worker participation in job decisions, is quietly emerging from the deep background in the United States.

By the year 2000, American workers will demand, and receive, a bigger voice in decisions that affect their job performance.

Participatory workplace projects—ranging from autonomous work teams to well-oiled labor-management panels—will thrive, especially in industrial plants.

Worker-community ownership of U.S. firms will expand slightly as profit-minded corporations sell off aging, unprofitable, plants that provide jobs to thousands of workers in the nation's industrial belt.

But "co-determination"—a European method by which workers and management share company policymaking—is unlikely to catch fire here. Management is unyielding and labor is uninterested.

This is the outline for the next 30 years provided by the experts—management, labor and independent—concerned with expansion of Quality of Work Life in the United States.

Today, "QWL" is a sometimes exotic, sometimes routine fact of life in many European and Japanese companies. Workers help design their jobs, representatives sit on corporate boards, sometimes even share ownership of the company.

Though QWL is in its infancy here, more and more American companies, large and small, are getting involved. Their practical experiences likely will help shape the nature of work in 21st century America.

Today's QWL projects come in all shapes and sizes.

Dana Corp. sends "front-office executives" to plants in places like Edgerton, Wis., and Lima,

Ohio, where workers are updated on corporate activities. In turn, the executives get the workers' reactions.

TRW's Turbine Components Division uses the Scanlon Plan, providing bonuses when employe suggestions bring cost savings to the company or improvements in the work environment. The plant's 1,100 workers shared $750,000 in bonuses during the first 12 months of the program.

In the newsroom of the Minneapolis Tribune, reporters have an advisory role in selecting middle-level editors.

Sperry Rand decided to get out of the library furniture business when its Herkimer plant failed to show sufficient profit. An employe group, unwilling to walk away from their work, bought the plant several years ago. Today Herkimer makes money, provides a local payroll of $3.5 million annually and employs 270 people.

The Rushton Mining Co. and AMSCO Equipment Co., in Jamestown, N.Y., have junked the assembly-line work approach in some areas and instead are using work teams, a process whose most famous practitioner is Volvo, the Swedish automaker.

At Rushton, in Pennsylvania, team members can handle any job in their section; they rotate jobs and all receive top pay. At AMSCO, a Jamestown, N.Y., division of American Sterilizer Corp., teams are responsible for decisions on scheduling, quality and production.

A labor-management panel called the "Policies and Procedures Committee" meets regularly at Rockwell International's Battle Creek, Mich., plant to decide on projects involving production and health and safety.

A Committee on Productivity at Kaiser Industries' steel plant in Fontana, Calif., meets monthly and workers also serve on panels in each

Source. The San Diego Union, October 29, 1978.

of the plant's 37 operating departments. Officials say committee discussions have brought substantial productivity increases as workers applied practical knowledge to reduce production delays and waste.

Despite a recent flurry of such activity, such "democratic workplace" projects are still rare in the United States.

There are several hundred so-called labor-management committees, where workers and management meet regularly to solve workplace problems. But the number of significant job projects where workers are involved day by day in job decisions probably is in the dozens, compared to an estimated 250 in West Germany alone.

The chief impetus for QWL efforts is the maturing of the American workforce.

"Most of our people, even the janitors, have high school (diplomas) and some college," says an insurance company executive. "So how do you tell 'em they're too dumb to help plan their own job?" According to an Ohio factory manager: "We've got an aggressive bunch of people; they don't like being told how to work a machine lathe by some guy from the Harvard Business School."

Worker participation in job decisions runs counter to long traditional production and "scientific" management practices in the United States. But now, for the first time, studies indicate that a majority of workers believe they are entitled to greater say about their work roles.

Management responsiveness to these trends is behind much of the QWL experimentation, but even their staunchest corporate supporters stress that these projects must pass the profit test if they are to survive and expand.

"Unions and management must both continue to adjust reasonably to pressures for democratic practices in the working place," says Cliff Garvin, chairman of Exxon Corp. However, he cautioned, quality of work-life efforts "that are instituted at the expense of organizational efficiency are, in my view, shortsighted and seriously flawed."

Exxon is one of many major companies interested in forging a more democratic work atmosphere, with QWL programs involving both blue collar and office workers. General Electric, General Motors, General Foods all have moved in

that direction. Perhaps the most ambitious plan is GM's, which has hundreds of projects.

One reason, a GM executive says, is that "to be competitive in the world market, we've got to tap human resources."

Adds an International Harvester executive, "Some of our European and Japanese colleagues have significantly lower costs when it comes to quality control and grievances. We've got to compete in these areas; on the ledger sheet, it's the same as if they were getting a price break on steel ingots."

If overall progress of the movement has nevertheless been slow, the reason seems to be the ingrained traditions of the workplace and wariness of drastic change on the part of both labor and management.

Union leaders fear work-improvement projects can be used either to circumvent collective bargaining or forestall organizing efforts in non-union operations. While some unions see QWL as a vehicle for making work more interesting and less oppressive, most labor leaders agree there are more important items on the union agenda.

"Labor at large should be more immediately concerned about the problems of the unemployed than those of the unhappily employed," says Lane Kirkland, second in command at the AFL-CIO.

Management's interest is focused by a desire to reduce personnel headaches and labor costs; employers seek to cut the costs of alienation—the "soaring pricetag of distrust," as one expert calls it—absenteeism, grievances, shoddy workmanship.

Yet the business community shows as much caution as labor. Even when top management is enthusiastic about worker participation efforts, there are often reservations at other levels in the organization—from executives worried over relaxation of work discipline or erosion of their own authority, or from cost-effectiveness people who sometimes view QWL as a frivolous attempt at social engineering.

As workers, union officials and managers build up more experience in job participation, opposition is likely to fade somewhat. The biggest obstacle ahead is the traditional organization of work, along "scientific management" lines, on the assembly line and, for that matter, in much white-collar office work.

These systems generally are not conducive to employe participation in job decisions, and officials who handle today's Quality of Work Life projects—management and labor alike—say they are being closely watched from above and below.

Meanwhile, there's extensive research. Groups like Edward Glaser's Human Interaction Institute in Los Angeles and the Harvard University Project on Technology, Work and Character run by Michael Macabee are working with employers and labor leaders to develop procedures to ease the adaptation of QWL efforts.

Wick Skinner, management organization expert at Harvard, says of the current crop of democratic work projects: "Although these experiments have generally been considered successful, their diffusion into broader usage has sometimes proved difficult."

Says the UAW's Bluestone: "No two projects are alike. The concept may be transferable; certainly there are general guidelines that apply across the board. But you can't stamp out one project to work like the next."

Glaser, a Los Angeles psychologist who helps GM and other companies implement QWL projects, says "There are failures. Lots of them for lots of reasons.

"I got a call from one company, one of the top 10 companies in the country, which has the attitude, "We're going to have worker participation if we have to shove it down their throats.

"Well, rule No. 1 probably ought to be pretty obvious: people have the right to decide whether to participate in their own salvation."

One indication that QWL is beginning to work its way into commoner usage is the launching of several projects in the federal bureaucracy.

To implement some QWL programs at the Commerce Department, Undersecretary Sidney Harman—a pioneer in the field—has hired Macabee and Robert and Margaret Duckles as "facilitators," who act as third-party mediators, forging compromises when problems arise and carrying messages and explanations from one side to the other. Macabee and the Duckles played this role at Harman's Bolivar, Tenn., plant, site of one of the most successful work democracy projects in the country.

People like Macabee and Glaser are optimistic about their work to broaden Quality of Work principles in the coming year. They are seconded by Reid Rundell, chief of personnel development at General Motors.

"Two years ago, I'd have said this whole area is too far out," Rundell says. But now, he reports, GM executives are so satisfied with early results that "our plan now is to expand QWL throughout the corporation as fast as possible."

Discussion Questions

1. What impact will the new QWL programs have on workers' opportunities to satisfy their social and growth needs on the job?
2. Discuss how the basic idea of QWL might be applied to any job you have ever held, including your role as student. How would it be done and with what results?

I QUIT

Mr. Nakamura, Director of Management and Organization Development for Midway Electronics, walked into the office of Mark Pritchard, the Training Supervisor, and said, "Mark, I've got good news." "Don't hold it back," said Mark. "Tell me."

"Well," began Mr. Nakamura, "though you've only been here fifteen months and you have already received two pay increases, the big news is that your pay will be increased by another $75.00 per month starting the first of the month. You have done a beautiful job here and we want you to know how much it is appreciated." To Mr. Nakamura's astonishment, Mark got quite upset.

"What's the matter?" He replied, "I don't know, it isn't the money. It's just that I have already decided to quit. I'm taking a job as Training Supervisor at the bank." "Well, they don't pay any better than we do," said Mr. Nakamura.

"That's not the point," said Mark. "I'm not going for the money. It's just that I don't really do any training here. I just arrange for conference rooms, speakers, luncheons. We hire these consultants who come in and give talks. Most of them are just like entertainers. They are so superficial. Look, I have an M.B.A. and I had eleven years of personnel and management experience even before I took this job. But I can't use any of that education and experience. I don't want to hurt your feelings, Mr. Nakamura, but all you give me is a dumb job. The bank is going to give me real training responsibility."

Discussion Questions
1. What light does motivation theory, as discussed in this chapter, shed on this situation?
2. If you were Mr. Nakamura, how would you respond?

SUMMARY AND PRINCIPLES

We have considered the behavior of people in light of human needs. These needs are arranged something like a pyramid, with physical needs at the bottom, social needs in the middle, and growth needs at the top. Only as satisfactions fulfill the physical needs do social needs come into operation powerfully. Only as satisfactions fulfill the social needs do the growth needs come to govern behavior.

So long as lower level needs remain satisfied, higher level needs direct behavior. If lower level needs become unsatisfied, however, they can again take over. Recall the case of the pioneers who began with good fellowship and lofty purposes, whose journey ended in starvation and cannibalism.

Even though all people may share the same set of needs, the importance of any one need varies from person to person, and from time to time within any person. This is because individuals and situations differ. Still, the pyramid provides a general description of common human need patterns.

Work provides a means of satisfying physical needs through money earned to buy necessities. Work also provides a means of satisfying social needs, because most jobs involve working with other people. Where it is a means to experiencing feelings of achievement, competence, and self-esteem, work also provides a means of satisfying growth needs. But the satisfaction of growth needs, particularly through work, is not the experience of everyone who works.

Jobs that are engineered to the point where they require only robotlike behavior are impoverished of growth satisfactions. Only jobs that contain possibilities of using unique human abilities can tap the motive power of growth needs. Fortunately, much has been learned about the power of such management strategies as goal setting, self-control, participative leadership, and job enrichment to design growth satisfactions into jobs. The payoffs, as the experiments at Volvo, Saab, and other organizations suggest, may be improved performance and increased satisfaction.

These results do not come easily, nor can anyone be sure that they will come at all in every case. Not everyone has strong growth needs that he or she seeks to meet through work. People lacking strong growth needs are not especially responsive to motivation-increasing strategies. Moreover, managers are not always free or able to change control practices, job designs, or their own leadership behavior, though they may recognize that such changes might be desirable. Even where managers have the power to make changes, the effectiveness of their actions will vary from one case to another. In one situation a change in leadership, for example, may produce important results. The same change in a different situation may have no effect on either productivity or satisfaction.

Although these problems exist, the outstanding truth is that there are abundant possibilities for making work more productive and satisfying through the use of an understanding of motivation.

Here are some principles:

1. Human needs are arranged in a pyramid with physical needs at the bottom, social needs in the middle, and growth needs, at the top.

2. Only unsatisfied needs motivate behavior.

3. If work is to motivate people, it must be seen by them as a path to satisfying their unmet needs.

4. Managers should examine work in their organizations. They should design jobs to arouse the motivation and performance that will lead to organizational effectiveness and human satisfaction by integrating human needs, effort, and organizational goals.

5. In managing motivation, managers must take into account such factors as the meaning of work to employees, the effects of job design changes on work flows and costs, and the results of increased motivation.

CHAPTER FIVE COMMUNICATION

LEARNING OBJECTIVES

At the conclusion of this chapter you should be able to:

1. Define communications.
2. Explain the communication process.
3. Describe the characteristics of one-way and two-way communications.
4. Explain the advantages and disadvantages of one-way and two-way communications.
5. Describe at least three types of communications patterns.
6. Describe several ways to improve communications skills.
7. Understand the barriers to effective communication.

ONE-WAY/TWO-WAY COMMUNICATION

I. Objectives
   A. To demonstrate the advantages and disadvantages of two-way communications.
   B. To examine the implications of one-way and two-way communications as management tools.
II. Premeeting Preparation
   A. Read the Instructions.
III. Instructions
   A. For the One-Way/Two-Way Communication Exercise:
      1. One member of the class will be selected to be the demonstrator.
      2. The remainder of the class will be participants.
      3. In each of the two parts of the exercise the demonstrator will direct the participants to draw figures on the forms that follow.

> *Time for Step A: 20 minutes*

IV. Discussion
   Your instructor will help you explore what happened in the exercises and their meaning for management.

> *Time for discussion: 20 minutes*

ONE-WAY COMMUNICATION

TWO-WAY COMMUNICATION

Communications may well be the key to the success of organizations, because without communications there could be no organizations. As soon as work is split among several people, it is imperative that there are some kind of communications among the people doing the jobs, and among the workers and the managers. If managers are unable to communicate their plans, and instructions for executing those plans to subordinates, they will probably fail as managers. It is also important that managers be effective in receiving communications, because if they are not, they will have a great deal of difficulty monitoring the progress of the organization and controlling performance. In many ways, communication acts as the glue that holds organizations together as well as the oil that keeps them running smoothly.

So what's the big deal about communications? We communicate every day, and it doesn't seem to be a particularly difficult task. Or does it? How often have you been stuck for just the right word to convey exactly what you mean? How often have you misunderstood a professor's instructions and done the wrong homework or read the wrong material? In your case maybe not often, but you can probably think of someone who "never seems to understand" and others who "never can take a hint." These are people who are having difficulties with the communications process. To see why they have these difficulties, let us examine the communications process.

THE COMMUNICATIONS PROCESS

The communications process entails more than just one person saying something and another person listening. It is a complex process that includes at least two people who must use their thought processes as well as their senses in a coordinated effort to transfer thoughts between themselves (Figure 5.1).

Six Steps   As you can see from Figure 5.1, the communications process includes at least six distinct steps: sender's thought, encoding, transmission, receiving, decoding, and receiver's thought. What makes the communications process so difficult is that at each of these six steps there is the chance for distortion or error. Even if there is only a small distortion at each step, by the time the message is finally converted into a thought by the receiver, it may be grossly distorted.

Sender's Thoughts   The place to begin to examine the communications process is at the original thought that triggers the entire process. The human thought process is a very complex affair, dealing with thousands of topics every day, some of which are communicated to others, some of which never leave the thinker's mind. Some of these thoughts are simple: I am hungry, whereas others are quite complex; the beauty of a sunset. It is relatively easier to convert simple thoughts into language than it is to convert complex ones. So the complexity

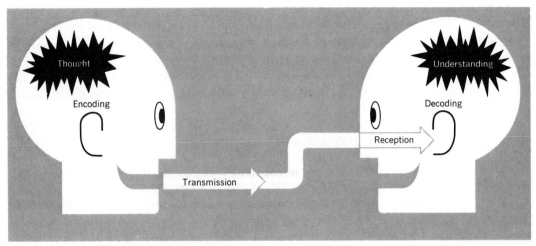

Figure 5.1   The communications process.

of the thought to be communicated can have an influence on the quality of the communication. The clarity of the thought is another factor that affects the communication. White or black may be clear, but a shade of blue is not. Think about it, try to describe the shade of a color you want to the person who mixes the paint without the aid of a picture. You would know it when you saw it, but you cannot describe it.

Encoding   Related to the thought process is how the thoughts are translated into language for transmission. Most of our communications use the language process as a medium for transmission, but some communications are done nonverbally, or without language. The shrug of the shoulders, the lifting of an eyebrow, the smile, and many other body movements can also be used to transmit messages. But here too, a translation of thought into movement must be made. Whereas "body language" is important, most communications take advantage of the fact that humans have developed language. How well an individual is able to translate thoughts into language is a function of the person's facility with the language. Some people seem to be able to handle the language better than others, and this ability, or lack of it, may cause errors in the communications process.

Transmission   The actual transmission of the message can also be a source of problems in the communications process. People talk too fast, their handwriting may be illegible, there may be other people talking or noise when the communicator is trying to transmit the message, and many other situations that make the transmission of a message difficult. This kind of interference with the actual transmission of the message is usually called noise. When we talk about noise in a system we mean anything that interferes with the actual transmission of communications.

Reception How well the receiver receives the message will also have an impact on the quality of the communication. The receiver may be thinking about something else and not really hear what was said. How many times have you had to say: "Pardon me, I didn't catch what you said," as someone was speaking to you? There are any number of reasons why the receiver may not receive the same message that the sender sent, but all of them bring about the same result: inaccurate communications.

Decoding After the message has been received, it must be decoded by the receiver, that is, the verbal message is converted into thoughts. As with each of the previous steps, there are many things that can go wrong with the message here. A word that means one thing to the sender may mean something quite different to the receiver, the imagery used by the sender may not create the same imagery for the receiver, or the complexity of the idea being transmitted may be lost in the transmission. The conversion of language into thought is a process ripe with the possibility for distortion.

Understanding The final step in the communications process requires the receiver to convert the decoded thoughts into a meaningful message. The receiver must get the idea the sender was trying to communicate. Such factors as the situation, the past experiences of the sender and receiver, and the complexity of the situation all have an influence on how well the receiver will understand what the sender is trying to communicate.

All in all, it is a fairly complex process. With the possibility of distortion at each step in the process, it is amazing that we do as well as we do in communicating with one another. As we shall see, the fact that communications take place in an organizational setting may further complicate the process.

DOWNWARD COMMUNICATION

In any organization, as in any group, communications flow three ways. First, communications flow downward from the leader to the other group members. This downward flow of communication is likely to contain the

Information information that the leader has accumulated from linking activities with other groups and his or her expertise in various activities. Downward com-

Feedback to munication is likely to be heavy in information content. At the same time,

Subordinates downward communication is likely to contain feedback from the leader to individual group members concerning their performance. Rewards for effective performance and punishment for ineffective performance are also likely to be part of the downward communication flow.

One-Way Too often, this downward flow is one-way in nature, for example, when a superior passes orders down to subordinates (Figure 5.2). The leader assumes that they understand exactly what was told them, and is quite upset if the results obtained fall short of expectations. Why? Well, remember the results of the one-way/two-way communication exercise? In most cases the

one-way communication tends to be less accurate and the recipients tend to be less confident in the communication. But it is fast, and in situations in which speed and unquestioning obedience (such as in the military in a combat situation) are important, the communicator may not have any choice but to use a one-way communication channel.

Now, you're probably saying to yourself, "So what, that was just verbal communication. All I would have to do is put the order in writing and there should be no question. It might take a few seconds longer, but my order will be clearly understood." If only it were so. Written communications are open to misunderstanding just as are verbal messages, particularly if they are the slightest bit vague.

Written Orders   One of history's great tragedies, later immortalized in poetry to make it seem glorious, was the Charge of the Light Brigade. During the Crimean War (1854–1856) while the British and French were fighting the Russians, Lord Raglan, British Commander in Chief sent a message to Lord Lucan, commander of his cavalry. The message read, in part: "Lord Raglan wishes the cavalry to advance rapidly to the front, and to prevent the enemy carrying away the guns. . . ." Since the two men were separated by a distance of several miles and about a half hour's ride, Lord Lucan followed his orders and launched the Light Brigade in an attack against the wrong guns. The result of this misunderstanding: 147 men killed and one famous poem. Moral of the story: one-way communication, no matter how transmitted is open to misunderstanding.

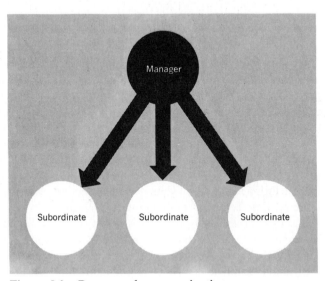

Figure 5.2   Downward communication.

Many Levels   If this kind of distortion can occur in a message between two levels in an organization, imagine what can happen when it filters down through several levels of an organization (Figure 5.3). Suppose, for example, the president of a firm learns that he is going to represent his industry at a Senate hearing on pollution control. He mentions to the Vice-President of Manufacturing that he could use some data on their firm's pollution control actions to beef up his presentation, particularly if the Senators really get on him. The Vice-President now sends a memo to all plant managers stating that she wants a report from all plants specifying exactly how and when all funds for antipollution control devices were spent. The plant manager, not sure of what's going on, orders his accountant, superintendent, and maintenance supervisor to develop and provide information on past expenditures. This result is a far cry from the original casual request, but it is possible.

There is another effect of one-way communications that might have shown up in the exercise. That effect relates to how the communicator and the person receiving the communications feel about the communication act itself.

Frustration   Receivers of one-way communication may feel frustrated and annoyed that they are unable to clarify points about which they are uncertain or confused. The sender, on the other hand, may feel more comfortable with one-way communication because no one can question the orders, and the sender doesn't receive any adverse feedback. The sender tells; others listen. No questions, no complaints; rather like a dictator.

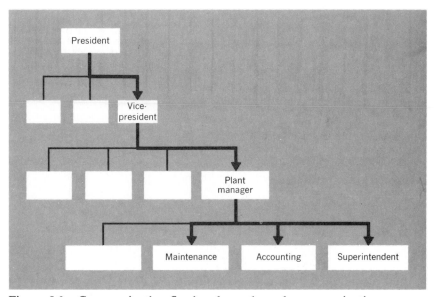

Figure 5.3   Communication flowing down through an organization.

UPWARD COMMUNICATION

Feedback on Conversely, communications also flow upward in the organization from indi-
Performance vidual members to the leader. This upward flow of information is likely to
contain information on performance. Such formal devices as budget reports,
project reports, and profit and loss statements are examples of upward communication of performance information. Feedback of leader performance
also flows upward in most organizations. This kind of communication, although shown as one-way in Figure 5.4, is in fact usually part of a two-way
system. If the manager is strictly a one-way communicator, he is not likely to
be too responsive to any noninformation communications directed toward
Usually Two-Way him from his subordinates. We are more likely to find that upward communications are welcomed by the manager when they are part of a two-way
system—information flowing upward and downward, through the organization through formal communication channels (Figure 5.5).

LATERAL COMMUNICATIONS

Coordination Finally, there is a substantial amount of communication that flows laterally
within the organization. Production supervisors are likely to communicate
extensively with maintenance supervisors and quality control supervisors in
an effort to coordinate the activities of these diverse, but interrelated groups.
Production workers are similarly likely to engage in extensive communica-

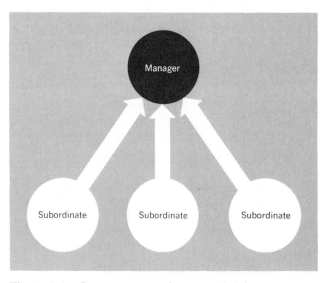

Figure 5.4   One-way upward communication.

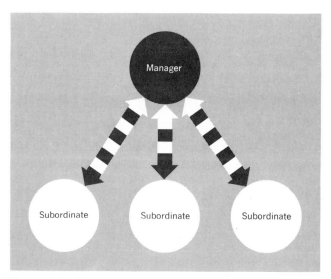

Figure 5.5   Two-way communications.

tions with employees from maintenance and quality control both in a business and a social sense.

This type of lateral communication can either be through formal or informal channels. When formal communications channels are developed between individuals at the same level in an organization, or individuals at different levels in different sections of an organization, they are usually designed to facilitate coordination. If there were no lateral communications channels in the theoretical organization shown in Figure 5.6, anytime the production manager wanted to make contact with the maintenance manager, the communication would have to be through the plant manager. An awkward situation, to say the least. But if we add lateral communication channels to this organization (Figure 5.7), we can tremendously facilitate the coordination and hopefully, the overall efficiency of the entire organization.

Grapevine   If, on the other hand, the lateral communication is of an informal nature it often takes on the form of the "grapevine" (see Chapter 3 for more on informal organizations). Where would any organization be without its grapevine spreading information (often rumor) faster than a forest fire? George in the Personnel Department tells his cousin Mary in the Tool Crib who in turn tells Charlie in the Machine Shop who is on the bowling team with her, etc., etc., etc. (Figure 5.8).

Grapevines exist in all organizations, and are the communications channels of the informal organization. The grapevine passes information that the formal organization does not, or will not, transmit. They arise from the interaction of people, because the grapevine is usually made up of people who know the person to whom they pass the message. Because the grapevine

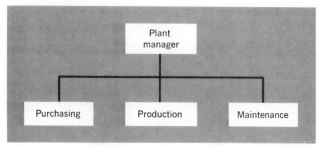

Figure 5.6   Organization with no lateral communication channels.

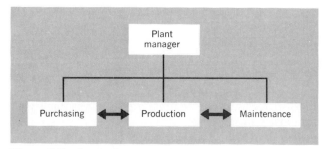

Figure 5.7   Lateral communications.

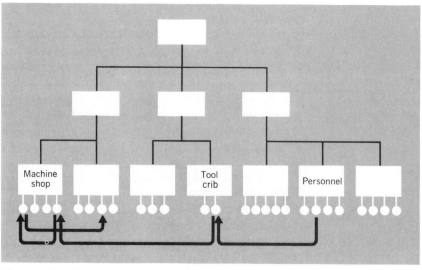

Figure 5.8   The grapevine.

stretches throughout an organization, it has the ability to carry a tremendous amount of information quickly through the organization. In his studies of the grapevine, Professor Keith Davis has found the following to be true of grapevines:

1. Grapevines tend to be accurate. Davis found that the grapevine is 80 to 90 percent accurate in transmitting noncontroversial information.
2. Grapevines work by word of mouth.
3. Grapevines can carry a great deal of information.
4. Grapevines are faster than most formal communications.
5. The grapevine is influential.
6. Because it is influential, misinformation (rumor) can be quickly spread throughout the organization.

A study by Professor Alex Bavelas attempted to determine what kind of communications network would prove most effective in the solving of problems. Bavelas studied four types of networks: chains, circles, Y's and wheels, each characterized by a different information flow. In each of the networks, an individual could only communicate with that person with whom he was connected, as shown by the solid lines in Figure 5.10. The greater the number of persons with whom a person could interact, the more central he would be in the organization. Bavelas developed an "index of relative centrality" to indicate who was most central, or most powerful in the organization. The higher the number, the more central the person.

The research showed that the more centralized the structure of the group the more accurate it was at simple tasks. In the more centralized group the individual who was most central was the leader. That individual was recognized by other group members as the leader. The central person was in contact with more people, and was privy to more information than anyone else in the group. Because the most central person was most involved in what

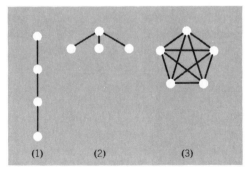

Figure 5.9   Typical communication patterns.

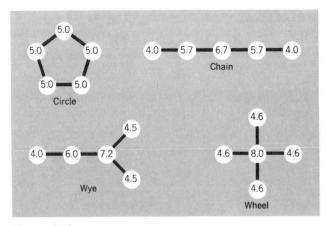

Figure 5.10

the group was doing, and knew what was going on, he was also the most satisfied person in the group.

OBSTACLES TO EFFECTIVE COMMUNICATION

Method of Communication There are many obstacles to effective communication. Obstacles fall into four categories. First, how the communication is made will often prevent its effective utilization. Most of us speak too rapidly or too slowly; we speak or write using confusing and often contradictory words. We often also utilize technical or unfamiliar words in an effort to impress our listener. All of these problems can prevent effective utilization of the communication.

Climate Second, the group or organization climate within which the communication takes place is often a barrier to its effective utilization. Communications between a warden and a prisoner, for instance, are likely to be very difficult because of the nontrusting climate that exists between the two individuals. Communication between police and gang members is often inhibited by the same lack of trust. Communication between the production department and the quality control department is also likely to be inhibited by a similar set of anxieties and concerns. Many subordinates in an organization often question whether their boss really wants to hear any bad news. As a result, much of the bad news in an organization never gets reported to higher levels until the problem has reached a crisis level. Then everyone hears about it.

Barriers Third, organizational barriers often prevent effective communication among individuals. It is often difficult to reach the right person with the right information at the right time. For example, giving information about a cost control procedure to a production manager who is under pressure to make a shipment that afternoon is very likely to result in ineffective communication. The student who has his or her mind on trying to cram for a calculus examination is likely to be nonreceptive to information concerning the customs of fourteenth-century monks coming from the history professor at the front of the room. Thus, one of the tricks in effective communication is to get the right information to the right person at the right time.

Inter-Personal Factors Fourth, one of the largest barriers to effective communication resides in the interpersonal factors involved in the communication process. We have already mentioned what some of these factors may be. As has been pointed out, communication is more than just the words that flow between each of us. We also express to each other our feelings, concerns, and attitudes. These are far more private than information, and therefore more threatening. Because of their high threat potential, people react more strongly both positively and negatively to them. Furthermore, much of our communication is *Nonverbal Cues* not done with words at all, but rather with such nonverbal cues as the way we shift our feet or hold our hands or the position of our head or the way we are looking at the person with whom we are communicating. These nonverbal forms of communication are often more honest than the traditional verbal or written forms. It is not uncommon for a person to say one thing but to convey, nonverbally, the impression that he or she means just the opposite.

Several Levels A large amount of the communication that takes place between two parties is conducted at several levels. In the case of a husband and wife, communication at the verbal level might concern everyday household activities, whereas nonverbally both parties communicate a host of more personal feelings. The observation that most of us communicate in a multiplicity of ways (both verbally and nonverbally) and that there are often conflicting signals that we give about what we really mean to communicate is the first interpersonal barrier to effective communication.

Managing Communications The second interpersonal barrier lies in the fact that most people spend a great deal of time attempting to "manage their communications." Many of us spend a considerable portion of our energy in not saying what we actually mean or feel. For instance, the person who was just rejected for a job is likely to spend a good portion of energy trying not to show disappointment.

Selective Listening A third barrier stems from the fact that listening tends to be a selective process. We hear basically what we want to hear. And when we are concerned with our own problems, it is difficult to hear anyone else's.

Of all the barriers to effective communication, the interpersonal barriers are probably the most vexing. As a professor, it is difficult to look out upon student faces whose blank looks clearly communicate, nonverbally, their lack of interest in the subject matter. As a manager, the inability to reach employees is a mystifying and frustrating feeling. "Why don't they understand?" is a commonly heard plaintive wail that echoes throughout the land.

Momma by Mell Lazarus. Courtesy of Mell Lazarus and Field Newspaper Syndicate.

METHODS FOR IMPROVING COMMUNICATION

Know Thyself Fortunately, there are ways to improve communication skills. First, there must be an awareness of the difficulties that plague communication. Aristotle's injunction, "Know thyself" is relevant at this juncture. It is important for you as a manager to analyze your motives and discount your prejudices in advance. Remember that the other people in the communication process see the world through their own eyes, not yours. It is an old saying, but very true: "If you would sway John Doe, it would be wise to see the world through John Doe's eyes."

Acceptance Second, not only is it important to be aware of these differences, but more significant, it is imperative to accept them as real and natural. Many of us in our own mind accept the fact that others are different from us, but relatively few of us accept the fact in our gut as well. It is necessary to understand honestly and forthrightly that not everyone sees the world the way we do, and that we cannot change them to see our viewpoint. Many of the unhappy marriages in our society can be traced to the unwillingness of one or both of the parties to accept the other as he or she really is and not as the other party would like him/her to be.

Listen Third, it is possible to develop sound listening skills. Unfortunately, we are all members of the 45/50 club, the largest club of losers in the world. That is, we often hear only 45 percent what is told to us and then remember only 50 percent of what we hear. This means we actually receive less than 25 percent of what others tell us. Thus, much of what people tell us we never hear. We tend to be people who talk without listening.

Use Your Brain One of the ways to improve our listening skill is to utilize the vast capacity of our brains. Although most people speak at between 150 and 200 words a minute, and we can read at 300 to 500 words a minute, our brains are capable of processing information at a rate of more than 2000 words a minute. This means that there is great excess capacity, and when this excess capacity is not utilized, the brain wanders from the subject and loses interest in what is going on. When listening to someone else speak, it is possible to summarize constantly in your mind. Keep asking yourself: "What is the main idea?" and "What is the data that the individual is utilizing to support his argument?" Attempt to anticipate the speaker's next comments. These "tricks" will enable you to utilize the capacity in your brain to focus more specifically on the speaker, thus improving the amount of material that you actually hear the person saying. In addition, we can learn to listen with our "third ear." That is, we can alert ourselves to various nonverbal cues that are an ever-present part of the communication process. With these techniques you can improve your listening skill and train yourself to receive more of what the sender is telling.

Feedback Fourth, it is important to build in ways to check the accuracy of the communications you receive. It is vital that there be feedback channels, or ways to find out from the person or persons involved with you in the communication process whether what you think they said and what you think they feel is in fact what they really said and what they really feel.

None of the above-mentioned means of improving communication skills will be effective unless the climate of the group is such that it is "safe" for people to tell one another what they really think. In the absence of this trusting environment, even the best listening skills will be used only to distort the communication process.

In short, there are ways to improve communication skills, and communication skills are at the heart of effective management. The manager needs to hear as well as be heard, and to be truly effective, the manager must create a climate in the organization in which effective communication can take place.

U.S. FIRMS, WORRIED BY PRODUCTIVITY LAG,
COPY JAPAN IN SEEKING EMPLOYEES' ADVICE

EARL C. GOTTSCHALK JR., STAFF REPORTER

America is importing a lot more from Japan than cars, television sets and calculators. It's also bringing in management techniques made in Japan.

Deeply troubled by slumping productivity, a growing number of major American companies are copying what many management experts believe is the key to Japan's productivity gains: small groups of employees that meet regularly and are trained to spot and solve production problems in their areas.

The groups, called "quality circles," are meeting regularly at 65 companies, up from only 15 a year ago. Companies using the circles include General Motors, Ford Motor, Northrop, Rockwell International, International Harvester and American Airlines.

Most companies say that involving employees in management decisions results in both increased productivity and cost savings. Northrop, the Los Angeles aircraft maker, says it's getting at least a two-for-one return on the cost of maintaining its circles. "The idea has tremendous potential to improve productivity," says Lawrence Ward, vice president of the American Productivity Center, a group that develops programs to try to increase productivity.

Cash and Recognition

Employees are profiting, too. Northrop, for example, pays its circle members about 10% of the money it saves every year from their suggestions. Some companies give out awards and prizes for ideas. At other companies, circles meet after work and are paid at overtime rates. But equally important, management experts say, is the fact that employees get recognition by a company when their ideas are acted on.

Source. The Wall Street Journal, February 21, 1980.

"In order to compete with the Japanese in the world market, we must get the whole employee," says Bruce Handshu, a senior engineer with North American Philips' Magnavox unit. "We've only been getting the workers' hands and feet. Now, with quality circles, we're getting their brains and know-how, too."

Curiously, the idea for quality circles came originally from U.S. business-management consultants. The Japanese picked up the idea after World War II as a means of improving the quality of their products. But today, with eight million Japanese workers involved in the system, it's more often used to increase production.

Since 1950, Japan's annual productivity growth rate has been four times that of the U.S. and twice that of major European nations. U.S. productivity growth now is the lowest of all major industrial nations. If current U.S. productivity trends continue, by 1990 American workers will be not only behind those in Japan in terms of output per hour, but also behind workers in Canada, Germany and France.

In efforts to improve their productivity, some U.S. companies have experimented with everything from stock and cash-bonus plans for workers to the omnipresent suggestion box. Nothing seems to have worked. And so, belatedly, American companies now are trying to learn from the Japanese.

Growth From "Fear"

Quality circles were first tried in the U.S. in 1974 by Lockheed's space and missile unit in Sunnyvale, Calif. Jeff F. Beardsley, president of a business-consulting firm in San Jose, Calif., believes the rapid growth of the circles is due to fear. "American companies are seeing their marketplace being taken over by Japanese competition in automobiles, electronics and many other industries. We're realizing that we have to do something different."

Quality circles can be found both on the production line and in the office. At Northrop, circles have spread from aircraft production into finance, industrial-relations and compensation departments. In San Diego, International Harvester's solar-turbines division plans to increase its 22 circles to 50. Workers seem to be enthusiastic. Larry Moss, a 31-year-old aircraft assembler at a Northrop plant, says, "It's the best thing that's happened in a long time around here. We've saved the company a lot of money. It gives you a feeling of accomplishment when a solution your circle thought up is enacted by management. You feel you can put in your two cents' worth."

The basic idea of the quality circle is quite simple. A plant steering committee, composed of labor and management, decides which area of a company could benefit from a circle. Eight to 10 workers are asked to serve on a circle; they meet once a week on company time with their immediate supervisor and with a person trained in personnel or industrial relations. This specialist trains the workers in elementary data-gathering and in statistics. The circle members learn how to talk the language of management and to present their ideas to executives using such business-school methods as "histograms" and "scatter diagrams."

"They don't just bitch about a situation," says Wayne S. Rieker, president of QC Circles, a Saratoga, Calif., consulting firm. "They investigate it and prove in dollars and cents how their solution will save the company money." Workers also are encouraged to share ideas, with the rule being that there won't be any criticism or ridicule from others. "We've found that the quiet introvert usually has the answer," says Duff Porter, a quality-circle coordinator.

Not a "Fad"

When a circle believes it has come up with a solution to a problem, it passes it on to management. Mr. Beardsley, the quality-circle

consultant, says there have been few instances where management hasn't accepted a circle's recommendations.

General Motors has about 100 quality circles operating in various plants of its Buick, Chevrolet, Fisher Body, Cadillac and Oldsmobile divisions. "This isn't a fad," says Delmar L. Landen, GM's director of organizational research and development. "It's part of a fundamental shift toward a new outlook on worker participation in decision making."

The circle at a GM plant in Michigan decided it should do something about the large number of automobiles leaving the assembly line with flat tires. Their analysis eventually traced the problem to a defective tire stem. The part was replaced, and the company's annual saving turned out to be $225,000.

An assembly-line circle at the solar-turbines division of International Harvester found a way to simplify the production of a compression disc for a turbine. As a result, several production steps were eliminated and $8,700 a year was saved. And the group at American Airlines' maintenance and engineering center in Tulsa came up with savings of $100,000 a year by simply replacing old hand grinders with new, more efficient tools.

At Northrop's aircraft plant in Hawthorne, Calif., a quality circle of mechanics assembling the F5 military fighter found that workers kept breaking expensive drill bits when they bored into the titanium on the tail of the aircraft. After a lengthy analysis, the angle of the drill was changed slightly, resulting in fewer broken bits and savings of $28,000 a year.

Mixed Union Reaction

Even the government is trying the circle approach. At the Navy's largest shipyard, in Norfolk, Va., about nine circles are in operation in such departments as supply, production and personnel. One circle found a simpler way to move the huge generators that feed electricity from shore to ship. That suggestion resulted in an annual saving of $10,000.

Union reaction to quality circles has been mixed, although the United Auto Workers union is favorably disposed—provided that the system doesn't result in any layoffs and doesn't increase the work pace. Irving Bluestone, a UAW vice president, says that the circles can benefit both workers and company through reduced labor turnover and improvements in quality. The circles, he says, have reduced the need for discipline, resulting in fewer grievances. "It brings out the best in the employee," says William T. Horner, an official in the UAW's GM department. But other unions argue that the system also can be used to weaken the need for a union by bringing management and workers closer together. In addition, they assert that circles don't enable union members to share directly in increased productivity.

Even some management people worry that increased productivity will lead to job losses and will be an eventual stumbling block to the program. At one Midwestern plant, for example, a worker in a circle devised a way to keep rust from forming on a product. His job was to brush off the rust as the product moved down the assembly line. Although he lost his job, the company reassigned him to another position.

So far, layoffs haven't been a problem, experts say. And some companies agree in advance that no one on a circle will be laid off as the result of a suggested improvement. Workers concede that the idea that they might be costing someone his job is at the back of their minds when they make a suggestion to management.

But many workers find the circles challenging. "I had never dared talk to some of these executives before, and here we were telling them how to solve a problem," recalls Janet Burcham, a 24-year-old scheduler in Northrop's facilities department. When Northrop adopted one of her circle's suggestions, at an annual saving of about $10,000, "it really improved my self-image and gave me confidence," says Mrs. Burcham. "Now I feel I can do anything."

Discussion Questions

1. What kinds of communications are involved in the quality circles?
2. What kinds of communications barriers are the quality circles overcoming?
3. Do you feel that a quality circle could be used in this classroom? Why? How?

A CASE

THE EARLY WORK SCHEDULE

Mrs. Mabel Thomas was employed to work with the food service of Community Hospital. The job for which she was employed required that she work two days a week from 5 A.M. to 2 P.M. The other three days she worked the regular day food schedule from 8:30 A.M. to 5:30 P.M. When she was employed either she failed to hear information about the early work schedule or the employment clerk forgot to tell her. She feels sure that if the early schedule had been mentioned to her, she would have heard it, because under those conditions she would not have taken the job.

During the first two weeks the job required Mrs. Thomas to work the regular day shift in order to have an instructor show her how to do the job; consequently, Mrs. Thomas thought she was on the regular day shift. She vaguely remembers that near the end of her first two weeks her supervisor mentioned something to her about beginning her regular schedule, but she did not understand what the supervisor meant and she did not inquire further. The result was that Mrs. Thomas failed to report for work on the early schedule on the day required. When she did report for work at the regular hour of 8:30 A.M., her supervisor criticized her for lack of responsibility. Mrs. Thomas said she could not work the early shift for family reasons and resigned.

Discussion Questions
1. What kinds of communications barriers affected the communications in this case?
2. What kind of communication pattern do you see in this case? Could it have had an effect on the problem?
3. How might Mrs. Thomas' misunderstanding have been prevented?

Source. Keith Davis, *Human Behavior at Work* (New York: McGraw-Hill Book Company, 1972), pp. 418–419.

The ability to communicate effectively is a key skill for all managers. As we have seen in this chapter, there are many aspects to effective communication: the communication process, the type of communication (one-way or two-way), what is being communicated (information or feedback), the organizational climate in which the communication is taking place, and the interpersonal relationship between the communicator and the person receiving the communication. The advantages and disadvantages of one-way and two-way communications should have been clearly demonstrated, and the distortions that can take place in the communications process also shown.

By examining the barriers to effective communication, we can begin to see some of the ways to improve communications in organizations. Specific techniques for improving communications were also presented to show that the individual can work on his or her own communications skills in an effort to improve them. Good communications alone are not the total answer to organizational effectiveness, but any organization that doesn't have good communications is an organization that is likely to have problems.

Here are some principles:

1. Communication is a complex process, and to ensure accurate communications there must be a minimum of distortion at each step in the process.

2. Distortions in the communications process can occur in the sender, the receiver, or through noise in the transmission.

3. Most downward communication contains information or feedback to subordinates about their performance.

4. Most upward communication contains information about what has to be done, information about what has been done, and information to allow management to monitor performance.

5. Most horizontal communication contains information to facilitate coordination or information of a social nature.

6. Managers must be good senders as well as good receivers of communications if they are going to be effective.

7. Two-way communication is usually more accurate than one-way.

8. One-way communication is usually faster than two-way.

9. Communications tend to become distorted as they pass through a number of people.

10. Barriers, both structural and interpersonal, exist that affect the accuracy of communications.

11. Communications skills can be improved.

CHAPTER SIX LEADERSHIP

LEARNING OBJECTIVES

At the end of this chapter you should be able to:

1. Define leadership and distinguish between management and leadership by giving an example of each.
2. Describe the five sources of leader influence.
3. Identify the basic contribution of the Ohio State studies, Blake and Mouton's Managerial Grid, Likert's 4-system and Path-Goal Theory.
4. Define three factors according to Tannenbaum and Schmidt, which influence the appropriateness of a leadership style.
5. Describe Fiedler's Contingency Theory approach to leadership including the three situational variables, and when each leadership style is effective.
6. Explain two management approaches to improving leadership performance.

ASSESSING YOUR LEADERSHIP STYLE

I. Objectives
  A. To examine some of the dimensions of leadership.
  B. To explore your personal leadership style.
II. Premeeting Preparation
  A. Read the instructions.
III. Instructions
  A. For this exercise each person will work alone.
  B. Read the instructions on page 135.
  C. Fill in the LPC Form (page 137).

  > *Time for Step C: 10 minutes*

IV. Discussion
  Your instructor will help you explore what happened in the activity and its meaning for management.

  > *Time for discussion: 30 minutes*

INSTRUCTIONS

People differ in the ways they think about those with whom they work. This may be important in working with others. Please give your immediate, first reaction to the items on the following two pages.

Below are pairs of words which are opposite in meaning, such as "Very neat" and "Not neat." You are asked to describe someone with whom you have worked by placing an "X" in one of the eight spaces on the line between the two words. Each space represents how well the adjective fits the person you are describing, as if it were written:

FOR EXAMPLE: If you were to describe the person with whom you are able to work least well, and you ordinarily think of that person as being *quite neat,* you would put an "X" in the second space from the words Very Neat, like this:

Very neat : _____ : __X__ : _____ : _____ | _____ : _____ : _____ : _____ : Not neat

               8   7   6   5   4   3   2   1

    Very   Quite Some- Slightly Slightly Some- Quite Very
    neat   neat   what   neat   untidy   what untidy untidy
                 neat   untidy

If you ordinarily think of the person with whom you can work least well as being only *slightly neat,* you would put your "X" as follows:

Very neat : _____ : _____ : _____ : __X__ | _____ : _____ : _____ : _____ : Not neat

               8   7   6   5   4   3   2   1

    Very   Quite Some- Slightly Slightly Some- Quite Very
    neat   neat   what   neat   untidy   what untidy untidy
                 neat   untidy

If you would think of that person as being *very untidy,* you would use the space nearest the words Not Neat.

Very neat : _____ : _____ : _____ : _____ | _____ : _____ : _____ : __X__ : Not neat

               8   7   6   5   4   3   2   1

    Very   Quite Some- Slightly Slightly Some- Quite Very
    neat   neat   what   neat   untidy   what untidy untidy
                 neat   untidy

Look at the words at both ends of the line before you put in your "X." Please remember that there are *no right or wrong answers.* Work rapidly; your first answer is likely to be the best. Please do not omit any items, and mark each item only once.

LPC

Think of the person *with whom you can work least well*. The person may be someone you work with now or may be someone you knew in the past. The individual does not have to be the person you like least well, but should be the person with whom you had the most difficulty in getting a job done. Describe this person as he or she appears to you.

Pleasant	: ___ : ___ : ___ : ___ : ___ : ___ : ___ : ___ : Unpleasant
	8 7 6 5 4 3 2 1
Friendly	: ___ : ___ : ___ : ___ : ___ : ___ : ___ : ___ : Unfriendly
	8 7 6 5 4 3 2 1
Rejecting	: ___ : ___ : ___ : ___ : ___ : ___ : ___ : ___ : Accepting
	1 2 3 4 5 6 7 8
Helpful	: ___ : ___ : ___ : ___ : ___ : ___ : ___ : ___ : Frustrating
	8 7 6 5 4 3 2 1
Unenthusiastic	: ___ : ___ : ___ : ___ : ___ : ___ : ___ : ___ : Enthusiastic
	1 2 3 4 5 6 7 8
Tense	: ___ : ___ : ___ : ___ : ___ : ___ : ___ : ___ : Relaxed
	1 2 3 4 5 6 7 8
Distant	: ___ : ___ : ___ : ___ : ___ : ___ : ___ : ___ : Close
	1 2 3 4 5 6 7 8
Cold	: ___ : ___ : ___ : ___ : ___ : ___ : ___ : ___ : Warm
	8 7 6 5 4 3 2 1
Cooperative	: ___ : ___ : ___ : ___ : ___ : ___ : ___ : ___ : Uncooperative
	8 7 6 5 4 3 2 1
Supportive	: ___ : ___ : ___ : ___ : ___ : ___ : ___ : ___ : Hostile
	8 7 6 5 4 3 2 1
Boring	: ___ : ___ : ___ : ___ : ___ : ___ : ___ : ___ : Interesting
	8 7 6 5 4 3 2 1
Quarrelsome	: ___ : ___ : ___ : ___ : ___ : ___ : ___ : ___ : Harmonious
	8 7 6 5 4 3 2 1
Self-assured	: ___ : ___ : ___ : ___ : ___ : ___ : ___ : ___ : Hesitant
	8 7 6 5 4 3 2 1
Efficient	: ___ : ___ : ___ : ___ : ___ : ___ : ___ : ___ : Inefficient
	8 7 6 5 4 3 2 1
Gloomy	: ___ : ___ : ___ : ___ : ___ : ___ : ___ : ___ : Cheerful
	8 7 6 5 4 3 2 1
Open	: ___ : ___ : ___ : ___ : ___ : ___ : ___ : ___ : Guarded
	8 7 6 5 4 3 2 1

Source. Fred E. Friedler, *A Theory of Leadership Effectiveness* (New York: McGraw-Hill Book Co., 1967), Table 3–1, pp. 40–41.

"Great leaders are born, not made" was a frequently heard statement in corporate board rooms. "Either a person has it or they don't." If you were one of the lucky ones to "have it," you were in. If not—well, there were lots of second-rate nonleader jobs around. Fortunately for most of us, these simplistic, elitist notions that the world is divided up into a few leaders and a bunch of followers is no longer seriously accepted in American management circles. Good managers can be made—and in fact, are being produced in larger and larger quantities by our educational system. This chapter will review what leadership is, how it actually functions in an organization, and some ways to improve leadership performance.

LEADERSHIP IS NOT MANAGEMENT

First, what is leadership? Many people confuse leadership with management, yet the two are very different. In a simple way, management is what this whole book is about—planning, organizing, directing, coordinating, and controlling. The activities of management concern not only the people in the organization but the physical aspects of it as well—its plant, equipment, materials, and money. The manager's job is to blend all of these diverse assets together to form an organization moving, more or less together, toward some commonly defined objective. Leadership, on the other hand, is a tool of management, a technique for influencing the people in an organization. Thus management is a much broader function dealing with the coordination and direction of things as well as people toward the accomplishment of given objectives. Leadership is a much narrower activity, involving influencing the way people behave in organizations (Figure 6.1). A good leader, therefore, may not be a good manager, although a good manager will probably be a good leader.

Now that we know what leaders are not (e.g., they are not necessarily management), it is logical to ask what leaders are, what leaders do, and how we know a leader when we see one. Every group has a leader. Because groups vary in size from only a few members to 200 or 300 members, every business organization of any size will have a number of leaders.

All of these leaders help their groups and individual members accomplish goals. Leaders do this by performing two general sets of activities: task directed activities, including planning, getting resources, and distributing assignments; and member satisfaction activities, including providing emotional support and helping people meet their particular needs. Furthermore, these leadership activities are often performed by many individuals within a group. Leadership is not necessarily vested in a certain person or position. It is more a function of what is done, rather than who does it. And, in the leadership

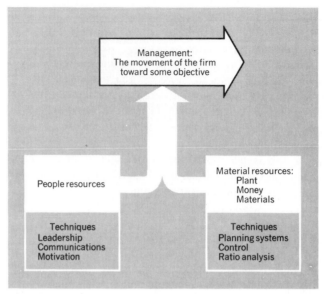

Figure 6.1

area, it takes two to tango. Without a follower, there is no leader. Therefore, a leader is someone who performs task direction and member satisfaction activities which help groups and individuals attain group objectives, and who, in doing so, influences others to follow.

THE FOUR LEADERSHIP ACTIVITIES

Leadership Is
a Reciprocal
Influence Process

Regardless of the size of the group, each leader performs four essential activities: controlling the internal activities of the group, enforcing the group's norms and values, linking the group with other groups, and protecting the group from outside pressures and threats.

Control Internal
Activities

Let us consider these four activities in greater detail. Every leader is responsible for controlling the internal activities of the group. Because groups are different in terms of their objectives (the objectives of the street gang group will be quite different from those of a production department at a local auto assembly plant) the nature of the activities that leaders will control varies widely.

A leader of a group in a factory, for example, may control people's break times, or give helpful hints to make the job go faster, of which the management time-study efficiency expert is not aware. In a street corner group, the leader might control who performs various activities, ranging from who carries the bowling balls for the group, to who puts the "kiss" on the opposition. Thus, the leader controls the resources that the group has at its disposal.

Enforce Group Values The second important activity that the leader performs is that of enforcing the group's norms and values. In a very real sense, the leader is the informally recognized "bouncer" of the group who is responsible for rewarding those group members who abide by the norms and code of the group, and for punishing those group members who stray from those norms. In a work group it is the leader's job to confront the rate busters and convince them by whatever means are necessary to conform to the group's production standards. Although much of this convincing takes the form of either conversation and perhaps a low level of social pressure, (e.g., isolating the individual—the "cold shoulder"), it is not unusual for the "fink" to find lunch boxes disappear, oily rags in machines, missing tools, and maybe even slashed tires and broken windows. We have all seen similar situations emerge in social groups where certain individuals are kidded because their dress does not match those of the other members of the group. The key for the kidding, in terms of when it begins, how long it goes on, and the seriousness with which it is conducted, is usually set by the leader. Thus, the second important function or activity that a leader performs for a group is enforcing the rules of the group, rewarding good performance and adherence to the group's norms and values, and punishing those who deviate.

Linking with Other Groups The third important activity of the leader is linking the group with the many other groups that exist in the organization. No group is self-sufficient. Every group relies upon information, materials, supplies, and other resources that are essential to its function. The leader of an informal work group in a factory is the link with both the management representatives (e.g., the supervisor) and the union representatives (e.g., the steward). This linking activity is a third major function of a leader.

Protection from Outside Pressures Because of this linking activity, the leader also serves to protect the group from influences and pressures that may arise from outside sources. The gang leader, for example, by being the focal point of contact between the police and the community, protects the other members of the group from the pressures that come from these two other groups. Similarly, the leader of the informal work group who goes to the supervisor and argues for a lower time study or for more wash-up time is protecting the individual group members.

In general, the leader may be labeled as the individual who is "one of the group" and the "best of the group." In many ways the leader is the embodiment of the group's norms and values, the living symbol of the purpose that the group fulfills for individual members. Thus, the leader performs those activities and functions (or sees to it that they are performed) which are instrumental to the accomplishment of the group's objective—and this is true whether the objectives are to produce a specific number of cars in a day, to score a basket, or have a party on Saturday night.

HOW LEADERS INFLUENCE GROUP MEMBERS

The key to leadership is influence. A leader is a leader, therefore, only to the extent that others follow the leader's direction. A leader without a follower is not a leader at all. Therefore the question might be raised, "Why do followers follow a certain leader?"

In general, followers follow in order to satisfy their needs. People are willing to be influenced, if they see the influence as being in their best interest. Thus, as Figure 6.2 indicates, there is a definite relationship between the needs of the followers and the leader's source of influence. There are five reasons why a person would follow a given leader. These five sources of leader influence are: coercion, reward, expertise, reference, and legitimacy.

Coercion   Coercion as a source of influence flows from the ability of the leader to dispense punishment to the individual member. This punishment can take the form of verbal abuse, perhaps a mild amount of physical abuse, and up to and including, if you believe "The Godfather," the pain of death. In addition, the assignment to less desirable activities is another use of coercion. All of these appeal to a follower's need for survival and safety.

Reward   Reward is the mirror image of the previous strategy. The pats on the back and the other symbols of success for acceptable performance lead individual members to behave in ways that secure this reward. As outlined in the chapter on motivation, our needs for status and recognition lead us to behave in ways that will satisfy these needs. A leader can satisfy these needs through dispensing the group's rewards. The thumbs up sign from the leader of the informal work group, or the big raise from the boss are all valuable rewards dispensed by the leader.

FOLLOWER NEEDS	LEADER INFLUENCE SOURCE
Self-Actualization	
Esteem	Reward (Recognition) Referent
Belonging	Affection Reward (Belonging) Legitimacy Referent Expertise
Safety	Coercion Reward (pay)
Physiological	Coercion

Figure 6.2   Follower needs and leader influence.

Expertise   The leader's expertise in various activities is a third influencing factor. The leader is usually recognized as an expert in something. Whether it is winning games, keeping the boss happy, or telling the best jokes, individual members recognize the leader as being "better" and therefore accept the leader's word as "correct." In this process, members satisfy needs for belonging (following the right person) and esteem (basking in the reflected glow of the leader's expertise status).

Reference   Reference as a source of leader influence results when the individual member identifies with the leader. This identification occurs because the followers want to be like the leader because of their respect and admiration. The person who follows because of referent influence says, "I want to act in a way that earns the admiration and respect of the person that I respect and admire." In essence, the individual group member wishes both to be liked by and to be like the leader. This appeals to a follower's need to belong.

Legitimacy   Finally, leaders often exert influence because followers believe that the leader has a legitimate right to do so. This legitimate right is usually based on some formal position the leader holds. For example, a leader in an informal work group is often one of the more skilled people in the group, often holding a slightly higher position. Even that tiny status differential can invest the leader with a certain amount of legitimacy in influencing behavior. In following legitimate leaders, followers satisfy needs for belonging.

The Need for
Multiple Sources of
Leadership   It should be apparent to you, based on your experiences, that many of these sources of influence appear together. In fact, very few leaders are effective using only one of these five sources of influence. The supervisor in a bank may well have legitimate sources of influence, as well as a large measure of coercion and reward influence sources, but without other sources of influence (e.g., the expert and/or referent sources), the leader's effectiveness may be reduced. This implies that in order to be an effective leader of any group (particularly of a work group) it is important to develop as many multiple sources of influence as possible. The manager who relies solely upon the legitimate source of influence is not likely to be an effective leader.

EFFECTIVE LEADERSHIP STYLES

Leaders Are
Different from
Followers,
Sometimes   Research first tried to discover in what ways leaders were different from followers. It was primarily believed that leaders share some personality traits in common, which enable them to lead effectively. This assumption, in fact, underlies most leadership selection tests. Unfortunately, volumes of research were largely fruitless. Although leaders turned out to be somewhat more intelligent, somewhat better adjusted, with strong achievement and human relations orientations, none of the differences between leaders and followers were very large. There seemed to be too many "other factors" that affected which leader was effective in which setting.

Ohio State Researched Initiating Structure and Employee Consideration Leader Activities

Shifting the emphasis from what leaders were to what leaders do, researchers at the Ohio State University identified two types of leader behavior: Initiating Structure, and Employee Consideration. Initiating Structure supervisors, who plan and schedule the work of subordinates in a directive way, were rated very highly by their superiors and generally had high productivity and low cost and scrap rates. They also had higher grievance and turnover rates. Employee Consideration supervisors, who emphasized cooperation and mutual trust and respect, had low grievance and employee turnover rates, but lower productivity rates as well. Some supervisors high in both Initiating Structure and Employee Consideration had high productivity performance and only slightly higher grievance rates. But, there was substantial unexplained variation between group performance and leadership styles. That is, many Initiating Structure leaders had low performance groups, and many Employee Consideration leaders had high performance groups.

Blake and Mouton's Managerial Grid Identifies Current Style and Trains Both Concern for People and Production

Following closely the Ohio State researchers, Blake and Mouton developed the Managerial Grid. They took the two kinds of leader behavior and relabeled them Concern for People and Concern for Production. They developed a questionnaire which identifies a leader's current style along these two dimensions. They have also developed a six part training program designed to help leaders develop a concern for both people and production. After several years of research, they concluded that most leaders still retain the high people, high production orientation learned in the training program. The Grid approach seems to work best when whole groups of leaders who work regularly together are trained together. In this way, each can reinforce the others efforts.

Likert Concluded that System 4 Leaders Were More Effective Than System 1 Leaders

Professor Likert, also focusing on what leaders do, related leader activities to group effectiveness. Based on research at the University of Michigan and later confirmed at the University of Southern California, he identified four separate management systems: System 1—exploitative/authoritative; System 2—benevolent/authoritative; System 3—consultative/democratic; and System 4—participative/democratic. He concluded that supervisors of high productivity departments had employee-oriented, supportive leadership styles, emphasizing member participation and satisfaction. Supervisors who practiced employee-oriented leadership had lower turnover, more cooperation, and higher employee satisfaction. Other research, however, indicated that not all high-producing units were characterized by employee-centered or human relations leadership, nor did all human relations oriented supervisors have high producing units. Thus there were still "unexplained" factors.

Leaders' Actions Must Be Paths to Member's Goals

House, Mitchell, and Evans concluded that effective leaders' actions must be paths to the follower's goals. Leaders help members get to their goals by: (1) clarifying both the goal and what is needed to get there; (2) making effective performance the way to meet member needs; and (3) providing the necessary resources, information, and coaching. They pointed out, however, that factors in the situation affected which of the two kinds of leadership behaviors, (e.g., Consideration or Initiating Structure) would be most effective.

THREE FACTORS THAT INFLUENCE LEADERSHIP STYLE EFFECTIVENESS

It is abundantly clear to those who practice management that there are specific circumstances in which one kind of behavior is more valuable than another. This suggests that the effective leader must be able to diagnose those factors in a situation that calls for a particular leadership style. Tannenbaum and Schmidt identified three such groups of factors: (1) factors in the situation, (2) factors in the members, and (3) factors in the leader.

Factors in the Situation

Several characteristics of the situation influence the most effective leadership style. Four factors seem important. First, the pressure of time exerts a major influence on the leadership style that will be appropriate in a given situation. In emergencies, when a job requires an immediate decision (the example of the fire in the theater), it is difficult for a leader to involve other people in making the decision.

Communication Patterns The nature of the communication pattern is a second situational factor. Certain jobs restrict person-to-person contact between group members as, for example, many assembly-line jobs. When this occurs, it is more difficult for a leader of even an informal social group to solicit member opinion concerning activities.

Group Size The size of the work group is a third factor. Where the work group is small, relatively homogeneous, and located in close proximity to each other, consideration-oriented leadership styles are encouraged. When the group is large enough that personal interaction may be difficult, the leader may have to rely more upon directing and controlling activities to insure accomplishment of the group's objectives.

Task Complexity Complexity of the task itself is the fourth factor. Where the task to be performed is complex and requires imagination and ingenuity on the part of the individual group member, such as in a research organization, employee consideration leadership is likely to permit the individual group member to make innovative contributions. Close supervision would only frustrate the individual member's need for independence of action. On the other hand, when jobs are routine in nature and specialized, requiring a high degree of coordination (such as on the automobile assembly line), more initiating structure leadership would be necessary in order to insure the accomplishment of the group's objective.

"Yes, he's definitely assuming leadership. A case of the right ant in the right place at the right time, evidently."

Drawing by Richter. © 1971 The New Yorker Magazine, Inc.

Thus, the pressure of time, the communication patterns involved, the size of the work group, and the complexity of the task to be done are all elements in a situation that determine the effectiveness of a given leadership style.

Factors in Members

The second set of factors that determines the effectiveness of a leadership style reside in the needs and aspirations of individual group members.

Member Personality First, individual member personalities differ. Where individuals have high needs for independence and are focusing on status recognition needs, consideration leadership style seems to be the most effective. Conversely, when individual group members have high needs for predictability and order as well as for security and stability, initiating leadership would be the most effective strategy.

Member Expectations Each group member has a unique set of expectations. Members who expect to be consulted on decisions (e.g., research scientists) are often upset by a leader who makes unilateral decisions. A research laboratory, for instance, whose leader adopts a strongly directive, initiating structure style should not be surprised when turnover and absenteeism go up and the number of new research proposals go down. Thus, the expectations of the individual group members are a powerful factor influencing member willingness to accept a given leadership style.

Factors in the Leader

People are encouraged to "apply for" and accept positions of leadership because such positions fulfill a set of needs for them.

Leader's Personality   The personality of the leader is one important factor. For example, the leader who cannot tolerate uncertainty and has a strong need to exercise power over others is likely to be most comfortable with the initiating structure style of leadership. On the other hand, a leader interested in being liked above all else would be most satisfied with a consideration-oriented leadership style. In general, leaders seek those leadership roles that are most compatible with the leader's personality.

Leader's Expectations   Past experiences determine expectations concerning preferred leadership style. A leader who has been successful with a consideration-oriented leadership style in the past is most likely to try that leadership style in any new situation. Similarly, the initiating structure leader is most likely to attempt to plan and direct the work of others in a new situation.

Leader's Confidence in Members   Last is the leader's confidence in individual group members' abilities. Leaders who believe that individual group members have the ability to perform the task are more likely to practice consideration-oriented leadership. Leaders who have low confidence in individual group members' capability are more likely to exercise initiating structure leadership.

In short, Tannenbaum and Schmidt pointed out that leadership style, in order to be effective, must meet the demands of factors in the situation, the individual group members, and the individual leader. They have provided us with a checklist of important factors to consider in choosing a leadership style in any situation. They assumed that leaders could (and would) vary their leadership style to fit the situation.

CONTINGENCY APPROACH—FIEDLER

Professor Fiedler was bothered by the assumption that the leaders could be like chameleons and change leadership style at will to fit the situation. He too had investigated leadership and also came to the conclusion that situational factors were crucial. He defined three such situational factors: leader/member relations—the feeling of trust, loyalty, respect, and friendliness between the leader and the followers; task structure—the routineness or clarity of what to do in the job; leader power—the leader's ability to hire, fire, discipline, and reward employees. His research discovered that initiating structure leadership works best in situations that are either very easy or very hard for leaders. Such situations exist when they have either very little or very great power, when the task is either very structured or very unstructured, and when relations with members are either very good or very bad. On the other hand, situations of moderate difficulty are best handled by leaders who emphasize the employee consideration approach. Probably most situations fall into this category.

Besides re-emphasizing that situational factors are important in leadership, Fiedler challenged the motion that leaders should change to fit the situation. He suggests instead that engineering the job to fit the leader is a lot easier than engineering the leader to fit the job. He suggests that leaders could work in changing their relationship with their group, for example, improving it somewhat to facilitate consideration-oriented leadership (if that style is more comfortable to the leader) or, the task itself could be considerably more routinized, thus making initiating structure leadership more effective. Fiedler called this approach, organizational engineering, or engineering the organization for leadership effectiveness. Many organizations have tried his approach—and it seems to work.

WAYS TO IMPROVE LEADERSHIP PERFORMANCE

Fit the Situation to the Leader There are two basic strategies to improve leadership effectiveness. The first is to select leaders to meet the situation. This is the most popular approach and is the basis for much of the testing done in organizations today. In general, this works as long as the cutoff levels are low, that is, as long as many leader candidates make it past the initial barriers. It is not very successful in pinpointing with great accuracy the most effective leader for a given position. The second alternative is to engineer leadership jobs to fit the needs of the situation and the leader. This is Fiedler's organizational engineering. Both strategies have been followed with some success by various managements. Job Enlargement and Management By Objectives are both efforts to engineer the nature of the task to fit the needs of individual group members and their leader.

A third strategy and one that underlies both the selection and engineering approach, is to train leaders in analyzing situations. Whether leaders vary their leadership style or modify the situation, the leader must be skillful in analyzing the situation. The most important factors to know include: (1) the needs and expectations of the followers, (2) the structure and routineness of the task, (3) how followers feel about the leader, (4) the leader's formal power, and (5) time pressures. The skill in diagnosing situations is likely to be the single most important determinant in leadership success. As such, many organizations are likely to make major investments in training leaders in this critical skill. In any event, the improvement of leadership performance and organization is likely to be a high priority item for most organizations over the coming decade. Many of you will be actively involved both in being "improved" and in doing the "improving" of others.

SUMMARY

In summary, an effective leader is one who diagnoses important factors in a situation, who is able to either vary leadership styles to meet the needs of varying situations, or who can change the situation to meet personal preference. Leadership styles vary essentially along two dimensions—"supportive of others" dimension and a "concern for task accomplishment." The mix of these two elements will be determined by factors in the situation, forces in the individual, and factors in the leader.

FACTORY BLENDS U.S., JAPANESE STYLES

Management of Sony's San Diego Plant Keyed to Flexibility

DAVID SMOLLAR, TIMES STAFF WRITER

"It's a Sony!" says the tagline to advertisements for one of Japan's best-known electronic products.

"... from San Diego!" might well be added to reflect the six-year success of Sony Corp.'s sprawling color television plant in the Rancho Bernardo Industrial Park.

The facility is the most successful overseas venture of Sony, Japan's trend-setting television maker, as well as the largest consumer electronics factory in San Diego County.

Inside the more than seven-football-field-long plant, a workforce of 1,000 Americans assembles 450,000 Japanese-designed color sets per year. That number makes up 65% of all Sony TVs sold annually in the United States and well over 10% of all Sony retail sales worldwide.

The plant now is undergoing a $14 million expansion, the second since it opened in 1972, to complete a picture tube manufacturing area. Completion this fall will boost employment by 200 persons and raise yearly TV production to 650,000 sets. It will make the plant largely self-supporting by reducing the number of components brought from Japan.

"San Diego is now the biggest effort of Sony in its worldwide marketing strategy," said Masayoshi (Mike) Morimoto, plant general operations manager.

Indeed, Sony—with the $40 million facility here and a $20 million stereo tape plant in Dothan, Ala.—has pioneered investment in the U.S. among Japanese firms aiming to cut both marketing costs and to hedge against possible congressional action limiting exports to this country.

The increased visibility of Japanese corporations in the U.S. has sparked interest about their methods of industrial management. Among questions asked:

—Have such companies exported their management systems, sometimes called "Japan, Inc.", along with their products?

—How extensive are traditional Japanese concepts of group decision-making, "bottoms-up" communication and family-style personnel practices in subsidiaries here?

American businessmen and others have scrambled to understand these characteristics.

A look at Sony here shows a style different from many American companies, especially in a more paternalistic treatment of workers. But it also reveals management as far from pure Japanese.

As such, Sony is in the forefront of Japanese firms that are successfully adapting to the American environment.

"Sony is above all an example of what any well-managed firm does, particularly a multinational. It is only secondarily a Japanese company," says Richard Tanner Pascale, Stanford University professor who has studied Sony's operations extensively.

Adds Harvard College Professor Ezra F. Vogel, another expert on Japanese management, "The main difference (between American and Japanese firms) is the communication between the top and bottom people. I don't think decision-making is different but Japanese have greater sensitivity and respect for people on the operating line who then understand what the company wants."

Plant operations manager Morimoto, 38, a Japanese with an advanced degree in business

Source. Los Angeles Times, June 4, 1978.

from Columbia University, has been in San Diego since the factory opened with 40 employees and one assembly line in 1972.

"Before, we brought everything to San Diego from Japan," Morimoto said in an interview. "But now we want to buy everything in the U.S. So this means more planning, purchasing and engineering capacity here."

The plant, which produces all Sony 17-, 19- and 21-inch color televisions, now has five assembly lines on one shift turning out 40,000 sets each month. A second shift will be added to one line when the expanded picture tube facility is completed, creating a fully integrated television plant. At present, the front half of the Trinitron tubes are imported from Japan.

Yearly payroll is $10 million. Sony spends an additional $25 million per year nationwide on various components for assembly at the plant.

In explaining management practices, Morimoto referred to both the American and Japanese flags in front of the Sony plant as symbolizing "our hybrid of Japanese and American thinking.

"I don't like the terms 'Japanese management' or 'American management'," he said. "In the United States, there are plenty of large companies like IBM and General Motors but their management policies are very different."

Morimoto believes the autonomy given him from Tokyo headquarters has helped Sony run its plant here profitably.

"I like the delegation of authority," he said. "U.S. subsidiaries in Japan always must refer to a manual two inches thick prepared by the home office. If the manual doesn't have the answer, the manager must call headquarters instead of deciding for himself."

"We have no thick manual at Sony."

Morimoto suggested American companies would be more successful in Japan if they followed this practice.

"You must give the officer in charge as much authority as possible," he said. "If the manager always has to call home, he will lose credibility with his staff, because they will wonder whether Detroit can make a better decision 9,000 miles from the scene."

Shiro Yamada, a senior vice president of Sony

Corp. of America who has been based in San Diego since 1975, also sees Morimoto's flexibility as the key factor.

"If Mike always had to call Tokyo, we could not motivate the local people—let them understand what our mission is—as well as we have done," the 55-year-old Yamada said.

That notion of "mission" is important to firms in Japan, where most of the male workers remain at one company under a lifetime employment system.

"Because of that system, Japanese workers expect the company to take care of them and no one can be laid off," Morimoto said. "Even without good management, you can depend on high morale. Here we need to set a system very well."

Yamada said he appreciated the plans of many American workers at Sony to stay only until they accumulate enough savings for either college or another job.

"Because of this, the Japanese worker looks more loyal," he said. "But as long as the American works hard while signed up for Sony, fine."

As a result, Sony assumes a higher yearly turnover here than in Japan. "If we followed the rules just like in Japan, we'd have problems," Yamada said.

Sony trains almost all of its workers here itself, 65% of whom are women and whose average age is in the mid-20s. The employees are non-union and two elections among employees to affiliate with the Communications Workers of America have failed.

"To run a plant effectively it is necessary to keep morale high and have good, close communications," Morimoto said. "If a union intervenes, then it's hard to maintain good relations."

A tour through the cavernous, color-splashed assembly rooms revealed the fruits of Morimoto's efforts.

Many of the smiling, yellow-smocked workers turned from the assembly line to shout a "Hi, Mike!" greeting as Morimoto passed by. Morimoto responded with numerous first-name greetings.

One employee stopped the manager and asked about the possibility of a relative getting a job in the plant. She showed no hesitancy about discussing particular job problems. The informality between Morimoto and the line workers reflected a cheery air seldom seen along assembly lines where routine has traditionally been called boring.

Morimoto said that absenteeism is about 3%, "good but not terribly so," although lower than daily percentages for many American industrial firms.

Morimoto said that many job functions along the assembly lines are rotated. "In general, it's beneficial both for the company and the employee," he said. "It helps cut down absenteeism and also helps the workers get promoted."

When the 3:30 p.m. buzzer sounded ending the day shift, several workers remained on the line to finish uncompleted tasks.

"I really appreciate it when someone stays to finish up the jobs," Morimoto said. "I like the worker to be concerned."

Morimoto said that quality television production relies on teamwork since all assembly lines produce identical sets.

"So we try to establish criteria by which we assess the performance of each line," he said. "If we find that the product improves, then the supervisor and the workers will all lunch together or perhaps have a party or picnic."

Sony pays no individual bonuses for increased performance, although wages are competitive to other local firms and promotion is based on quality work, he said.

Morimoto cited ex-U.S. Navy personnel as among the best maintenance workers Sony has anywhere.

"They are versatile," he said. "None have ever been inside an exhaust oven before (used to vacuum picture tubes) but they can take one look and know how it works."

Said Yamada, "Not only do they have technical skills but they are well-disciplined and familiar with teamwork, the philosophy of one ship, one submarine."

In Yamada's view, management under Morimoto has been "very Japanese-like."

"Mike has been treating the employees just like a family," Yamada said. "I changed nothing when I came here but just continued what I had been doing in Tokyo (Yamada headed up a Sony picture tube production plant in Azawa, Japan)."

Yamada said the San Diego plant "has no manager's cafeteria, just one large room where everyone sits together. There is no sign in the parking lot of the general manager but everyone can park in the same spaces. Just as in Japan."

But to Stanford's Pascale, Morimoto's style more than the nature of Japanese management explains Sony's success.

"That man is a genius," Pascale said. "He is the finest example of what I call an 'integrator', necessary for a company to relate Japanese traditions and management to American ideas."

Pascale said that Zenith, the largest American televison maker, also has a common cafeteria and a common parking lot.

"What are often cited as special Japanese characteristics are simply good management," he said. Further, Pascale said that other aspects of management and employee relations in Japan, such as company songs and company vacations, are not used here. They would be viewed as encroachments on American feelings of individualism, he said.

"The difference rather is in someone like Morimoto, who has a marvelous capacity to pat a person on the back, establish rapport and the like," Pascale said. "He is at home both with Japan's reserved group style as well as with that of his American workers."

Professor Michael Yoshino of the Harvard Business School said that Sony is more innovative and international-minded than the typical Japanese firm which remains inward-looking and traditional. For example, Sony does not recruit management exclusively from top Japanese universities, which most large companies do, but also fills positions by hiring from other firms.

"The top management like Morita (Akio Morita, chairman of Sony) have had a lot of experience by living in the U.S.," Yoshino said. "They know how difficult managing a plant here can be. They haven't made the mistake of many Japanese companies by traditionally rotating managers every two years."

Half the Sony plant's 32 managers are Japanese

and half Americans, but with Japanese in the key areas of accounting, inventory and general management.

Morimoto said that all of them are consulted when a decision is reached.

"Individuals must not take too much responsibility upon themselves alone," he said. "I had a purchasing manager before who was always saying, 'I, I, I'. Why didn't he say 'we'? After all, it was Sony that was buying all the materials, not the man himself. I don't understand such an attitude."

Pascale said that this consultation technique is not uniquely Japanese although it is often said to be part of the nation's philosophical underpinning.

He quoted a senior Sony executive he had interviewed: "To be truthful, probably 60% of the decisions I make are my decisions. But I keep my intentions secret . . . whatever the outcome they (the managers) feel a part of the decision."

The best American managers instinctively do the same thing, Pascale said. But his studies of Sony and other firms show that the Japanese themselves value a mystique about their management system, he added.

"They are very skillful in bringing (to the U.S.) the mythology and some of the symbols of employee relations," he said. "But by-and-large, they behave very much like American companies."

In fact, according to Pascale, Sony's success so far has not been duplicated across-the-board by other Japanese firms in the United States.

"Sony is illustrative of the very best," he said.

"But overall, if Japanese subsidiaries are looked at as profit centers independent of home offices, you'd find a very, very mixed bag. Many are no more efficient than their American counterparts."

Harvard's Vogel said that Japanese will invest more and more in the United States as they build a cumulative base of experience.

"You will have a great expansion when the time is right because Japanese companies have developed a terrific capacity to compete," Vogel said.

Morimoto said that Sony plans to produce 25-inch models in San Diego eventually if the demand for color televisions continues to increase.

But Sony's success here does not automatically translate into a primer for Sony elsewhere or for other firms, he added.

"We started from scratch here and in the United Kingdom (with a plant in Wales) but we purchased an ailing company in West Germany," Morimoto said. "So Sony has different technical and marketing policies depending on the situation."

Yoshino of the Harvard Business School said that other Japanese firms must evolve a hybrid system along the lines of Sony's.

As for Sony, Yoshino said its next challenge will be to integrate American managers into top management where they can communicate directly and effectively with Japan.

"We want to hire more capable American managers," Morimoto agreed. "Maybe some day we will run this entire thing with only Americans."

Discussion Questions
1. Describe the sources of influence that Mr. Morimoto uses to establish leadership.
2. If you were ruler of the universe, would you require all managers to adopt Mr. Morimoto's style?

SELECTING A PRESIDENT

You have to decide on the selection of a president for a company which you own. The search has narrowed to two men, one of whom is named Johnson and the other named Brown. Before you are descriptive statements of the two men, prepared by a consulting psychologist.

Johnson

He is a persistent pusher and an enthusiastic team leader. Energetic, frank, and direct, he does not hesitate to speak his mind to prevent what he feels are mistakes or to suggest a better way of doing things. He does not mind a difference of opinion or a fight, but also gladly and easily helps and protects members of his staff when he thinks they need it. He has the reputation of being generous. He encourages and invites others to behave in the same straightforward way.

Johnson's method of directing includes periodic and thorough discussions of important matters with his close top staff members. He is very independent in reaching his conclusions and making his decisions, and he also likes to have the benefit of other people's experience and judgment. Johnson has the ability to make people think out loud and contribute constructive criticisms and positive ideas. He judges people by their personal qualities rather than by the positions they occupy. He leads a very alert and tense life, but he thrives on it. He initiates rather than reacts, modifies undesirable situations, rather than adapting to them.

Johnson enjoys the power he exercises, but he genuinely likes people. One of his striking characteristics is great liveliness, both physical and mental.

Brown

He is a very quiet and thoughtful person. He is available for aid in overcoming obstacles and seeing that things are done according to schedule and plan, but he likes to give his subordinates the feeling of independence and allows them a great deal of personal initiative. He encourages each individual to try his best.

Brown is active in many community affairs. He has a strong belief in the importance of adequate communication. He has frequent conferences with each of his top associates singly, and works hard to make each person feel that the decisions were arrived at jointly. Brown does not like group meetings. Rather, he prefers to confer with one person at a time, which enables him to establish a more intimate rapport with each of his associates, but also to influence and control them better. Brown creates the impression that he is superior and experienced, who is there to set an example and to help rather than to boss. The most noticeable feature of Brown's type of leadership is that things happen in a calm and apparently unhurried way.

Discussion Questions

1. What other factors in the situation would you need to know before you could make a decision?
2. Assume you had a very competent, well-running group of executives who will report to this president and that you have a stable product line that is marketed through many large distributors. Which person would you choose and why?
3. Assume now that the corporation is relatively new in a very competitive nuclear instrument manufacturing market, where the emphasis is on growth. Assume that there are young, aggressive, recently appointed executives in your organization. Do these product and personnel factors make any difference? Why or why not?

More words have been written trying to analyze and understand leadership than any other single management activity. Despite all of these words, the subject is still like the planet Venus—shrouded in deep clouds and largely hidden from view. Leadership is a station in life to which many aspire, which few obtain, and fewer still retain. We have taken the position that effective leadership is a function of the situation one finds oneself in—and that basically three factors in that situation influence what style will be effective. These three factors are (1) forces in the leader, (2) forces in the follower, (3) factors in the situation.

In this chapter you have had the opportunity to review and experience several of these factors that influence leadership style. The experience, for instance, was designed to show you the leadership style, instrumental or supportive, with which you were most comfortable.

The issue discusses how one group of leaders is attempting to implement a supporting leadership style in situations that have traditionally encouraged instrumental styles. Many of these efforts have been in repetitive task situations, which favor instrumental styles.

Their success thus far is testimony to the basic vitality of the management system, which rewards performance even though that performance may have been done differently in the past. As the article points out, they are safe with their leadership style as long as it works! And they have been accurate in diagnosing the needs of the followers and structuring the situation to permit the success of their style.

In essence, your problem is just the reverse of theirs. With an understanding of the needs of the situation and the followers, you can choose two different leadership styles. Unfortunately, most leadership positions are filled without adequately diagnosing the three critical factors that determine leader success. No wonder we have such high turnover and such generally poor performance!

This need not be, however. Better leaders can be produced by either specific training or organization engineering. Many of you will be actively involved throughout the course of your careers in that improvement process.

Here are some principles:

1. Management is more than just leadership. Management involves both the people- and thing-oriented activities of a company (e.g., money, material, and physical assets), although leadership is a technique for influencing the people aspects only. Good managers will be good leaders, although good leaders need not be good managers.

2. Leadership involves followership. Without followers there can be no leader.

3. Leaders are capable of securing followers because of their ability to reward or coerce group members, be an expert, be a reference, or be legitimate. Leaders rely mostly on multiple sources of influence in order to secure followers.

4. An effective leader will take three factors into account when determining leadership style. These factors are the needs of the situation, the needs of group members, and the leader's own needs. Whether the effective leadership style is task oriented, employee oriented, or a mixture of the two will vary from situation to situation, depending on these three factors.

5. The leader-member relations, task complexity, and power of the leader will influence the success of the leader's style. Fiedler suggests that situations be tailored to fit leaders' styles rather than altering leaders.

6. Leaders need to diagnose the situation within which they operate in order to lead effectively. Leaders can then choose either to vary their leadership style or change the situation, whichever is easier.

CHAPTER SEVEN POWER, INFLUENCE, AND CONFLICT

LEARNING OBJECTIVES

At the conclusion of this chapter, you should be able to:

1. Distinguish power from influence.
2. Define the two formal and two informal bases of authority.
3. Describe the bases for expert power.
4. List several power tactics.
5. Discuss five sources of conflict.
6. Illustrate five steps managers can take to manage conflict.

INTERGROUP NEGOTIATIONS

I. Objectives
   A. To experience group decision making.
   B. To experience intergroup negotiations.
II. Premeeting Preparation
   A. Read the instructions.
III. Instructions
   A. For this exercise, form as many groups of six to eight students as class size permits. (Be sure, however, there is an even number of groups.)
   B. Each group will be designated either a red group or a blue group.
   C. Teams will then be paired, each red team having a blue team assigned to it.
   D. The red and blue teams will not be allowed to communicate among themselves in any way—verbally or nonverbally—except when told to do so by the instructor.
   E. When the instructor begins the exercise, each group will make a series of five decisions. The red group chooses A or B. The blue team chooses X or Y. The values resulting from each possible combination are depicted in the payoff schedule in Figure 7.1.
      AX: Both teams win 3 points.
      AY: Red team loses 6 points, Blue team wins 6 points.
      BX: Red team wins 6 points, Blue team loses 6 points.
      BY: Both teams lose 3 points.
   F. Remove the Intergroup Negotiations Score Sheet (Figure 6.2)
   G. After each decision round, the instructor will also post results on the chalkboard.
   H. The five decision rounds will proceed as follows. Each will be started and stopped by the instructor.

		Blue Team	
		X	Y
Red team	A	+3 +3	+6 −6
	B	−6 +6	−3 −3

Figure 7.1   Blue team.

Round 1: Discuss your ideas and make a group decision. At the close of the round, write your group's decision on your score sheet.

Time for Round 1: 3 minutes

Round 2: The same as round 1.

Round 3: This is a special round. The payoff points will be doubled.

Step A: Each group will select a representative who will talk with a member of the other group of the pair. Instruct this representative in what strategy he or she should follow.

Time for Step A: 2 minutes

Step B: Instruct the two representatives to meet and discuss their strategies.

Time for Step B: 3 minutes

Step C: The representatives return to their groups and the groups make the decision. At the close of the round, write your group's decision on your score sheet.

Time for Step C: 3 minutes

Round 4: The same as rounds 1 and 2.

Time for Round 4: 3 minutes

Round 5: The same as round 3 except that payoff points will be tripled.

Please note negotiations will take place again with the 2 minutes to plan, 3 minutes to negotiate, and the 3 minutes to make the decision.

Time for Round 5: 8 minutes

IV. Discussion

Your instructor will help you explore what happened in the exercise and its meaning for management.

Time for Discussion: 15 minutes

Power—getting it and using it has fascinated managers and students of management alike for years. The magic of getting someone else to do something that you want has been likened to the charismatic callings of Joseph Smith and President Kennedy, in stirring the imagination of millions to seek greater contributions to themselves and society, and the devilish work of Reverend James Jones in Jonestown, leading 912 people to their suicide-deaths. Yet, for all of this fascination, power has been very infrequently studied. It is almost as if there is some black magic surrounding the subject which obscures understanding. This chapter will examine the mystical subject of power, and the equally confusing subject of conflict.

DEFINITION: POWER AND INFLUENCE

Power Is Getting Your Way Power is one of the most difficult concepts for most students to understand. For reasons probably buried in our history, many Americans rebel against the thought of having and/or using power. Yet, power fascinates us. Many of us have a schizophrenic view of power: desiring it secretly, whereas publicly denying any interest; both admiring and resenting those who exercise power; publicly condemning "power grabbers," whereas buying books by the millions on ways to exercise power (witness the overwhelming popular success of such books as *Power: How To Get And Use It* (Korda) and *Looking Out For No. 1* (Ringer). Because of this ambivalence, power has been infrequently studied systematically, although it is clearly an important part of the manager's job.

Influence Is Changing Someone Else's Attitude or Behavior Reflecting this ambivalence, many different definitions of power and influence have been put forth. Without getting trapped in the semantic jumble, for our purpose influence is the change in attitude or behavior that results directly or indirectly from the examples or actions of another. If your instructor can change your behavior to write a paper on a Saturday night rather than go out and party, or to have a more positive attitude toward a possible management career, you have been influenced. Power, on the other hand, is the ability to exert influence to get things done the way you want them to be done. Power, therefore, is influence over things and people. It is a specific kind of influence that is directed toward the accomplishment of the individual's objectives.

For example, if I refuse to discuss some matter with you, and don't answer your telephone calls as a result, you are influencing my behavior (e.g., not returning your phone calls). But you are not exercising power over me because you are not accomplishing your objectives.

SOURCES OF POWER

There are many sources of power. There are many answers to the question, "Why do people obey?" We have examined several of these in the Leadership chapter, using the Raven and French typology: reward, coercion, expertise, reference, and legitimate. In this chapter, we will examine some of the factors underlying two of these sources of power: legitimate and expertise.

Legitimate Power

Authority Is Power Granted by an Organization Legitimate power, for instance, is often called authority, in that it is power granted by an organization. There are two types of authority: formal and informal. There are two views of why formal authority is usually obeyed. The classical view is that all authority flows from the top down. At the top of the authority pyramid are the people who elect legislators to pass laws. These laws grant certain rights of private property. The owners of private property (stockholders in the case of corporations), working within the legal framework, elect a board of directors, who in turn choose a president with certain legitimate power or authority. The president, in turn, delegates a portion of this authority to the vice-president, who in turn, delegates a part to department heads, who delegate a part to managers and supervisors. Thus, people who join an organization agree in advance to accept the authority of their supervisors and managers, recognizing that it has been, in the final analysis, granted by themselves in the first place as voters.

Formal Authority Is Traditionally Viewed as Top Down This view of formal authority is descriptive and idealistic. Although most of us obey legal directives such as traffic laws and no smoking regulations, there are a large number of rules which are not obeyed. For example, it is estimated that at least 50 percent of automobile drivers usually exceed the posted speed limits. And, most people ignore the "Don't walk on the grass" signs. There are some missing links between top-down authority and complete compliance.

Formal Authority Can Also Be Viewed as Acceptance A second view of the origin of the origins of formal authority can be traced to Machiavelli's *The Prince,* which found its way into the management literature through Chester Barnard's proposal of the acceptance theory of authority. Barnard argued that authority, like beauty, exists in the eye of the beholder. Barnard focused on the reasons why people comply as seen from the follower's point of view. He said that people obey when: (1) They understand what is wanted; (2) they believe it is consistent with both their objectives and those of the organization; (3) they are physically and mentally capable of doing it. When these conditions are met, formal authority will be effective, according to Barnard, because it falls within the individual's zone of acceptance. The acceptance approach, although comforting, does not explain all of the power used in an organization. For example, it does not explain the power exercised over peers and colleagues at the same organizational level. Neither does it explain the frequent power exercised by subordinates over their superiors. Other factors, besides acceptance are important.

Informal Authority Comes from Social Exchange In addition to the formal basis of authority, there are two important informal ones. First, authority is often based upon a social exchange process. People are often willing to allow others to exercise authority over them in exchange for certain benefits. This is the familiar horsetrading, "I'll do this for you, if you do this for me." As long as the benefits are equal to or exceed our costs, we are usually willing to go along. In dealing with a peer, for example, this exchange process is likely to be most apparent. One agrees to support the other on a certain issue, and the other agrees to support the first on yet a second. Or, a boss agrees to allow an employee to leave a little early on certain days, in return for the employee staying a little later on other days to finish some "rush" work. This "you scratch my back and I'll scratch yours" view of authority is apparent in many organizational interactions.

Access to Information Is Another Basis for Informal Authority In addition, access to information often is the basis for authority, and information is not concentrated only at the upper end of the hierarchy. It is not unusual, for instance, for individuals lower in the organization to have information not possessed by higher level persons. One of the authors, for instance, as a Personnel Assistant, a very low-level management position, was able to secure information about a union organizing campaign that enabled him to exercise considerable authority over individuals who were several levels higher in the hierarchy. Staff personnel often acquire knowledge about the organizational transgressions of superior-line officials (overspending of budgets, misclassification of employees to get higher salaries, permitting paid time off in violation of company policies, etc.). This "guilty knowledge" can often be traded for authority.

Thus, through both a social exchange process and the access to information, authority can be acquired and exercised informally by individuals who are lower in the formal hierarchy. Authority, as legitimate power, is granted by an organization either formally or informally, and is one basis for power.

Expert Power

Expert Power Is Based on One Person Being Recognized as Knowing More Than Another Expertise, as another basis for power, is not derived from an organization, but rather from the perceived competencies of the parties. For individual A to permit individual B to exercise expert power over him, individual A must first recognize that he/she knows less about the subject than individual B. For example, a supervisor will not allow just anyone to set a time standard, but is likely to permit the Time Study Engineer to do so. Secondly, the symbols or credentials of the expert need to be clear. A college degree often gives the credential required to be regarded as an expert. Thirdly, following the expert's opinion needs to be rewarded. The time standard had better be correct, or else the supervisor is likely to not follow the Time Study Engineer's advice next time. In all cases, the nonexpert is willing to follow in order to realize the positive benefits of the expert's knowledge.

Power Bases Are Potential Only Regardless of the base, legitimate authority, expertise, reward, coercion, or referent, they are only a potential source of power. Simply having them does not guarantee power in and of itself. Power, to be effective, must be accepted by the influencee. Ordering someone to come in on time and work hard will not, by itself, necessarily produce on-time, good performance behavior. Neither will requiring class attendance, or reading the textbook, necessarily result in perfect attendance or effective studying. The linkage between these potential sources of power and the effective exercise of power seems to lie in the leadership ability of the individual. These five power bases are inherent in all management jobs. Individual managers differ, however, in their ability to use them to accomplish theirs and the organization's ends.

There Are Two Faces of Power: "Power Over" or Personal Power, and "Power With" or Socialized Power Some managers use what David McClelland called the negative face of power. This is a dominating, domineering "power over" approach to power where the manager puts power in personal "I want" terms. Contrasting with this is the positive or socialized face of power. Managers in this mode use power as a means of finding group goals and developing individual competencies and the group's ability to succeed. This use of "power with" stressing we (the group) needs has been demonstrated to be more successful in developing effective personnel and enhancing the manager's power. Thus, which of the two faces of power the manager chooses to use will affect the manager's effectiveness in translating the potential into effective power.

Power Tactics Regardless of the technique, managers use several strategies in exercising their power. The particular strategy used at any point in time is dependent upon the relative power of the parties, the situation, and the personal preferences of the individuals. Fallow has listed 16 strategies for getting one's way including the following:

Assertion voicing your opinions loudly and often;

Bargaining doing something for the other if they'll do something for you;

Deceit talk fast and even lie a little;

Emotion either put on a sweet face and try to look sincere, or put the other person in a good mood;

Expertise claim a lot of experience in handling similar situations;

Fait acompli just do it and talk about it later;

Persistence stick to the point regardless;

Thought manipulation let the other person feel it was his/her idea;

Threat do it or else.

In a similar way, George Strauss found that managers use power by: (1) appealing to rules, (2) evading rules, (3) engaging in personal politics,

(4) persuading with reason, and (5) changing the organizational interactional system. All of these tactics (and the list can go on and on) will vary from situation to situation and manager to manager. All are efforts to use the potential power at the manager's disposal to get the job done. These tactics are neither moral nor indecent; they are a necessary ingredient in the managerial stew.

In short, power is the fuel that drives the organization and its members down the appointed path. Without it, the organization would sit like a rusting car, immobile in its current position. Yet like most fuels, it has its toxic by-products that may be dangerous to one's health. In some ways, this book describes techniques for dealing with these potentially hazardous by-products.

CONFLICT IN THE ORGANIZATION

If everything worked according to plan, there would be little or no conflict in organizations. Individuals would cooperate and work would proceed smoothly. But, as most of us can readily testify, organizational life, paraphrasing Mark Twain, is one damned conflict after another. Most human interactions are characterized by disagreement and conflict, and those that occur on the organizational stage are no exception.

Conflict has only recently been recognized as an integral part of organizations. For much of the past, and indeed in many organizations today, conflict is viewed as the snake in what would otherwise be an organizational Garden of Eden. To be sure, some conflict is built into organizations, as, for example, inspection departments that are designed to check on production departments. In the federal government, separating the legislative, executive, and judicial branches build in conflict among them. But, a great deal of conflict arises from other sources as well. Accordingly, we need to consider how such conflicts originate and what strategies managers can use to cope with them. We will examine five such sources of conflict: individual differences, jobs that conflict, competition over scarce resources, status differentials, and work flow problems.

SOURCES OF CONFLICT

Individual Differences

Sometimes individuals whose attitudes and typical behaviors simply cannot mesh are assigned to work together. For example, a professor was assigned the duty of counseling graduate students and helping them plan their programs. Her approach was to be as accessible and supportive as possible, believing that in this large, impersonal school, students needed to feel someone was interested in helping them personally. Her secretary, who had been secretary to the previous counselor (who was less accessible and more formal) placed a sign on the door which requested that anyone knock before entering. She seemed to enjoy having some power over students, and was not popular with them. Because access to the professor was through the secretary's office, and because the professor wished to be more accessible, she had the sign on the secretary's door removed and replaced with one that read "Please Enter." Relations between the professor and the secretary became increasingly strained. The door signs were merely representative of the personality differences between the two. Eventually, the secretary began having severe chronic headaches that culminated in her resigning.

Individual Differences Sometimes Are Based on Personality Clashes and Cultural Differences

We often assume that individuals from other cultures share our values and interests. Unfortunately, this is most often not the case. Consider, for instance, the American business executive accustomed to making quick business decisions dealing with a Japanese executive who has been trained to review patiently all of the facts with all of the people concerned before deciding. Many American business executives have lost lucrative business ventures in the Orient because they misread the Japanese deliberateness as disinterest. Similarly, South American executives have much less regard for meeting precise time requirements than do Americans. Many Americans have been irritated and frustrated when the Brazilian executive who was supposed to arrive at 8:00 actually arrives at 9:00 because that is customary behavior in the Brazilian business culture. These cultural and value differences often give rise to conflict.

Clashes caused by individual differences, however, are probably not as common as one might think. Many conflicts appear to be caused by individual differences, but actually have their origins in the formal organization. There are several varieties of conflict induced by the design of the formal system. Earlier we suggested that sometimes organizations are designed with built-in checks and balances. One group is empowered to block or implement the action of another. Checkers who evaluate engineering drawings prepared by designers provide one such example. Purchasing agents who process requisitions initiated by engineers or others provide another. Both the checker and the purchasing agent are meant to assure that the drawing or requisition complies with established standards. If not, it gets sent back. You can imagine how this makes the originator feel, especially when there are serious time pressures.

Jobs That Create Shared Responsibilities and Checks and Balances Can Cause Conflict

In addition, many responsibilities in an organization are shared between an operating line official and a staff specialist. In this sharing are the seeds of conflict. Consider, for example, the manufacturing superintendent, (a line official) who shares with the budget analyst (a staff position) the responsibility for approving overtime. The manufacturing superintendent usually argues for overtime on the basis of meeting schedules, whereas the budget analyst resists in order to reduce costs. These shared responsibilities are another source of conflicts caused by job design. In addition, some jobs serve boundary or linking functions between two or more groups, and this often results in conflict. Consider, for example, the sales engineering person who serves as the link between sales and engineering. Such a person must please both departments, which often have conflicting interests. The personnel manager similarly links the organization with outside job seekers. Particularly in jobs where new employees are difficult to find (and therefore may ask salaries in excess of what the organization is willing to pay), this exposes the personnel manager to conflict. All of these, checkees versus checkors, shared responsibilities, and linking responsibilities, are job conditions that build in conflict.

In cases of this sort the conflict persists even if the people who occupy the jobs are replaced by new employees. The main cause of the conflict is in the job, not in the people. The result is that when an employee in such a job is performing satisfactorily, conflict is a normal occurrence.

Competition over Scarce Resources

Scarcity Can Lead to Conflict Another normal condition in organizations is insufficient resources—people, materials, money, time—to meet all of the needs. Both production and engineering need more time, yet the master schedule can allow only one of them a slight extension. The chief engineer and the superintendent of production both plead their cases. The outcome is often that one wins and the other loses.

The budgeting process often brings this conflict into sharp focus. All of the budget requests in most organizations usually add up to significantly more than the organization can spend. So, the rationing process begins, and there are inevitable winners and losers. Zero-based budgeting is one method used by some companies to ration their scarce monetary resources. And, money isn't the only scarce resource over which competition and conflict occurs. For instance, in a matrix organization, competition often exists between product managers for the best people to work on their project and for the salesperson's time and effort in emphasizing their products. In short, because the organization has limited resources (money, people, materials, and time) conflicts emerge over the division of the fixed pie.

Status Differentials

Status Differences Can Often Lead to Conflict All organizations are based on status differentials. Sometimes the status assigned a person differs from that which action on the job seems to permit. A classic example of this type of problem is the conflict that occurs between food suppliers (waiters/waitresses) and counterpeople in restaurants. Supposedly, the counterpeople are of higher status, but the work situation requires them to react to directions given by lower status waitresses and waiters. The result is conflict.

Consider the case of the young, highly trained engineering manager and the older, less technically trained staff specialist. In such situations, the relatively equal status accorded to the staff's specialist is likely to be challenged by the engineering manager with the words, "But they just don't understand the business."

Work Flows

Work Flows Cause Conflict Finally, the way the work flows in an organization is often a source of conflict. Sometimes, conflict emerges when people in different departments must depend on each other to complete their work. The credit department, for example, is often in direct conflict with the sales group, because the salesperson is dependent upon credit approval in order to have a sale count toward the monthly quota. Unpredictability is also likely to cause conflict. When work comes in spurts, with heavy demands at times and light demands at others, and the particular pattern cannot be predicted, resentments and conflicts will likely result. And, the conflict potential is heightened when people cannot get the information they need to do their jobs. Imagine, for instance, that you were told to do a certain assignment in this class and were not permitted to ask the instructor questions to clarify expectations, and furthermore, the material necessary to do the assignment work was not in your textbook and you didn't know where to find it. We bet you'd be very angry! Yet, this situation occurs frequently in organizational life, and is a source of continual conflict. In short, work flows that create interdependence, unpredictability, and inadequate information can cause conflict.

MANAGING CONFLICT

Modern management thinking accepts conflict as a normal part of operating organizations, much like friction is a normal part of operating machines. But this has not always been true. For a long time, conflict seemed to be regarded as something sinful that should be stamped out as promptly as possible. Now

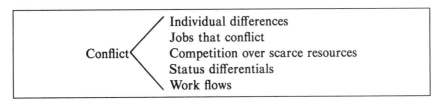

Figure 7.2 Sources of Conflict.

it is more likely to be seen as both potentially valuable as well as inconvenient, depending on the situation. Conflict is no longer viewed as an evil to be avoided, but rather an organizational fact of life that must be handled. Here we shall consider several ways that managers deal with conflict. Any manager might wish to use more than one of them, depending upon the particular situation.

Avoidance and Denial

No Problem This is the course of smiling even though it hurts, and agreeing even when we don't. It amounts to sweeping the conflict under the rug, pretending that it doesn't exist or isn't serious anyway in hopes that it will go away. This is the most common way of coping with conflict. Avoidance of directly facing disagreement has a long tradition and is the accepted means of coping with conflict in many cultures. In such cases, the conversation is roundabout and the matter is eventually dealt with indirectly or through intermediaries. Of course, when the issue is unresolved, it remains to surface again. This is the weakness of avoidance and denial. This conflict management technique is most useful when the issues are not important, when there is little chance of winning anyway, and when the costs of continuing the conflict are greater than the benefits of winning. This tactic enables the situation to cool down and people to gain pespective. In this way, present avoidance may lead to future resolution.

Dominance

I Win, You Lose This is the next most common method of handling conflict. Just order a settlement, based on the terms you like, and if you have the power, you can probably make it stick—this time. But, the loser of the battle lives to fight again on another issue, with better weapons and probably with more ferociousness. So victories won in this way are often Pyrrhic victories—short-term benefits which impose long-term costs. This win-lose situation often results in poor cooperation and continued plotting of ways to "get even" in the future. This type of conflict resolution tactic does suit some circumstances, however. It is valuable in emergency situations, when quick decisive action is vital, or when important issues and unpopular decisions need to be made (e.g., layoffs, budget reductions, etc.). In the right situation, dominance represents the best short-term resolution of the conflict, but needs some additional long-term strategies in order to prevent the issue from being pushed underground.

Smoothing

We All Really Agree This is the managerial equivalent of pouring oil on the troubled waters. Lawrence and Lorsch found that effective coordinators coped with conflicts by relying on jokes and kidding to make disagreements seem less important. They maintained friendly relationships by emphasizing common interests, playing down differences, and avoiding known problems. This strategy is particularly useful when the parties at conflict are approximately equally matched and their goals are mutually exclusive. This strategy also achieves temporary solutions to complex issues, particularly when there is a time pressure. But, this approach yields a short-term reduction of the conflict without solving any of the longer-term issues. As such, smoothing may only postpone the frustration and hostility which are often the long-term by-products of dominance.

Appeal to Higher Authority

Kick It Upstairs When people can't agree, often the easiest solution is to let the boss decide. The boss often has a broader perspective, and not being personally involved, can often see the issues more objectively. Of course, someone usually wins, and someone loses, so this method suffers from some of the same problems as dominance. But, it is especially useful when both parties are "dug in" and the conflict needs to be settled.

Establish Policies and Rules

Go by the Book The establishment of rules and policies can often reduce conflicts. The establishment of credit policies, for instance, can reduce the conflict between sales and credit. The establishment of quality standards often reduces the conflict between production and quality control. Policies and rules in general increase the amount of predictability in the relationships between people and groups. This reduces the amount of conflict. Rules, of course, cannot be made for every situation. But wherever possible, they are useful conflict-reduction techniques.

Appeal to Neutrals

Can You Help Me? Sometimes conflicts can be appealed to neutral third parties, such as omsbudsmen, personnel departments, or some noninvolved colleague. In such cases, the third party investigates the situation and makes recommendations for solutions. Many organizations assign this investigatory function to the personnel department, particularly in conflicts involving bosses and their employees. Efforts to resolve conflicts in this way succeed only sometimes, because the parties often cannot hear the other side, and the third party must be very skillful in overcoming this emotional blockage. This technique has been used with considerable success in union-management and international conflict situations. One of the more famous examples was President Carter's Camp David agreement between Israel and Egypt, where the President played the role of the neutral third party.

Changing the Work Flow

Let's Do Things Differently Because how jobs work together often causes conflict, changing the work flow is one way to reduce conflict. Sometimes it is possible to separate the warring parties by putting a linking group in between them. The conflict between production and engineering is often reduced by putting between them a third linking group called manufacturing engineering. Their task is to take engineering drawings and specifications and translate them into manufacturing procedures that are understandable to production people. Other times, jobs can be unified to reduce conflict. This is particularly useful when the conflict can be traced to divided responsibilities, as when, for example, sales and advertising are separated. Making jobs "whole" can reduce conflict. In either case, defining jobs more completely can reduce conflict. Most often conflict emerges because the responsibilities of various jobs are not precisely defined. As people hurry to complete their own tasks, they inevitably step on other people's organizational toes. Clarifying these gray areas in and of itself can reduce conflict. In short, by changing the work flow in an organization, either separating or unifying jobs or defining them with more precision, it is possible to reduce the amount of conflict.

Intergroup Confrontation

Let Me Tell You . . . Sometimes conflicts between groups in an organization become fierce. Production can war with quality control, engineering can war with sales, and so on. When this conflict reaches the war stage, drastic measures are necessary. Intergroup confrontation, as proposed by Bechhard, is one such structured measure. In this strategy, each group meets separately and drafts two lists, one of how they see the other group and another of how they feel the other group sees them. These lists are shared, without comment or explanation. The separate groups then generate a list of what the other group does that frustrates them, and a list of what they expect the other group will say they do that is frustrating. These lists are shared again without comment. The groups again meet separately to list what the other group can do to reduce the conflict, and what they believe the other group will want them to do. These lists are then discussed between the two groups. Usually by the third round (the "what can be done to reduce conflict" lists) much of the emotions surrounding the conflict have been spent. The groups by then are usually ready to listen to each other. This technique has worked successfully in a number of situations, but it has also, in some situations, led to an escalation of the conflict. This is a high-risk, high-return strategy. It is useful when the conflicts between the two groups have reached the all-out war stage.

Selection and Training

Finding New People or Training the Old Ones Selection and training deal with conflict by changing the people. Through selection, for instance, it is possible to form work groups on the basis of personal compatibilities. This has proven successful in reducing conflicts in submarine crews and problem-solving task forces. It is also possible, for instance, to put people in conflict-ridden jobs—as linking or boundary jobs tend to be—who have the capacity to smile through it all and not pass on the conflicts to others. Transferring individuals who are involved in personality clashes with others in the group is also possible. Thus, selection can reduce conflict by changing the cast of characters. Training, on the other hand, seeks to change the characters who are present on the stage. It is possible to train people in conflict-handling techniques, as one way to manage conflict. It is also possible to train individuals in their specific job responsibilities so as to improve their individual performance, thus reducing one of the causes of conflict, namely, inadequate performance. Both selection and training seek to change the people so as to manage conflict.

Find Superordinate Goals

The Greater Enemy One of the best ways to manage conflict is to find some greater enemy against whom to compete, rather than conflict with each other. Professor Muzafer Sherif of the University of Oklahoma conducted a classic series of "natural" experiments on group behavior. These studies, known as the "robbers cave" studies, used groups of boys at a summer camp as subjects. By designing the activities of the boys so that they formed groups to accomplish goals and competed with other groups for prizes, the experiments created groups with intergroup friction and conflict. Under these conditions, contact between groups was ineffective and stressful. To reduce the intergroup conflict, Sherif arranged for the boys to be cast into a problem situation in which effective action could not be achieved by one group alone, but only by the cooperation of both groups in a pair. For example, interdependence was created by a water shortage, a defective vehicle, and by other means also requiring intergroup cooperation to overcome the obstacle. In the face of a common overriding or superordinate goal, cooperation developed. And the experience of cooperation in solving a mutual problem led to a reduction in intergroup tension and hostility. Group incentive plans in industry, which tie individual pay to group performance, are another example of a superordinate goal designed to reduce individual conflicts. Sales contests that pit one location of a fast food company against others is another example. Such plans work best when the members of the groups are interdependent with each other.

Bargaining

Let's Make a Deal Bargaining requires confrontation and involves give and take. The original demand isn't imposed when true bargaining occurs. Some compromises are involved so that the final agreement meets only some of the original preferences. This is the familiar mode by which union/management agreements are negotiated. Bargaining also determines prices at which services are rendered and goods sold in many instances. It is also the implicit means by which the terms of all manner of interpersonal relations are arranged. Two bargaining strategies have been identified. The first, distributive bargaining, involves competing for a larger share of a fixed pie based on the assumption of a fixed amount of benefits. Thus, there is a winner and a loser in this bargaining strategy. The second, integrative bargaining, revolves around finding solutions in which both parties can be winners. As such, it is based on the assumption that the benefit's pie is expandable. Distributive bargaining strategies are most common in organizational life. The major weakness in bargaining as a means of conflict resolution is that it may lead to mutually unsatisfactory outcomes, if neither side obtains what it wanted in the first place because it has made compromises.

Consensus Problem Solving

Although each of the means of coping with conflict we have discussed is useful, the one that receives the most enthusiastic play today in the management press is one that involves confrontation and effort to find the best solution which will integrate the desires of the conflicting parties. This is called consensus problem solving and it involves the following characteristics.

Here's How I See It 1. Present your own position as clearly as possible.

2. Listen to the other position as effectively as possible. (A good test is for both parties to state the other's position in acceptable terms before assuming those positions are correctly understood.)

How Do You See It? 3. Do not avoid or deny disagreement where it exists. Don't give in just to make uncomfortable disagreement go away. Instead, explore the reasons for disagreements and yield only for good reasons.

Integrative Solutions 4. Do not quickly appeal to authority or resort to arbitrary devices such as flipping coins.

5. Do not assume you are in a combat where one must win and one must lose. Search for the best solution. Try to open your mind to integrative solutions, those that go beyond your original ideas on the problem.

Where consensus is reached it often amounts to a more creative and unresented solution than either party envisioned at the outset. Although it has great merits, however, it is infrequently used. Dealing with conflicts are "gut searing" experiences, and few of us are likely to enjoy them. Furthermore, once conflicts become open, they may not go away, but get worse. It is also terribly time consuming, so although it offers great benefits, it is infrequently used.

Stimulate Conflict

We Need More Disagreement Sometimes conflicts needs to be stimulated in order to encourage differences of opinion, which are essential to creative and innovative decisions. Additional conflicts, for instance, could have been fruitfully used in President Kennedy's decision concerning the Bay of Pigs invasion of Cuba in 1962, and President Nixon's Watergate conspiracy. The easiest way to do this is to avoid using many of the conflict-reducing strategies spelled out above. For example, not acting as a court of last resort, the manager can encourage the conflict to persist. Furthermore, the manager can push the people to settle the matter among themselves. By bringing in outsiders, and taking other steps to increase uncertainty, conflict can be stimulated. One method, dialetical debates, has been used in the planning process to stimulate conflict. In this method, both sides of a position are forceably presented to a third party, who challenges both parties to respond to specific facts. Based on the facts and assumptions discovered during the conflictful debate, a better decision can be made. In some ways, this is like the adversary proceedings in a court of law. There are many steps that can be taken to stimulate additional conflict. Surprising as it may seem, many organizations suffer from too little conflict and too much "me too-ism" and "going along-ism." Conflicts are a common manifestation of organizational life. They can help the organization in the way that pain helps the body: by forcing awareness of and responses to a problem. The possible responses to conflict are several, and part of becoming a skillful manager is learning both how to use and control conflict so that it aids effective performance and development.

TEACHING HOW TO COPE WITH WORKPLACE CONFLICTS

It is nothing if not comical: Sixteen middle-aged executives, divided into teams, race against the clock—and each other—to build a device out of assorted junk that will catch raw eggs gently enough to keep them from breaking. They get the junk from an auctioneer who "sells" such things as metal strips and pieces of string, for which each team can bid up to $55,000. In the background a videotape machine quietly records the sights and sounds of the competition.

Later, the executives watch themselves in action. To their distress, they see themselves mocking their teammates, throwing out authoritarian orders, and showing impatience. Although their goal was to beat the other teams, they discover that most of their conflicts were with persons on their side.

The egg drop exercise, developed by Vector Management Systems Inc., of New York, to open a three-day course on managing conflict, is one of a growing number of techniques offered by consultants who teach managers to recognize and deal with on-the-job conflicts. The techniques may be as simple as self-administered and self-scored questionnaires, such as those offered by Houston-based Teleometrics International Inc. to let managers analyze their own styles of dealing with conflicts. But they also include psychologist-scored surveys that allow subordinates and peers to rate managers on their ability to handle conflicts, as well as courses that run as long as nine days. The disparate methods have one thing in common—a belief that conflict, when properly recognized, is not debilitating to job effectiveness and can actually enhance it.

"There's a lot of energy wasted because many people work toward eliminating conflict," says Kenneth Sole, a psychologist who runs conflict seminars at NTL Institute for Applied Behavioral Science in Bethel, Me. "My goal is not to have fewer conflicts, but to make conflicts productive."

Source. Business Week, February 18, 1980.

Charles Reiner, Vector's president, notes that there are five ways to deal with conflicts: compromise, competition, avoidance, collaboration, and accommodation. "As psychologists we've worked studiously to suspend value judgments about the five styles," he says. "We try to give course participants an ability to use all of them, and by the end of our seminar their bias against or for any one style is considerably reduced."

Increasing tension

The proliferation of conflict seminars comes at a time of increasing tension in the workplace. The influx of women and minorities into the work force has caused problems that can rarely be resolved by fiat. The growing popularity of avant-garde management structures such as matrix management, in which many corporate employees wind up reporting to two bosses, has reduced many executives' authority to issue orders, making their interpersonal skills far more important. And in general, corporate management over the last decade has become far more amenable to judging managers by their behavior patterns as well as by bottom-line performance and has shown an increasing willingness to spend time and money on behaviorally oriented programs.

John W. Humphrey, president of Forum Corp., a Boston behavioral consulting firm, calls the trend an evolution from resolving conflict to managing conflict to working with conflict. "We've gone," he says, "from something that says, 'Get it out!' to something that says, 'Learn how to use it.'"

Acting it out

The techniques of teaching managers how to use conflict vary as much as the consultants who develop them. Vector, for example, includes a commercial movie, *Twelve Angry Men,* in its course because the jury members in the film use a variety of styles to resolve their conflicts. After each showing, the course participants analyze the conflicts and how to resolve them.

Other consultants rely more heavily on role-playing. In one exercise, Forum Corp. sets up groups of three people and gives them a hypothetical problem. One participant might play the part of a research manager, another a product manager, and a third an engineering department head. They have to figure out how to allocate scarce resources for each department. Situation Management Systems Inc., of Boston, offers courses on "Positive Power and Influence" and "Negotiating Skills" that deal heavily with resolving conflicts. They wind up with each trainee playing himself or herself, and a fellow participant acting as the trainee's boss or subordinate.

Not surprisingly, such methods have their detractors. One of them, Kenneth R. Hammond, director of the University of Colorado's Center for Research on Judgment & Policy, has been a conflict troubleshooter for such disparate organizations as the Denver Police Dept. and an international pharmaceutical company. He pays little attention to behavioral styles, concentrating instead on separating facts from values. "People assume that if they solve the emotional problems, the cognitive aspect will solve itself, but then nobody focuses on issues," he maintains.

By focusing on issues, Hammond says, he resolved a two-year conflict between the Denver Police Dept., which wanted a new bullet with greater stopping power, and community leaders, who saw the request as bloodthirsty and possibly racist. He got the warring parties to rank in importance such values as stopping power, injury, and threat to bystanders. He discovered that the community as a whole would accept a bullet that had increased stopping effectiveness without increasing injury. Within six weeks, the police settled on ammunition that would flatten out and knock a person over on impact. As Hammond saw it, the solution had been elusive because of emotions. "When they couldn't agree," he says, "they attributed it to unpleasant motives, such as

'You hate blacks' or 'You want a lawless society.'"

To NTL's Sole, such real-life issues are the stuff of which conflict courses must be made. He also eschews role-playing and artificially created situations and arranges to have an equal distribution of warring factions in his workshops, allowing conflicts to arise naturally. He tries to have the same number of men and women, for instance, and to include a large smattering of minorities. With the participant distribution forming a built-in powder keg, he lets simple issues—such as whether or not to allow smoking—form the conflicts that will be analyzed. "We get a participant pool that guarantees differences but also guarantees pools of support," he explains. "My workshops are kind of a social microcosm, and the issues that emerge mirror issues in society."

Racism and sexism

In contrast to comprehensive efforts such as Sole's nine-day workshop, a number of corporations are putting in less sweeping programs of their own. More often than not, they are designed to resolve specific conflict problems within an organization. Northwestern Bell Telephone Co., for instance, has a program to combat racism and sexism. "We teach women and minorities to develop support systems and to confront people who use sexist or racist language," Larry L. Waller, staff manager for awareness training, explains.

At Sperry Vickers, a Troy (Mich.) division of Sperry Corp., a switch to matrix management, with its dual ladder of authority, dramatically increased conflict two years ago. B. Richard Templeton, manager of human resources and organization development, has since distributed conflict analysis questionnaires to managers and their subordinates and has been holding informal self-assessment meetings to help them understand how their behavior is perceived by their colleagues.

Templeton grants that the matrix system still causes clashes, but he says that his program is helping resolve the conflicts at an early stage. "It's like setting a course for the moon," he says. "The best place to make a course correction is as early as possible, before you're hopelessly off track."

Tailor-made seminars

Conflict consultants sometimes develop seminars to a company's specifications. Union Carbide Corp., for one, has sent nearly 200 managers through a tailor-made Vector course over the last two years. Stephen J. Wall, Carbide's manager of corporate management development, reports that informal feedback has been very positive. "The thread that runs through the comments is that people are startled to discover their own patterns of response to conflicts," he says. "Now they say they can see what's coming and actually plan strategies to deal with it." Wall, who took the course before he bought it for Carbide, says he discovered that he had a tendency to be an accommodator and used to give in to unreasonable requests. "Now whenever I feel I'm about to give in, I roll it around in my head first," he says.

It is almost impossible to put a dollars-and-cents value on such behavioral awareness, but every conflict course graduate with whom BUSINESS WEEK spoke insisted that the course was worth the few hundred dollars it typically cost. Marilyn Loden, an organization development specialist at New York Telephone Co. and a graduate of Sole's program, noted that she had just had a conversation with a recalcitrant employee; it was difficult for her, but it cleared the air in the office. "A year ago I would have been stewing about the fact that he wasn't working out, but I would have said nothing," she says.

Raymond A. Murphy, a Carbide manager of systems software, and Leicia Marlow, a Carbide data processing applications manager, liked the Vector course so much that they have assigned several of their own employees to attend it. "Watching my people at staff meetings now, I see more conscious attempts to understand where the other guy is coming from," Murphy notes. "We've had people who were overassertive before who are now curbing their responses, while others who had sat back and watched have learned to be assertive."

The ability to choose among several styles as the situation requires is probably the most important result of all the courses. Marlow, who concedes that she needed help in becoming more assertive, insists that the course was far more complete than standard assertiveness training. As she sums it up: "It wasn't necessarily altering behavior; it was broadening it."

Discussion Questions
1. What sources of conflicts are discussed in the article?
2. What steps that managers can take to manage conflict are spelled out in the article?

You are Sam Jones, a supervisor in the grinding department for the Abalone Eyeglass Manufacturing Company. There are 14 people who work in your department. Your efficiency ratings are good and your scrap and rework are low enough. You don't have the best department, but it's far from the worst; in fact, you rank just about average. You know that your department has the capability to do far better, and that unless it does, your chances for keeping your job are out the window. You have just recently been promoted to the job of supervisor.

You've worked in the grinding department for about 6 years. During that time you've been going to college in the evening and are about two-thirds of the way through to your bachelor's degree. You figure that that's the reason you were chosen to be the supervisor of this group over several other longer-service employees, at least one of whom had a better production record than you did.

In fact, the basic problem in the department seems to be this one individual, Johnny Bench. Johnny is 37 years old, about the same age as you, married, with three children, and has been with the company for 11 years. That's 5 more years than you've been there. He's always worked in the grinding department and knows its operations quite well. He was the top producer until you were promoted. In the 6 years that you've known and worked alongside of Johnny he's always been somewhat of a smart aleck. He know all the rules and walks just to the edge of them. He's never caught, but then again, he's never done all of his job. You know he could be the top producer and organize the rest of the crew so that they too would exceed the standard. But, you suspect he is the ringleader in keeping production down. His lateness pattern is typical. He's late 5 or 10 minutes a couple of times a month, usually when he knows that you need that little extra. It's never enough to discipline him—just enough to annoy you.

His production record in the last several months has been on the downside. Yesterday you noticed that he had been storing parts, that is, saving good production pieces by labeling them as "rework" to be put back in the line when he wants to slow down. Although this is clearly against company policy, all of the people, including yourself, have done this as a matter of practice.

In the several months that you have been supervisor, your boss has put increasing pressure on you to get the performance of your unit back to its top-rated position. She's even made some thinly veiled threats that if you couldn't do it, she'd find someone who could. How would you handle the problem of Johnny Bench?

Discussion Questions

1. What are the sources of conflict between Johnny Bench and Sam Jones?
2. What sources of influence or power might Sam Jones use to get Johnny Bench to produce more?
3. How would you handle the conflict between Sam Jones and Johnny Bench, and why?

No topic raises as many management eyebrows and piques as much management interest as those of power and conflict. Like evil—and the morning sun—these are always with us. Our ambivalent feelings about these crucial organizational processes assure that they will continue to be lively subjects of continuing debate. Managers must get things done, and power is necessary to do that. Power itself, getting your own way, is a form of influence. Influence, in turn, is changing someone else's behavior or attitude as a result of either direct or indirect action. Power is usually based on five sources: reward, coercion, expertness, referent, and legitimate. Legitimate power is called authority. There are two views of the sources of formal authority. Traditionally, authority has been thought to flow from the top down in an organization. Machiavelli and Chester Barnard have proposed instead, that authority rests on the acceptance of the influencee. In addition, authority flows from such informal sources as the social exchange process, a version of the familiar "you scratch my back and I'll scratch yours," and the access to "guilty knowledge" information by individuals who are lower down in the hierarchy. Thus, authority (or legitimate power), as one power base, flows both up and down and laterally in an organization.

Expertise, as another power base, on the other hand, is based on the follower's recognition that someone else knows more about a certain subject. Even here, acceptance plays a part in the effective use of power. In fact, acceptance by the influencee seem to be the crucial ingredient in the tasty power stew.

One of the ways in which power is used in an organization is to deal with conflicts. If everything were perfect, conflicts might never exist. But organizations are imperfect mechanisms, designed by imperfect people. In addition, conflict is often designed into the organization. The chapter examined five sources of conflict: individual differences, jobs that conflict, competition over scarce resources, status differentials, and work flows. Managers need to manage conflict because it is an inevitable part of the organizational scene. Conflict is usually managed either by dominance, avoidance, bargaining, smoothing, appeals to higher authority, establishing rules and policies, changing the work flow, intergroup confrontation, selection and training, or consensus problem-solving. In fact, in many situations, managers may need to stimulate conflict in order to clear out some of the group-think cobwebs. Each of these approaches has its merits, and the skillful manager uses that method, or combination, which best fits the situation.

Here are some principles:

1. Power, defined as getting your way, is a special kind of influence. Influ-

ence is changing another person's attitude or behavior either directly or by example.

2. Power is usually based on five sources: the ability to reward others, punish others, be an expert and know more than others, want to be copied by others as a referent, or granted by an organization to make legitimate.

3. Legitimate power, called authority, flows from the top down in an organization, is based on a social exchange beween people, or on the basis of some specific knowledge, usually possessed by low-ranked employees. In any event, acceptance of authority by the influencee is crucial to its effective use.

4. Expertise, as another power base, is based on the recognition that another individual knows more about a situation. It too seems to be based on acceptance.

5. Conflict is an inevitable part of organizational life. It is neither good nor bad. Conflict arises out of individual differences, jobs that conflict, competition over scarce resources, status differentials, and work flows.

6. Managers have many ways of dealing with conflict. They range from such personal strategies as avoidance or dominance to restructuring the work flow to providing structural mechanisms to deal with the difficulties. In fact, conflict sometimes needs to be stimulated to encourage creativity and innovation. The effective manager learns to match the conflict needs of the situation to the particular conflict management technique.

III.

ORGANIZATION

In the following five chapters we shift our emphasis from the individual and the small group of which he or she is a part, to the much larger organizational setting. We live in an organizational society—one dominated by large, formally organized social units often called "bureaucracies." We belong to many of these large organizations. "Big Education" is what most of us are now involved in. Universities with 30,000 students, 4,000 faculty members and 5,000 staff members are not unusual. When we work it will most likely be for a "Big Business" with thousands of employees, located in many different locations and even counties, with thousands of stockholders who you as an employee will never see. You may be represented by "Big Labor"—a union will negotiate your salary and economic terms of employment. You will be protected by "Big Government" who delivers your mail, regulates the prices you pay for most things, passes and enforces laws and even tells you what you may or may not build on your own property.

Our purpose in the chapters that follow is not to slay the dragon of bureaucracy. In truth, we need bureaucracy or else our complex society could not exist. Instead, we will highlight seven ways in which these bureaucracies work. First, in Chapter Eight, we examine the fundamental decision-making process that individuals in the organization use to execute and implement the plans necessary to attain the organization's objectives. Second, in Chapter Nine, we examine how these organizations decide what they are going to accomplish—their objectives. Next, in Chapter Ten, we examine how organizations plan their activities to accomplish their objectives. Fourth, in Chapter Eleven, we examine how organizations set up a hierarchy of authority to ensure that the necessary work really gets done. Next, in Chapter Twelve we examine one way organizations set out to accomplish their objectives, namely by dividing the work to be done. Sixth, in Chapter Thirteen, we review how organizations recruit and select individuals to carry out the plan. And, lastly, in Chapter Fourteen, to ensure that all of the various parts of the organization really work together to attain its objectives, we examine the control cycle. Throughout, our emphasis is on the ways managements seek to deal constructively with the "fact of organization."

CHAPTER EIGHT DECISION MAKING

LEARNING OBJECTIVES

At the conclusion of this chapter you should be able to:

1. Distinguish between the rational and administrative approaches to decision making.
2. State the seven steps in decision making.
3. Explain a breakeven chart, the usefulness of ratio analysis, statistical decision-making techniques, decision-tree analysis, economic order quantity technique, and network analysis.
4. Describe the four shortcuts most commonly employed in the decision-making process.
5. Discuss three reasons why group decision making is more effective than individual decision making.
6. State three ways in which a manager can improve decision-making ability.

LOST IN THE DESERT

I. Objectives
   A. To experience both individual and group decision making so that you can compare and contrast these two styles.
   B. To experience some of the frustration involved in decision making under conditions of uncertainty.

II. Premeeting Preparation
   A. Read the instructions concerning group decision making on page 191.

III. Instructions
   A. All persons are to rank *individually* these items as they believe the experts have ranked them.

   > *Time for Step A: 5 minutes*

   B. The entire class shall then be divided into groups of not more than 10 members, preferably 7. The groups are then to take 20 minutes to reach a consensus decision, following the instructions in the following sheets.
   C. Individual members are not to change their rankings, but record the group's ranking on the sheet provided.

   > *Time for Steps B and C: 20 minutes*

   D. After the 20-minute decision period, the instructor will record the group scores and instruct the class to complete the group score sheet, which is attached.
   E. The winning group would be that group with the lowest group score. In the event of a tie, the winning team would be that group whose score improved most over the average of its individual group member scores.

   > *Time for Steps D and E: 10 minutes*

IV. Discussion
   Your instructor will help you explore what happened in this exercise and its meaning for management.

   > *Time for discussion: 15 minutes*

Source. Copyright: Human Synergistics, © 1970. Used by permission.

THE SITUATION

It is approximately 10:00 A.M. in mid July and you have just crash landed in the Sonora Desert in southwestern United States. The light twin engine plane, containing the bodies of the pilot and the co-pilot, has completely burned. Only the air frame remains. None of the rest of you have been injured.

The pilot was unable to notify anyone of your position before the crash. However, ground sightings, taken before you crashed, indicated that you are 65 miles off the course that was filed in your VFR Flight Plan. The pilot had indicated before you crashed that you were approximately 70 miles south-southwest from a mining camp which is the nearest known habitation.

The immediate area is quite flat and except for occasional barrel and saguaro cacti appears to be rather barren. The last weather report indicated that the temperature would reach 110°—which means that the temperature within a foot of the surface will hit 130°. You are dressed in light weight clothing—short sleeved shirts, pants, socks and street shoes. Everyone has a handkerchief. Collectively, your pockets contain $2.83 in change, $85.00 in bills, a pack of cigarettes, and a ballpoint pen.

The Problem

Before the plane caught fire your group was able to salvage the 15 items listed on the next page. Your task is to rank these items according to their importance to your survival, starting with "1" the most important, to "15" the least important.

You may assume that the number of survivors is the same as the number on your team and the team has agreed to stick together.

DECISION FORM

Below is a list of the 15 items your group was able to salvage before the plane caught fire. Your task is to rank these 15 items in the same order as the survival experts did. Place the number *1* by the item that you think was ranked as the most important; place the number *2* by the second most important item, and so on through the number *15,* which is your estimate of the least important item.

Items	Your Individual Ranking
Flash light (4 battery size)	_____
Jack knife	_____
Sectional air map of the area	_____
Plastic raincoat (large size)	_____
Magnetic compass	_____
Compress kit with gauze	_____
.45 caliber pistol (loaded)	_____
Parachute (red and white)	_____
Bottle of salt tablets (1,000 tablets)	_____
1 quart of water per person	_____
A book entitled, *Edible Animals of the Desert*	_____
A pair of sunglasses per person	_____
2 quarts of 180 proof Vodka	_____
1 top coat per person	_____
A cosmetic mirror	_____

DECISION BY CONSENSUS
Lost in the Desert

Instructions. This is an exercise in group decision making. Your group is to employ the method of *group consensus* in reaching its decision. This means that the prediction for each of the 15 items must be agreed upon by each group member before it becomes a part of the group decision. Consensus is difficult to reach. Therefore, not every ranking will meet with everyone's complete approval. Try, as a group, to make each ranking one with which *all* members can at least partially agree. Here are some guides to use in reaching consensus:

1. Avoid *arguing* for your own individual judgments. Approach the task on the basis of logic.
2. Avoid changing your mind *only* in order to reach agreement and avoid conflict. Support only solutions with which you are able to agree somewhat, at least.
3. Avoid "conflict-reducing" techniques such as majority vote, averaging, or trading in reaching decisions.
4. View differences of opinion as helpful rather than as a hindrance in decision making.

GROUP SCORE SHEET

On this sheet you are to determine (a) the difference between your rank number for each item and the experts'. (*Example.* You rated mirror as 10, but the experts rank it 1; the entry in the *Difference* column will be 9); (b) The difference between the group rank and experts' rank for each item. Absolute values are to be used only—that is, if experts rank the salt tablets 15 but you ranked them 7; the difference is to be recorded as 8, not −8. Then total each Difference column.

	Difference Between Expert and Individual Score, Absolute Value	*Individual Score*	*Expert Score*	*Group Score*	*Difference Between Group and Expert Score, Absolute Value*
Flash Light					
Jack Knife					
Sectional Air Map					
Plastic Raincoat					
Magnetic Compass					
Compress Kit					
.45 Pistol					
Parachute					
Salt Tablets					
Water					
Book					
Sunglasses					
Vodka					
Top Coat					
Mirror					

"Give me a good decision maker and I'll make a great manager" has been quoted over and over again as the watchword of corporate presidents across the country. For, in truth, one of the most fundamental activites of a manager is the making of decisions—decisions about people, production, materials, equipment, and scheduling. Virtually every aspect of a manager's job requires decision making. Many people, in fact, believe that the best way to study management is to study who makes what decision and how the decision gets made. Similarly, many management consultants believe that the best way to improve the effectiveness of an organization is to improve the effectiveness of the decision-making process. In this chapter we will not be concerned with the question of who makes what decision; that topic was covered in the chapter on organization structure. Rather, we will focus on the process of decision making, some of its limitations, and ways to improve it.

The process of decision making is not easy even though we do it all the time. Contrary to popular thought, the easiest decisions are those in which you have little stakes and little information. The more facts you have, the more important the decision is to you, or both, the harder it will be to make. Consider for a moment the following examples. If you have to choose between two cars—a Chevy and a Ford—and you know only that the Ford is cheaper, you can decide on the Ford without much further thought. But, if in addition, you know the Chevy has a higher trade-in value, you might have to think a little longer. Yet, the information that the Ford comes in brighter colors, the Chevy is peppier, the Ford has a nicer interior, the Chevy gets more miles to the gallon—gives a great deal more information about both cars, and your process of reaching a decision is considerably more complex. It must be pointed out, however, that you now have a greater chance of choosing the best car. Despite all the information you do have, you are still missing many important facts, including probably the most critical one—will you like the car after you get it?

Decisions Are Made   This illustrates two important insights into the decision-making process.
Without All   First, decisions must always be made without complete information. The
the Facts   trick is to secure "enough" information before the decision is made, and not adopt the position (even secretly) of "Don't confuse me with the facts; my mind is already made up." Second, the critical factors in any decision are likely to be weighed differently by various persons. The Ford's lower cost for instance, may appeal to someone but turn others off. This unique weighing is a product of many factors that will be explored further in this chapter. Suffice it to point out at this juncture that in all kinds of decisions—personal and business—all the facts are never known, although the more information factored into the decision the better the decision is likely to be.

Two schools of thought have emerged concerning the study of managerial decision making. These are: the scientific or rational approach and the administrative approach.

RATIONAL APPROACH TO DECISION MAKING

The school of thought originated with the writings of Jeremy Bentham and John Stewart Mill. They set forth the following principles:

1. All decision makers (that includes all of us) seek to maximize the utilities or benefits derived from any decision.
2. The utilities or benefits we seek to maximize out of every decision are a combination of maximizing pleasure and minimizing pain.
3. In order to maximize pleasure and minimize pain, we know and evaluate impartially all of the facts relevant to the situation.
4. Because of this impartiality (or rationality), there is a finite set of definite principles that can be learned and practiced.

In response to these principles, a great body of management principles has emerged from the pens of such famous writers as Fayol, Urwick, and Koontz. These lay out a correct path for a manager to follow. These principles cover such aspects of management as delegation (always delegate authority with responsibility), and span of control (most managers can effectively coordinate the activities of only between four and seven subordinates performing similar tasks). These guides to decision making were considered absolute, in that all a manager need do is correctly apply the correct principle in the proper situation to be assured of a correct decision.

Most of you know already that this ideal kind of decision making occurs very rarely. Few of us know all there is to know, or can be so objective in any setting.

ADMINISTRATIVE APPROACH TO DECISION MAKING

Professor Herbert Simon in the late 1940s challenged the assumptions that a decision maker was all-knowing and a maximizer of anything. Professor Simon argued that no one could possibly know all of the implications of all of the possible available courses of action. Rather, Simon argued, all of us are limited to consider only those facts we know of—and the facts we "know" tend to be a simplified version of the real, very complex situation. And second, that simpler version tended to be influenced by personal considerations such as values, aspiration levels, and previous successes or failures.

Several principles of decision making have emerged from the research concerning this approach. They are:

1. People always simplify the decision process by not considering all the facts.
2. Those "facts" people choose to ignore or consider are influenced by personal characteristics such as values and attitudes.
3. Most people look for the first satisfactory decision and do not keep mulling over the problem until the best decision is apparent.
4. Failure to achieve success will lower decision standards, whereas easy success will tend to raise minimum standards.

Two research studies have supported the utility of these principles. Cyert and March, using these concepts, predicted 96 percent of actual price decisions made in a large retail department store. G. E. Clarkson reported similar success in predicting the decisions of trust officers in stock investments in large banks. There have been many other research studies that support parts of the administrative decision-making theory. Most management texts today partially, are based on this approach. Whether this theory is correct we leave for you to test in the research laboratory of your own experience.

THE DECISION-MAKING PROCESS

This car selection system mentioned above can be used to illustrate the managerial decision-making process most frequently used (Figure 8.1).

State the Problem 1. STATE THE PROBLEM. Decide what you want to do—in this case, find the most satisfactory car. If what you really seek is a long-term investment, it is better to admit it to yourself, for even the most "scientific" decision making requires honest information.

State the problem
Determine your goal
Select a method of measurement
Build a model
Collect the facts
Use the model
Decide

Figure 8.1 The decision-making process.

2. DETERMINE YOUR GOAL. Set forth your likes and dislikes with care. Keep them simple, (never mind great detail over preferences in food, clothing, magazines, etc.), but all your important preferences must be there.

3. SELECT A METHOD OF MEASUREMENT. One of your objectives might be to find an inexpensive car; another objective might be to find a prestige car. You can measure the first element directly by specifying a car costing so many dollars. The second element is harder to measure and probably you must settle for indirect measures.

4. BUILD A MODEL. Specify the relative importance of each of the critical elements of your likes and dislikes. How important, for instance, is good styling versus low gas consumption? Adding up all the pluses and minuses gives you a "perfect" car, much like the pluses and minuses concerning plant location give a company the "perfect" location.

5. COLLECT THE FACTS. Now that you have a decision "model," find out all you can about each car in the area in which your model calls for information.

6. USE THE MODEL. Now insert the values for each car that is still in the running and see which one gets the best score. You may decide to make your selection right now simply by choosing the one with the highest overall score. Or you may realize that there are many other factors that do not seem to fit into your model. If this is the case, you still have to consider those stubbornly subjective factors and somehow take them into account in making your choice.

7. NOW CHOOSE. Striking the best balance between all the pluses and minuses and all the subject factors that do not fit into the quantitative numbers, choose the car that you think will be best for you.

These are the steps in the decision process. It may seem to you that going through all these steps for such a simple decision is like using an elephant gun to shoot a fly. Yet, the example should give you a good feel for the process of making all kinds of decisions; easy ones about whom to date, as well as difficult ones concerning where to locate a new plant. From this little exercise in fantasy and from your own experience, it should be apparent that not all the important factors in any decision can be weighed and measured. In fact, most of the significant factors can only be estimated. We call those factors that can be assigned numerical weights *quantitative factors,* meaning that they can be measured precisely. The factors that do not lend themselves to easy quantification are called *qualitative factors*. In the car example, the price and weight of the car would be quantitative measures. In typical business situations, many economic and financial factors are easily quantified (e.g., the projected cash flow for a quarter, or sales for the last year), whereas some others can definitely not be quantified (such as the possible responses of employees to a new automation program). Other factors, such as the attitude of consumers, can be estimated and then quantified. Every manager is confronted with the difficult task of deciding first which items can be quantified, and which can be estimated with what degree of reliability. For instance, a projection that it will rain next March 24th is not useful, but the result of an extensive survey of consumer attitudes toward a new product may be quite useful in the decision-making process. Thus, the fundamental difference between quantitative and nonquantitative factors in the decision making process lies in their ability to be expressed in useful, numerical terms.

QUANTITATIVE TECHNIQUES

Fortunately, there is a growing number of management decisions that can be expressed in numerical terms and, therefore, are open to solutions using quantitative techniques. Generally speaking, quantitative techniques fall into three general categories: (1) break-even analysis, (2) financial ratio analysis, and (3) statistical methods. This section will explore all of these briefly.

Advantages of Quantitative Techniques

Managers are often confronted with an almost endless and overwhelming amount of information upon which they must make a decision. The basic problem, as we have previously pointed out, is not finding the information, but sorting out the valuable from the irrelevant and weighing the various pieces of information. One of the basic advantages of using quantitative techniques is that it enables the manager to handle a larger volume of information in the decision-making process. Bringing more information to bear on the decision often improves that decision. Second, quantitative techniques require the statement of clear assumptions and the weighing of criteria. In this way, the assumptions underlying the real preferences of the manager get expressed. This forced thinking-through often brings hidden preferences to the surface. Third, once the criteria are weighed (see Step 4 of the steps in the decision-making process) their application becomes less subjective. The personal mood of the manager, therefore, becomes less important. It is not unusual for a person to have a bad morning, and to allow a bad mood to overtake and modify the previously specified criteria in making a decision. (Computers don't have burnt toast for breakfast.) Thus, the ability to handle more information, to examine the assumptions more systematically, and to reduce the influence of emotionalism in the decision-making process are three major advantages of utilizing quantitative technique.

Disadvantages of Quantitative Techniques

On the negative side of the equation, many quantitative technique specialists are often accused of having an answer and then seeking a problem that may or may not fit their answer. Because the quantitative technique involves a set of assumptions, the manager must be sure that the assumptions of the technique actually fit the problem at hand. For instance, employing a quantitative technique that is based on the days of sunshine in San Diego in order to predict economical inventory lot size for automobiles of a Detroit car dealership is obviously useless. Yet some quantitative techniques which assume that the attitude of employees toward work will be unchanged by the introduction of a computer-based information system are equally without value. In addition to the assumption problem, it is also probably true that most of the important concerns in management—such as motivation, cooperation, and other human factors—are difficult to quantify. Although there have been efforts to do so, much of the human behavior consideration in management remains beyond the scope of quantitative techniques. Last, but not least, it costs a great deal to quantify many factors. To decide the best inventory level for a given product may not be too difficult, but for a firm with several hundred or even a thousand products in a rapidly changing market, the costs of doing the same analysis would be staggering, and hardly worth it, because the analysis would be obsolete almost as soon as it was completed. Thus, the inapplicability of some assumptions, the inability to quantify many significant behavioral factors, and the high cost, all serve to limit the utilization of quantitative techniques in management.

Break-Even Analysis

The first and possibly simplest form of quantitative technique utilized in the management decision-making process is the break-even analysis. A break-even chart clearly shows how varying sales levels affect the profitability of given product lines. The chart rests on the assumption that all costs in a business can be classified into one or two categories.

Fixed Cost. These are costs that in the short run do not vary with sales volume. For instance, rent, electricity, or interest on borrowed money all go on, regardless of sales volume. The salaries of some administrative officials, the president, and the personnel manager do not vary depending on sales volume. These are fixed costs and are illustrated in Figure 8.2 as a straight line.

Variable Cost. These are costs that vary in the short run, usually directly with sales volume and production. Thus, most labor and materials are considered variable costs, in that the more you sell the more of these commod-

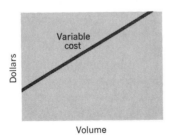

Figure 8.2

Dollars

Fixed cost

Volume

ities you use in the construction process. Variable costs are usually shown as a diagonal line, indicating that the more you sell, the more you will spend on these activities (Figure 8.3). The slope of the line is a function of the nature of the business. Some firms, restaurants, for instance, have a deep slope; that is, as sales increase, costs increase sharply, whereas other firms such as steel fabrication firms have a very moderate slope.

Mixed Costs. In fact, many costs are partially mixed and partially variable. Electricity, for instance, may be fixed for a portion of the time, (e.g., the lights in the office), but variable in that the more product that is produced, the more machines run, and the more electricity is utilized. In turn, labor may not be totally variable. In the short run you may not lay off idle workers but put them on maintenance work. Thus, the seemingly straight line for either fixed or variable cost may in fact be a series of stepped curves looking like the one in Figure 8.4. Regardless, costs should be classified into either fixed or variable on the basis of their predominant characteristic, to utilize a break-even analysis.

A break-even analysis can be plotted once you know the fixed cost, the variable cost, and the sales volume figures for a given product. To illustrate the use of a given analysis, let us assume that the financial data for the Magic Widget Product Company is as follows on the next page:

Figure 8.3

Dollars

Variable cost

Volume

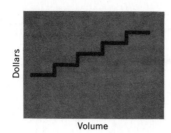

Figure 8.4

Dollars

Volume

Widget sales price = $10 per widget
Variable costs = $6 per unit
Fixed costs = $200,000 per year

With these numbers it is now possible to plot the break-even point for the production of magic widgets. Figure 8.5 shows that the break-even point for magic widget production is $500,000 in sales. Sales below that will result in a loss; sales above that will yield a profit. The chart also shows the impact that varying sales levels have on profitability. Thus, an increase in sales of 17 percent from $600,000 to $700,000 results in a 100 percent profit. This assumes that sales price and fixed and variable cost remain constant. This is one reason why so many firms are sales-volume oriented, because a small increase in sales can result in a large increase in profit.

The break-even analysis is useful in several management decisions. First, in evaluating new product production, the break-even analysis identifies the sales volume required for profitability, and when the sales estimate doesn't equal that level, the product should not be produced. Second, this analysis focuses attention on the critical factors in producing a profit. For example, what would the impact of lower sales price be even though volume may increase? The increased volume may not generate sufficient additional revenue to lower the break-even point, but may actually increase it. The ability to shave variable cost can also be questioned as a result of this analysis. Lowering variable cost can result in a dramatic lowering of the break-even point. This quantitative technique enables a manager to examine more systematically the relationship between costs and revenue and profits for a given product. As such, it is a valuable decision-making aid.

Ratio Analysis

Numbers are the language of business, and it is difficult for a modern manager to function without some fundamental knowledge of accounting and budgeting. Some of the most useful knowledge can be generated through analysis of various financial ratios. Operating managers, for instance, are

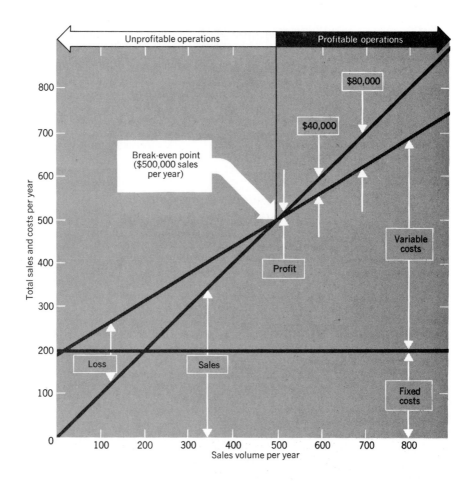

Figure 8.5 The Magic Widget break-even chart.

often interested in ratios that show the effectiveness with which various resources under the manager's control are used. Several of these ratios are shown below. Gross profit margins by product, for instance, are good indicators of which products should be emphasized. Similarly, inventory turnover can indicate the efficiency of the production forecast system. In the same vein, average collection period can indicate the effectiveness of the credit and billing departments.

As another example, various leverage ratios indicate the ability of the financial manager in utilizing the corporation's financial resources. The ability to get other firms such as suppliers to partially underwrite the company is an important additional source of funds for the organization. Probably the most important ratio of all, however, is the return on investment, or ROI. This is often used as the "litmus paper" test of business success. This yardstick will be frequently used to evaluate your performance as a manager.

1. Current ratio	$\dfrac{\text{Current assets}}{\text{Current liabilities}}$
2. Acid test ratio	$\dfrac{\text{Cash}}{\text{Current liabilities}}$
3. Inventory turnover	$\dfrac{\text{Sales}}{\text{Inventory}}$
4. Working capital turnover	$\dfrac{\text{Sales}}{\text{Net working capital}}$
5. Fixed capital turnover	$\dfrac{\text{Sales}}{\text{Net working capital}}$
6. Average collection period	$\dfrac{\text{Receivables}}{\text{Average daily sales}}$
7. Operating margin/product	$\dfrac{\text{Operating profit / Product}}{\text{Sales}}$
8. Sales margin/product	$\dfrac{\text{New profit after taxes / Product}}{\text{Sales}}$
9. Productivity of assets	$\dfrac{\text{Gross income less taxes}}{\text{Total assets}}$
10. Return on capital—ROI	$\dfrac{\text{Net profit after taxes}}{\text{New worth (or investment)}}$

Statistical Analysis Techniques

The most widely practiced quantitative aids in decision making involve statistical techniques in reducing costs, improving efficiencies, minimizing distribution costs, or finding the optimum product mix. There are four basic steps in utilizing these statistical analytical techniques.

1. Specify all the alternatives you wish to consider in the decision.
2. Assign each alternative a specific probability of success. Thus, if you believe that there is a 90 percent probability of getting an A in this course, you should assign a probability of 0.9 to that alternative. On the other hand, if you believe that your probability of getting an A is 40 percent but getting a B is 90 percent, then the alternative of getting an A would be assigned a probability of 0.4 and getting a B would be assigned a probability of 0.9.
3. Assign a common unit of value, usually money, in which these probabilities can be evaluated. This possible value can often be computed by

multiplying the expected profit or loss expected from the sale or production of the specific item by the number of items likely to be sold or produced.

4. Calculate the expected value (usually monetary value) using the following formula:

(The probability of success) $\times$ (the profit) + (the probability of loss) $\times$ (the expected loss) = value

The probability of loss or profit is determined by calculating the amount of product to be sold or produced, multiplied by the amount of profit or loss per item.

For example, let's assume a factory is seeking to determine if it should produce product A or product B. Let us assume the following values for these products:

	Product A	Product B
Production level	100	50
Profit level	$ 20	$ 35
Expected profit	$2000	$1750
Expected loss (cost not covered times number of units produced)	−4000	−1750
Expected probability of success	.8	.6
Probability of failure	.2	.4
	.8 $\times$ (+2000) + .2 $\times$ (−4000) 1600 − 800 = 800	.6x (+1750) + .4x (−1750) 1050 − 680 = 370
Expected value	$ 800	$ 370

Given this example, the firm would produce product A even though the risk of loss is greater; so is the probability of gain. Although the little example contains only two products, the same formula could be, and often is, used to examine the relative merits of producing several alternative products, as well as determining the optimum production mix of these products, (perhaps 50 of A and 20 of B would yield the best optimum production mix). In these cases, a computer would be used to analyze the data.

Several parts of this example illustrate some of the uses and limitations of statistical aids. When the alternatives are many and the numerical values can be assigned to them, the basic objective is to determine the optimal, best single mixture of them to choose; then these procedures are very valuable. Note, however, the necessity to add in subjective estimates. The probability estimates are all judgmental and changing them even 10 percent would dramatically affect the outcome. Thus, even with the use of quantitative techniques that enable the manager to handle more information more systematically, there is still considerable opportunity for decision making of a qualitative, subjective, judgmental nature.

Decision Tree Analysis

Decision tree analysis enables the manager to evaluate the future consequences of present action, particularly when there are either/or alternatives to be evaluated. If, for instance, you are trying to decide whether to study for a test or party on a particular Saturday night, the decision tree analysis would enable you to:

1. Identify the future possible actions that would be caused by current action, (for instance, not studying for a test will likely result in a poor grade);
2. Estimate the probability of each of these alternatives occurring. (There is a high probability, for instance, of getting a low grade on a test for which you have not done the reading);
3. Weigh the potential benefits and costs of each alternative; (weighing the cost of studying for the test and the likelihood of getting a good grade on it, versus the cost of not studying for that test and the probability of getting a poor grade).

As another example, the ABC Machine Company is considering the purchase of two new drill presses. The total cost of these is $400,000. These presses will be more efficient, but will cost more to operate. Certain individuals in the firm believe the company should spend $50,000 for repairs on the old drill presses and forego the purchase of this new equipment. After calculating the possible output demands and the accompanying probabilities, it is possible to develop a decision tree as shown in Figure 8.6. As you can see, the gain in net expected payoff on purchasing the two new presses is $2,385,000 ($3,325,000 less $940,000).

Decision tree analysis is a systematic way to examine the potential future consequences of current actions. It provides a way to weigh the cost/benefit of each action against the likelihood of its occurrence in order to evaluate its value. Its major advantage is that it systematizes decision making. It requires lots of information and the making of many subjective estimates. Many organizations use decision tree analysis in evaluating investment decisions, such as the repair and/or replacement of equipment. It it a valuable

Act	Expected Profit[a]	Probabilities	Event	Conditional Profit
Purchase Two New Drill Presses for $400,000	$3,325,000	.6	High Demand Gain $1,500,000 Year for 5 Years	$5,000,000
		.3	Medium Demand Gain $200,000 Year for 5 Years	1,000,000
		.1	Low Demand Gain $50,000 Year for 5 Years	250,000
Make Repairs on Old Drills for $50,000	$940,000	.6	High Demand Gain $250,000 Year for 5 Years	$1,250,000
		.3	Medium Demand Gain $120,000 Year for 5 Years	600,000
		.1	Low Demand Gain $20,000 Year for 5 Years	100,000

[a]Disregarding the Cost of Interest and the Discounting of this Income to the Present

Figure 8.6   Decision Tree—Expected Payoff from New Versus Old Machinery.

tool, but it is time consuming and does not provide answers. Rather, it is a logical reasoning process that weighs the benefits of current action against their future potential costs.

Economic Order Quantity

Inventories represent one of a company's most costly investments. Many organizations have as much as 30 percent of their sales dollars tied up in inventory. The trick is to have enough inventory on hand to meet production requirements, while minimizing both the cost of carrying the inventory and reordering it. Economic order quantity statistical techniques have been developed to determine the best point at which to order new material. Two costs need to be balanced. First, there are carrying costs, including interest storage and insurance and taxes. These must be balanced with ordering costs, which include record-keeping time, purchasing time, and shipping and receiving time. Ordering large lots of material lowers ordering costs, but increases carrying costs. Figure 8.7 shows how these costs can be compared. The most economical order quantity would be that point A on the graph where carrying and ordering costs are equal.

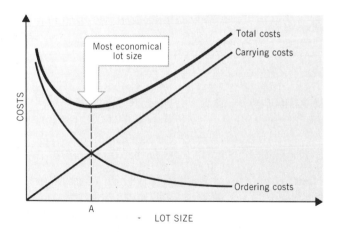

Figure 8.7

Network Models-PERT/CPM

Network models have been used by managers to control such large complex tasks as building a space station, constructing a dam, or designing a preventative maintenance program for a large plant. These networks show how one activity leads to another, and when put together, make up the final product. It helps the manager identify the critical path, that activity with the least amount of flexibility. There are two kinds of network models. PERT is used for nonrepetitive projects where costs are proportional to time spent. The construction of a space station or a large dam are examples of projects where PERT has been successfully used. CPM, on the other hand, is useful in repetitive projects, such as airplane construction or designing a preventative maintenance program, where costs are not proportionate to time spent. Both techniques focus the manager's time and effort on those few critical activities that will make the most difference. This enables the manager to anticipate potential future problems, and take action today before they occur.

FOUR SHORTCUTS TO THE DECISION-MAKING PROCESS

Because of the inability to measure accurately all of the elements in a decision, the decision-making process is always subject to limitation. No matter how bright we are, it is impossible for us to know all the factors relevant to a decision or how they interact with each other. Even if we could know everything, the relative importance of various factors would likely vary from time to time, and person to person. Therefore, there are limitations imposed by our humanness that cannot be overcome. Because of these limitations on our ability to know and handle all the facts, we use a number of shortcuts in the decision-making process. In the next few pages we will discuss four of these shortcuts.

Simplifying

First, because the world is literally infinitely complex and we have a difficult time grasping its complexity, we all tend to simplify it. One of the best ways to simplify the world is to use stereotypes. This negative sounding word, because it comes out of the racial and religious discrimination field, actually describes the process whereby we attach to individuals or things the characteristics we believe are true for the group. Thus, college professors are supposed to be sort of far out, forgetful people. So when we meet one, we automatically believe that person will act that way. On the positive side, stereotyping (one form of simplifying) enables you, the decision maker, to focus on fewer issues, thus both shortening the decision cycle and making it more efficient. On the negative side, if the stereotype is inappropriate, you can easily reach a poor decision because you proceed from incorrect assumptions. Managers are guilty of simplifying all the time. The long-haired hippie can't be any good even though he or she is a straight A student and the most brilliant scientist since Einstein. Or the sales for next year for buggy whips, for instance, will be a simple extention of last year's sales, despite that young upstart, Ford, and his automobile. Although it is easy to point fingers and laugh at the often ludicrous results of using simplified models, without them we would all be hopelessly mired in the quicksand of "all the facts." Thus, simplifying the world is a necessary part of the decision process, though it sometimes causes serious problems.

Psychological Sets

The second method we all employ to aid in the decision process arises out of our own unique frame of reference. It is important to realize that individual differences exist in the way we see the world, and that these differences influence the decision-making process. The principal impact of these psychological sets is in the differing weights each of us will attach to the "facts." For example, the production manager is likely to attach a different set of importances to a machine breakdown than would a quality control manager. At least some of the difficulty in reaching agreement in the exercise can be attributed to these differences in the psychological sets of group members, leading to differentiated evaluations of the same set of facts. Thus, our use of individually different psychological sets in the decision process enables us to make decisions efficiently, but can lead us often to ludicrous results.

Focus on Unknowns

Third, because each decision we face is infinitely complex, we are forced to focus on only a small, manageable portion of the problem. We quickly by-pass what we think we "know," to focus on those facts or alternatives of which we are not certain. It often happens that groups in the exercise easily rank the first few items and probably the last few. Most often, difficulty is encountered in the middle ranks—and probably most of the time was spent exploring those. This is an example of the human tendency in decision making to focus on those alternatives ("facts") of which we are not certain, and to spend most of our time searching for new information concerning them. This tendency to search for new information concerning unknowns is almost independent of their relative importance to the decision. For example, during staff meetings it is not uncommon to discuss extensively the most irrelevant but unknown material, thereby limiting time to discuss the more important issues. The time consumed in committee meetings can be traced to this human tendency. This search and concentration on the unknown issues is a third characteristic of the decision-making process.

Satisfactory Not Excellent Decisions

Finally, regardless of the search activities, there is a tendency for all of us to reach a decision before all the facts are in. We are usually happy to get the issue decided and off our back, rationalizing to ourselves that even if it isn't the best decision, it is one that is "good enough." For example, in the exercise, the desire to reach a decision and get it over with may well have led you to agree to a certain ranking order that you knew was not the best, but would "do." Or, the tendency of managers is to hire the first acceptable person to come along without waiting for the "best" person who might show up later. As a result, virtually all decisions are less than perfect. That shouldn't disturb you, because we've been making our decisions that way since the beginning of time and apparently have been doing all right. This discussion of the methods of decision making is intended to point out some of the potential difficulties, because it is possible, with knowledge and understanding of the limitations, to take some steps to improve our decision-making abilities. In short, then, simplifying, the use of psychological sets, the tendency to focus on the unknown, and the desire to reach satisfactory instead of excellent decisions are ways in which we handle the unmanageable world.

WAYS TO IMPROVE DECISION MAKING

Group Decisions

Given these decisional processes, there are at least four ways to improve managerial decision-making behavior. The first should be obvious to you as a result of your exercise. In all probability, most groups reached a better decision (measured by a lower score) than the average of the individual in that group. The use of groups to make decisions, therefore, is one method to improve decision making. Why do groups generally reach better decisions than individuals? The standing joke is that a camel is a horse designed by a committee. The answer apparently lies in the groups' ability to provide additional information, to moderate the screening effects of the individual stereotypes and psychological sets, and to prevent early decisions. Thus, a group can reduce some of the confirming tendencies in us all, by exposing us to more information and forcing us to hear at least part of it.

This is obviously not true of all groups. Many staff meetings, for instance, turn out to be battlefields on which the organization war is fought between various departments. Where groups are given the set of instructions you were given in the exercise (and actually follow them), the decision outcome is substantially better than either individual decision making or decisions made by groups not so instructed. This suggests that although groups can be an effective way to improve decision making, the climate or atmosphere within which they function is a critical concern. The matrix organization and organizational development type strategies that are designed to build better organization climate are discussed elsewhere in this book. It is sufficient at this point to underline that groups, given the right conditions, can be one way to improve decision making.

Computerized Aids and Techniques

A second method to improve decision making is to employ computerized aids and techniques to handle the quantifiable elements in the decision and to quantify as many of them as possible. Decision tree analysis and ratio analysis, management information systems, and mathematical models are several such aids available to the manager. These may be integrated into the manager's own decision-making style and reduce the number of subjective judgments. Such aids also enable the manager to handle a much larger quantity of information, thus helping to assure that a better decision will be reached.

Self-Training

A third strategy for improving decision making is for the manager to follow Socrates' injunction, "Know thyself." A manager can be trained to be more aware of individual personal psychological sets operating in different kinds of situations. Feedback from trusted people can be helpful in this regard. This can enable the manager to discount prejudices and secure more accurate information. The combination of more accurate information, information less distorted by the psychological set, and a larger quantity of information should produce better decisions.

Training in Decision Making

A fourth method is to receive actual training in the decision-making processes. Many consulting organizations offer courses in improved decision-making techniques. The principal strategy of these courses is to train the manager to search more carefully and completely for information before reaching a decision. This one ability—to seek, receive, and use larger amounts of information concerning the decision—is the key, they believe, to more effective decision making. In essence, all of these strategies basically aim to accomplish the same objective—improve the manager's ability to handle larger amounts of information. This is based on assumption that such a strategy improves the quality of the decision finally reached. If this is so, and we believe from experience that it is so, the good decision maker, as we said in the quote in the beginning of the chapter, can become a great manager.

SUMMARY

The most fundamental responsibility of a manager is decision making. There are two basic decision-making strategies—one using quantitative techniques such as break-even analysis, ratio analysis, and such statistical tools as decision tree analysis and network models, and the other employing more subjective qualitative techniques. Quantitative techniques enable a manager to handle more data in a more systematic way. There are still judgmental factors, however. Regardless of the approach employed, most of us use the shortcuts of stereotyping, psychological sets, focusing on unknowns, and settling for satisfactory but not excellent decisions. Employing group decision making, quantitative decision-making aids, and self-knowledge are several ways to overcome these confirming rather than searching tendencies.

IN-BASKET

You are Geoff Morgan and have been named the new President-General Manager of the Swiss Kitchens Division of a large company.

Last year, Susan Hill, Inc. purchased the Swiss Kitchens Company of Oakland, California, an important subcontractor with sales in both frozen and nonfrozen bakery foods.

You arrived yesterday afternoon (Monday, October 28) and found that your predecessor, Eileen Harris, had left to accept a position with another company without seeing you. Since yesterday, you have been busy meeting your new staff. (A partial organization chart is shown in Figure 8.8 below.)

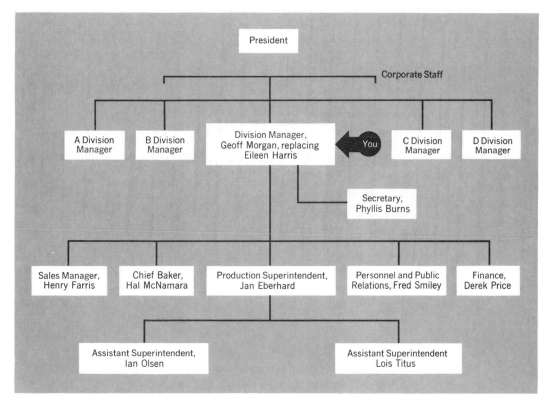

Figure 8.8   Partial organization chart of Swiss Kitchens.

The Problem

In one half hour you must leave to fly to Chicago, Illinois, to attend the quarterly President's meeting of Susan Hill, Inc. Subsidiaries. You will return next Monday, November 4, six days from today. The following correspondence is in your in-basket and looks as if it should be handled before you leave. Some of the items are holdovers that your predecessor, Eileen Harris, left for you to handle.

You are to go through the entire packet of papers and take whatever action you think seems appropriate. Write down every action you would take, including notes to your secretary, yourself, and others. Draft or write letters where appropriate. Write out any plans or agenda for meetings or conferences you would call. If you call conferences during the next half-hour, indicate the time you would allot for each. Also record any telephone calls made. A calendar is on page 215 to aid in your planning.

When you have completed the items in your in-basket:

1. List any other action you would take not directly involved with this correspondence.
2. List the major problem areas that you face in your new job as general manager and give your tentative thoughts on how you would handle each situation.

Discussion Questions

1. How would you describe your own decision-making style in terms of the model you used?
2. Describe some of the difficulties you encountered as Morgan in the decision-making process, and how you handled them.
3. Are there some decisions Morgan should not be making? If so, which ones? Why? How does he delegate them? To where does he delegate them? Why? If not, Why?
4. Does Morgan need more information on some of these decisions? If so, which ones? Why? How does he go about securing the information? How does he make certain that he has the information next time?

SUNDAY	MONDAY	TUESDAY	WEDNESDAY	THURSDAY	FRIDAY	SATURDAY
10/20	10/21	10/22	10/23	10/24	10/25	10/26
10/27	10/28	10/29	10/30	10/31	11/1	11/2
11/3	11/4	11/5	11/6	11/7	11/8	11/9

Figure 8.9   REMEMBER: You are Geoff Morgan, new President of Swiss Kitchens. In one half hour you must leave and will be gone for six days. You will return on Monday, November 4. Write out every action you take on every item.

7895 Red Fox Drive
San Francisco, CA.

October 25

Ms. Eileen Harris
President/General Manager
Swiss Kitchens
Oakland, California

Dear Ms. Harris:

I am the owner of 472 shares of stock in your company, my wife also
owns considerable stock (520 shares). I have been concerned about
the erratic performance of the stock in the New York Stock Exchange.
It has not shown the growth that I would have hoped and expected.
The glowing news releases sent out by your company several years ago
induced me to purchase your stock -- and it has been a disappointment
ever since.

I retired recently after serving more than 35 years in the legal
profession. The last twenty have been with the Attorney General's
office investigating and prosecuting stock frauds. My recent retirement is the cause of my concern over your stock prices.

I would like very much to have an appointment at your earliest convenience to discuss what plans you have to reverse these disappointing
results. I will telephone you next week if I haven't heard from you.

Sincerely yours,

Felix Jones

Felix Jones
Attorney-at-Law (Retired)

FJ/mnk

<u>MEMO</u>

October 28

TO: MR. MORGAN

FROM: PHYLLIS BURNS

I'm sorry I didn't mention it today, but I need to take Tuesday
(tomorrow) off. I thought I would be seeing you this afternoon,
but didn't. I hope you don't mind. I will be taking care of
somethings downtown in the morning, but I expect to be at the
doctor's all afternoon. If you need me I can be called there.
The number is 886-9970. I hope this doesn't cause too much in-
convenience on the day you leave for Chicago.

Phyllis

10/28

<u>Personal</u>

Mr. Morgan —
I hated to interrupt you because
I can see how busy and hassled
you were during your first days
here — hence the memo. But
super critical problems have come
up and I must talk to you about
them as soon as possible! I
cannot be there on Tuesday
since I must be in court to
answer a traffic citation. But
may I see you the first thing
Wednesday morning?

Ian Olsen
Ass't. Superintendent

October 29th --

TO: GEOFF MORGAN

FROM: JOYCE ROGERS, DIVISION MANAGER
           FRUIT DIVISION

SUBJECT: Possible Competition with Customers

Before Swiss Kitchens was purchased by Susan Hill, Inc., we sold
approximately one quarter of our fruit crop to Parsons Farms. It
now seems that Swiss Kitchens is in direct competition with Yummie-
Munchies, their pastry subsidiary. We have noticed a distinct
cooling in our relations with the Parsons' people. We have worked
hard to procure their contracts and have established an excellent
long term relationship, which now seems threatened. While they
have not brought the subject up specifically, the contract is due
for negotiation shortly and they may cancel.

It is absolutely imperative that we take steps now to re-assure
these major customers that the presence of Swiss Kitchens in our
corporate family will not result in a competitive disadvantage
for them. I plan to be in Chicago and would like to draft specific
plans with you at that time to deal with this serious problem.

           JR:kih

           cc: President

October 28

TO: EILEEN HARRIS

FROM: JAN EBERHARD, PRODUCTION

I contacted Grainbelt Flour last Tuesday, concerning the retroactive
price boost they wanted. Mr. Stone, their marketing man, stated that
if we wouldn't go along with these demands, we could take our business
elsewhere. I talked him into waiting until November 2 for a reply,
but he was reluctant to wait that long for a decision. Please act
on this immediately.

Jan

October 22 --

PERSONAL AND CONFIDENTIAL

TO: PRESIDENT/GENERAL MANAGER

FROM: LOIS TITUS (Assistant Superintendent, Production)

SUBJECT: NOTICE OF RESIGNATION

I am sorry that this is on such short notice, but I am herewith
submitting my intention to resign after 22 years of service to
Swiss Kitchens. When I first began, we treated our employees
fairly and produced a quality product. What I have been asked to
do recently is against my principles. I cannot continue, so I
must do what I have to do!

PERSONAL   October 24

Mr. Geoff Morgan
President/General Manager
Swiss Kitchens

Dear Geoff:

I am sorry ████████ to have to leave before you get on the job. I am
sure there are a number of things I am not able to help you get
caught up on. Anyway, best of luck. I know you will do an excellent
job. There are some "holdovers" in the basket that I thought you
should handle.

One problem I want to tell you about. Phyllis Burns, who is your
secretary, will be operated on soon for gall stones. She has delayed
the operation for several months because of the pressure of work, but
Phyllis tells me it must be done now.

I know this couldn't come at a worse time for you, but I wanted you
to know the facts and that the recovery period will last two weeks.
She will be back on the 19th.

I am sure between now and her operation, she can give you a general
picture of what is going on. You can rely on her judgment.

Best of luck on the job. I am sure you will get full cooperation
from the staff (or almost all of them). Don't hesitate to call on
me if I can be of help.

Cordially,

Eileen Harris

Decision making is a key management function. A good decision maker is worth her weight in gold to corporate power brokers. In this chapter you have seen and experienced some of the difficulties in decision making. Decisions must be made without complete knowledge of the facts or consequences—and they must be made by imperfect human beings who are swayed by stereotypes, psychological sets, and a frequent strong desire to reach some conclusion even though it may not be the best one. You experience many of these limitations. Consider the Exercise, for instance, and the shortcuts many of you used in reaching a set or rankings. Or, the In-Basket Exercise where probably, under the pressure of time, you reached certain decisions just to get that piece of paper off your desk and settled; whether it was the best action to take or not probably was not as important as just doing something about it. In many important ways, the problems confronting you as a student are very similar to those you experienced in this chapter. You do not really know what the future holds for you, yet you are forced to make decisions concerning your future without knowing many of the critical facts—and that decision is likely to be a product of a strange mixture of stereotypes, hope, and fact.

Given all of the difficulties with decision making, we have also sought to stress that there are several important ways in which better decisions can be reached. The use of group decision making, where a cooperative climate exists, the use of computerized aids (models and the like), and special training are all ways to improve the process. As with most management techniques, we must settle for something less than perfection in its execution, but being conscious of our shortcomings, and determined to at least partially overcome them, holds the key to personal decision-making success.

Here are some principles:

1. Persons seek to be systematic in making decisions. In an effort to do so, most individuals generally follow the pattern of stating the problem, determining the goal, selecting a measurement instrument, building a model, collecting the facts, using the model, and deciding.

2. Quantitative techniques can enable the manager to handle more information in a systematic way, thus improving decision-making ability.

3. Break-even analysis is a simple device that can help the manager plan varying production levels for given products by relating variable costs and varying sales levels given a certain amount of nonvariable fixed costs.

4. Ratio analysis is used to evaluate the financial effectiveness of various

departments. Profitability of various products and the contributions of such units as billing, inventory and material control, and sales, can be effectively evaluated utilizing these techniques.

5. Most of us cannot handle all of the information available to make most decisions. So we typically use stereotypes and psychological sets to choose the "important information." We further tend to focus on what we do not know, thus overemphasizing the importance of these unknowns. When the decision time comes, we all tend to accept a satisfactory solution rather than waiting for the "best" one.

6. The combination of a larger quantity of information, less distortion by psychological sets and stereotypes, and a commitment to search and evaluate before deciding produces better decisions. These conditions for improved decision making can be fostered by:

(a) Decisions made by a group, especially where the group climate is cooperative, tend to be better than individual decisions. This is because the group provides additional information input into the decision and moderates the effects of individual stereotypes and psychological sets.

(b) Increased awareness of early decision tendencies and the desire to change them is a good way to improve individual decision-making ability.

(c) Quantitative techniques can provide additional information when organized in a systematic way.

CHAPTER NINE GOAL SETTING

LEARNING OBJECTIVES

At the end of this chapter you should be able to:

1. Explain three characteristics of organizational objectives.
2. State the three general types of organizational objectives.
3. Explain two factors that effectively influence the shifting nature of organizational objectives.
4. Describe the negotiation process during which organizational objectives are determined.
5. Describe the relationship between objective setting, planning, and organizational structure.
6. List four stakeholders and discuss their relationship to the organization.
7. State two "watch them" and "ask them" strategies for ascertaining demands of stakeholder groups.

PAPER AIRPLANE MANUFACTURE

I. Objectives
   A. To experience the effects of environmental influences on performance.
   B. To experience the process of initially establishing goals.
   C. To experience the process by which goals may be modified through experience.
II. Premeeting Preparation
   A. Read through the instructions.
   B. Read and be familiar with the rules of the game spelled out in instruction Step C.
   C. Bring about 20 sheets of blank paper to class with you.
III. Instructions
   A. Divide the class into groups of six persons.
   B. Each group of six is to practice producing two different designs of paper airplanes. Each person in the group must work on (e.g., do one of the production steps) *all* products. Thus, there is a necessity for a division of labor involving the entire group of six. Also each group must produce a mix of both designs such that not less than 40 percent or more than 60 percent of either design is produced.

   > *Time for Steps A and B: 5 minutes*

   C. Each group now is to decide on a production goal—for example, the number of each design of Paper Airplane the group will produce during a 5-minute period.
      1. During this 10-minute period, the group will receive various pieces of information that may affect this ability to effectively produce the estimated number of Paper Airplanes.
      2. The object of the exercise is to maximize the group's profit. The group's profit will be determined as follows:
         a. One dollar of profit for each acceptable Paper Airplane produced up to the estimated amount.
         b. Twenty cents profit for each acceptable Paper Airplane produced over the estimated amount.
         c. Twenty-five cents reduction from total profit for each Paper Airplane estimated but not produced.
      Thus, the formula for determining the group profit is: number of Paper Airplanes produced up to estimated amount times $1, plus the number of Paper Airplanes produced over the estimate times $.20, minus the number not produced but estimated times $.25. That group with the highest profit in the class shall be the win-

ner. The instructor might wish to collect a small sum ($.50 to
$1.00) to be awarded to the winning group.

    d. The group's estimate may be no lower than 40 Paper Air-
planes in the 5-minute period.

    e. The number of Paper Airplanes your group plans to produce is

Design 1	_____
Design 2	_____
Total	_____

Time for Step C: 10 minutes

D. Produce the Paper Airplanes.

Time for Step D: 5 minutes

E. Calculate the group's profit using the following table:

	Design 1	Design 2
1. Number of airplanes of each design produced up to estimated amount × $1.00	_____	_____
plus Number of airplanes of each design over estimate × $.20	+_____	+_____
minus Number of airplanes of each design not produced but estimated × $.25	−_____	_____
2. Report the group's total to the class so that the winning group may be determined.	_____	_____

Time for Step E: 5 minutes

IV. Discussion

Your instructor will discuss with you the meaning of this exercise and its
implications for management.

Time for discussion: 20 minutes

"Would you tell me, please, which way I ought to go from here?"
"That depends a good deal on where you want to go to," said the Cat.
"I don't much care where," said Alice.
"Then it doesn't matter which way you go," said the Cat.

Lewis Carroll, *Alice in Wonderland*

As the quote from Lewis Carroll suggests, where you want to go makes a great deal of difference in terms of what you do. As it is with Alice, so it is with every organization. Differing objectives give rise to differing actions. Because the objectives of the Democratic Party are very different from those of General Motors, it does different things. Similarly, a company that attempts to maximize sales volume will act differently from a company that seeks to maximize profit, even though both may be selling the same product in the same market to the same customers. One will write almost every sale, whereas the other company may take only the cream. Another example is IBM, which concentrates on the sale of large-scale computer installations, and has thus opened the market of serving smaller users to other companies. The objectives of IBM to concentrate their efforts emphasizing profitability rather than completeness of coverage, led to this opportunity for other firms. Thus, objectives for any organization are important keys influencing what that organization does.

RELATION OF OBJECTIVES TO MANAGEMENT

Objectives: an Essential First Step The setting of objectives is the essential first step in the managing of an organization. Objectives flow from analysis by the management of the situation confronting that organization. Once objectives have been set, they become the key criteria against which all decisions are evaluated. Thus, if your firm desires to be number one in its industry, all management decisions can be evaluated in terms of that objective.

Once objectives have been set, plans can then be drawn to attain them. Objectives essentially answer the question "Where is the organization headed?," whereas plans generally concern "How the organization will get there." Thus, the establishment of objectives is the essential first step in the planning process. As a result (and to make a point to which we will return later during this chapter), how objectives are established becomes a very important element in influencing all of the managerial steps that follow.

Relationship of Objectives to Plan Furthermore, plans become blueprints for action, some of which are in accordance with the plan but some of which are not. Therefore, plans trigger control systems that feed back data on performance. To some real extent this process of then trying to understand why performance has or has not been in accordance with the plan raises all of the questions of motivation, leadership, communication, and so forth, discussed later in this section. Concerning objectives, however, when behavior is not in accordance with the plan, it may be traced to any number of conditions, some of which are specified below (see Figure 9.1).

1. The objectives may not be attainable given the plan. For example, a company wishing to begin the production of automobiles that does not allocate an extensive enough capital budget to purchase buildings and equipment will never achieve its objective. Individuals within the company, therefore, will not be able to perform in accordance with the plan.

2. The objectives may not be understood by the individuals within the organization. The objectives of an organization to "become a major factor in the office copier field" may be too vague to be used by the individuals in the organization as a guide for action. Salespeople, for example, may be left wondering "Do I try to write every order regardless of profit?" or "Do I concentrate on a few accounts in order to gain a foothold in the area, and not worry about sales volume?"

3. Objectives may not be acceptable to organizational members. This particularly arises when individual departments or groups may be short-changed as a result of the objectives. For example, the objective to "enter and become a major factor in a commercial aircraft industry" is likely to be viewed by members of a government aircraft department with some suspicion and even open hostility. There would likely be a tendency not to support this objective on the part of those who would likely (or feel they may) lose company resources as a result.

Thus a good deal of management decision making hinges around a topic of organizational objectives. They are the first steps in any management process.

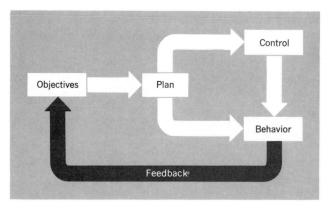

Figure 9.1

As we saw in Figure 9.1, once the objectives are set, plans are developed to accomplish the objectives. To carry out the plans, the organization must be structured in such a fashion as to be able to marshall resources and organize the people needed to bring the plan into action (Figure 9.2).

FOUR CHARACTERISTICS OF OBJECTIVES

A View of the Future But what are objectives? Objectives have four characteristics. First, objectives are what organizations would like to accomplish, what they would like to be. As such, they usually represent more of a view of the future than a picture of the present—and a future that the organization would prefer to see. For example, an organization such as Avis may have as one of its objectives to be number one in the car rental business, obviously a preferred picture of the future over today, because as of this writing Hertz is far larger. Or a state college may have as one of its objectives a quality Ph.D. program, even though current levels of funding prevent the mounting of even a solid Master's program. Or a local community hospital may have as its objective the offering of a complete medical service even though current levels of activity prevent purchase of any but the simplest form of equipment. Thus, objectives are what organizations would like to be in the future.

Theodore Levitt, in a series of case studies, has pointed out that organizations that do not "meet the market" or make a product that sells, will soon be out of business. Although this is so obvious as to be self-evident, some of the cases Levitt cites are not obvious. The railroads, for instance, failed to see themselves in the transportation industry, and thus lost a large profitable

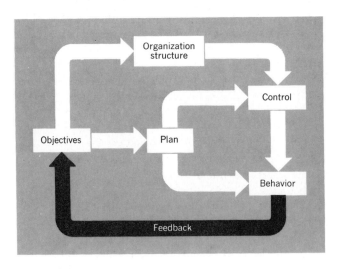

Figure 9.2

market to the trucking industry. Similarly, the movie industry failed to see itself in the entertainment business and thus initially lost a large market to the TV screen (a trend that has recently been reversed, by the way). Thus, the need to meet the market in order to survive as an organization is very strong.

Multiple   Second, objectives are multiple in nature. In general, organizations pursue three different types of objectives—a productivity objective (the production of a marketable product or service)—a satisfaction objective (the satisfaction of employees)—and a survival objective (the management of internal conflicts and the utilization of information from external sources). Your organization in the game probably had these three objectives and you probably devoted some time to each one. Most organizations devote most of their time to productivity objectives—producing Paper Airplanes in your case—though a good deal of the socializing, banter, and joking that probably took place during the production time is designed to accomplish both the satisfaction and survival objectives. A cold and impersonal group, one that devotes all of its energy to production, often has difficulty in attracting and retaining members. It is particularly true that when the demands of the market change over time, it becomes increasingly important to devote time to survival activities such as finding out what the market wants and attempting to influence what it wants in order to be more compatible with organizational abilities. In fact, as the demands of the market pressed on your organization, you undoubtedly were pulled in the direction of devoting more time to that activity and less to the task of producing current production. Because there are many objectives, every organization must decide on priorities. For example, with a shipping deadline hard upon it, an organization is likely to assign the highest priority to the attainment of its productivity objective and prompt shipment of the goods required at the expense of its being a good corporate citizen. And given the constant pressure on production and shipment, it is not hard to see why broad social goals can easily be overlooked. Recall the pressures on your own organization as demands from outside groups changed. Thus, the multiplicity of organizational objectives and the inevitable creating of priorities that occurs are the second characteristics of objectives.

Change over Time   Third, organizational objectives change over time. The March of Dimes is an excellent example. With the development of the Salk vaccine, came the virtual extinction of polio as a major childhood disease. Rather than disbanding, the March of Dimes Foundation switched to a concern for birth defects. In a less dramatic way, organizations switch their objectives through acquisitions, mergers, or entry into new fields. Gulf Oil, for instance, through its acquisition of General Atomic, modified its market objectives from merely the petrochemical field to the total "energy" industry. The movement of tobacco companies such as R. J. Reynolds to include other consumer items is another example. Or the decision by the General Motors Board of Directors to commit $150 million to the correction of problems of pollution and its plants represents a shift in organizational objectives. The objectives of your own organization in the game probably changed over time, for instance. Thus, organizations change their objectives over time in response to a number of pressures.

Guideposts for Behavior Finally, organizational objectives serve as guideposts for behavior of individual organizational members. To a large extent, organizational objectives light the way for individual employees. Maintenance employees in the general hospital, for instance, act very differently than maintenance employees in the production plant, both in terms of wages received and attitudes. This is true even though these people may perform the very same tasks. The fundamental difference lies in the nature of the organizational objectives.

DIFFERENT KINDS OF ORGANIZATIONAL OBJECTIVES

Process and Results Objectives Objectives of organizations are broad and have many faces, though they may be classified into two general categories—results objectives and process objectives. Examine the objectives of Inland Steel, for instance, and notice that relatively few objectives are results oriented (Exhibit 9.1). Number 10, for instance, "To make an annual return on sales and invested capital as good or better than any other company in the industry" is a results objective—that is, it states in specific end-measurable results that which is desired. Notice, however, objective 2 concerning ethical behavior and objective 4 concerning product improvement stress the way in which the business will be conducted. Thus, most of Inland's objectives are process objectives, in that they stress how the company will carry out its business, not what results it will seek to attain. Both process and results objectives are established by organizations to guide their activities and the actions of persons within the organization.

Overlapping Objectives Not only are there generally two different kinds of objectives, but there are also different levels of objectives. In all large organizations objectives are arranged in an overlapping way in which the objectives of one unit contribute to the objectives of the next higher unit (Figure 9.3). At the top of the organization, for example, the entire organization has a given general direction. Each division, in turn, has a set of objectives that, taken together, enables the organization as a whole to move toward its general objective. Each department also has its own objectives that enable the division to accomplish its objectives. Each person within the department, in turn, has a set of personal objectives that, when coordinated with the objectives of all the other persons in the department, enable the department to accomplish its objectives.

Reasons Why Objectives May Not Be Followed There are several instances, however, where this simple-sounding process whereby all the objectives of the departments fit together does not work—and the results are often disastrous for the organization. A large aerospace company, for instance, asked each of its departments to report its plans for the coming 10 years. When all of these departmental plans were assembled,

Exhibit 9.1 The Objectives of Inland Steel Company

1. To endeavor constantly to improve the caliber of our personnel at all levels of our operations with the objective of having the best team in the field. This can only be done by employing the most careful methods of selection, training, and promotion. Without attaining this goal most of the others can never be reached. With it, they are all possible.

2. To conduct all phases of our business under the highest standards of ethics and morality. This includes a policy of nondiscrimination in employment and promotion. Merit and experience alone should govern, and all should have equal opportunity irrespective of race, color, or creed.

3. To foster harmony throughout our organization; provide satisfactory working conditions; properly reward our employees by adequate compensation, and offer them the opportunity of acquiring a stock ownership in the company. The objectives of these moves are, of course, to make Inland a place not only where men and women want to work, but where they will be happy in their work, and seek to do their best in the common interest.

4. To continually improve our methods and our facilities so that our costs will be as low or lower and our quality as good or better than our competitors.

5. To serve our customers so well that we will merit a volume of business from them relatively as great or greater than that enjoyed by any of our competitors.

6. To expand our plants and enter new lines of activity whenever the undertaking appears wise and the investment sound in relation to the financial condition of the company.

7. To encourage our people to play their full part in the affairs of their community—civic, philanthropic, religious, educational—and thus take their places as good and useful citizens.

8. To lend our best efforts to improve and assist the communities in which our operations are located.

9. To inform our employees, stockholders, customers, and the public fully and regularly regarding our plans, our progress, and our problems.

10. To make an annual return on our sales and our invested capital as good or better than any other company in the industry.

---

it was discovered that, based on these plans, the firm would be in seven different businesses other than which they were in now, and none of which they had the capital to enter. What happened? Why did this occur? All too *Objectives May Not* often managers assume that objectives are established and clearly under-*Have Been Set* stood by all members of the organization when, in fact, they are not. Often objectives are not even present. It is not uncommon to examine a company's operations and realize that several individual departments are not contribut-

Figure 9.3 Overlapping organizational objectives.

ing at all to overall company objectives—and may even be frustrating the ability of other departments in meeting their objectives. This often occurs because top management does not keep a hierarchy of objectives in mind and simply does not know which departments contribute to the overall objectives. These useless departments may be hardworking and very efficient, but they simply may not be needed in the first place.

Objectives Are   In addition to the absence of objectives, often objectives are not clearly *Misunderstood* understood by the individuals within the organization. This misunderstanding is often due to the manner in which objectives are established in the company. Most often, objectives are determined by the top management and given to the other individuals in the company. As a result, individuals do not often know all of the shades of gray represented by the words contained in the final statement of the objectives. Furthermore, individuals in different jobs often have different points of view that stem from their different positions. Thus, a sales manager is likely to emphasize sales volume at the expense of profit per sale. The production manager is likely to emphasize meeting production schedules, whereas the quality control manager is likely to be more concerned about the quality of the product rather than the quantity. These differences in viewpoints (illustrated by the fable of the blind men and the elephant) often gives rise to misunderstandings concerning organizational objectives. Regardless of these problems, most companies obtain most of their objectives in a reasonably efficient manner.

LOST OR MISPLACED OBJECTIVES?

Objectives, once established, are not set in concrete. Once determined, they are often modified and even in some cases, abandoned by large segments of the organization. Research conducted by Professors Merton, Blau, and Thompson have discovered a process called "goal displacement" wherein new goals or objectives arise in certain subgroups to replace official company objectives. For instance, Professor Blau discovered in a state unemployment bureau that job placement counselors really didn't want to find the unemployed persons jobs (as was the official objective of their agency). Rather, they tried to find jobs for only the most easily placed persons and tended to ignore the others. Simplifying their work seemed to be a more important objective than finding jobs. In the same vein, social welfare case workers were often found to go around the rules to the point of even deliberately violating the law, by providing benefits to some welfare recipients not technically entitled to them. These welfare case workers obviously valued the personal objective of ameliorating human suffering over the organizational objective of enforcing welfare regulations. Along the same lines, entire departments often become so wrapped up in their own pursuits that their goals become more important than the overall company objectives. The classic case of the quality control department rejecting a large number of parts without consideration of the workability of the specification is a case in point. The sales department that sells to anyone regardless of credit standing, just to boost sales volume, is another. "Sell now and collect never" may be their motto. These are but several examples where the goals and activities of individual departments often become so important that they overcome and even subvert the overall company objectives.

Professor Thompson has discovered a tragic but sometimes comical example of goal displacement. Studying individuals working in large organizations, he discovered that for some people, the rules themselves take on a certain holiness. Even when the rules clearly frustrate the intent of the regulations, some person will stick to the letter and not the spirit of the law. We have all, at one time or another, encountered one of these persons known as "bureaucrats" whose basic answer is "It doesn't have to be right, it is the rule."

THE PROCESS OF OBJECTIVE SETTING

Directive Goal Setting: Advantages and Disadvantages Most often, objectives are established by the top management and given to the balance of individuals in the organization. This top-down establishment of objectives is called directive objective setting. When objectives are established in a directive manner, the objectives are determined by the top management and given to other organizational members basically without their participation or contributions. Often this is the most efficient manner in which objectives can be established in an organization, taking the shortest length of time. Because top management often sees the relationship between the organization and its outside client groups (see the following discussion concerning stakeholders), the objectives established in a directive way are likely to be good ones, in that they take into account important factors in the environment. Thus, directive objective setting may result in good objectives, established in the most efficient way. These objectives, however, may be either not accepted or not understood by other individuals in the organization who have not participated in the objective setting process. Thus, it is not uncommon for the question to be raised both vocally and silently, "What do they really mean by that?" Beyond the disbelief and questioning implied in the quote, there may actually be areas for misunderstanding. Objectives are often broadly stated, and there are few specific guidelines for behavior in a given situation. For example, the marketing manager who knows that one of the company's objectives is to attain a market share of 25 percent, may not know whether the price should be lowered a little in order to secure a very large order. It is also possible and probable that as the everchanging market shifts, previously established objectives may become less relevant to the new situations. The often low level of commitment to the objectives of the organization may in part be a result of this directive process. This is not to say that directive objective setting is a poor management practice. Probably most objectives are established this way, and most organizations accomplish most of their objectives. The relative efficiency of this objective setting process often offsets the sometime inefficiency in the way individuals in the organization attain these objectives.

Participative Objective Setting: Advantages and Disadvantages In contrast to the directive strategy, where objectives flow from the top down, many companies have involved individuals of the organization in establishing the company's objectives. Most often, individuals meet in departmental groups to draft objectives for their departments and then meet with other departments to coordinate these objectives. Overall company objectives are then constructed on the building blocks of the objectives of these subunits, such as departments and divisions. This process is most useful in making objectives clear to members of the organization. This clarity occurs because individuals have participated in the process and, therefore, are familiar with all of the nuances of meaning that lie in and behind the final words in which the objectives are finally stated. Because objectives are clearer, there is often more consistent performance to attain them. The process of establishing these objectives, however, can be very time-consuming. One supermarket organization, for instance, took 15 months to define its objectives in this participative manner—and no doubt, at least some of the objectives would then have to be modified to meet the conditions that had undoubtedly changed during the 15-month period. In addition, if the company's objectives are determined by internal individuals only, often the focus of these persons is not on environmental concerns outside the organization that may be vital to the company's survival. The authors know of a private school serving learning-disabled children that, because internal faculty members established the school's objectives, closed for all the traditional school holidays, not taking into account the needs of the children and parents for a continuing contact even during vacation periods. As a result, the school lost children and was eventually forced to close.

Some research by Raia and then confirmed by Meyer, Kay, and French suggests that participation in establishing the objectives may be a key factor in securing successful execution of the plan. Studying the Work Planning and Review program conducted at General Electric, which provided for joint determination of objectives and methods to reach them, the researchers concluded that managers using the participative W.P.R. System:

1. Were likely to take action to improve performance;
2. Received help and support in the attainment of their objectives;
3. Planned better;
4. Made better use of their abilities and experience.

Thus, participative objective setting may result in more commitment to the objectives, once they are established, but the process of establishing the objectives may take a long time and may overlook important environmental factors. To reduce these problems, top management often establishes general company objectives in a directive way, and then permits individual participation in the determination of department objectives. In any event, the crucial management decision on how to establish objectives must weigh the cost of establishment, evaluated in time, energy, and money terms, versus the benefit of clarity and commitment.

Thus, organizational objectives are the first step in the management process. Objectives determine where the organization is going, and establishes the groundwork for the plan that determines how the organization will get there. Objectives also influence the determination of the organization's structure, which lays out who will do what to implement the plan and accomplish the organization's objectives.

TWO PRESSURES TO CHANGE

Prepotency Principle In short, there are many organizational objectives that, because they establish what the organization would like to be in the future, guide current actions of individual members. The priorities for these objectives vary over time, as do the nature of the objectives themselves. This changing characteristic of organizational objectives can be attributed to two pressures. First, when one organizational objective is fulfilled, another arises to take its place. There is probably a hierarchy of objectives ranging from the most basic and pressing concern for organizational survival to other concerns for human growth and fulfillment. Figure 9.4 represents a graphic presentation of this hierarchy. Obviously, if the organization cannot survive, other objectives cannot possibly be met, whereas once survival is assured, other objectives

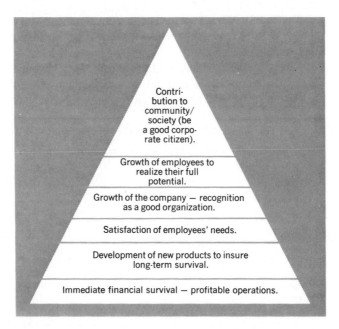

Figure 9.4 Hierarchy of organizational objectives.

become possible. This mechanism whereby as one objective is satisfied and another arises to take its place as a guide for action is called "prepotency" and will arise again in the discussions about motivation. This is the first source of changing organizational objectives.

Agreement Process with Stakeholders The second pressure for shifting organizational objectives arises from the very way in which objectives get established. In general, the initial company objectives are set by a sort of agreement that emerges between groups existing outside of the company and the company itself. These outside groups, known as stakeholders, have important things that the company needs to survive. The company needs customers, for instance, to purchase products and services. The company also needs suppliers to supply raw materials. All of these groups (and many others) must be heard from in the objective setting process that occurs between the company and its environment. Usually this company-environment objective setting process goes on before objectives are determined within the company. Agreement is necessary between the stakeholder groups and the company before internal objective setting may take place. This agreement emerges as a result of a constant, on-going negotiation between the organization and these important other groups. In understanding this negotiation process, there are two separable topics. First, there is the matter of who the "important groups" or stakeholders are and, second, there is the matter of how the negotiation process is actually conducted.

DEFINITION OF STAKEHOLDER GROUPS

Turning our attention to first things first, it might be an oversimplification, but in its most basic form, an important other group or stakeholder may be any group or individual who has something that the organization needs. In general, in order to survive, organizations need materials, human resources, money, customers, and facilities. Thus, the organization needs customers to purchase its products, materials suppliers to supply raw materials, finance people to supply money, and people to design, produce, and distribute its products. In order to induce these stakeholders to supply what the organization requires, the organization must supply something of equivalent value in return. Thus, customers must be induced to part with sufficient cash in order to purchase the firm's products, enough to cover the firm's costs and hopefully a profit. In turn, material suppliers must be induced to provide the material of sufficient quality and delivery schedule in return for cash. And assembly line workers must be induced to push the right button at the right time, in return for cash and a host of other things. Unfortunately for the modern organization, this list of stakeholders grows almost daily. New demands are placed on the organization from consumer groups, minorities, and a growing list of government agencies. In each of these instances, the organization is confronted with new demands, actions that these stakeholders want the organization to perform on the threat of withholding what the organization needs. For example, minority groups frequently threaten to boycott a firm's products if that firm does not hire more minority employees. In the game, similar threats were made by various groups and your organization had to respond.

To compound the manager's problem, these many and growing lists of stakeholder groups often present divergent and conflicting demands. Imagine for instance, the problem of a construction company manager confronted with demands from minority groups for more minority carpenters, and the demand from the carpenter's union for the exclusive employment of graduates of the "white only" apprenticeship program run by the union. In this situation, the manager is caught between the threat of a boycott and the threat of a strike, and can only hope that something can be worked out that will satisfy both groups without a major confrontation. In the exercise, your organization experienced these conflicting demands and the difficulty in dealing with them.

Complicating the matter still further is the observation that the groups' demands change over time, thus rendering it almost impossible to know in advance at any point in time, how to respond. For example, minority groups originally demanded more minority employees without regard for skill level, then changed to a minority percentage at all organizational and skill levels that match the level in the general community population. The shifting nature and often conflicting characteristics of the demands of the stakeholder groups combined with the growing list of stakeholders renders the manager's job very challenging.

THE NEGOTIATION PROCESS

Boundary Positions to Negotiate It is even more interesting how the process of negotiation takes place. We will discuss three dimensions of this negotiation process. First, much of negotiation that takes place between the organization and the stakeholder groups is centralized in certain special jobs in the organization called boundary positions. An example of a boundary position is the personnel manager who is specifically charged with the responsibility of dealing with such stakeholder groups as the union, community groups, minority employment groups, employment groups, employment agencies, state and federal health and safety agencies, group health and accident insurance carriers, and personnel representatives in other companies. The purchasing agent is another example. He or she is usually charged with the responsibility for dealing with the material suppliers and distribution agencies (such as trucking firms) and state and federal regulatory agencies. Sometimes in the game you played, this form of specialization emerges where one person is designated as the negotiator or boundary job holder. In short these contacts tend to be centralized in certain specific boundary occupations. This enables the other non-boundary jobs to concentrate on the task at hand, without being subject to the pressures from external groups.

Discover Stakeholder Needs Second, these boundary positions use various strategies and techniques in discovering the demands and expectations of these stakeholder groups. Although the ouija board and astrology have never received widespread use in ascertaining what stakeholders "really want," undoubtedly some managers, after a particularly frustrating day, might be willing to try them—at least once.

"Ask Them" Strategies Seriously, these ascertaining tactics fall into two general categories—the "ask them" and the "watch them" categories. If you really want to discover what a stakeholder group wants (as some of you undoubtedly discovered during the game), there is no substitute for a direct face-to-face question: "What do you want?" There are several different, though closely related, "ask them" strategies. The most popular is the survey. Market research surveys, for instance, are very popular ways to ascertain buyer preferences for products, both old and new. In fact, an entire industry employing thousands of persons has arisen to conduct and interpret market research studies. By questioning a small percentage of the population, known as a sample, a firm hopes to find out what all of us might think of purple as a color for men's shoes, for instance or of a new style of car. Surveys are often also conducted among employees to find out what they really want.

Oftentimes, it is difficult or impossible to ask members of a group directly what they want and expect to get a valid answer. Hostilities between groups—such as between management and labor—or the absence of established channels of communication often make it difficult to ask stakeholder groups directly. In these cases, organizations rely on such indirect techniques as grapevines or third-person intermediaries such as mediators. (In a recent rent strike, for instance, a mediator was able to get the landlord and the striking renters to talk to each other for the first time.) Even when direct face-to-face communication is possible, often the relationship is filled with game playing and hostility. In labor-management relations, for instance, it is not uncommon for both sides to say one thing but mean something else. A skilled negotiator soon picks up subtleties and words between the lines. All of these—surveys, grapevines, mediators, and listening for what isn't said—are "ask them" techniques designed to help the organization to find out what stakeholder groups really want.

"Watch Them" Strategies   A second basic find out strategy allowing stakeholder groups to tell you what they want is by watching them. Analysis of sales activity for a product is one of the best ways to find out customer tastes. The failure of the Edsel to sell, even after market surveys had indicated the saleability of a medium-priced car is an outstanding example. (The surveys were correct, however, of course, as American Motors Rambler proved—only the design of the Edsel was poor.) Actually observing employee behavior is an excellent way to discover what really turns them on and off. With students, for instance, one of the best ways to find out student preferences is to observe which courses they register for, and where they choose to live. Students express preferences for courses with class cards much like consumers express product preferences with dollars. Thus, both by watching and by asking, an organization can find out the demands and expectations of various stakeholder groups.

EFFORTS TO INFLUENCE STAKEHOLDER DEMANDS

Advertising   Third, although up to now we have stressed the flow of information and demands from stakeholder groups to the organization, it should be apparent to you that most organizations make aggressive efforts to bend the demands of stakeholder groups to suit the needs of the organizations. Many organizations in the game probably exerted some effort to do just that. There are three principal ways an organization seeks to influence stakeholder expectations. Advertising, for instance, is one way in which organizations attempt to shape the needs of one important stakeholder group, the consumer, to accept what the organization has to offer. Detroit, for instance, for years has insisted that the American public wanted big cars rather than compact models, and spent billions of dollars in advertising to convince the American public of that preference. Only the success of American Motors' Rambler and Germany's VW caused a shift of the Big Three's production schedule. The advertising effort put in to sell a new product (such as color TV) in an effort to awaken a new need in consumers, is another example of the use of advertising by a company to shape consumer demands to fit the product and capability of the firm.

Lobbying   Lobbying is another way in which organizations seek to mold the demands and expectations of external groups, particularly governmental units. Virtually every aerospace company has a lobbyist in Washington, buttonholing Congressmen and Senators, urging them to vote for particular programs. Two classic examples of lobbying are the automobile industry's successful effort to postpone the effective date of pollution and safety requirements and the education industry's successful effort in convincing the federal government in 1966, for the first time, to fund local school district programs. From lobbying for zoning ordinances and favorable tax rulings at the local level, to canvassing customers to vote against a statewide antipollution measure, to persuading Senators to vote for the Chrysler bailout, most organizations attempt to shape the demands and expectations that government agencies hold for their firm through lobbying activities.

Involvement in   A third way organizations seek to influence the demands and expectations
Decisions   of stakeholder groups (and the way most frequently chosen by student organizations in the Paper Airplane game) is through the process of involving dissident groups in the decision-making process. This is known as the process of cooptation. For example, in order to get a bond referendum passed for a new school building, school administrators often organize a citizens advisory committee composed of leading local citizens to help plan the building. It is expected that in return for such participation, the individuals will "endorse" the new building and work actively for its passage in the referendum. Difficult issues between labor and management may be assigned to a joint committee to study the problem. This often results in both sides seeing more of the other's points of view and compromising their original position. The classic often-cited example is the Tennessee Valley Authority that involved both union officials in their decision-making processes concerning employees and local residents in decisions concerning plant location and electric power distribution. This involvement modified the expectations of TVA held by these two stakeholder groups in such a way as to make them satisfiable by TVA. Although the term *cooptation* often implies a Machiavellian way of seducing some person or persons to betray their true interests, in reality it is very similar to the widely practiced "you scratch my back and I'll scratch yours." Through cooptation and involvement, outsiders become more aware of, and more sensitive to, the needs and problems of the organizations, thus leading them to modify their demands on the organization.

In short, organizations seek to mold the demands and expectations of stakeholder groups through the process of advertising, lobbying, and cooptation. Regardless of the process, these activities are usually centralized in specific jobs called boundary positions often involving a two-way communication process between the organization and the stakeholder groups which have some resource that the organization needs. In this communication process, the organization seeks to discover what the group wants and at the same time to shape what the group wants to make it easier for the organization to comply.

SUMMARY

In summary, organizational objectives are statements of future goals that an organization hopes to attain, are multiple in nature, shifting in character, and serve as guideposts for individual organization member behavior. Organizational objectives are initially determined as the result of a constant ongoing negotiation process conducted between various stakeholder groups and the organization. These stakeholder demands are then utilized within the company in either a directive or participative manner to generate a series of objectives specifying either results desired or preferred ways to accomplish them, arranged in a means-end hierarchy. Once established, objectives that specify what the company wants then lay the groundwork for plans that specify how the company will accomplish its objectives and an organizational structure that specifies who will do what to carry out the plan. Stakeholders include consumers, suppliers, various government agencies, local community groups, and employees. They seek to have the organization engage in certain actions and communicate their demands to the organization in various ways. At the same time, the organization, through lobbying, advertising, and coopting activities conducted by specific boundary jobs, seeks to influence the stakeholders to modify their demands to be more compatible with organizational capabilities. Through this dynamic, mutually interactive influence process, the initial objectives of an organization are established.

WALDENBOOKS: COUNTERING B. DALTON BY APING ITS COMPUTER OPERATIONS

Gone are the days of musty bookstores laden with a formidable array of classics and tended by a literate but scatter brained proprietor. The once-genteel business of bookselling is now among the most competitive in retailing. And Waldenbooks and its hard-charging rival, B. Dalton Bookseller—by far the largest of the nation's three dozen or so chains—are waging a decidedly unbookish battle for the spot at the top of the stack.

Together, the two bookstore giants sold nearly 125 million titles last year. Because both have roughly doubled in size in the last five years, they now control about a fifth of all book trade at retail, and each has become a significant contributor to its parent—Carter Hawley Hale Stores Inc. in the case of Walden and Dayton Hudson Corp. for B. Dalton.

On the face of it, both owe their prosperity to the same formula: Following people to the suburbs, the two brought mass-merchandising flair to the highly fragmented bookstore business, building nationwide chains of cheery, well-organized units in large shopping malls and filling them with paperbacks and bold displays to lure the casual reader.

The differences

Beneath the surface similarities, however, the two pursued sharply diverging courses. Walden focused on amassing a large network of outlets stocked with a slimmed-down selection of the most popular titles. B. Dalton took the opposite tack. To develop an image as a broad-line bookstore, it put as many as 25,000 titles in a typical unit. In part as a result, Dalton expanded more slowly, concentrating instead on building an organization, including a computerized book-tracking system. That set-up was superior to Walden's manual inventory controls, which produced a surplus of some books and a scarcity of others.

The effects of those different approaches to growth are beginning to show. Not surprisingly, Walden has established a third more stores around the country—560 outlets compared with B. Dalton's 380 units. But despite its substantial edge in outlets, the Stamford (Conn.) retailer is on the verge of losing its long-standing preeminence in volume. Four years ago, Walden logged an estimated $105 million in revenues, compared with Dalton's $84.1 million. By last year, however, the two were virtually neck-and-neck in sales—about $180 million for Walden vs. $174.4 million for B. Dalton. More telling, Walden's $110 or so in sales per sq. ft. was outdistanced by Dalton's $130. While neither company releases data on profits, industry sources estimate that B. Dalton came out slightly on top.

Even more worrisome for Walden, B. Dalton—having built a solid marketing image and inventory-control system—is now adopting the very expansion strategy Walden has pursued so singlemindedly. After adding roughly 40 stores a year through much of the 1970s, Dalton opened 61 units last year and plans to add about 70 a year for the next several years. "We spent a number of years designing a system of people and equipment that could support our growth," says President Floyd Hall. "Now we have all those things in place, and are accelerating our growth."

Conversely, the growth-minded Walden is hurriedly adopting many of Dalton's operating efficiencies in hopes of expanding per-store sales and profits. To accomplish that, Carter Hawley Hale last January brought in a new Walden president, Harry T. Hoffman, who had built Ingram Book Co. into one of the nation's largest book wholesalers. Walden's previous chairman, Russell L. Hoyt, was named vice-president for corporate development for CHH. "Russell Hoyt is a

Source. Business Week, October 8, 1979.

great entrepreneur," explains CHH President Philip M. Hawley. "But now it is time to build a strong management system, and Harry Hoffman is one of the strongest managers in the book business."

Hoffman has no plans to jettison Walden's emphasis on growth. In fact, the chain is shooting to double the number of its stores, to 1,000, by 1984. Over that period, however, Hoffman also hopes to boost sales per sq. ft. in constant dollars by at least 40% by redirecting the chain's marketing program toward a broader audience and by getting a firmer grip on inventory control.

By all accounts, it was B. Dalton's decision to computerize early that lies behind its snappy sales record. From the moment it is ordered from the publisher, each Dalton book is coded by number and monitored by central computer. Thus Dalton's corporate managers can call up weekly sales reports, by title and topic, for every outlet, city, or region, and use the data to restock fastsellers, drop slow movers, and choose new books to buy.

Walden's corporate managers have no such precise tally of which books are where—and when. Some store managers copy the titles of big sellers by hand, while others keep rough counts in their heads, but the consequence lies in its sometimes stuffed, sometimes empty bookracks. "Because it didn't know what its inventory was, Walden often reordered on top of stock it already had, then couldn't sell the books," says the sales manager of a major publisher. "We're in the dark," Hoffman concedes. "There's no question computerization has helped Dalton. They are able to respond to sales trends more rapidly than anyone else in the business."

Pressing to close that gap, Hoffman plans to install a point-of-sale terminal in every Walden store over the next two years. Like Dalton's, the $4 million-plus system will be linked to a central computer that will track each book from delivery to reordering. At the same time, Hoffman has ordered each Walden unit to sweep out sluggish sellers and reduce the number of copies stocked on titles that remain. To date, Walden's level of returns to publishers is running 30% ahead of last year, and while it usually receives full credit on that merchandise, industry sources estimate the shipping charges it must bear on such returns

could run into the millions. Yet Hoffman believes that the interest savings from the 20% inventory reduction will offset the costs involved.

'Broaden the market'

Because better inventory controls will also help keep fast-selling books in stock, it will probably boost Walden's store sales, too. "If a customer is looking for *The World According to Garp,* he's not willing to buy *The Joy of Sex,*" explains one competitor. "If you don't have the book, you've often lost the sale."

But Hoffman is aiming to do more than satisfy customers looking for a specific title. "The industry has been interested in selling books, not in selling reading," he says. "Our goal is to broaden the market for books."

To lure what he calls the "sometime reader"— the 40% of the adults who read newspapers and magazines but not books—Hoffman is augmenting his focus on operations with a host of marketing changes. Walden has developed a new store design that is intended to make the store more inviting to the window shopper. Customers will encounter a newly fattened selection of hardback books, in fiction as well as such fast-growing nonfiction categories as economics. As a result, says Hoffman, Walden's title selection now matches that of Dalton. "As new titles come out, we want to keep up and keep the reader coming back to see what's new," explains Joyce Rhoda, director of purchasing. The chain is also hoping to increase store traffic and sales by adding magazines.

Beyond that, Walden plans to double its advertising budget over the next 12 months, to more than $3 million. While most of its promotions have focused on single titles, usually best-sellers, its advertising will now tout a shelfful of books on a wide range of subjects in hopes of catching the less avid readers.

Battle of the future

Despite the operating improvements now in the works, CHH insists Walden did not err in stressing fast expansion first. "It is hard to close a differential of 150 stores," says Hawley, referring to the task facing B. Dalton. "In the end we will be far out ahead in terms of sales." But some observers are not that sanguine. "Walden has enough to do in its existing stores," says the head of a rival chain. "I question whether they can continue to expand so rapidly and still correct the problems there."

With Dalton now pursuing Walden's strategy of aggressive growth and Walden adopting Dalton's long-standing emphasis on controls, the competition in bookselling is likely to become hotter still. "Dalton is the better bookseller so far," says a veteran bookchain executive. "But if anybody can help Walden overtake them it is Harry Hoffman." Chortles a senior book buyer at Walden: "The honeymoon for the enemy is over."

Discussion Questions

1. How have Waldenbooks' goals changed?
2. How have changing stakeholder demands affected the direction that Waldenbooks' goals have taken?

GOLDEN TRANSIT COMPANY

At the turn of the century in 1901, a group of civic-minded citizens of Golden City formed a public corporation and received from the city a franchise "to operate a public transportation system." The Golden Transit Company, the corporation thus formed, grew with Golden City; and in 1946 at the close of World War II, its annual statement showed a capital surplus of $1,200,000 in the form of cash and negotiable securities. In addition, the corporation owned substantial real estate holdings, including a 12-story office building.

The end of the war also marked a turning point in the fortunes of the Golden Transit Company. Golden City expanded from its postwar population of 300,000 to more than 700,000 by 1960 and, in the process, the geographic area of the city grew from an area of 30 square miles to more than 120 square miles. The length of existing bus routes had to be increased and, in many cases, new routes were established. With the advent of a system of freeways, Golden City residents contributed their share to the booming automobile market. The transit company had to purchase additional rolling stock, some of which was an overdue replacement of equipment worn out during the war years when replacements were impossible. Much of the equipment, however, was to serve new bus lines and was purchased in an effort to make public transportation more convenient and to attract new customers. In addition, a continuing spiral of rising costs and subsequent fare increases began. The seeming result was that with each fare increase, the number of passengers declined. Though the frequency of service was greatly reduced on many routes, no routes were completely eliminated. The earnings of the company were poor and, as a result, the stock of the company was traded on the local over-the-counter market at $11 per share, despite the fact that financial analysts estimated a book value of $23 per share.

In the spring of 1961, sales of the stock became more active, and during the remainder of that year it traded at prices ranging between $12 and $14 per share. By the year's end, the reason for the increased market activity of the stock became apparent. It was revealed that National Busways, an out-of-state corporation, had purchased 60 percent of the outstanding stock. Early in 1962, National's slate of directors was elected and a new management for the Golden Transit Company was appointed. During 1962 the following events occurred.

Source. Reproduced by special permission of Southwestern Publishing Company, 5101 Madison Road, Cincinnati, Ohio 45227.

1. Two requests were submitted to the Golden City council for fare increases. The new management stated that it was a public corporation entitled to make a profit, and that if the fare increase were not granted, it would be necessary to further reduce service and eliminate unprofitable routes. The first request was denied by the city council, with the result that 10 relatively new routes serving suburban areas were discontinued. The city council was still considering the second request for a fare increase.

2. The real estate holdings, including a 12-story office building, were transferred to a holding company controlled by National Busways. The income from this property was no longer available to offset the operating losses of the Golden Transit Company. A large part of the capital surplus was used to purchase another transit company in an adjacent state.

3. Golden Transit Company had been somewhat tardy in establishing adequate retirement and disability insurance plans. However, they recognized these obligations to their employees and devised a plan whereby disabled persons and some of those who had retired could continue working with the company on a part-time basis performing light duty. A total of 51 persons were employed in this category. All of this group were discharged by the new management with the comment. "We're running a bus line—not a charity."

4. A citizen's group, whose chairman was a prominent Golden City attorney, was investigating the steps necessary to revoke the charter under which National Busways was operating the Golden Transit Company.

Discussion Questions
1. What were the objectives of the Golden Transit Company as it operated until 1961?
2. How and why did those objectives change when National Busways took over the company?
3. How could the citizen group influence the new management to modify its goals and to be more compatible with citizen interests?
4. If you had the power, would you bar this type of takeover from taking place? Be certain to consider the impact of changing stakeholder demands as well as the demands of changing stakeholders.

Probably one of the most important and least understood management activities is the process of determining the objectives of the organization. Until recently, both textbooks and business leaders would glibly state that "maximizing profit" was their basic objective—and most of us naively swallowed the words. Many students of organizations have known for years that management pursued objectives other than profit, but that information was largely trapped in the scholarly journals. The emergence of organized subgroups in the community representing such interests as blacks, women, students, civic interests, and environmental concerns have stripped away the veil of secrecy and now we see the very complex objectives that most organizations pursue. We also now can see more clearly how organizations react to stakeholder pressures, and in turn, how they seek to structure stakeholder expectations to be compatible with organizational capabilities.

In this chapter you have had the opportunity to see and experience some of the process of establishing objectives. The impact of changing stakeholder demands should have been clear to you during the Paper Airplane exercise. Unfortunately, many organizations become insensitive to stakeholder's demands, and when they do, they face the real problem of losing an important source of support.

The changing and shifting nature of organizational objectives, and several of the pressures that force these changes were highlighted during this chapter. Reactions to stakeholder demands are a major pressure for a shift in objectives, and this was true in the Paper Airplane manufacturing game (where the minority coalition forced the hiring of minority employees), Waldenbooks, and the Golden Transit case (where a new stockholder milked the corporation of its major assets and forced the community to increase support of the transit system).

Finally you have had the opportunity to review several methods that organizations use to deal with these stakeholder demands. Much as in your little Paper Airplane manufacturing company, most organizations must divert energies from the production of current products and services to deal with these demands. The way you dealt with them—negotiation, capitulation, or cooptation—all are typical methods organizations use to moderate these stakeholder demands. The process of negotiation between stakeholder groups and the organization can be likened to charming a cobra—both fascinating and deadly—and for most organizations the stakes are life or death.

Here are some principles:

1. Company objectives establish the company's future image and guide the current action of individual members.

2. Companies pursue multiple objectives, which specify both results desired and preferred methods to accomplish these results.

3. Company objectives are arranged in a means-end hierarchy, ranging from the broadest aims of the entire company to the specific objectives of the smallest department or subunit.

4. Company objectives change over time, largely in response to pressure from the prepotency principle and external stakeholder groups.

5. Company objectives are initially determined through negotiation with an ever-changing pattern of external stakeholders, conducted by specified company boundary positions.

6. Companies seek to influence stakeholder groups and expectations through involvement and pressure strategies.

7. Once initial objectives arising from stakeholder demands have been fixed, internal objective setting takes place, either in a directive or participative manner, balancing the costs of establishment and the benefits of clarity and commitment in time, energy, and money terms.

8. Company objectives, by establishing where the organization is going, lays the groundwork for planning, which establishes how the company will get there, and organizational structures that determine who will do what to carry out the plan to accomplish the objectives.

CHAPTER TEN **PLANNING**

**LEARNING
OBJECTIVES**

**LEARNING
OBJECTIVES** ────────────────────────────────────

After studying this chapter you should be able to:

1. Describe four phases of planning.
2. Discuss the importance of forecasting.
3. Distinguish between strategic plans and tactical plans.
4. Discuss the advantages of planning.
5. Discuss the disadvantages of planning.

THE PRODUCTION MANAGER'S IN-BASKET

I. Objectives
   A. To take the role of a production manager.
   B. To receive and respond to the correspondence in your in-basket.
   C. To cope with developing circumstances that pose changes for established plans.
II. Premeeting Preparation
   A. Read the instructions.
III. Instructions
   A. For this exercise each student will work independently.
   B. Here is the situation:

   You are the Manager of Production at Video TV, Inc. You report to the President and direct the operation of four departments: Chassis Fabrication, Electronics, Final Assembly, and Shipping. A partial organization chart is shown as Figure 10.1.

   One of your major customers is the department store chain, Korbel's. They have on order 4000 color consoles that are marketed under their own brand name. The contract calls for shipping these sets by September 14.

   Video TV has a few other retailers to whom it supplies sizable quantities of TV sets under various brand names. It also produces and ships the Video TV line of sets to other retailers.

   Following closely on the heels of the Korbel order is an order of 2200 color consoles for Amerex Discount Department Stores. This order is to be shipped by October 12.

   A schedule is developed for each major order, showing the time it is to spend in each department. These schedules are integrated into a master schedule that is displayed on the wall in the office of the production control assistant. That portion of the schedule for Korbel's order that covers the period from August 1 to September 15 is shown as Figure 10.2

   Note that each memo fills only the upper half of the page. You are to use the lower half to write a reply to each memo.
   C. Turn to the memos, remove them from the book, examine them, and prepare your responses.

   > *Time for Step C: 20 minutes*

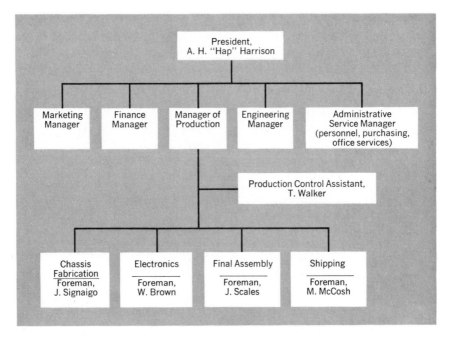

Figure 10.1   Partial organization chart for Video TV, Inc.

IV. Discussion

Your instructor will help you explore what happened in the exercise and its meaning for management.

Time for discussion: 20 minutes

Each Monday morning your principal subordinates report to you in writing concerning the status of work in their departments. Several memos arrive in your in-basket on Monday morning, August 6.

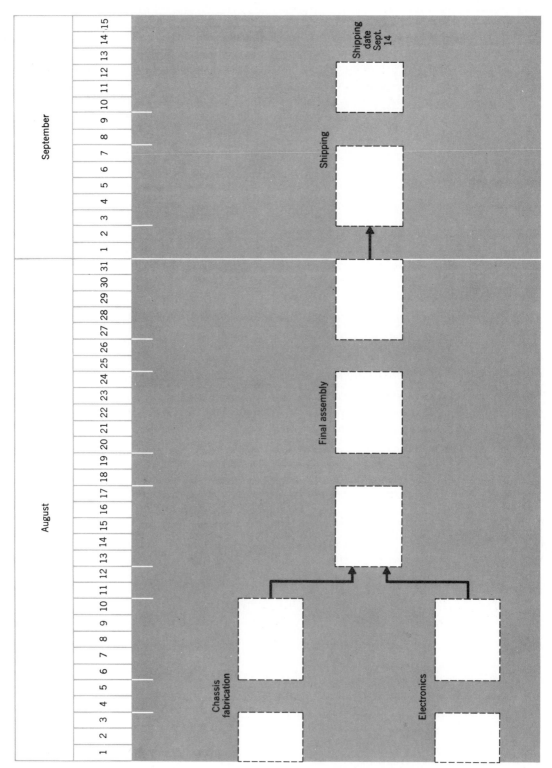

Figure 10.2 Schedule for Korbel's Department Store order.

To: Production Manager
From: Willie Brown, Electronics Foreman

I agree last month to take on four "hard-core" trainees as part of Personnel's Affirmative Action Employment Program. I've had trouble with two of them not showing up regularly. This has put us in a bit of a bind on the Korbel order. Will two or three days' slippage in the schedule cause any serious problems?

To: Production Manager
From: J. Signaigo, Chassis Fabrication Foreman

Everything is on schedule for the Korbel order. The only possible delay could come if Purchasing doesn't obtain the Z type brackets needed by Wednesday of this week. I checked last Friday and they said the supplier wanted a week's extension, but I told Purchasing we absolutely couldn't live with that. Unfortunately, this supplier is our sole source; we can't get the brackets from anybody else any sooner.

To: Production Manager
From: John Scales, Final Assembly Foreman

We will have the decks cleared and be all ready to work on the Korbel order by the 15th. As you know, we have a tight schedule on our rework commitments, so it is extremely important that we get this job on time. Any delays in our receiving the Korbel work mean unavoidable delay in the rework and quite possibly in the Amerex order, which comes up next.

To: Production Control Manager
From: M. McCosh, Shipping Foreman

It is either boom or bust down here, as you know. Right now we have two men idle most of the time. Of course, we'll need them when the Korbel job comes along. The question is: Do we want to lay them off for a while or find something for them to do?

To: Production Manager
From: Hap Harrison, President

I was playing golf Saturday with Ned Korbel (President, Korbel's Department Stores). He tells me that they are planning a fall sale on TV's. They want to shift the sale days forward from the second week in October to the first week. He said they could only do this if we could ship the 4000 sets they have on order September 7 instead of September 14. I told him we could probably help him out.

What do you say?

Planning refers to spelling out means of accomplishing goals or objectives. As the In-Basket Exercise demonstrates, planning operations are performed not in a static world, but in living systems where hardly anything is nailed down.

We will do well to keep this feeling for the situation in mind as we proceed to discuss how planning can help impose order despite what may seem to be formidable forces for chaos.

THE PLANNING PROCESS

There are several steps involved in the planning process. They overlap and are not neatly taken in sequence in real situations. But we can discuss each step and see how it can contribute to the creation of effective enterprise.

Forecasting   First, planning involves looking to the future and attempting to forecast conditions or "states of nature" that will exist. An American manufacturer of tape recorders, or motorcycles, or steel might, for example, be trying to decide when the flood of Japanese imports might recede. If such manufacturers saw the flood coming in the first place, of course, they might have sought to compete more effectively or, failing that possibility, to reduce capacity or to find new activities.

Of course, forecasting is not easy. Uncontrollable forces can buffet the individual firm about in a storm of change. Indeed, this is a point often raised by managers to rationalize their failure to try to forecast. But because forecasting is difficult and because many events cannot be controlled does not mean that it is not useful.

Some claim that all forecasts are "wrong." If this is the case, why bother? The value of forecasting to the manager may not be so much in the accuracy of the forecast, but in the fact that the planner must stop and think about the future. What kind of economic conditions will be facing my firm? How will the world energy crisis affect my production processes? Will people still want to buy the kinds of products I am now selling? These are the kinds of questions the planner must think about as he or she is attempting to get a handle on what the world both inside and outside of the firm will be like.

Some forecasts are readily available, such as projections of the Gross National Product, whereas others, such as consumer preferences for clothing five years from now, may be quite difficult to determine. Threats of oil embargos, lines at gas stations, and a general concern about the energy problem have made shambles of the forecasts of American automobile manufacturers for any particular year, but in general, their forecasts that small cars will take an increasing share of the market are quite accurate.

The manager may have to make an assumption about some future fact or event if a forecast cannot be made. We don't know what OPEC will do about oil prices in the future, but we would be safe in assuming that they will go up. How far we do not know, but we would probably make some major goofs if we assumed that energy costs will remain the same for the next five years. In a situation such as this the exact amount of increase may not be as important to us as a true understanding of the direction of energy costs and how they may affect all of our business plans.

Problems and Second, and closely related to forecasting, planning involves trying to find
Possibilities opportunities and obstacles in the present and future. This would be the real purpose of a motorcycle manufacturer's trying to foresee the incoming herd of Kawasakis, Yamahas, and Hondas. Does this mean that the manufacturer must passively breathe their exhaust? Or does it mean grabbing up franchises and converting dealerships to handle the new products? Or possibly getting to work to design a better, less-expensive product to compete with the new wave of imports?

The same facts speak differently to different mentalities. For the entrepreneurial mind, a key part of planning is vigorous and imaginative search for alternative courses of action. The goal is to profit from the course of events. The problem is to figure out how (Figure 10.3).

Detailed Planning Third, and a partial answer to figuring out how to profit from the course of events, is exploring the path from A to Z. An intent to profit is apt to remain a mere hope without conscious mental effort to trace the course from intent to objective. The manager can mentally travel the course pointed out by the new proposed course of action, investigating the rules affecting a partial or total conversion of dealerships from American-made motorcycles to Hondas.

One characteristic of effective executives is that they perform this phase of planning realistically and thoroughly. The inept manager does not. This

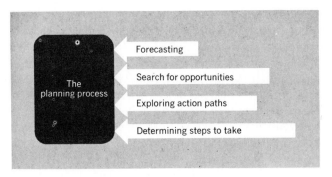

Figure 10.3 The planning process.

manager may get lucky, but is far more likely to trip over obstacles that were never looked for on the ground when hopes were in the sky. The effective manager takes pains to think through the course that must be followed, trying to anticipate the obstacles that must sooner or later be faced if success is to be achieved. The good manager does not limit this type of analysis to overall company plans, but applies it to all of the specific managerial problems that are part of the everyday operation of the firm.

Action Plans   Once the preceding steps have been taken, the final step of the planning process is to spell out the means of accomplishing the goal. This is the action plan. In reality, it often leaps to mind before preceding planning steps have been taken. Often action is taken before any planning at all occurs.

PLANNING AND PERFORMANCE

Professors Allan C. Filley of The University of Wisconsin and Robert J. House of York University, Toronto, reviewed research on planning to see whether planning is related to effective management. They found a number of laboratory experiments and studies of corporations which indicate that effective managers do plan more than less effective managers. In addition, more planning, up to a point, was related to organizational effectiveness. Companies with established planning programs were shown to out-perform those without formal planning. Finally, as you would suspect, research suggests that flexible plans are more likely to aid in achieving effectiveness than are plans that remain locked in place after circumstances change significantly.

TYPES OF PLANS

Planning activities differ in how detailed and specific they are and in the time period they cover. Activities that are more general and often cover a longer time period are strategic plans. Those that are more specific and detailed and often cover a shorter time period are tactical plans.

Programs and   Strategic plans include programs and policies. Programs specify certain
Policies objectives of special importance and the means of reaching them. For example, a large pulp and paper manufacturer established a program to fight pollution. A central office was created for this purpose and a manager placed in charge of the program. This individual's job was to develop means of curtailing or eliminating the flow of pollutants from the plant into its environment. The pollution control manager's authority was unclear, and it did not always exceed that of departmental managers responsible for production and sales quotas. As a result, the pollution control program was fairly vague,

and there was a relatively ineffective authorization to try to convince busy managers under conflicting pressures.

In another case, a state developed a program to combat alcoholism. The program director controlled substantial amounts of money that could be allocated to state agencies in proportion to the contribution of their activities to the prevention of alcoholism and rehabilitation of alcoholics. Agency heads found they depended upon the alcoholism program manager for funds to carry on activities they wished to implement. This program was more than a fuzzy objective. It was supported with authority and practices that gave it teeth.

Policies are another type of strategic plan. They provide general guides for action. In some cases, the policy guides decision making in a situation. A department store, for example, may have a policy of accepting all merchandise returned within 10 days of purchase unless the merchandise shows wear or damage. The clerk or manager still may exercise discretion, but there are some guidelines to help them (Figure 10.4).

To be sure, policies and programs shade into one another. They shade into more specific and detailed guidance, too. But for convenience's sake, we draw a line somewhere along the dimension of how specific and detailed that guidance is. The less discretion the plan leaves for decision making, the more it takes on the qualities of tactical planning.

Procedures, Rules, Budgets, and Schedules Tactical plans include such items as procedures, rules, budgets, and schedules. Procedures, for example, might go so far as to spell out the steps to be taken in handling customer complaints and merchandise returns. Standard regulations or procedures are common for an immense variety of business activities, ranging from the purchasing of supplies to the servicing of merchandise after sale. In fact, an early experience in the work careers of most salaried employees in large business organizations is the discovery of a thick volume or set of volumes called S.O.P. or Standard Operating Procedures.

Figure 10.4 Planning elements.

Rules are the most specific directions. "No Smoking," for example, leaves nothing to decide, unless it is whether or not to obey the rule.

Quantitative Plans   Budgets and schedules are quantitative or numerical plans. Budgets are usually expressed in terms of dollars, and schedules are expressed in terms of time. How much simpler the manager's job would be if only either the budget or the schedule had to be satisfied. Instead, usually both must be satisfied. The rub is that the action that satisfies one often interferes with satisfying the other.

A balanced response to multiple, conflicting standards is necessary. Because this is easier said than done, however, the practice of planning usually entails a continuous or periodic problem solving and change.

PLANNING: ADVANTAGES AND DISADVANTAGES

The advantages of strategic and tactical planning are many. General plans permit delegation to employees, who can exercise discretion and better handle the special qualities of individual cases, without loss of control. Specific plans can control the bounds of that discretion as intended by higher level managers. In other words, planning simultaneously permits decentralizing and centralizing decision making.

Strengths   Planning also provides known and approved means of handling routine situations or situations with recurring elements. It would be the height of inefficiency if every issue were handled in a novel way. It would be as if the organization had no memory and no core of preferences and values. Customer complaints, salary reviews, promotions, purchasing of supplies, customer relations, and other matters could then be handled by the whim and caprice of diverse personnel. Inequities and stupidities might be the results.

Employees, too, might be upset. People find routine and clarity desirable, not oppressive, when they are able to help deal sensibly with complex matters. The lack of policies, programs, and rules can be as disturbing as the presence of ineffectual ones.

Another particularly valuable feature of planning is realized when superiors and subordinates sit down together and talk over what the goals are and how they are to be reached. It is not entirely clear from research whether performance is always better if goals are set by superiors or by subordinates. But there is good reason to believe that the subordinate who discusses goals and the means of reaching them with his superior has an edge over the subordinate who may be equally highly motivated, but who has not explored the path from A to Z with his superior, with others, or with both. Even if the discussion does not increase motivation, it does generate useful information.

Weaknesses   Planning, too, has its problems however, and they can be serious enough to cancel out the benefits in some instances. For example, procedures, rules, and regulations can loom so large in the minds of some employees that they crowd out any sense of the basic purposes which they were meant to implement. Means become ends.

When this happens, the purchasing agent is scrupulously attentive to obtaining three bids, documenting every step of the procurement of supplies, and meeting other procedural requirements. Under ordinary circumstances, this is all to the good. But when it prevents the purchasing agent from helping an engineer who must buy a part to cope with a crisis, it looks like red tape (Figure 10.5).

There is a tendency to take the course of least resistance. If following the plan seems easier and more likely to be rewarded than exerting the effort to provide a special response to novel circumstances, then following the plan, however ill-suited it may be, can be seductive. Plans can be made irrelevant by changing circumstances; the risk is that they still may guide action.

Contradictions   We have already touched on another problem that occurs in planning: the problem of inconsistency between elements of planning. The schedule sets one target, the budget another, procurement regulations still another. A program to employ more minority group members might impose still another requirement to be served.

The manager can't please everybody, and plans don't always simplify decision-making. What they may do, however, is help the manager keep in mind the price to be paid for choosing one course over another. As in the In-Basket Exercise, if you wish to (and if you could) accommodate "Hap" and Ned Korbel, who has asked that you move up the delivery date from September 14 to September 7, then you must consider the effects on the training program, the equipment maintenance needs, the purchasing problem with the subcontractor, and the costs of overtime. Because these requirements are inconsistent doesn't mean the planning was defective, but it does reflect the inconsistencies that the manager faces in the complex world.

THE SPIRIT OF PLANNING

Perhaps what is most important to the success of planning is not the mechanics but the spirit. Planning both reflects and helps to set a climate for work. That climate can be one of trust and support, in which the mutual problem is to help do the best job and gain the most satisfaction from it. In sharp contrast, the climate can be one in which the felt problems are to avoid getting caught and punished for an error, to look good as opposed to doing the best job, and to look better than one's colleagues.

Planning Climate   Whatever techniques are employed, planning will inevitably reflect the spirit or climate in which it is conceived. Techniques that require trust, openness, and mutual support will fail where the hidden agenda is to set traps, to beat out somebody, or otherwise to deceive. Similarly, techniques of directive planning will fail without direction from above.

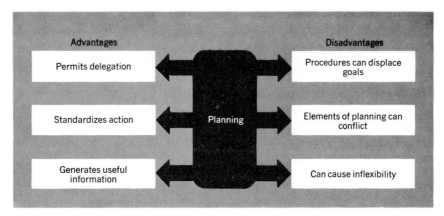

Figure 10.5   Mixed results from planning.

These conditions for success may seem obvious, but they are not always applied in practice. In planning, incongruities are all too common between the professed and the practice.

SUMMARY

We have seen that planning consists of a number of subprocesses and that each subprocess or phase affects the others and each can be a source of advantage or disadvantage. The weight of the evidence is that careful planning pays off. However, the risk is that these management processes can subvert the real objectives of the enterprise by becoming all important in the eyes of managers. Effective managers remain alert to this possibility.

HOSPITAL WAS READY FOR THEM

Emergency plan put into effect

SARA SCHWIEDER, INQUIRER STAFF WRITER

Only minutes after yesterday's train crash in Southwest Philadelphia, about 80 injured commuters suddenly flooded the emergency room at Misericordia Hospital, spilling into waiting rooms and corridors in a throng of blood-soaked confusion and tears.

They found wheelchairs and stretchers waiting. Doctors, nurses and emergency medical technicians also were ready.

The first task was to separate the most seriously injured from the others and wheel them to the emergency room, with hospital bracelets identifying each one. After that, those with more minor injuries were treated.

Dozens of boxes of bandages, splints and braces waited near a makeshift treatment room, and shortly after the first waves of patients had been processed through the specially beefed up admissions department, cartloads of hot coffee and tea appeared.

The source of the hospital's calm under pressure is its emergency diaster plan, which was invoked about 8:30 a.m. yesterday, only minutes before dozens of accident victims appeared.

Under the plan, which is painstakingly practiced at area hospitals twice a year, every detail is thought out and drilled into the staff so it can respond to a disaster coolly, hospital officials said. A city agency coordinates and supervises the disaster plans in Philadelphia and its four suburban counties, with help from the Philadelphia County Medical Society.

"You have to have everything ready to go in a minute when you hear that a disaster has been called on the loudspeaker," said John F. Sherlock, director of development and public affairs for the Mercy Catholic Medical Center, which operates Misericordia as well as the Fitzgerald Mercy Hospital in Darby.

"You have to be ready to go immediately. It is life-saving and life-protecting in a hospital. No one can have second thoughts about where they're supposed to be; everybody knows exactly where they're supposed to be."

Yesterday's accident occurred during the daytime, when most of the administrative and medical staff was already at the hospital, Michael J. Pavlo, the hospital administrator. But if an accident occurs at night, some of the staff is summoned from home, he said.

Yesterday at Misericordia, about 30 doctors and 40 nurses, and ultimately more than 300 hospital workers, performed their tasks under the provisions of the hospital disaster plan, Pavlo said.

A nurse on each floor keeps an up-to-date list of which patients could be discharged a day or two early if the hospital should run low on beds during an emergency. But yesterday, few were needed because only nine of the 80 treated had to be admitted, Pavlo said.

The Hospital of the University of Pennsylvania, which treated 68 of the accident victims, also relied on its disaster plan, which had been recently reviewed and tested in anticipation of the visit of Pope John Paul II. "The fact that we were anticipating problems with the Pope helped," one official said.

Although the hospital staffs probably will hold

Source. *Philadelphia Inquirer,* October 17, 1979.

critique sessions on how well their disaster plans worked, the patients at both Misericordia and University of Pennsylvania hospitals seemed to have already formed complimentary conclusions:

"You couldn't have asked for better treatment than we got here (University of Pennsylvania Hospital)," said one women with a big bandage on her chin.

Discussion Questions
1. What kind of assumptions underlie the "disaster plan"?
2. Does it make sense to plan for something that may never happen? Why or why not?

LONG-RANGE PLANNING

The Easiride Taxicab Company, located in a large midwestern city, had steadily increased its market share and profitability over 25 years. Its basic strategy was steadily to acquire licenses to operate cabs in this city, trying to obtain a few each year. After 25 years, the company had acquired 74 out of 197 licenses issued. In 1945, it had owned 12.

Like many other U.S. cities, this one had an entry control law, which restricted the total number of taxicabs that could operate in the city. In 1920, when the law was passed, 150 licenses were available. The number was increased to 197 in 1945 but this number had not been increased by 1968. The population of the city and nearby suburbs was 426,000 in 1920; 688,000 in 1950; and 1.1 million in 1966.

As the population grew and the number of taxicabs stayed the same, two things happened. First, each cab's earning power increased; demand for rides rose, while the supply of cabs did not. The Easiride Company planned its operations well with two-way radios and careful scheduling, so that by 1967 each cab was in use almost 20 hours per day, as compared to an average of nine hours per day in 1950. The firm was quite proud of its intensive utilization of its cabs, and profits per cab had more than tripled since 1950.

The second thing that happened was that the citizens grew increasingly restive about taxicab service. It was impossible to find a cab on a rainy night, and many irate citizens constantly complained to the press and the politicans about the terrible service.

The cost of obtaining a license in 1920 was $10—the price of the filing fee. By 1930, any firm wanting a taxi license had to buy it at a price of $3,000 or more from someone who already owned one. In effect, a man had to buy his job as a taxi driver. By 1967, the available licenses were being sold for $21,000 and more. Easiride knew every license owner, and one secret of its success was to offer quickly to buy an available license when it came on the market, which happened when an owner died or decided to cash in his capital gain.

Easiride's profits rose from $12,000 in 1945 to $227,000 in 1967. The firm planned to acquire at least 20 more licenses by 1970, and it already had spotted the owners of these licenses and had made arrangements to buy them when the owners were ready to sell.

Source. Richard N. Farmer, Barry M. Richman, and William G. Ryan, *Incidents for Studying Management and Organization* (Belmont, Calif.: Wadsworth Publishing Co., 1970), pp. 22–23. Reprinted by permission of the publisher.

In the 1967 city election, a new mayor was elected on a reform platform. The mayor had once studied transportation economics, and one of his first acts was to modify drastically the taxicab control law, patterning it after that in Washington, D.C. This new law provided that anyone who was bondable, had a valid chauffeur's license, bought insurance, and passed a test to prove his knowledge of city streets could get a license to operate a cab.

Within a year, over 300 cabs were in operation in this city, including many operated by former drivers for Easiride. Some of its best men took advantage of the new law to go into business for themselves. Within 18 months, over 600 cabs were in operation. The cost of a license fell to $25, the fee which the city charged for registration and testing. Cab fares fell from an average of 45 cents per mile to 15 cents, and Easiride went bankrupt late in 1969.

Discussion Questions
1. Analyze this incident from the standpoint of good planning practice. Where did Easiride go wrong? Why?
2. What major planning issues are present here?
3. Would a company owning many chain supermarkets be likely to have this kind of problem? Why or why not? How about the manufacturer of a soft drink with a copyrighted name?

Planning involves forecasting, finding opportunities and obstacles, exploring the path from A to Z, and spelling out the means of accomplishing goals.

Planning activities divide into two main types: strategies and tactics. Strategies are more general and often involve a longer time span. Programs and plans are the major types of strategies. Tactics include procedures, rules, budgets, and schedules.

The advantages of planning are principally that it permits delegation without loss of control, helps clarify proposed courses of action, and generates useful information. But these benefits are often accompanied by some disadvantages. Plans can displace goals, for example, by making procedures seem more important than end results. Plans can also block quick action and lose relevance to changing circumstances, thus encouraging undesirable behavior.

Here are some principles:

1. Forecasting isn't always easy, but it can be useful.

2. Planning discussions should not be hurried or slighted. They often reveal new information and teach much.

3. Careful planning makes delegation easier.

4. How detailed plans should be depends on how much room should be left for subordinates to exercise discretion in light of special and changing circumstances.

5. Managers must guard against plans, for example, procedures and rules, taking on more importance than intended and actually displacing goals.

CHAPTER
ELEVEN

ORGANIZATION STRUCTURE

LEARNING OBJECTIVES

After studying this chapter, you should be able to:

1. Describe four contributions that structure makes to the functioning of organizations.
2. List four principles of authority.
3. Discuss four key factors in organizing.
4. Define the conditions under which centralization and decentralization may be used.
5. Explain the two coordination strategies and the environmental and task conditions under which each may be successful.

GREETING CARDS, INCORPORATED

I. Objectives
   A. To accomplish a task within an organizational framework.
   B. To try to outproduce another organization working on same task.
   C. To compare alternative organizational structures.
II. Premeeting Preparation
   A. Read the instructions.
   B. The instructor will assign you to a company. Read the directions for that company. The instructor may also assign you to a management position in that company.
   C. Think about the instructions and directions, but do not discuss the exercise with others before class.
III. Instructions
   A. The instructor may draft a few students to assist in the exercise.
   B. For this exercise the remainder of the class will divide into two groups of equal size.
   C. Each group will operate as a company producing greeting card verses.
   D. Each greeting card consists of a two-line verse. The verses may be serious or humorous. They are designed for various occasions such as birthdays, Christmas, graduation, and so on. Sample verses for a graduation are shown below.

Graduation

It's been many years of parents' bills,
For books and board and certain frills.

* * *

But now it's graduation and a job.
You're on your own at last, you slob.

Quality Standards: Verses that are to meet acceptable quality standards must have correct grammar, spelling, and punctuation. The two lines must rhyme. Poetic license is also allowed.
   E. Pages 293 through 307 are forms on which you are to write your verses. Each page contains six verses.
   F. Each company will be assigned a set of instructions to follow. If the instructor assigns you to Company A, read the directions on page 289. If the instructor assigns you to Company B, read the directions on page 291. The instructor will name persons to fill the management positions in each company.

G. Each company will meet to plan how its operations will be carried out.

> *Time for Step G: 8 minutes*

H. Two work periods will follow.
1. In the first period your company, in response to purchase orders, is to produce as many cards as possible for the following occasions.
   a. Birthdays
   b. Valentine's Day
   c. Get well

> *Time for Step H:1: 8 minutes*

2. In the second period your company, in response to new purchase orders, is to produce as many cards as possible for the following occasions.
   a. Graduation
   b. Christmas and New Year
   c. Mother's Day

> *Time for Step H:2: 8 minutes*

I. At the close of each work period, the instructor or one of the assistants will pick up the verses each company has prepared. The verses will then be checked for quality, and unacceptable ones will be rejected as will duplicates.
J. After the second work period is completed and the verses have been handed over, you should turn to page 309, headed Opinion Survey. Answer its questions.
K. After you have completed the Opinion Survey, score it by summing the numbers you selected as a response to each of the items. Put the total score at the top of the page and turn the page over to the secretary of your company.
L. Productivity and Opinion Survey results will be tabulated for each company and presented to the class.

> *Time for Steps K and L: 5 minutes*

IV. Discussion

Your instructor will help you explore what happened in the exercise and its meaning for management.

> *Time for Discussion: 10 minutes*

COMPANY A

Directions

You have 10 minutes to review these directions and plan to implement them.

Your company is a business firm producing greeting card verses. Your organization structure is depicted in Figure 11.1. Your instructor has already assigned persons to fill each job in the chart.

The responsibilities of the General Manager include the overall direction and coordination of the company. The general manager is the boss, and is responsible for conducting the planning session and for the success of operations according to this structure.

The responsibilities of the Production Design Manager include generating the ideas for greeting card verses within the limits of purchase orders. This department must create the ideas and pass them along to Production.

The Production Manager's department is responsible for actually writing complete verses. This department takes the ideas given by Product Design and develops them into complete products. Then, it passes the complete verses to Quality Control.

The Quality Control Department is responsible for the inspection, and accepted verses are to be passed to the secretary. Verses defective in some way may be changed or corrected by Quality Control or passed back to Production for rework.

The secretary will receive and count all verses supplied by Production. At the end of each work period the secretary will hand the verses over to the instructor or the assistant. At the same time the secretary will inform the instructor of the total number of verses produced in that period and how many there were of each of the three product types specified in the purchase order.

As stated in the general instructions for this exercise, the person who receives the verses will check them for quality. Unacceptable ones will be rejected as will duplicates.

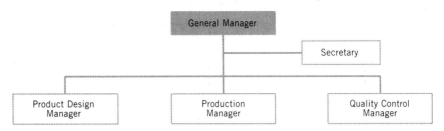

Figure 11.1   Organization structure of Company A.

The company secretary will have one additional duty. At the end of the second work period the Opinion Surveys are to be completed and scored by each person, including all of the persons assigned the jobs in the organization chart. These are to be turned over to the secretary who is responsible for adding the total scores for all of the Opinion Surveys and dividing by the total number of persons in Company A. The secretary may need to draft some persons to assist in the prompt and accurate completion of this chore.

COMPANY B

Directions

You have 10 minutes to review these directions and plan to implement them.

Your company is a business firm producing greeting card verses. Your organization structure is depicted in Figure 11.2. Your instructor has already assigned persons to fill each job in the chart.

The responsibilities of the General Manager include the overall direction and coordination of the company. The general manager is the boss, and is responsible for conducting the plan session and for the success of operations according to this structure.

The responsibilities of each Product Manager are identical. Each one is responsible for the complete preparation of one type of greeting card verse, as assigned by the General Manager, in each work period.

The secretary will receive and count all verses supplied by the Product Managers. At the end of each work period the secretary will hand the verses over to the instructor or the assistant. At the same time the secretary will inform the instructor of the total number of verses produced in that period and how many of each of the three product types are specified in the purchase order.

As stated in the general instructions for this exercise, the instructor who receives the verses will check them for quality. Unacceptable ones will be rejected as will duplicates.

The company secretary will have one additional duty. At the end of the second work period the Opinion Surveys are to be completed and scored by each person, including all of the persons assigned the jobs in the organization chart. These are to be turned over to the secretary who is responsible for adding the total scores for all of the Opinion Surveys and dividing by the total number of persons in Company B. The secretary may need to draft some persons to assist in the prompt and accurate completion of this chore.

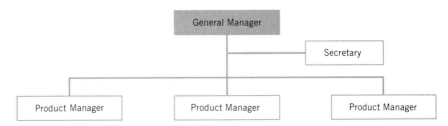

Figure 11.2   Organization Structure of Company B.

GREETING CARDS, INCORPORATED

Verses
Company _____ (Please indicate A or B)

1. _____

   _____

   * * *

2. _____

   _____

   * * *

3. _____

   _____

   * * *

4. _____

   _____

   * * *

5. _____

   _____

   * * *

6. _____

   _____

GREETING CARDS, INCORPORATED

Verses
Company _____ (Please indicate A or B)

1. _____

_____

* * *

2. _____

_____

* * *

3. _____

_____

* * *

4. _____

_____

* * *

5. _____

_____

* * *

6. _____

_____

GREETING CARDS, INCORPORATED

Verses
Company _____ (Please indicate A or B)

1. _____

   _____

   * * *

2. _____

   _____

   * * *

3. _____

   _____

   * * *

4. _____

   _____

   * * *

5. _____

   _____

   * * *

6. _____

   _____

GREETING CARDS, INCORPORATED

Verses
Company _____ (Please indicate A or B)

1. _____

_____

* * *

2. _____

_____

* * *

3. _____

_____

* * *

4. _____

_____

* * *

5. _____

_____

* * *

6. _____

_____

GREETING CARDS, INCORPORATED

Verses

Company _____ (Please indicate A or B)

1. _____

   _____

   * * *

2. _____

   _____

   * * *

3. _____

   _____

   * * *

4. _____

   _____

   * * *

5. _____

   _____

   * * *

6. _____

   _____

GREETING CARDS, INCORPORATED

Verses
Company _____ (Please indicate A or B)

1. _____

   _____

* * *

2. _____

   _____

* * *

3. _____

   _____

* * *

4. _____

   _____

* * *

5. _____

   _____

* * *

6. _____

   _____

GREETING CARDS, INCORPORATED

Verses

Company _____ (Please indicate A or B)

1. _____

_____

* * *

2. _____

_____

* * *

3. _____

_____

* * *

4. _____

_____

* * *

5. _____

_____

* * *

6. _____

_____

GREETING CARDS, INCORPORATED

Verses
Company _____ (Please indicate A or B)

1. _____

   _____

$$* \ * \ *$$

2. _____

   _____

$$* \ * \ *$$

3. _____

   _____

$$* \ * \ *$$

4. _____

   _____

$$* \ * \ *$$

5. _____

   _____

$$* \ * \ *$$

6. _____

   _____

OPINION SURVEY

Please check the number on the following scales that best reflects your feelings

1. Satisfaction with job

1	2	3	4	5
My job is not at all satisfying		My job is moderately satisfying		My job is especially satisfying

2. Satisfaction with other people in the company

1	2	3	4	5
I do not at all enjoy the other people in the company		I have mixed feelings about the other people in the company		I especially enjoy the other people in the company

3. Sense of competence

1	2	3	4	5
I do not feel at all that I am doing my job well		I feel I am doing my job with average effectiveness		I feel I am doing my job especially well

4. Satisfaction with organization

1	2	3	4	5
I do not at all like the way this company is set up and operated		I feel moderately satisfied with the way this company is set up and operated		I feel especially pleased with the way this company is set up and operated

THE TEXT

A key management function is designing the organization structure. By that we mean establishing a formal network of authority—who reports to whom about what. The structure usually is depicted in a chart that shows the locations and reporting relationships of the units and management positions in the organization.

Although the formal organization structure is not the total operating reality, it is a key factor in determining what a living organization is like, how well it performs, and how the people within it feel. The exercise you have just completed, "Greeting Cards, Inc." offers a laboratory-like glimpse at the effects of structure on performance and satisfaction. We will return to the lessons of Greeting Cards, Inc., later in this chapter. But for now let's look at how structure combines people and tasks into an operating reality.

WHAT STRUCTURE DOES

Specifies Authority and Responsibility Structure contributes to the functioning or organizations in several ways. First, as we have already said, structure allocates authority and responsibility. It specifies who is to direct whom, and it specifies who is accountable for what results. Without some clear understanding of obligations and expectations, some employees might perform too little, others too much, and others might merely engage in irrelevant activities. Every actor—the person on the assembly line, the salesperson in the field, the chemist in the laboratory, and the manager in the office—has a role to play. The structure helps them know what the role is and how it relates to other roles.

Provides Communication Second, structure provides communication and coordination. By grouping together activities and people, structure facilitates communication among people centered on their job activities. People whose work must mesh or who have joint problems to solve often need to share information. In some cases this need may mean that the electronics engineers ought to be grouped in one department to help them communicate and pool the technical expertise they can bring to the design of the TV set. In other cases it may mean electronics engineers ought to be scattered among new product development groups comprising other specialists as well, to be sure the new innards of the TV set will fit within the chassis. The former arrangement stresses communication among specialists, the latter coordination between specialists.

Locates Decision Making Third, structure determines the location of decision-making in the organization. A department store, for example, might develop a structure that leaves pricing, merchandise selection, sales promotion, and other matters largely up to individual departments to assure that varied departmental conditions are considered. In contrast, a highly integrated oil refinery might concentrate production, maintenance, and scheduling decisions at top levels

Drawing by Brickman © 1973 Washington Star Syndicate, Inc.

in the structure to assure that interdependencies along the flow of work are considered.

Balance and Emphasize Activities Fourth, structure can create the proper balance and emphasis of activities. Those more critical to the firm's success might be placed high in the organization. Styling and design in a high fashion clothing manufacturer, or research in a pharmaceutical firm, for example, might be singled out for reporting to the president to stress their importance.

STRUCTURES AND THE PRINCIPLES OF AUTHORITY

Unity of Command In determining who reports to whom about what, managers generally follow four principles of authority. The first principle is the unity of command, which states that each person should work for only one boss. The principle is often followed, although those of you who have worked in an organization know that many nonbosses often have bosslike authority. A customer, for instance, is not the direct boss of the salesperson, but negative comments from the customer to the sales manager can get the salesperson in deep trouble. So, although each person usually reports to one official boss, there are many other authority figures around.

Scalar or Chain of Command Second is the chain of command, or scalar principle. This states that authority flows in an unbroken line from the top of the organization to the bottom. Employees are expected to check first with their boss before making agreements with people in other departments. This principle demands that manufacturing supervisors, for instance, check first with higher-level managers before agreeing to change production schedules to meet a particular sales request. This principle helps to insure consistent action up and down the organization ladder, and helps keep all organizational eyes on the same target.

Parity Principle   Third is the parity principle. This stresses that authority and responsibility must go hand in hand. Authority without responsibility leads to anarchy. Responsibility without authority leads to frustration—and an early managerial grave. Under this principle, individuals are assigned the authority necessary to carry out their responsibilities.

Span of Control   Fourth is the span of control. This concerns the number of individuals reporting to each manager. The span of control significantly affects the number of levels in an organization. The wider the span of control (i.e., the more individuals reporting to each managerial position), usually the fewer the levels in the organization, and the shorter the communication channels. Spans of control vary widely from 1 or 2 individuals to as many as 24, with 8 as an overall industry average. The width of the span of control in a given situation is based on the ability to effectively manage that number of subordinates. Some organizations, such as department stores, for instance, have flat structures with a large number of relatively autonomous department managers reporting to a single store manager. In those situations, each department can be run as an independent business, (and, in fact, often is leased to an independent subcontractor). In contrast, a smaller span of control is needed in an oil refinery, where the production process requires a high degree of interdependence.

Structure is based on these four principles. In designing who reports to whom about what, managers aim to have: (1) each person work for only one boss (the unity of command); (2) an unbroken line of top to bottom authority (chain of command); (3) authority matching responsibility (parity); (4) a manageable number of individuals reporting to each position (span of control).

KEY STRUCTURE DECISIONS

In deciding on a structure, a manager must make at least three key decisions. The manager must first decide how jobs will be grouped together into organizational subunits called departments. Managers can usually choose between two basic departmental structures, functional or product, and two combinations of these, matrix, and/or project.

Departmentation determines whether, for instance, all of the engineers work together in one department or are scattered throughout several departments, depending on the products with which they are working. Next, the manager needs to decide whether these departments will be centralized or decentralized. These departments are centralized if most of the important decisions are made at the top of the organization. If most are made by lower-level personnel, then it is decentralized. In addition, a manager must decide how these departments, centralized or decentralized, will be coordinated. It is important that all of the departments move toward the same goal, at approximately the same rate. So, the manager needs to decide how to divide up the work of the organization into subunits called departments, which are either centralized or decentralized. The manager then needs to decide how to put these pieces back together to coordinate them.

KEY FACTORS IN CHOOSING A STRUCTURE

In selecting a a structure, a manager must consider several key factors. These include (but are not limited to): environment, task and technology, people, and coordination requirements.

Environment

Stability and Diversity The environments of organizations vary in at least two important ways: stability and diversity. For example, some firms, such as paper products producers, face a relatively steady and predictable demand for their products or services. Others, such as computer companies, face rapid and unpredictable changes in demand. Firms can vary along the dimension of stability in other ways as well. Labor markets can be more or less stable, suppliers more or less reliable, technology more or less stable, and political and economic conditions more or less predictable. But whatever the relevant areas and rates of change outside the firm, they amount to conditions to which the firm must adapt if it is to be successful.

In an effort to study the impact of environmental stability on organizations, Tom Burns and G. M. Stalker of the University of Edinburgh, Scotland, studied 20 Scottish and English firms engaged in electronics and other industries. They observed that successful firms in stable environments organized differently than those in rapidly changing ones. Those firms facing stable environments developed a mechanistic management style, whereas those facing unstable environmental conditions adopted a more organic style. Mechanistic styles were characterized by: functional organizational structures, specialized and fragmented work roles, explicit job descriptions, working chains of command, a tendency for superiors and subordinates to interact rather than a tendency for interaction among co-equals, and for superiors to give directions in those interactions. Organic systems were characterized by loosely defined responsibility with an emphasis upon contributing competence to the common task rather than carrying out a limited range of specific duties, tendency to interact laterally with co-equals rather than vertically with superiors or subordinates, and for these interactions to emphasize exchanges of information rather than the giving of directions.

The same is true of diversity. For example, a chain of supermarkets may face a wide range of socioeconomic conditions from area to area. Or consider the manufacturer of electronic products. Its research and development staff may face a scientific world requiring long-term studies and analyses of products five years in the future. Simultaneously, its sales staff may face fiercely competitive short-run marketing competition, and be worried about meeting next month's sales quota. The firm's effectiveness depends on each group being different in the face of diverse subenvironments.

Lawrence and Lorsch researched the effect of environmental diversity on organization structure. They found successful organizations operating within stable environments, such as container and basic material producing firms (steel and paper), had little internal diversity. That is, production people were not much different from salespeople in both attitude and orientation. This may be why such organizations had mechanistic structures. On the other hand, organizations operating within unstable environments, such as electronics firms, had much greater internal diversity. In general, stability in the environment is associated with more mechanistic and formalistic organizational structures, centralized planning, formalized job descriptions, and tall hierarchies. On the other hand, organizations confronting rapidly changing environments seem to adopt more organic structures with decentralized planning, with more of an emphasis upon group problem-solving, less-defined job descriptions, and a more team-oriented participative approach.

Tasks and Technology

The nature of the tasks to be performed and the technology with which they are to be performed is another factor to be considered in selecting a structure. The Greeting Cards, Inc. exercise you performed at the beginning of this chapter provides an illustration. A useful starting point in analyzing the results of this exercise is to consider the behavior called for by the firm's major task: composing rhyming verses. The individual employee's contribution is to write different kinds of verses. Success at this kind of work requires creative imagination, idea generation, and problem solving. The exercise is designed to discover if, by varying only the structure and by trying to keep other conditions constant, we obtain differences in productivity and satisfaction associated with performance of the same task.

Of course, we don't know what happened in your class. But in a large number of classes where Greeting Cards, Inc. has been used, the people in Company B seem to write more verses and enjoy the work more in product organizations. This is not always the case of course. Sometimes the results are reversed. This is sometimes because the organization doesn't operate according to the plan. It can also be due to other causes, such as concentration of gifted verse writers in one group. More often than not, however, Company B wins.

Why? The answer seems to be that breaking up the whole task of composing a verse of satisfactory quality into fragments—product design, production, and quality control—and assigning these subtasks to different people, creates a number of problems that damage productivity and satisfaction. No group has a responsibility for more than a piece of the total effort and product. Coordination between groups doesn't always go smoothly. Production personnel sometimes find it hard to understand the incomplete notions given them by Product Design. Production people are sometimes unable to use some of their own ideas, and they may resent rejections by Quality Control. There is also often a confusion over who will prepare each type of card. And, employees often feel frustrated at doing only pieces of a whole unit of work.

Technical Excellence

But let's consider another situation. Suppose that the task calls for high levels of training and knowledge, as distinct from the lack of special training of the verse writer. Requirements for technical expertise may point toward a structure that puts all the engineers together. Grouping all of the electrical engineers in one department, the propulsion engineers in another, and the mechanical engineers in still another, can foster interaction centered on professional accomplishment in each discipline. Although emphasis on the product as a whole may be weakened, needed technical excellence may be concentrated on electrical, propulsion, and mechanical components and systems.

Centralization/Decentralization

Alternatively, other tasks might call for concentrating skills of a different sort in a different way. To recall an earlier example, a chain of department stores may find wide variation in consumption patterns from region to region. Accordingly, a territorial structure that decentralizes sales promotion responsibilities may be able to take advantage of local circumstances known best by local store managers.

In contrast, as another earlier example suggests, a large producer of chemicals or petroleum products may need to concentrate production planning at high levels in its structure. Only at high levels would there be sufficient marketing, purchasing, production information, and competence to commit massive economic resources. In this instance, task and technology call for the opposite of decentralization.

The late Professor Joan Woodward of Britain's Imperial College of Science and Technology studied the relationship between technology and organizational structure in over 100 manufacturing firms. She found that successful firms with different technologies had different organizational structures. Unit production firms, those producing single products to order (anything from a tailor-made suit to a large and complex airplane), averaged three levels of management from top to bottom in the organization structure. Mass production firms (e.g., automobile and TV manufacturers) averaged four levels. Process chemical firms (continuous flow production, e.g., petroleum, chemicals, pharmaceuticals), averaged six levels. In unit production firms, first-line supervisors had an average span of control of 21 to 30 subordinates. In mass production firms, the figure was only 11 to 20. The most successful firms in each type of industry had structures that were the medium for their industry.

Woodward concluded that there was no one best way to organize for all production tasks. Instead, her data suggested some aspects of structure help firms to cope successfully with the distinctive problems posed by its type of technology.

Coordination Requirements

The key problem that an organization faces often provides a good clue to its coordination requirements. The problem experienced by a manufacturer of computer equipment provides one example. The firm faced a key problem of incorporating technical innovations in its products rapidly and frequently in order to keep pace with competitors. One group, Sales, had regular contacts with customers. The salespeople were in close touch with changing customer needs and with the product innovations of competitors. Another group, Product Engineering and Development, was a separate functional department. There was no systematic interaction between the salespeople and the people who might have used their information in developing products. Cooperation between Sales and Research was strategic in this case. Consequently, a critical problem in organization design was to provide adequate collaboration or integration at these strategic points. For major products, the structure provided a product group that included sales, product development, and other personnel. The results were remarkable. Not only was sales-product development interaction increased, but this collaboration resulted in a sharp increase in patent applications and sales volume.

In another case, a container manufacturing plant, the main issue was keying volume of output to demand. Here, linkage between sales and production was critical. A good production planning system, with strong leadership and tight controls, was all that was necessary to obtain required collaboration. In other cases where collaboration requirements are not so simply handled, intermediary jobs, such as liaison people, expediters, and coordinators, are created to link departments. Committees are also used to provide contact and share decision making. A good example is the Change Review Board in aerospace firms, which is used to examine the implications of proposed product changes.

Lawrence and Lorsch discovered that the best clue as to how much integration is needed and where it was needed (say, between sales and production, and/or between product development and sales) is the dominant competitive issue faced by the firm. For example, a food firm needs to match closely the production of their perishable products to the demand for them. The firms that had achieved the closer collaboration of production and sales were more successful. For plastics firms, however, technological innovation was a more critical business issue, and the firms that had closer coordination between product development and sales were better able to handle that issue.

People

A final clue as to the appropriate structure is the level of education or talent of the employees. High talent personnel are normally hired to exercise discretion within their spheres of competence. People of modest education are often hired to fill well-established routines. People in unit technologies, for instance, tend to be mainly highly skilled tradespeople. The skilled tool and die maker, for instance, must utilize all of the equipment in the shop to produce a prototype, one-of-a-kind model. Similarly, a skilled research and development scientist applies generalized knowledge to a specific chemical or metallurgical problem. On the other hand, people in mass production technique industries can be less experienced because their jobs are more predictable. An automobile assembler, a clerk in a large insurance office, or a bank teller needs to know less because their job is more standardized. Employees in a process technology need to be highly trained, but in a limited sphere. Oil refinery technicians, for instance, are responsible for millions of dollars of equipment and must know what to do if dial readings reach certain levels. But, this high degree of training has a narrow application. There are few other jobs to which it could be usefully applied. In general, broadly experienced people are most likely to be found in unit technology companies, narrowly experienced people in mass production activities, and highly trained but narrowly experienced people in process situations.

It is important to organize in a way that contributes both to the firm's productivity and the satisfaction of individual members. Examination of the firm's environment, the nature of its task, the critical coordination requirement, and the characteristics of its personnel constitute a first step. Each type of departmental structure—functional, product, matrix or project—has distinctive advantages. The choice is determined by one central consideration: Which structure will help the organization cope most effectively with its situation?

TYPES OF DEPARTMENTAL STRUCTURE

To realize the several contributions that structure can make to the organization, the manager must choose from two basic structural designs, or any combination of them. Each has its distinctive quality and emphasis. The advantages of one often are the disadvantages of the other. Each departmental structure involves a trade-off, and requires that individual managers focus on the most important dimensions of their situation. The basic forms are departmentation by function or product, and the two most popular combinations are matrix and project.

Functional Departments

This involves grouping jobs according to the similarity of skills required or tasks performed. In typical manufacturing firms, this would group together all engineers in the engineering department, all welders in the welding department, all accountants in the accounting department. In a hospital, all operating personnel are grouped in the O.R. Department, all X-ray technicians in the Radiology Department, and all food service personnel in the dietary department. This is depicted in Figure 11.3.

Functional Departments Group Jobs According to Similar Skills

Functional departmental structures seem to be most successful when environmental conditions are stable (as in the basic materials industry, paper and steel), and mass production techniques are used (as in the production of automobiles or processing of insurance claims). Functional department structures, for example, provide the greatest institutional commitment to permanence. They help the firm establish routines and patterns suited to predictable environments and to realizing economies of scale. They emphasize the differences between research and sales by clearly splitting them apart and establishing each as a separate entity. Where stable patterns inside the firm help get the job done, functional structures can help create those patterns.

Best in Stable Environments and Mass Production Technologies

Technically Superior Products

Functional departmental structures often lead to superior technical performance. By putting all of the engineers together in one department, they can learn from each other, pick up new ideas, and receive encouragement and support from other people who share their technical background. An MIT study, and the Lawrence and Lorsch results, confirm that technically superior products are most often produced by functionally organized departments.

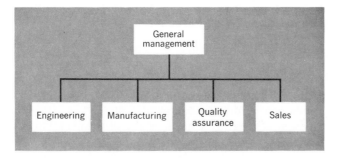

Figure 11.3   Functional organization.

Employee Stability   Functional departments also provide employees with the greatest sense of stability and predictability. By providing a set of standardized regulations and clear standards of performance, employees come to know what is expected and how to succeed.

Less Interdepartmental Cooperation   Such department structures are not without their disadvantages, however. Often, functionally organized departments refused to cooperate with each other in the pursuit of overall organizational goals. The Engineering Department strives to design the "world's best product," which the Production Department cannot economically produce. The Sales Department often strives for maximum product-line flexibility, which the Engineering Department cannot possibly design. This tunnel-vision problem often creates functional empires which are constantly at war with each other, washing out many of the benefits of improved efficiency.

Client Needs Sometimes Get Lost   Furthermore, in the emphasis on technical superiority, client needs often become lost. All of us have been confronted with the maddening, "I know it's not right, but it's the rule." This is one of the disadvantages of functional departments which emphasize internal regulations to the detriment of the client's interests.

Slow to Change   In addition, although the commitment to permanence is one of the strengths of the functional departmentation strategies, it is also its greatest weakness. Tomorrow may not necessarily be an extension of yesterday. Markets change and firms must change with them. The railroad's focus on fixed rail transportation, rather than the movement of goods regardless of method, causes them to lose out to the profitable trucking business. Automobile companies are notoriously slow to change, and have seen foreign car imports eat into their market. Functional structures are slow to change, and this is one of their chief disadvantages.

In short, functional departmentation concentrates technical competence which often produces improved technical performance and efficiency. It works well in a stable environment, and is particularly suited to mass production techniques. In such organizations, however, client needs can get lost, departmental objectives may become more important than overall company objectives, and change may be too slow to meet marketplace demands.

Product Structure

Product Departments Group Jobs According to Similar Objectives or Clients   This involves grouping jobs on the basis of common goals and objectives. Many companies are organized around a common purpose, each self-contained unit being a microcosm of the organization as a whole. Departments can be organized around a product, as for example, the Chevrolet Division of General Motors, or the police department in your city (Figure 11.4). It may also be organized around a particular customer or market as, for example, the commercial products division of most aerospace companies, the intensive care wing of the local hospital, or the women's wear department of the local department store. Product-type departments are also organized according to geography (Figure 11.5). Many retail chains, such as Sears Roebuck and J. C. Penney, and food stores such as Safeway, have semi-autonomous regional product-type departments. All of these combine dissimilar activities to create departments that focus on a common objective.

Best in Unstable Environments and with Unit and/or Process Technologies

Product departments are most suited to rapidly changing environmental conditions, and either unit or process-type technologies. Product, territory, and client-centered organizations are more flexible. They are to organization design what modular building units are to architecture—ad hoc components that can be added or dropped as necessary with relative ease. For example, as a big advertising agency loses one client, it can drop its ad hoc client-centered unit (Figure 11.6). Structurally aided flexibility inside the organization helps the firm cope with instability outside of it. Hence, where instability is a major feature of the environment, more fluid structures have an advantage.

Adaptable and Innovative

A product-type department focuses more on client needs, and is more adaptable to rapidly shifting customer requirements. A Harvard University study of 285 businesses showed that product organized firms did a better job

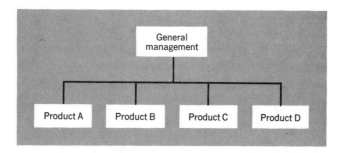

Figure 11.4 Product organization.

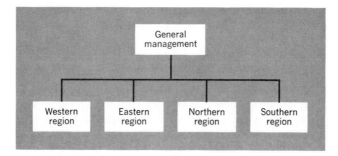

Figure 11.5 Territorial organization.

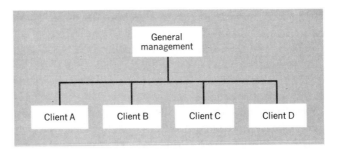

Figure 11.6   Client-centered organization.

in adapting to changing customer needs by creating and selling new products. With the shift in customer demands in some industries averaging every 6 to 18 months (e.g., computers and electronics) this is a major advantage.

Better Business Performance Product organizations focus people's energies on the needs of a given customer or product. As a result, improved business performance is often realized. The MIT study found that government contractors who were organized on a product basis had a better record of meeting schedule and cost deadlines. A product organization may not produce the best product, but it often produces a product that best meets customer demands at the best costs.

Less Technical Expertise All is not perfect in the purpose organization, however. Product organizations are usually not the technical leaders in their fields. Spreading out engineers to all product departments often prevents the synergistic interaction among them which is necessary to generate new technological breakthroughs. Product departments are refiners of older ideas, not the developers of new breakthrough ones.

Higher Employee Anxiety Furthermore, because of the instability in the organization, employees in product departments experience tension and anxiety. Their performance standards are less clear-cut, and there are fewer past guidelines upon which to rely. The more frequent job transfers required in a product organization (as some products die and others are born) contribute to this general employee anxiety.

Duplicate Services Furthermore, product organizations have frequent duplication and overlap. It is not uncommon for each product department, for instance, to have its own purchasing activities, despite the savings of mass purchasing. Duplicate accounting and personnel activities are also frequently found in product organizations.

In general, where the environment is rapidly changing and client needs rather than technological excellence are the key to success, product departments may be advantageous. Technical capability is lowered, however, and employees pay a higher price in anxiety. Where the environment is relatively stable, technological superiority is the key to success, and the technology can be routinized and standardized, functional departments may be more valuable. In an effort to overcome some of the limitations of each departmental design, and capitalize on its strengths, many organizations have turned to two hybrid department structures—the matrix and the project.

Matrix

Matrix Organizations Provide Both a Functional and a Product Boss This structure involves both departmentation by function and product. It overlays a product structure on a functional one as shown in Figure 11.8. The dotted lines in the figure represent a special organization clustered around Product A, and comprise personnel who are members of various functional departments. They "belong" to Engineering, but they apply their talents to Product A and work for the manager of that product. The Product Manager parcels out the work on the product, and "contracts" for help from the functional departments. As the chart shows, there are two lines of authority in a matrix organization. Each exercises equal influence. The result is that each person works for two bosses—a functional boss and a product boss. This forces people to think about both the demands of their specialty and the needs of the customer. For example, the electronics engineer must be con-

Factor	Function Departmentation		Product Departmentation	
	Advantage	Disadvantage	Advantage	Disadvantage
A. Efficiency of resource use, production/operation	+			−
B. Coordination cost		−	+	
C. Willingness to adapt and change		−	+	
D. Ease of measurement of output and results	+			−
E. Preparation of broadly trained managers and employees		−	+	
F. Preparation of well-trained specialists	+			−
G. Interdepartmental conflict		−	+	
H. Client satisfaction		−	+	

Figure 11.7   Advantages and Disadvantages of Function and Product Approaches to Departmentation.

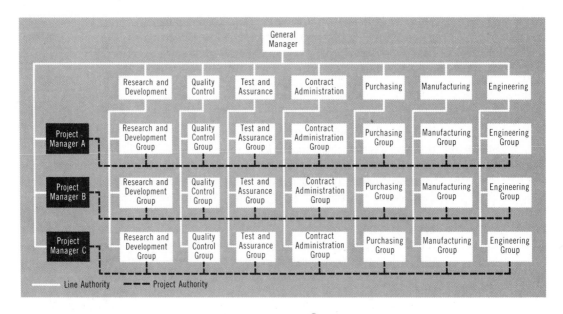

Figure 11.8   Matrix organization.

cerned with both designing a product that can be praised technologically by other engineers in the functional department, and yet meeting the customer needs for costs, quality, and performance, as demanded by the product manager.

Increase Flexibility   Matrix organizations generally increase operating flexibility. By pushing decisions down to lower organizational levels, the organization can respond more rapidly to changing market conditions. Furthermore, by focusing energies on certain specific programs, the matrix structure helps the organization

Better Operating Results capitalize more quickly on market opportunities. Operating results are better with a matrix organization, particularly where complex products are being produced in a rapidly changing environment. Shell Oil, for instance, turned their chemical operations from a loss to a profit through adopting the matrix structure.

Costly Conversions   But, there are disadvantages. The conversion to a matrix structure takes time, a great deal of retraining, and often managerial turnover. Shell Oil, for instance, took 4 difficult years to convert fully, and it cost them a number of

Authority/ Responsibility Gap executives who could not adapt. The responsibility/authority gap is one of the most difficult problems to overcome. Most managers have been raised on the parity principle, matching authority with responsibility. The matrix organization violates this principle by assigning the Product Manager responsibility for the product without the corresponding authority to control the people who work on it, but still report to the functional department.

This often causes high employee uncertainty and anxiety. The shifting sands of authority, one day function manager, one day product manager, leaves employees in the dark as to which boss to follow when.

On balance, matrix department structures seem particularly suited to situations that demand high technical product excellence to meet rapidly changing customer demands. This has led many organizations in the aerospace, electronics, computer, and health care industries to adopt such structures. In general, matrix department structures are more costly to operate, extracting a high price in employee anxiety, but in the right setting, yield better operating and technical results.

Project Structure

It often takes considerable time, money, and managerial blood to get a matrix organization to run smoothly. Many organizational activities would be over before the benefits of the matrix could be realized. To overcome this shortcoming, many organizations have adopted a temporary task force approach called the project structure. This project structure is composed of a temporary group of specialists, drawn from the various functional departments. They are assigned to work full-time on a short-term basis, 6 months to 3 years, as part of a special project team. When the project is completed, the individuals return to their original functional departments. The aerospace industry used this departmental structure in their many space and missile projects. General Motors recently adopted this project-centered approach to develop and implement its down-sizing strategy in the production of its new line of smaller cars—for example, Citation.

A Project Structure is a Temporary Product Department The project structure is a product department that is temporarily grafted onto a functional structure. It is particularly useful in situations requiring the application of high technical knowledge to the solution of a specific product problem. This application can usually be done in a short time period. And, it does not disturb other departmental activites. With the success of the General Motors strategy, many other organizations will likely adopt this departmental structure.

The four department structures discussed above are efforts to balance the functional advantages of stability and technical excellence with the product advantages of flexibility and business performance. All of these efforts ultimately must relate to the conditions in the environment, technology, coordination requirements, and people.

EXTENT OF CENTRALIZATION AND DECENTRALIZATION

Decision Making Can Be Either Centralized at the Top or Decentralized at Lower Levels Managers must also decide where decisions should be made in the organization. Decision making can be centralized either at the top, or decentralized at the lower levels. No organization is completely centralized or decentralized. Some decisions are almost always made at the top, such as strategic decisions and 5-year budgets. Some are almost always made at lower levels, such as hiring or job assignment decisions. Still, most organizations can be characterized as centralized, when most important decisions are made at the top, or decentralized, when they are made at lower levels.

Stable Environments Favor Centralization The information demands on managers are the key factors in the centralization/decentralization balance. These information demands, in turn, are influenced by the environment, technology, and coordination requirements. Lawrence and Lorsch discovered that in stable environments, for instance, that usually less information was needed to make decisions, because past experience was a good guide. As such, centralized decision making was more probable in those settings. Just the opposite was true for firms in rapidly changing environments. In rapidly changing environments, a great deal of information was needed to make decisions. Decentralized decision *Routinized* making was most effective under these circumstances. Mass production and *Technology, as in* process technologies similarly facilitated centralization. Woodward found *Mass or Process* that where production technologies were standardized and routinized, as in *Firms, Facilitates* the production of TV sets, the processing of bank checks or the production of *Centralization* chemicals, centralization of decision making was usually successful. On the other hand, where production was more customized, as in aircraft or printing press manufacturing, decentralization was the route to corporate success.

Few Key Coordination Points Favor Centralization Chandler found few key coordination points favored centralization of decision making. He reported that successful steel companies, which emphasized production efficiency and had few coordination points, were centralized. Electrical manufacturers, such as General Electric, which stressed growth through diversification and needed several key coordination points, were more decentralized. Apparently the information needs to manage growth are greater than those needed to manage internal efficiency.

The balance of centralization and decentralization in an organization is another important organizational structure decision managers must make. The key situational factors of environment, task and technology, and coordination requirements will shape the manager's decision on where decisions should be made.

COORDINATION TECHNIQUES

Both Vertical and Horizontal Coordination Is Needed Putting the pieces back together is another important organization structure decision. Managers need to coordinate both vertically along the chain link of superiors and subordinates, and horizontally among different departments. The Engineering Department must design the products sold by the Sales Department in such a way that they can be produced by the Production Department. And, the Vice President of Sales has to be certain that all of the salespeople are selling the same product at the same price. Without coordination, there is no organization and no management. Vertical coordination is generally accomplished through the principles of authority. Horizontal coordination techniques vary with the situation confronting the organization.

Coordination by Plan Involves Policies, Strong Leadership, and Appeals to Hierarchy There are two general horizontal coordination strategies—coordination by plan, and coordination by feedback. Which coordination strategy is likely to be most effective will depend upon factors in the environment and technology. Coordination by plan is usually successful under the following conditions: The environment is stable or slowly changing (as in the paper, steel, and automobile industries); the technology is repetitive and standardized; and there are few key coordination points. In this strategy, coordination is achieved by pre-establishing policies that specify in advance what activities will be performed by whom and when. Strong, directive leadership is needed to insure the plan is followed. And, there should be a formal hierarchy that specifies a common superior who can resolve coordination difficulties.

Coordination by Feedback Involves Intermediaries and Task Forces Coordination by feedback is needed when the organization faces a rapidly changing environment, tasks that are nonroutine, and many coordination points. In these situations, original approaches are needed to solve unique problems. Coordination is achieved through specific intermediary persons, such as expeditors, liaison representatives, customer coordinators, and project coordinators. These individuals are responsible for linking and coordinating among many different departments. Sometimes, task forces and committees are used as a coordination by feedback device. Lawrence and Lorsch reported that successful plastic and food companies (facing rapidly changing environments) used cross-functional committees and teams as a coordination device.

Insuring coordination among the organization's many diverse parts is an essential managerial responsibility. Depending on the stability in the environment, the routineness of the task, and number of coordination points, the manager may choose either coordination by plan or feedback.

SUMMARY

Managers make important decisions about who reports to whom about what. These decisions affect the organization's productivity and individual member satisfaction. There are three basic organization structure decisions to be made: departmentation by function, product, matrix, or project; the extent of centralization and decentralization in decision making; and coordination by either plan or feedback. The right structure is one that meets the demands posed by environmental stability and diversity, task routineness, coordination requirements, and the people in the organization.

THE ORGANIZATIONAL UPHEAVAL

There was a time when a table of organization—sometimes familiarly known as a "T/O"—showed a neatly arrayed series of boxes, each indicating an officer and the organizational sub-units for which he was responsible. Every bureaucracy of any size, whether a corporation, a university or a government agency, had its own T/O, providing its managers with a detailed map of the organizational geography. Once drawn, such a map became a fixed part of the organization's rule book, remaining in use for years at a time. Today, organizational lines are changing so frequently that a three-month-old table is often regarded as an historic artifact, something like the Dead Sea Scrolls.

Organizations now change their internal shape with a frequency—and sometimes a rashness—that makes the head swim. Titles change from week to week. Jobs are transformed. Responsibilities shift. Vast organizational structures are taken apart, bolted together again in new forms, then rearranged again. Departments and divisions spring up overnight only to vanish in another, and yet another, reorganization.

In part this frenzied reshuffling arises from the tide of mergers and "de-mergers" now sweeping through industry in the United States and Western Europe. The late sixties saw a tremendous rolling wave of acquisitions, the growth of giant conglomerates and diversified corporate monsters. The seventies may witness an equally powerful wave of divestitures and, later, reacquisitions, as companies attempt to consolidate and digest their new subsidiaries, then trade off troublesome components. Between 1967 and 1969 the Questor Corporation (formerly Dunhill International, Incorporated) bought eight companies and sold off five. Scores of other corporations have similar stories to tell. According to management consultant Alan J. Zakon, "There will be a great deal more spinning off of pieces."[1] As the consumer marketplace churns and changes, companies will be forced constantly to reposition themselves in it.

Internal reorganizations almost inevitably follow such corporate swaps, but they may arise for a variety of other reasons as well. Within a recent three-year period fully sixty-six of the 100 largest industrial companies in the United States publicly reported major organizational shake-ups. Actually,

---

[1]Zakon cited in "Finding Buyers for the Bad Buys," *Business Week,* September 13, 1969, pp. 49–51.

Source. Alvin Toffler, *Future Shock* (New York: Random House, 1970), pp. 115–119.

this was only the visible tip of the proverbial iceberg. Many more reorganizations occur than are ever reported. Most companies try to avoid publicity when overhauling their organization. Moreover, constant small and partial reorganizations occur at the departmental or divisional level or below, and are regarded as too small or unimportant to report.

"My own observation as a consultant," says, D. R. Daniel, an official of McKinsey & Company, a large management consulting firm, "is that one major restructuring every two years is probably a conservative estimate of the current rate of organizational change among the largest industrial corporations. Our firm has conducted over 200 organization studies for domestic corporate clients in the past year, and organization problems are an even larger part of our practice outside the United States." What's more, he adds, there are no signs of a leveling off. If anything, the frequency of organizational upheavals is increasing.

These changes, moreover, are increasingly far-reaching in power and scope. Says Professor L. E. Greiner of the Harvard Graduate School of Business Administration: "Whereas only a few years ago the target of organization change was limited to a small work group or a single department . . . the focus is now converging on the organization as a whole, reaching out to include many divisions and levels at once, and even the top managers themselves." He refers to "revolutionary attempts" to transform organization "at all levels of management."

If the once-fixed table of organization won't hold still in industry, much the same is increasingly true of the great government agencies as well. There is scarcely an important department or ministry in the governments of the technological nations that has not undergone successive organizational change in recent years. In the United States during the forty-year span from 1913 to 1953, despite depression, war and other social upheavals, not a single new cabinet-level department was added to the government. Yet in 1953 Congress created the Department of Health, Education and Welfare. In 1965 it established the Department of Housing and Urban Development. In 1967 it set up the Department of Transportation (thus consolidating activities formerly carried out in thirty different agencies), and, at about the same time, the President called for a merger of the departments of Labor and Commerce.

Such changes within the structure of government are only the most conspicuous, for organizational tremors are similarly felt in all the agencies down below. Indeed, internal redesign has become a byword in Washington. In 1965 when John Gardner became Secretary of Health, Education and Welfare, a top-to-bottom reorganization shook that department. Agencies, bureaus and offices were realigned at a rate that left veteran employees in a state of mental exhaustion. (During the height of this reshuffling, one official, who happens to be a friend of mine, used to leave a note behind for her husband each morning when she left for work. The note consisted of her telephone number for *that* day. So rapid were the changes that she could not keep a telephone number long enough for it to be listed in the departmental directory.) Mr. Gardner's successors continued tinkering with organization, and by 1969, Robert Finch, after eleven months in office, was pressing for yet another major overhaul, having concluded in the meantime that the department was virtually unmanageable in the form in which he found it.

In *Self-Renewal,* an influential little book written before he entered the government, Gardner asserted that: "That farsighted administrator ... reorganizes to break down calcified organizational lines. He shifts personnel ... He redefines jobs to break them out of rigid categories." Elsewhere Gardner referred to the "crises of organization" in government and suggested that, in both the public and private sectors, "Most organizations have a structure that was designed to solve problems that no longer exist." The "self-renewing" organization, he defined as one that constantly changes its structure in response to changing needs.

Gardner's message amounts to a call for permanent revolution in organizational life, and more and more sophisticated managers are recognizing that in a world of accelerating change reorganization is, and must be, an ongoing process, rather than a traumatic once-in-a-lifetime affair. This recognition is spreading outside the corporations and government agencies as well. Thus *The New York Times,* on the same day that it reports on proposed mergers in the plastics, plywood and paper industries, describes a major administrative upheaval at the British Broadcasting Corporation, a thorough renovation of the structure of Columbia University, and even a complete reorganization of that most conservative of institutions, the Metropolitan Museum of Art in New York. What is involved in all this activity is not a casual tendency but a historic movement. Organizational change—self-renewal, as Gardner puts it—is a necessity, an unavoidable response to the acceleration of change.[2]

For the individual within these organizations, change creates a wholly new climate and a new set of problems. The turnover of organizational designs means that the individual's relationship to any one structure (with its implied set of obligations and rewards) is truncated, shortened in time. With each change, he must reorient himself. Today the average individual is frequently reassigned, shuffled about from one sub-structure to another. But even if he remains in the same department, he often finds that the department, itself, has been shifted on some fast-changing table of organization, so that his position in the overall maze is no longer the same.

[2]Organizational change is discussed in "Reorganizing for Results" by D. Ronald Daniel in *Harvard Business Review,* November-December, 1966, p. 96; also in "Patterns of Organization Change" by Larry E. Greiner in *Harvard Business Review,* May-June, 1967, pp. 119–120.

The result is that man's organizational relationships today tend to change at a faster pace than ever before. The average relationship is less permanent, more temporary, than ever before.

Discussion Questions
1. How is the rapid pace of organizational change likely to affect people?
2. How will attitudes and values toward one's job and one's place in the organization need to change to fit the pace of organizational change?

BUTLER ADVERTISING

Butler Advertising is a middle-sized agency. For many years it had been organized along functional lines. All the creative types were in one major creative group. It was divided into such departments as Art, Copy, TV and Radio Production, and Newspaper and Magazine Production. The other major groups were Marketing and Account Executive.

An account executive was assigned to manage each account. He was to direct a team drawn from creative and marketing personnel, and provide service for the client.

The account executives complained that although the creative and other personnel were supposed to contact the client only after checking with the account executive, they were actually making contacts directly. They would "play up their big ideas" to the client and make arrangements that the account executive would hear about only later.

To cope with this problem, top management reorganized the agency. The old functional departments were broken up into new organizational units built around each client. This strengthened the position of the account executive, and he was able to control his team better.

Under the new arrangement, employees were physically regrouped according to the new organization. This meant, for example, that artists no longer sat with other artists exclusively. More likely the artist sat with a copywriter, a market research person, a TV production person, and so on.

After several months another change also occurred. Formerly, a person had been evaluated mostly on his or her skill as a professional. Now what seemed more important was the ability to satisfy the client. Meeting a deadline was valued more than the niceties of artwork. This seemed to be good for the business of meeting client requirements, but it had serious effects on those people whose job satisfaction came mostly from being good artists, writers, or whatever.

In fact, these people grumbled a great deal and several of them quit within a year—they said the job wasn't what it used to be.

Discussion Questions
1. What were the strengths and weaknesses of the original structure?
2. What were the strengths and weaknesses of the new structure?
3. How was the behavior of the creative staff related to the structure of their organization? How did structure affect performance and satisfaction in this case?

Designing the organization's structure is a critical management task. Structures prescribe authority and responsibility relationships. They influence patterns of coordination and communication. They determine the location of decision making. Their overall contribution is to provide a balance and emphasis of activities. Three structure decisions were discussed: departmentation, centralization, and coordination. Almost all managerial structure decisions are based on the four principles of authority: unity of command, chain of command, parity, and span of control.

Several alternative department structures are in common use. We considered functional, product, matrix, and project types. We also considered a number of factors—environment, tasks and technology, coordination requirements, and people—which affect the suitability of each type. There is no easy way to make sure you will choose the best department structure. But careful consideration of key factors—environment, technology, coordination, and people—provides a reasonable method of weighing the advantages of each type.

Managers must also decide where decisions will be made in the organization. If the information demands are not high, as in stable environments and routinized technologies, centralization of decision making is possible. Where rapidly changing environments and unique tasks add to the information load, decentralization seems to be the wise choice. Coordination of all departments is also an important managerial decision. In turbulent situations, coordination by feedback seems most important. When situations are more stable, coordination by planning and strong leadership seem more appropriate.

Finally, lest we leave a false impression that structure is something managers design once and for all, we need to point out that organizing, like other management processes, is a continuing function. The key factors change. Stable environments become unstable. Tasks and technologies change. Accordingly, structures must be changed or they will cease to make a positive contribution to performance and satisfaction. Indeed, reorganizing rather than organizing is probably a more apt term for the job of structuring.

Here are some principles:

1. Functional department structures have particular advantages where concentration of technical expertise and economies of scale are important. They are often indicated where environments are stable and tasks are routinized.

2. Product department structures have particular advantages where diverse and unstable environmental conditions exist. They can help the organi-

zation's subunits adapt to conditions that vary by product, territory, or client.

3. Organizing is a continuing management function. As conditions and strategies change, so should the structure.

4. Organization design must take into account the diversity and stability of the environment, the tasks and technology involved, the characteristics of the people involved, and the need for coordination within the firm.

5. Most organizing decisions are based on the principle of authority: unity of command (one boss), chain of command (the unbroken link of authority from top to bottom in an organization), parity (matching authority with responsibility), and span of control (the number of subordinates).

6. Centralization or decentralization of decision making will vary with information needs. In stable environments and routinized tasks, less information is needed to make decisions, so centralization is possible. In changing environments, and developmental tasks, decentralization is needed, because a larger amount of information is needed in order to make a decision.

7. Putting the pieces back together again through coordination is another key organizing decision. Coordination by plan, involving preplanning policies, strong leadership in implementing them, and a hierarchy to settle disputes is most likely in stable structures. In rapidly changing structures, coordination by feedback, involving intermediaries and task forces, is more likely.

CHAPTER TWELVE DIVISION OF LABOR AND JOB DESIGN

At the conclusion of this chapter you should be able to:

1. Define the division of labor and two positive and two negative results of it.
2. Describe three job redesign strategies and several limitations on their use.
3. Define staff and line, and give an example of each.
4. Outline three functions of staff.
5. Explain three factors that lead to conflict and communication difficulties between staff and line.
6. Explain three strategies to reduce line-staff conflict.

PLANNERS AND OPERATORS

I. Objectives
    A. The class will be divided into 9- to 11-person teams that will compete against each other in assembling as quickly as possible a multiple-piece puzzle into a predetermined shape. Teams will be divided into a 4-person planning group, a 4-person operators group, and 1 to 3 observers.
    B. To experience some of the feelings associated with line-staff difficulties.
    C. To gain insight into some of the assumptions underlying the division of labor and some possible ways to rethink the assumptions.

II. Premeeting Preparation
    A. Read the briefing sheets for planners, operators, and observers, Figures 12.1 to 12.3.

III. Instructions
    A. Selection of teams at the beginning of the exercise.
        1. The professor states that this is a simulation in which people in specialized tasks work together to produce a common result. The group is divided into 9- to 11-person groups that are subdivided into 4-person planning teams and 4-person operating teams and 1- to 3-person observer teams. Observers step out of the room to be briefed by the professor, operators step out into the adjoining room or go to a separate part of the large room. Planners begin to meet just to get acquainted.
        2. The professor hands out the puzzle material to planning teams and planners begin their task. Time limits are stressed. The planning gets underway (see Figure 12.1).
        3. The professor briefs observers out of the earshot of both the planners and operators teams on what to look for in the planning and assembling stages of the exercise (see Figure 12.3).
        4. The professor then goes to the operating teams to review their task with them during the waiting period. Essentially this is to discuss: (1) how they feel while waiting to be instructed, and (2) how a person can prepare for an unknown task. They are told that their planning teams may summon them to the room at any time, but if they are not called prior to 5 minutes before the starting of the task, they are to report for work anyway (see Figure 12.2).

> *Time for Step A: 10 minutes*

B. Planning and assembly of the puzzle
   1. The planners have a maximum of 10 minutes to complete the planning. The planning team will call in the operating team to give them their instrutions for a minimum of 5 minutes. Thus, there is a total of 15 minutes of planning and instruction time.
   2. The professor calls time to begin assembly and instructs the planners to step back from the table and to remain silent as the operating teams begin.
   3. Operators complete the task according to their instructions, taking no more than 5 minutes.

   Time for Step B: 20 minutes

IV. Discussion
   Your instructor will help you to explore what happened in the exercise and its meaning for management.

   Time for discussion: 20 minutes

Figure 12.1 Briefing Sheet for Planning Team

The objective of your combined planning and operating group is to assemble the 16 puzzle pieces exactly as shown in the diagram in the shortest possible time during the assembly period. The planning team gets a packet containing 16 pieces of a puzzle. When the pieces are properly assembled, they will form a large square containing an empty place in the middle. A sheet bearing a diagram of the completed puzzle is provided to your team.

Your task is to do the following:

1. Plan how the 16 pieces can be assembled to make the puzzle.
2. Instruct your operating team to carry out your plan for assembling the puzzle.
3. You may call the operating team and begin instructing them at any time during the next 10 minutes.
4. The operating team must begin assembling the puzzle 15 minutes from now (but not sooner) and you are required to give them at least 5 minutes of instruction.

Before you start, read these rules.
During planning:

1. Keep the pieces in front of you at all times.
2. Do not touch the pieces now or during the instruction phase.
3. Do not assemble the square; that is the operators' job.
4. Do not mark on any of the pieces.

During instruction:

1. Give all instructions in words. Do not show the diagram to the operators. Do not draw any diagrams yourselves, either on paper or in the air with gesture. You may convey your instructions either orally or on paper.
2. The operating team must not move the pieces until the signal is given to start assembly.
3. Do not show any diagram to the operators.
4. After the signal is given for the assembly to begin, you may not give any further instructions; stand back and observe.

Figure 12.2   Briefing Sheet for Operating Team

1. Your team of four people will have the responsibility of carrying out a task according to instructions given you by your planning team.
2. Your task will begin 15 minutes from now.
3. Your planning team may call you in for instruction at any time during the next 10 minutes.
4. If they do not summon you during the next 10 minutes, you must report to them at your own initiative at the end of the 10 minutes.
5. Once you have begun the task, your planning team will not be allowed to give you any further instructions.
6. Finish the assigned task as rapidly as possible.
7. You may send notes to the planners and they may send notes in reply at any time during the planning or assembly stage.
8. While you wait for a call from your planning team, do the following:
   a. Individually, write on a piece of paper the concerns you feel while waiting for instructions.
   b. As a group, think of anything you can that might help you do the job. Write the things that are working for you on one sheet of paper and the things that are working against you on another.
9. During the assembly period, watch for the following behaviors:
   a. What evidence do the operating team members exhibit that instructions were clearly understood or misunderstood?
   b. What nonverbal reactions do planning team members exhibit as they watch their plans being implemented or distorted?

Figure 12.3   Briefing Sheet for Observing Team

You will be observing a planning team decide how to solve a problem and give instruction to an operating team so that they can carry out the solution. The problem consists of assembling 16 flat pieces into the form of a square containing an empty square in its middle. The planning team is supplied with a diagram of the assembled pieces. This team is not to assemble the pieces itself, but is to instruct the operating team how to assemble the parts in minimum time. You will be silent observers throughout the process.

Suggestions:

1. Each member of the observing team should watch the general pattern of communication but give special attention to one member of the planning team (during the planning phase) and one member of the operating team (during the assembling period).

2. During the planning period watch for the following behaviors:
   a. What assumption do the planners make about their own task? The capabilities of the operators? The rules?
   b. How does the planning team divide its time between planning and instructing? (How early does it invite the operating team to come in?)
   c. How does the group work together? Are there factions or is participation pretty well balanced?

3. During the instructing period, watch for the following behavior:
   a. At the beginning of the instruction, how do the planners orient the operators to their task? Does the operating team appear to feel free to ask questions of the planners?
   b. What assumptions made by the planning team are not communicated to the operating team?

Alternatively praised as the "saviour of the American economic way of life" and then "as the destroyer of the American worker," the division of labor, or task specialization, has been a controversial topic in management circles for some time. Actually, history shows that Americans neither invented nor fully developed the division of labor. Credit for that invention has been lost in antiquity, although it probably belongs to some ancient Neanderthal or pithancantropus. It is indeed as ancient as thinking-knowing man himself. It could be said that God created heaven and earth and the division of labor.

DEFINITION OF THE DIVISION OF LABOR

But before you can decide on the moral and/or economic issues involved in the division of labor you must first know what it is and what it is not. In its simplest form, when a job gets too much for one person to do, and two or more persons are employed, each to do a portion of the job, division of labor has emerged. Obviously, virtually every task in our society, from child rearing through to the production of the most complex electronic hardware, involved some division of labor. It should be apparent to you that because we do not grow all of our own food, make all of our own clothes, and so on, that no person is immune from the effects of the division of labor.

Vertical Division of Labor   There are two ways in which tasks get divided. The first is a vertical division into a ranking or hierarchy of authority based upon either status or economic wealth (Figure 12.4). Thus, the president of an organization is superior to the vice-president of that organization who in turn is superior to the clerk-typist employed in the office. Or, between organizations, the Supreme Court is superior to a business in deciding antitrust violation. All of these are examples of a vertical division of labor, one based on a hierarchy of authority.

Horizontal Division of Labor   The second way tasks get divided is horizontally or according to function (Figure 12.5). The division into planning and operating is one such example. Another is the machinists in a plant who are divided from the typists, who in turn are divided from the chemists. In essence, the nature of the work to be done is the principal factor determining how the work gets divided. This chapter will not concern the vertical division of labor; that will be discussed elsewhere. Rather, the focus here is on the horizontal division of tasks.

REASONS UNDERLYING THE DIVISION OF LABOR

Inability To Do Task Alone   Although the division is ever present, it is useful to explore some of the reasons underlying its widespread use. There are two most often cited rea-

Figure 12.4 Vertical division of labor.

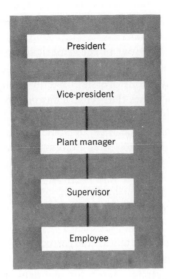

sons. First, is the inability of one person to do the entire task alone. Imagine the time and physical energy necessary for one person to completely build an automobile. It took some of the early automobile pioneers as much as 18 months to build one car. How many of you, for instance, have the time and energy to do a complete repair of your automobile? Very few of you, we wager, without giving up such other important activities as socializing and attending interesting classes. So physical and time limitations force work to be divided up among many people.

Inability To Know   The second reason lies in the inability of any of us to know everything
Everything necessary to perform a given task. Take car repair, for instance. Although many of you may know enough to change the oil and maybe even tune the engine, how many know enough to overhaul the engine, install new brake shoes, and realign the wheels? In all eventuality, very few of you have sufficient information to do even one and, even fewer, all three of these common tasks. The increasing complexity of automobile engines necessitates increasing specialization. Thus, in the well-equipped repair shop there are engine specialists and brake specialists, as well as general mechanics who change oil. Each of these individuals, because of his or her limited scope, is able to

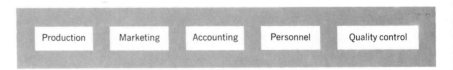

Figure 12.5 Horizontal division of labor.

keep up with the knowledge explosion in their particular specialty. What is true in automobile repair is also true in most other fields: medicine, law, finance, production, and management. The production supervisor is just too busy with the current job to keep up with new developments in engineering, equipment, materials, or motivation. Knowledge limitations are the second reason underlying the widespread use of the division of labor.

POSITIVE EFFECTS OF THE DIVISION OF LABOR

Less Training Time Division of labor often results in specialized jobs that are easier to learn. Consider the task of tuning up your engine, for instance. It would probably take you a lot longer to learn how to do it if you were also trying to master valve jobs and brake relining at the same time. Furthermore, it takes less prior experience just to learn how to tune engines, than it takes to be an all-*Aids Recruiting* around engine mechanic. So, you can hire a lesser skilled individual to be an "engine tuner-upper," and there probably are more of them available than skilled mechanics.

Adam Smith observed 200 years ago that specializing in production increased output. That is still true today. By limiting the number of activities done and the knowledge necessary to perform those activities, specialization *Increased Output* increases efficiency. Division of labor, then results in increased output—that *at Lower Costs* is, producing more physical products at lower cost. Evidence indicates that this does occur. In fact, much of the economic progress of such industries as automobile manufacturing can be attributed to this process.

NEGATIVE EFFECTS OF THE DIVISION OF LABOR

Output Up But There are, however, some negative unintended consequences of the division *Quality Down* of labor. First, although output tends to increase when tasks are divided, the quality level tends to go down. Difficulties with many mass-produced prod-*Decreased Job* ucts may be an example of such a quality problem. This quality problem may *Satisfaction* be indicative of a second negative consequence of the division of labor: decreased job satisfaction. Although the evidence is not totally clear, many people on specialized jobs often have low morale or job satisfaction, and this may be manifested in lack of concern about the quality of the product they produce. "I missed one of those damn steering column bolts just now, but who cares," may well be the attitude of some assembly line workers.

Increased Absence Third, as a possible correlate of this job dissatisfaction, persons perform-*and Turnover* ing finely divided tasks are more likely to be absent frequently and leave their jobs. In some mass production jobs these "personnel costs" can add as much as 20 percent to the cost of the labor in the product. This often wipes out the cost efficiencies mentioned under the advantages.

In short, then, division of labor is associated, on the positive side, with increased output, lower cost, and shorter training times and, on the negative side, with lower job satisfaction for some persons, and lower quality and higher absence and turnover rates. On balance, task specialization has contributed greatly to our economic progress, and extracted a social and human cost. The question is not, "Should we or shouldn't we specialize?" Rather it is, "How can we specialize to avoid the human consequences?"

OVERCOME NEGATIVE EFFECTS

Management has attempted many strategies to overcome the negative consequences of the division of labor. In the 1920s and 1930s, rest periods and social clubs were tried. In the 1940s and 1950s, human relations supervisory training programs were the rage, and in the 1960s and early 1970s, sensitivity training and organizational development efforts were the "things to do." All of these were efforts to change the people. None of them focused on the critical area of the task responsibilities under the assumption, perhaps, that the task could not be changed. The employee just had to endure the subdivision the way it was because that was the most efficient method.

Job Redesign Efforts

Challenging that assumption of the immutability of the task structure, many managements have tried a different approach. Three strategies have emerged, all of which modify the task in an effort to moderate the ill effects of the division of labor. They are job enlargement, job enrichment, and autonomous work groups.

Job Enlargement Adds Diversity, But Not Responsibility Job enlargement redesigns work to add additional tasks of the same skill and responsibility level. This provides a greater variety of work to do, longer work cycles, and greater diversity. The Maytag Company, for instance, applied the "horizontal loading" principle to the assembly of a 27-part washing machine motor pump. These were originally produced on an assembly-line conveyer by six operators. The job was enlarged so that four employees assembled the entire unit, thus giving each person a greater diversity of work to do.

Work can also be redesigned to "vertically load" jobs and give them greater responsibility. This is done by adding planning, control, and direct feedback elements. The addition of these managementlike tasks is what distinguishes job enlargement from job enrichment. At Maytag, for instance, after the water pump assembly job was enlarged, it was enriched when the group was given control over their work pace, the right to inspect their own product, and put their mark on it when it was done.

The results were very encouraging. Pump assembly time dropped 25 percent, representing a savings of approximately $2000 in the first year. Employees were also more satisfied with their jobs. Research performed by Kilbridge on the Maytag Company experience suggests that job enrichment does result in cost reductions and improved quality. In general, job satisfaction of employees was also reported to be higher. A significant minority of employees, however, expressed a preference for the nonenriched, traditional assembly-line type positions. Furthermore, productivity per person did not improve. Rather, waiting time was eliminated through being able to perform other tasks while waiting for the parts to be delivered. The Maytag series of studies suggests that job enrichment can result in an improved quality, in somewhat better overall productivity, and improved job satisfaction for many (but not all) employees.

Job Enrichments Add Responsibility Through Planning, Control, and Feedback Elements

American Telephone and Telegraph Company, Detroit Edison Company, Colonial Insurance Company, the Social Security Administration, and IBM have utilized job enrichment to promote productivity. The research results are mixed. For example, Robert Ford reports on 18 studies that have been conducted within AT&T. Job enrichment resulted in improved productivity and satisfaction in the Treasury, Commercial, and Controller's departments. In the Traffic, Plant, and Engineering departments the improvements were positive though modest. On the other hand, job enrichment resulted in no significant change on four other units. Apparently, job enrichment works in some settings, but not others.

Autonomous Work Groups Combine Vertical and Horizontal Loading with Group Responsibility

Autonomous work group designs were implemented to overcome many of the limitations of both job enlargement and job enrichment. This work design assigns responsibility and authority for the completion of several tasks to a group of employees. At the Kalmar plant of the Volvo Auto Works, for instance, employees work in teams assembling entire engines. The team is responsible for meeting a weekly production schedule, rotating work among its members, inspecting their own product, and handling customer complaints should there be any. These work groups have enlarged jobs in that they have a wide variety of tasks to perform; and enriched jobs in the sense of providing more planning, control, and feedback on their performance, while having responsibility as a group for the performance of the entire collection of activities and tasks.

These work designs have been implemented in over 500 locations in Sweden alone. They have been tried in a wide variety of American companies, including General Foods, General Motors, AT&T, and Polaroid. In general, turnover and absenteeism have been reduced, and, in some cases, direct productivity improvements have been realized.

Job Redesign Limitations

These work designs are not panaceas. The enthusiasm for job redesign as a means of assuring both productivity and employee satisfaction needs to be

*Some People
Don't Want
Challenging Work* balanced with a recognition of their limitations. First, not all employees hunger for enriched or enlarged jobs. Edward Lawlar, a motivation researcher, concluded that there are many people who are happy working in repetitive jobs. Hulin and Blood, Cohen, Wise, and Thayer all found a similar lack of universal desire for more challenging job assignments. And remember, Kilbridge found a significant minority at Magtag who preferred nonenriched assembly-line jobs.

*Costs of
Installation
Are High* Second, it costs a lot of money, patience, and lost productivity to implement a job redesign program. At Atlas Copco Mining and Construction Techniques, Inc., it took three years for productivity to return to the old standard. It takes time for people to learn new skills and willingly exercise

*May Ignore Other
Important Factors* new responsibilities. Third, in the enthusiasm for job redesign, other important factors such as pay, supervision, and working conditions are often overlooked. Enriching the job to make it more challenging, without adjusting the pay scale, could leave employees feeling manipulated, and cancel out any positive effects. Similarly, installing an autonomous work group structure with considerable group autonomy and not modifying a directive supervisory style will likely lead to conflict and reduced results.

The above limitations do not detract from these significant efforts to redesign work to make it fit human needs. Work that is performed within an organization must be divided. It is impossible for any one given member to know about everything that is required and to have the skill and ability to perform every job requirement. Jobs may be enlarged, where individuals perform a wide variety of tasks, each at the same skill and difficulty level. Jobs may be enriched, providing for planning, control, and feedback components. Or jobs may be combined into an autonomous work group structure, where groups of individuals are responsible for entire subunits. The thoughtful manager seriously considers the limitations of each design before embarking on any given one.

The division of labor and the creation of specialized jobs lead to increased output and reduced cost. Such specialization also produces high absenteeism and turnover and lowered quality levels. To combat the human and social costs of specialization, managers have sought to redesign jobs.

DEFINITIONS OF LINE AND STAFF

Another way in which tasks get divided in an organization is into the doing and the planning activities. Those groups responsible for performing the main mission of the organization get identified as "line" groups, with all other groups being defined as supportive or staff. Thus, in an automobile manufacturing firm, the production department is a "line" group. In a market research firm the marketing research department is the "line" group. In a school or university the faculty is the "line" group. Obviously the same functions could be "line" in one organization and staff in another, depending on the main purpose of the organization. The staff, therefore, is defined as the group that is not responsible for the performance of the central mission of the organization.

Why Staff Groups Emerge

Staff groups originally emerged as firms grew. As a company grows from a one-person firm, such as a retail store at the corner, to a huge 700,000-person organization such as General Motors, the top management is faced with increasing responsibility. The one-person retail store that grows soon needs an accountant to keep track of expenses and taxes. The store owner also needs an attorney to ensure compliance with all the relevant laws. Both of these people are staff. In the same vein, the president of a large corporation must keep abreast on the affirmative-action program to insure compliance with federal and state regulations. The special person hired to perform that task, often called an Affirmative Action Officer, would be a staff person. Thus, staff persons in organizations emerge in response to the company's needs to perform tasks that are not directly related to its central mission, but that must be performed if the company is to survive.

Historically, staff persons have always existed in companies, although they were usually few and performed aide-de-camp special assistant-type work for the manager. When Henri Fayol, the Father of Modern Administrative Thought, wrote in the 1880s, he largely ignored staff people, because in his day the typical companies may have had organizational charts that looked like the one shown in Figure 12.6.

Note that there are four line officials—the President and the three Plant Managers. The Accountant is a staff member who performs service-type functions, whereas the Staff Assistant to the President is more of an advisor and controller in the military sense of the word—often speaking for and with the authority of the chief. Fayol was concerned, even then, over the possibility that the staff assistant might usurp the authority of the chief. Imagine how Fayol would feel if confronted with Pepsi Cola's organization chart as shown in this management example.

As companies grew and technical processes became more complex, it became more necessary for the line manager to have more knowledge. Specialists who knew a great deal about specific technical activities but who had no line authority came into the company. This was the beginning of the employment of persons who knew, but who did not have the authority to do (staff specialists), alongside those who had authority to do but often did not know (line management). The number of these technical specialists caused some confusion in many companies, and this prompted Taylor, in the early 1900s, to propose a functional type of organization where each employee reported to a number of functional supervisors, each of whom was a specialist in some

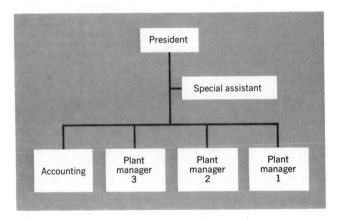

Figure 12.6

specialized area, and had line authority over the employees for that function. A typical organizational chart utilizing Taylor's functional management is shown in Figure 12.7.

Although Taylor's proposals for work specialization had a great impact on the business scene, his functional management idea never got off the ground. The confusion that arose in reporting to multiple supervisors and the possibilities for conflict undoubtedly contributed to the early death of Taylor's idea, although he was very correct in pointing out the difficulties posed by the separation of technical knowledge and administrative authority. In fact, over time, this problem has become far more difficult to solve.

As technical processes grew more complex, social concerns pressed in on the business firm. Unions and their threat, and changing cultural conditions encouraged firms to devote more attention to the personal needs of employees. Government, in all of its many forms, became more actively interested in the conduct of the firm's business, ranging from shipping regulations to advertising restrictions, from pollution control requirements to the restriction on who may sit on the board of directors. Government became an active partner in the business, with a growing interest and voice. And to compound the situation, consumer societal groups became active in making demands on the corporation. Under the burden of trying to deal with all of these "new" concerns as well as still run an "old" business and make a profit at it, management hired staff specialists in large numbers. The 1950s and 1960s may well have been the "specialist" years, and as is pointed out in Chapter 15, this trend is likely to continue and accelerate into the future. The result is that now a typical organizational chart might look like Pepsi Cola's, where in the modern organization, staff personnel constitute approximately 50 percent of the total employment. Although it varies from industry to industry, it is apparent that the percentage of staff personnel does not change once the

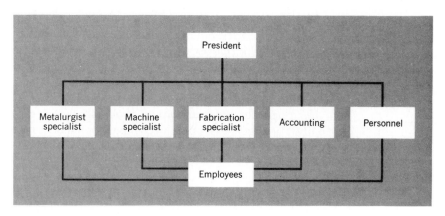

Figure 12.7

company grows to more than 500 employees or so. Even though this organization system has handled the problem of technical versus administrative authority well, there are unresolved conflicts that will be discussed in the next section.

BASIC FUNCTIONS OF STAFF GROUPS

Service Staff groups perform three basic functions. First, they provide a service to the line organization by performing certain necessary but time-consuming tasks. Some examples of these service-type activities include the maintenance of accident records, the processing of group insurance claims, and the maintenance of various accounting books and ledgers. These are all functions that the organization must have performed, but they are not central to the mission of the organization.

Advice The second basic staff function is to give advice on matters that fall within the group's particular area of knowledge. For example, the personnel department may recommend an executive salary payment program. This advice-giving function naturally arises from the assumption that the staff group in question is the expert in the organization concerning that particular area. This activity is not without its perils, however. Advice is about the only commodity that it is easier to give than receive. Furthermore, advice may not be sought, like a dentist visit, until the pain is very bad. In many ways, staff giving advice to the line resembles a parent giving a college-age son advice on dating patterns. In both instances, the advice is likely to be received with less than wholehearted enthusiasm.

Control In addition to the service and advice-giving activities, staff often also performs a control function in organizations. For example, in many companies all salary increases must be approved by the personnel department. This is done in an effort to maintain uniformity in administration of a salary program across many different units. Similarly, all purchases over a certain small amount of money (usually $100) often must be approved by the purchasing department. Thus, control by staff over line activities is usually provided to maintain uniformity of policy administration across all organizational units.

This need for policy uniformity often clashes with the line's need for flexibility. For example, it is not uncommon for supervisors to grant little policy exceptions to employees (such as extra coffee-break time or extra paid days off) in return for employee loyalty and the willingness to extend extra effort when necessary. This is a version of the highly effective "you scratch my back and I'll scratch yours" philosophy. This need for policy deviation flies straight in the face of the staff's need for policy uniformity—and highlights one of the basic facts of organizational life that you should have personally experienced in the Hollow Square exercise—namely, that staff personnel (planners) usually have a different set of needs, values, and expectations than line personnel (operators).

FACTORS LEADING TO LINE-STAFF CONFLICT

Different Backgrounds
There are at least four reasons for the differences between line and staff personnel. First, they usually come from differing backgrounds. Although this was not always the case in your exercise, staff people usually have more education (a B.A. or Master's degree) than line people, who often (though less frequently today) come up from the production floor.

Different Task Objectives
Second, staff personnel tend to have differing task objectives and responsibilities. In the exercise, for instance, the planner was concerned with evolving the best plan ("best" defined as most complete), whereas the operators were concerned with how to put the pieces together. In general, staff people seek to produce the best-looking set of plans, a consideration that often becomes an end in itself. This concern is just the opposite of the line's concern for the most understood plan.

Different Ways To Gain Recognition
These differing objectives may well be associated with the third basic difference between line and staff—the differing nature of their reward system. Staff people tend to be judged, both by others in their area and by higher

level officials in the company, on the basis of the plans they produce; hence, their desire to "package" these plans in the most attractive way possible. Line personnel, however, are rewarded on the basis of output, so their main concern is the plans utility. Although there is a correlation between the completeness of plans and their utility, as you probably experienced in the Hollow Square Exercise, there are other perhaps more important considerations. The differing nature of how both groups accumulate points in the organization game seems to drive a wedge between them.

Different Time Orientations

Fourth, staff and line groups often have widely different time orientations. Line officials are concerned with solving today's problems, because output must be accomplished today. Staff officials, on the other hand, are more concerned with the long run. A training officer, for instance, plans training programs months and even years in advance. Hence, when the training officer talks about a management-by-objectives program a year from now with the Plant Manager who was concerned about meeting today's production schedule, the two often pass like ships in the night without ever hearing each other.

Communication and Conflict Problems   All of these differences between line and staff produce differing orientations, differing perspectives, and serious communications and conflict problems. These problems may be traceable not to the inherited irrascibility of staff and line people but more to the structure that builds in divisiveness. The story is told of a person who had the good fortune to be both a staff and line official in the same organization. As a personnel officer, she installed a complete performance appraisal program. Although she was widely acclaimed for the program by other personnel people and top management officials in the company, she could not understand the less than enthusiastic response by operating line officials at her plant. When she became a line official she discovered why. Even though the plan looked great on paper, it was cumbersome, difficult to work with, and time-consuming. In short, it was very difficult for the line official to use. This little anecdote highlights the observation that many of the differences dividing line and staff arise out of the division of labor.

LINE-STAFF CONFLICT: DOES IT EXIST, AND WHY?

Dalton, in the early 1950s, reported some research which suggested the presence of sharp conflict among line and staff officials. As a result of some innovative research techniques, Dalton concluded that staff personnel were significantly different than their line counterparts. Staff personnel tended to be younger, better educated, came from a different social class, dressed differently, and had different recreational preferences than their line counterparts. In order to move ahead in the organization, the staff personnel were forced to play company politics. Staff personnel often performed a "fink" function: in which they carried tales from one divisional level to another. Staff personnel often formed alliances with various line managers, only to desert these alliances for better ones when the occasion arose. In short, Dalton found that staff personnel continually sought to undercut line management, to find their faults, and then "blackmail" them into support of their proposals.

In 1958, Alvin Gouldner, while conducting some research among faculty members of a small, private liberal arts college, discovered that certain individuals were oriented more toward their profession and discipline, whereas other faculty members were more committed to the institution. Using the Gouldner classifications, other researchers have discovered that staff personnel in general tend to be more committed to their profession, whereas line personnel tend to be more committed to the organization. This has been found to be true for employees in such diverse organizations as research institutions, advertising agencies, and labor unions. As a result, most management textbooks assume the existence of conflicts between line and staff personnel.

More recent research conducted by Dalton, however, suggests that this line-staff conflict assumption may be as out of date as the horsedrawn carriage. Dalton's data suggests, for instance, that personal differences between line and staff personnel may be disappearing. In the modern organization, both line and staff people appear to be educated, young, and ambitious to climb the corporate ladder. The nature and extent of line-staff conflicts seems to be a function of the climate in the organization, with some organizations experiencing little such conflict, whereas others experience a great deal. Conflicts that do exist, apparently revolve around the distribution of corporate resources and in that arena, alliances may be formed among staff people as well as between staff and line personnel.

Recent research by Ritzer and Trice suggests the possibility that individuals may be committed to both their profession and their organization. The presence of this dual loyalty, challenging somewhat the Gouldner concepts, casts an even larger shadow of doubt over the existence of an inevitability of line-staff conflicts.

Thus, with the growth of staff specialists, and the large number of college-trained people in general, the differences between line and staff may be narrower. Furthermore, many of the new organizational structures, (e.g., matrix or project organizations) which are discussed in the chapter on Organizational Structure, may also narrow the gap between line and staff, because in these organizational patterns eventually everyone is staff. It may be a good thing for you, too, that these conflicts are being reduced (if in fact they ever existed as sharply as had been projected), because most of you will spend at least some time in a staff position during your career.

Ways To Overcome the Line-Staff Conflict

Sharing Information Earlier During Planning Re-examination of the assumptions underlying the division of labor into line and staff suggest some management strategies to relieve these conflicts. The first assumption that time and energy constraints necessitate the division of labor can hardly be challenged. The time and energy costs in line-staff conflicts, however, may be greater than the time and energy benefits of dividing the labor. Sharing information earlier with the operating team in the exercise, for instance, may have reduced the time available for planning, but shortened the total time to assemble the puzzle. Thus, earlier sharing of information between planners and doers is one way to reduce these conflicts.

Involvement of the Doers in the Planning The second assumption of the limitation posed by the knowledge explosion is also very real. Yet, the knowledge of how to do a given task is as vital in the planning process as the knowledge of what to do. The Operations Research Specialist may have the most knowledge of how to program a computer to provide information, but unless the specialist also knows the use to which that information will be put, the numbers generated may be meaningless. The knowledge of the operator's skills, attitudes, and perceptions in the exercise, for instance, might have facilitated the planning process and made it more effective. Thus, increased involvement of the doing people early in the planning process is another way to reduce line-staff conflicts.

Matrix and Project Departmental Structure To Ease Coordination Costs Third, although experience clearly indicates that specialization of function leads to greater efficiency in the performance of a given task, experience also indicates that there is a greater difficulty and cost in coordinating many diverse specialities. For example, even though the planners and operators independently may have been very efficient in the performance of their specialized task, they were inefficient in the coordination among themselves in the accomplishment of their overall objectives—the assembly of the puzzle. Thus, a way to divide the task is needed so that the costs of coordination are reduced. The matrix and/or project departmentation are two examples of ways to divide work so as to reduce conduration costs. Both were discussed in greater depth in the Structure chapter.

SUMMARY

The division of labor, like death and taxes, is a permanent part of out industrial scene. Whether the tasks are divided vertically into a hierarchy or horizontally according to function, division is necessary because no single person can perform all the tasks or know all there is to know. This division of labor enables our society to produce more goods and services more efficiently. At the same time, there are negative effects of this division of labor, principally lower quality, less job satisfaction, and more turnover.

Jobs are also divided into line and staff activities, which gives rise to tension and conflict between these two groups. While these two groups may perform different functions, and a certain amount of conflict is inevitable between them, there are several management strategies that have substantially reduced this conflict. Managers have sought to redesign work to provide greater diversity (job enlargement), greater responsibility (job enrichment), and/or greater group responsibility (autonomous work group). These job redesigns, have frequently resulted in lower absentee and turnover costs and, in some cases, better productivity. Some individuals prefer finely divided work, however, and the extensive costs of retraining and the danger of overlooking other important workplace factors pose serious limitations to these redesign efforts.

THE BRAND MANAGER: NO LONGER KING

There is a basic article of faith, long enshrined in marketing mythology, that the only way to sell a large diversified line of consumer packaged goods is through brand or product managers.

As originated by Procter & Gamble in 1927 and refined down through the years, a product/brand manager is typically viewed as the president of his or her own little company. This person is a middle-management coordinator who focuses on a single product or small family of products. Drawing on specialists within the company, the product manager orchestrates everything from market research and manufacturing to sales, package design and advertising. In some companies, he or she has broad decision-making powers. More often, the product manager is a junior executive whose age is in mid-or-late 20s, and who makes recommendations to a marketing vice-president or some other higher level executive.

All through the 1950s and 1960s there was a stampede into product/brand management. Now, suddenly, that faith is beginning to falter. PepsiCo, Purex, Eastman Kodak, Levi Strauss, and some other major corporations are abandoning the system, and many more are making important structural changes. The implications are far-reaching, not only for the marketing function in large corporations, but for the whole corporate management structure itself.

Giant PepsiCo is on the leading edge of the trend. At the company's otherwise quiet, sylvan retreat in Purchase, New York, there is a lively difference of opinion that typifies the intense soul-searching that more and more companies are going through.

John Sculley, senior vice-president of the Pepsi-Cola division and a former Pepsi brand manager, claims that the brand manager system is in big trouble. "It's certainly dead and buried at Pepsi," says the 34-year-old marketer—and Sculley should know, because he is largely the one who killed it in 1970.

At the product level, however, some of Sculley's

lieutenants disagree. "Everyone can talk about all the problems of the brand manager system, but eventually Pepsi will have to get back to some of the system's basic principles," says Chris Hallenbeck, a Pepsi planning manager and a former brand manager at General Foods Corp. "Right now, our system is in flux. It is not working smoothly. And I am betting that it will evolve back toward some improved variation on what we had before."

Pepsi has moved major brand decision making upstairs and is reorganizing away from brand management toward a more specialized "functional" or job approach. Rather than a single brand manager who coordinates all jobs, Pepsi now has separate managers who specialize in advertising, promotion, planning, and other marketing duties for all brands. They report to a vice-president of market planning who handles all the coordinating that the brand manager previously supervised.

Many more manufacturers and processors—including, of course, P&G—are sticking with brand or product managers and remain entirely sold on the system. Yet even some of these companies are changing their organizational hierarchies and shifting their lines of authority and responsibility.

A System Under Pressure

Although marketing people may disagree on the future of brand management, they do agree that the system now faces its stiffest challenge yet, and that some important changes are inevitable. "Traditional brand management was fine when you were dealing with a big, undifferentiated market," says Sculley, "But today, consumer-goods companies are segmenting their markets by age, income, geography, and even by 'psychographics' or lifestyle." Yet brand managers, Sculley claims, are not trained to think that way. "They are usually younger guys who, if they are any good,

Source. Business Week, June 9, 1973.

quickly move to bigger and better assignments within their company. So they take a short-range view of building total volume and market share, and tend to neglect market segments, since this is more of a long-term proposition."

At the same time, the system is also coming under strong outside pressures from consumerism, environmentalism, and growing government regulation. "This means," Sculley adds, "that many decisions that the brand manager used to handle are becoming major policy decisions that can be made only at a higher level."

Edward D. Gottlieb, executive vice-president of a Los Angeles ad agency, has worked with product managers at Lever, General Foods, and Max Factor, and was himself a product manager at Revlon. He claims that an even bigger challenge to the system is the proliferation of new products and the corresponding drop in product life cycles. "Ten or 15 years ago," Gottlieb says, "a product manager could succeed on figures alone, just keeping up his market share. Now, with shorter product life cycles, he's got to consider things like social dynamics and future demand."

Stuart Schultz, director of consumer and market research for Genesco, Inc., the big apparel maker, agrees. "There is simply less continuity with almost everything," he says, "especially in the fashion business. We are getting calls from food product people who say they don't know how to deal with a life cycle of something like eight weeks. If this is the way of the future, the brand will mean less and less, and brand loyalty less and less."

"Whether the system can adjust remains to be seen," says M. B. Nease, associate professor of marketing at Emory University, "I think the system can adjust. But it will take some major changes in thinking," he stresses. For instance, Nease claims that brand managers must develop a broader perspective and, with management support, must enlarge the scope of their job to include "some kind of social audit." Nease concedes that the brand manager's emphasis on volume "creates a great deal of efficiencies that were not there before. But," he adds, "maybe it has not gone far enough, maybe the product has

some broader ramifications in society that should somehow be accommodated within the system."

P & G's Model Brand Setup
The company that started it all—giant P&G—continues to be the model for all other companies that set up brand-management systems. "This approach is so basic to our business philosophy and has been so successful," says Edgar H. Lotspeich, P&G advertising vice-president, "that no one to my knowledge has seriously asked whether we should try something else."

P&G breaks its system down into more than 50 brand groups. Each group usually handles one brand and includes a brand manager, assistant brand manager, and one or two brand assistants. The brand manager assigns the two or three assistants broad areas of responsibility, and within a tight framework of checks and balances, they work closely with corporate specialists on their brand's annual marketing plan development, ad copy, media planning and selection, sales promotion, package design, market research, and business analysis and forecasting.

The Tide brand group, for instance, might want to change its package design. The group would work with the art and package design department on the new design. The sales department would help evaluate how the change might affect shelf space, stacking, special displays, and trade reaction. The market research department would probably run some tests. And the manufacturing department would advise on costs and timetables.

The Key: Fine Tuning
The key to the system, however, is people and P&G's airtight recruiting and training programs. Another element is a well-tuned chain of command that includes a rigorous system of checks and balances. This is why so many companies that start out with a P&G-style organizational chart seldom obtain quite the same results.

Robert M. Fulmer, professor of management at Georgia State University, recalls working for

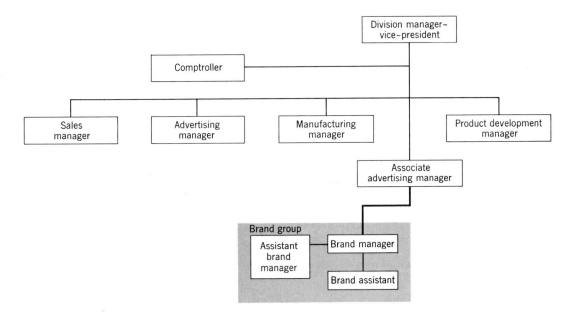

Figure 12.8   The old and the new in the management of brand marketing: P&G still makes one manager responsible for the whole job, but Figure 12.9 shows another approach.

P&G in the 1960s right after graduating from college, "I had been there three or four months," he says, "and I was asked to prepare a sales promotion involving an expenditure of maybe $300,000. My boss, the brand manager, read it and made a recommendation, I revised it, and then it went from the brand manager to the associate advertising manager. He pointed out certain areas and made suggestions. I revised it, and it went back again. This time the associate and manager sent it to the division vice-president. It came back with a couple of minor changes. Then it went to the marketing vice-president, and he ultimately presented it to the executive committee. This is the way authority is delegated and shared. But at this point, whose proposal was it?"

With its system, P&G has managed to strike the right balance in an organizational field that is marked by enormous oscillation. "On the one hand," says John Howard, marketing professor at Columbia University's Graduate School of Business, "you must hit the right balance between a centralized and decentralized structure. Then you must also balance an expertise by product (in the brand manager) with an expertise by job or function (in corporate specialists on sales promotion and so on)."

Because of this, Stanley M. Davis, associate professor of organizational behavior at Harvard Business School, claims that the modern brand system has almost become an anomaly. Although the brand manager has all the responsibility for a

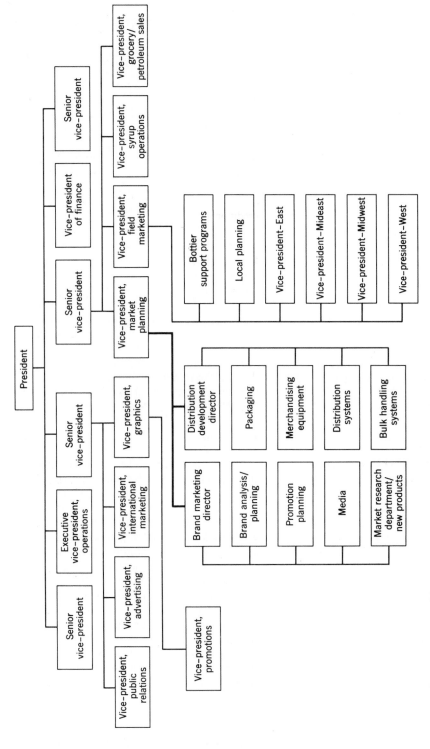

Figure 12.9 Pepsi-Cola has broken the job down into several functions.

product, he or she usually has no authority. Meanwhile, the "functional executives" or job specialists who are assistants, have authority but no brand responsibility. "This goes against one of the classical tenets of American management—the unity of command," says Davis. In older pyramid organizations, each member knew his place and to whom he reported. "Now you have ambiguity in the structure," says Davis. "Each member of the organization has to balance out conflicting desires from more than one superior. It requires a whole new way of thinking. You have to acknowledge conflict and be able to cope with it."

As one way of coping, Pillsbury, General Mills, and many other companies are simplifying their brand structures and trying to create a more "fluid" system. "Any highly structured organization is a problem," says H. Brewster Atwater, Jr., an executive vice-president at General Mills, Inc.

Five years ago, Atwater reorganized General Mills' Consumer Products Division into five decentralized mini-divisions, shortening communication channels and increasing the brand manager's flexibility and access to specialists—as well as the sales. Before the change, the division's rate of growth ran 6 to 9 percent a year. Since then, the growth rate has averaged 13 percent.

"What is fundamental is that your structure reflect the things that are important to your company and its growth," stresses Ronald Cox, marketing director for the Grocery Products Div. of Pillsbury Co. In Pillsbury's new "team approach," the product manager now acts more like a traffic manager than the president of his or her own little company. W. Haynes Kelly, product manager for all Pillsbury cake mixes, insists that this does not diminish the role. "It simply means that the other spokes of the wheel gain in importance," he says. "Market research is more important, because the niches are getting smaller and we have to find where our product fits. Consumer services are also gaining, since this builds the product and keeps us selling."

Closer to the Consumer

At the same time, Kelly claims that a team approach sharpens brand reflexes. He cites the 1970 Food & Drug Administration ban on cyclamates. "Our artificial sweeteners were all based on a cyclamate formula," Kelly says, "and the team hastily reformed on a crash basis to decide which way to go. The FDA decision came on Friday, and we all met Saturday morning." In this case, Kelly coordinated efforts among the legal department, which was trying to pin down Washington on specifics; research, which was working on a replacement product; marketing, which had to contact 30,000 supermarkets and either mark Pillsbury products with a warning sticker or destroy the product if the grocer wanted credit or a refund; and accounting, which handled refunds and credits.

One of the biggest complaints against product/brand managers is their preoccupation with the internal functioning of their own company. Because of the nature of the system, they must constantly work at getting their share of advertising, market research, sales promotion, and other services. "He just does not get involved enough with the ultimate user of the product and with other external marketing functions," says Richard L. Johnson, general manager of the Foodservice Marketing Dept. of H. J. Heinz Co. Now Heinz, which switched to product management in 1964, is trying to correct that with a new structure which combines product management and market management.

A few years ago, for instance, Heinz had a single product manager for bottled ketchup. This person handled both the food service and grocery divisions. Today each division has separate managers. As Johnson puts it, "There is quite a difference between selling ketchup to a retail grocery organization, which makes a profit on bottled ketchup, and to a restaurant chain, which gives the ketchup away."

Like many other companies, Heinz is also aligning related product groups under the same product managers. In the institutional feeding market, one product manager handles restaurant-pack soups, entrees, and puddings. Another oversees 14-ounce ketchup, bottled sauces, mustard, and other table condiments. "The next step," says Johnson, "would be to segment the food service market into an institutional market and a commercial restaurant market." Then the institutional market, he continues, could be further split up among schools, colleges, prisons, and hospitals. Similarly, commercial restaurants could be broken down into drug and variety stores, drive-ins, coffee shops, and fine restaurants.

Heublein, Inc., which jettisoned its old brand management system three months ago, is substituting a similar market management setup, partly in response to a slowdown in the liquor industry's growth rate. "The industry is losing out to beers and, most important, to wines," says Jerry Adler, a Heublein sales and marketing vice-president. "Yet, while some liquor segments, such as American-produced bourbon whiskey, are declining, others are exploding upward. To lock in on the marketplace, we had to evolve a system to capitalize on these changes."

Previously, Heublein had three product groups. Each group had a vodka brand and a separate manager for each brand. "We were structured with all kinds of people." says Adler, "We needed 30 people in a vodka meeting. That became untenable. No meetings were ever conclusive. No decisions were ever made."

Now, Heublein is switching from a brand emphasis to a broader market or "category" emphasis. One manager supervises all vodkas, another handles premixed cocktails and cordials, and so on.

"The category manager," says Adler, "is more flexible and better able to watch for regional, pricing, and attitudinal differences across his product group, and adjust prices, advertising, merchandising, publicity, and research to meet local needs. Where the category manager needs a new brand, he can create it. If the geriatric set should suddenly decide that drinking vodka will prolong life, the vodka manager could either reposition existing brands or create a new 'Golden Age' vodka."

Organizations in Flux

Among the companies that have scrapped brand or product management altogether, Eastman Kodak probably underwent the most massive restructuring. Since dumping the system in 1965, Kodak has reorganized entirely toward markets and channels of distribution. There are now separate Kodak marketing divisions for business systems, consumer products, international operations, motion pictures and education, professional customers, commercial and industrial markets, and radiography. Each is a self-contained profit center.

In the Consumer Markets Division, for instance, the line organization goes from salesperson to district sales manager to regional sales manager to field operations manager to division sales manager—who happens to be William S. Allen. "There are also trade-channel specialists," says Allen, "who keep an eye on identifiable outlet groups such as drug stores, supermarkets, photo specialty stores and so on. This way, we can watch for special needs and opportunities."

Barbara Pitre is a former product manager for the Levi's for Gals Division of Levi Strauss & Co., which just went through its second major product management shakeup in 14 months. She summarizes many of the complaints of the harried product/brand manager. "Before," she says, "I was a designer, fabric buyer, planner, expediter of paperwork, and overseer of production, I couldn't get to the root of a problem and find a solution. We weren't marketing the line. We were just merchandising it." The major problem, she says, was defining her market. "The product manager," she notes, "has been plodding along, figuring everything in the product was being greatly received by the consumer when we didn't really know how much merchandise was selling, for instance, because of retailer markdowns and closeouts."

Under the restructuring, which took place in April, the Levi's for Gals Division was split into two subdivisions organized along "functional" or job lines: Levi's for Me (misses' sizes) and Levi's Juniors (junior sizes). The product manager's job was divided into three separate functional jobs for each subdivision. There is a designer responsible for styling, an operations manager who handles production, and a merchandising line manager, the spot Mrs. Pitre moved into. She is now in charge of financial planning and marketing for the Levi's Juniors subdivision. Her main goals are profits and market share. All three managers report to a merchandising manager who, in effect, acts as product manager.

Gary Delles, merchandising manager for the Levi's for Me subdivision, says it is only a matter of time before other Levi Strauss divisions are restructured the same way. "In a fast-moving market like women's wear," he insists, "the product manager doesn't function fast enough. The concept becomes frustrating for the individual and wasteful by duplicating effort. It just doesn't get results."

How Much Authority?

Some brand experts feel that the future of brand management will continue to be one long grope for a workable system that may or may not come. "The product manager's role has varied all the way from office boy to czar," says Harold Koontz, professor of management at UCLA's Graduate School of Management. "Many companies are just now learning what P&G has known all along: Somehow, you have to work out a system of authority, not necessarily apparent on the organization chart. This allows the product manager to effectively cut across several operating lines."

As it is, says Richard H. Brien, group vice-president of marketing at Dart Industries, Inc., the brand manager's job is almost an organizational impossibility. "There is potential conflict at every turn," he says. "The job description inevitably reads 'market the brand,' but the man is never given the necessary authority on a straight power basis. His authority is always in terms of negotiation or persuasion. That's a heck of a strain on a guy."

"My biggest problem," says Bradford Watson, brand manager for spices and extracts at R. T. French Co., "is getting field salesmen to give my line the selling time it deserves in proportion to other lines they sell. Our salesmen tend to concentrate on high-profit lines, such as powdered sauces and gravy mixes, to boost their bonuses."

Another frustration: Watson has profit responsibility for spices and extracts, yet no voice at all in the biggest factor that affects profits—price.

James T. Evans, group brand manager at California Canners & Growers, a big fruit and vegetable processing cooperative, recalls similar frustrations at Hunt-Wesson Foods, where he once worked. "The top man there called all the shots," Evans says, "Products and markets are changing so fast, and consumers are asking for so much more, that the brand manager can't wait around for committees. The brand manager must make the decisions, and he must live or die with the bottom line. But many companies don't let him operate that way."

Evans claims that CCG does operate that way. He supervises two brand managers and personally handles two other brands: Diet Delight, a low-calorie fruit product, and Fruit'N Honey, which went on the market last month. In the Fruit'N Honey introduction, Evans made the final decisions on everything, including label design, media schedules, pitches to buyers and brokers, and even pricing. He claims he has full profit responsibility—and the authority to go with it.

On their side, Evans and other boosters of brand management—and they remain legion—are unwavering in their support. "The academicians can argue from their universities that consumerism will force a return to functional systems," says James Matson, vice-president of the Grocery Products Division of Pet, Inc. "However, looking from within a corporation, as long as there is emphasis on sales and earnings, there has to be accountability at the product/profit-center level. You can't spread this profit accountability among functional elements such as sales promotion, advertising, market planning, and so on. The right kind of marketing man can manage his brands to achieve sales and profit objectives and still be responsive to consumerism."

While Pepsi, Levi Strauss, and several other companies have reorganized away from product or brand management, even they have not entirely escaped the need for someone who performs some of the brand manager's broader duties. As Pepsi's Sculley notes, "The same planning, analytical, and

Figure 12.10   Pepsi's John Sculley on Brand Management

"The idea of Pepsi being No. 1 in all areas of the soft drink business may seem like a daydream," says John Sculley. After all, Pepsi has only 20.4% of the soft drink market compared with 34.8% for Coca-Cola Co. Yet Pepsi's youthful (34), energetic senior vice-president is convinced that Pepsi—somehow, some day—will catch up with its now distant rival. Sculley pins much of his faith on his company's shift from brand management to a "functional" organization. "As we all become more familiar with strategic planning," he says, "we'll learn how to use these resources better and better."

Sculley on the changing marketplace: "Since most companies started with a functional system, this may look like a step backward for us. But it's not. This is because marketing has changed so much in the last 15 years that the functions existing then are totally different now. The type of person Pepsi looked for 15 years ago needed strong advertising and publicity skills. Now, we are looking for people steeped in planning, distribution, finance, and economic analysis."

On brand management vs. a functional organization: "Trade merchandising needs are becoming so selective that there is simply more pressure to specialize by job rather than product. In their merchandising requirements, service stations are different from convenience stores, which are different from chain stores, and they're all different from discount stores. Back a few years ago, our merchandising people tended to perform strictly a liaison function. They contacted the customer and told him what was new in merchandising equipment. Today, with our new system, we are able to work much closer with bottlers and their customers on specific trade needs."

On coordinating functions: "This is no easy job. As priorities change in one functional group, there are usually immediate implications for other functional groups, and without good communications and a clear understanding of who does what to whom, an awful lot of wheel-spinning could take place."

On the chain of command: "We feel that a lean organization is usually the most effective organization, and we try to do away with the layers upon layers of management that often frustrate the young brand manager."

On profit accountability: "It's less than fair to say that functional departments have profit accountability. Yet I can't think of a brand structure with true profit accountability, either. Profits are made up of so many different pieces of the business today that it's hard to say that any brand manager has profit accountability. If he did, he would not be the brand manager. He would be the president of the company."

coordinating skills that a product manager needs in a brand organization are still very much required in a functional organization."

Neither Sculley nor anyone else, of course, expects brand management to pass totally from the scene. General Mills' Atwater probably best sums up the mood that prevails among marketing people today: "Because of market segmentation and other pressures, the product manager cannot be the see-all expert anymore. Our philosophy is that the product manager, while important, is no longer king."

Discussion Questions

1. What difficulties do you foresee in the switch in the brand manager concept at Pepsi Cola?
2. How does the brand management concept fit into the "traditional" line-staff organizational plans?
3. Does the Pepsi Cola model differ substantially from the Procter & Gamble model? Which would you prefer to work in? Why?

Ajax Manufacturing Corporation had a complex line-and-staff organization. Recently, Ned Forrester, who had spent his entire career in the production department, was elected president of the company. Shortly after assuming the presidency, Mr. Forrester wrote the following memorandum.

November 12

From: N. J. Forrester, President
To: All Vice-presidents
Re: Line and Staff Relationships

Since I have been in this company there has always been friction between line and staff. I want this to stop.

The purpose of our staff people is to advise and assist our line managers. If that advice is worth anything, our line managers ought to be willing to pay for it.

I propose that our staff departments be set up on a consulting basis. They are to bill the line departments for any work done at a mutually agreed-upon price. The entire budget of the staff departments will consist of money earned in this fashion. No line manager will be charged for any staff services he or she does not desire. As usual, line departments will be evaluated upon their profitability, after deduction of funds paid to staff departments.

I shall appreciate your prompt cooperation in implementing this policy.

N.J.F.

The memo from President Forrester represented a radical change because the budgets of staff departments had previously been determined each year by the president. Visibly upset by the president's memo, Jack Worthy, administrative vice-president, replied as follows:

November 19

From: J. P. Worthy, Administrative Vice-President
To: N. J. Forrester, President
Re: Line and Staff Relationships

Your proposal of November 12 would effectively wreck the accounting, production-control, industrial relations, public relations, and other staff departments for which I am responsible.

We do give advice to line functions, but we are also responsible for checking on, and in some ways supervising, the line. Most line managers would be glad to have us out of their hair; they certainly would not "hire" us, as suggested in your memo. I urge that you immediately withdraw your recommendation to put us on consulting basis.

J.P.W.

Discussion Questions
1. What assumptions did Mr. Forrester make about the nature of line-staff relations?
2. What assumptions about the division of labor between line and staff did Mr. Worthy make in his memo of November 19th?
3. If you were Mr. Worthy, what would you do? Why?

The division of labor, which until recently was lauded as the great American contribution to the world, has now been roundly condemned in the halls of Congress for causing widespread alienation among American workers. This chapter has focused on this inevitable process and sought to enable you, the student, to both see and feel some of the issues surrounding this controversy. We have taken the position that the division of labor is inevitable—and railing against it is as useless as King Canute commanding the tide to stop running. Rather, we have sought to demonstrate some of the positive effects of this division (without some amount of planning in the puzzle game, nothing would have been accomplished, as doers are notoriously poor planners), and some ways in which the potential negative consequences may be reduced (through job redesign). You have experienced some of the passion and emotions that surround this issue in the puzzle game, and can hopefully sense some of them in the case as well. These passions often obscure alternative ways of dealing with the real issue. The case is an excellent example of how emotions and vested interests often muddy the waters.

By not assuming that technology is fixed, as has previously been done, many companies, through job redesign, have taken positive steps to reduce the negative consequences of the division of labor. The Maytag experience is one of many successful instances, although there are limitations on wholesale adoption of this technique. Often such simple devices as earlier inclusion of line personnel in planning activities (as was suggested in the puzzle game) can work wonders in improving overall efficiency and reducing the cost of line staff divisions.

In the final analysis, though, there remain two fundamentally different perspectives—the line perspective and the staff perspective. This is dramatically illustrated in the case. Considerable effort is necessary to bridge the gap. Many techniques discussed in other parts of this text spell out several of these techniques. In any event, the division of labor is an inevitable part of the organizational scene. As such, we as managers must learn to effectively maximize the benefits of such division while minimizing its potential costs.

Here are some principles:

1. Division of labor results in increased organizational efficiency together with increased absence and turnover costs and lower quality.

2. The division of labor is inevitable given the growth in technical knowledge and social responsibilities of business enterprises.

3. Job redesign of either horizontal enlargement (greater diversity), vertical enrichment (greater responsibility), or autonomous work group (diversity

plus responsibility with group control) results in improved quality and job satisfaction for many employees, and is one way to reduce the negative consequences of the division of labor.

4. Staff personnel perform service, administration, and specialized control functions in a company.

5. Conflict exists between line and staff personnel which arises partially out of the different functions they perform.

6. Conflicts between line and staff personnel can be reduced through such management actions as the matrix organization.

CHAPTER THIRTEEN STAFFING

At the conclusion of this chapter you should be able to:

1. Explain the importance of the staffing function.
2. List and describe the steps in the staffing process.
3. Discuss how government legislation affects the staffing process.
4. Discuss how labor unions affect the staffing process.

THE PERSONNEL MANAGER'S IN-BASKET

I. Objectives
   A. To take the role of a personnel manager.
   B. To receive and respond to the correspondence in your in-basket.
   C. To cope with a number of problems that are related to the staffing function.

II. Premeeting Preparation
   A. Read the instructions.

III. Instructions
   A. For this exercise each student will work independently.
   B. Here is the situation:
      The Chentenham Division of the Wyncote Corporation manufactures outdoor antennas for television sets and C.B. radios that usually are sold in discount department stores. You are Dave Reimer and just came on board last week as the divisional personnel manager. Prior to this assignment you spent three years as a personnel recruiter for the corporate headquarters. You just stopped into the office to check your mail before taking a plane to the home office of the corporation. You find the following items (Figures 13.1, 13.2, 13.3, and 13.4) in your in-basket and have 20 minutes to deal with them before taking your plane. You can leave instructions with your secretary on how you wish the problems handled. Please write out the instructions you would leave your secretary.
   C. Turn to the memos, remove them from the book, examine them, and prepare your responses.

   | *Time for Step C: 20 minutes* |

IV. Discussion
   Your instructor will help you explore what happened in the exercise and its meaning for management.

   | *Time for discussion: 20 minutes* |

National Association for the Advancement of Colored People
September 26, 1979

Mr. David Reimer
Personnel Director
Cheltenham Division
Wyncote Corporation

Dear Mr. Reimer:

There is undoubtedly a file on the matter that is discussed in this letter. Because your employment with the Cheltenham Division of Wyncote is relatively new, I wish to begin this letter by summarizing the frustrating experiences we have had with your organization:

1. Over one year ago we contacted James Laughlin, then President of the Cheltenham Corporation. We informed him that we were upset over the fact that only six of your 150 production workers were black; and that no black employees were found in the office or the managerial ranks of the corporation. Mr. Laughlin stated that he was unaware of this and asked for time to investigate the matter.

2. We never heard from Mr. Laughlin again. All of our subsequent attempts to contact him by telephone were stopped by his secretary and our letters remained unanswered.

3. When Cheltenham was taken over by Wyncote, there was no response by the Wyncote Corporation to any of our inquiries on this matter.

4. From our own information, we find that the situation regarding employment of blacks has not changed.

In the light of these considerations, I intend to bring discrimination charges against the Cheltenham Division next week and to request that all of the ministers in the black churches in this town inform their congregations this Sunday of the situation.

Percy Grainger
Executive Director

Figure 13.1

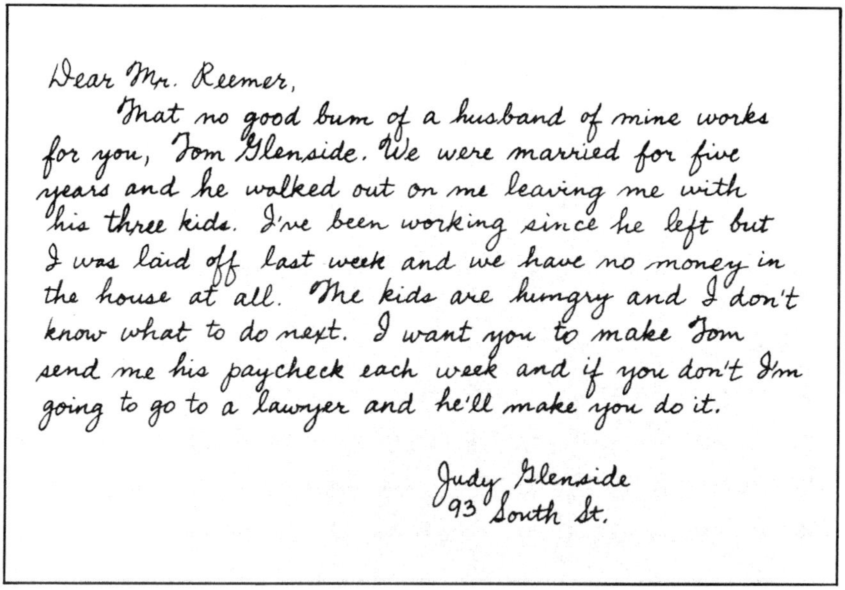

Dear Mr. Reemer,

    That no good bum of a husband of mine works for you, Tom Glenside. We were married for five years and he walked out on me leaving me with his three kids. I've been working since he left but I was laid off last week and we have no money in the house at all. The kids are hungry and I don't know what to do next. I want you to make Tom send me his paycheck each week and if you don't I'm going to go to a lawyer and he'll make you do it.

                    Judy Glenside
                    93 South St.

Figure 13.2

```
┌─────────────────────────────────────────────────────────────────┐
│                                                                   │
│                        INTEROFFICE MEMO                           │
│                                                                   │
│  Dear Dave:                                                       │
│      There is a difficult problem in connection with Joe Brown    │
│  the truck driver. You no                                         │
│  doubt recall that Brown was called into my office two weeks ago  │
│  and charged with                                                 │
│  stealing a case of antennas over the Labor Day weekend. Brown    │
│  denied the theft and                                             │
│  agreed to take a lie detector test. I just got the results of    │
│  the test. The operator asked                                     │
│  Brown specific questions on stealing antennas over Labor Day.    │
│  Brown denied the                                                 │
│  charge and the operator believed that he was telling the truth.  │
│  But at the end of the                                            │
│  interview, the operator asked a question none of us anticipated. │
│  He asked Brown if he                                             │
│  ever stole anything from us while working for us. Brown then     │
│  said no but the indi-                                            │
│  cators went crazy. The polygraph operator is convinced Brown     │
│  lied in response to this                                         │
│  question and is convinced that he has stolen from us while in    │
│  our employ. I suspended                                          │
│  Brown for three days and I would like to get your OK to fire him.│
│                                                                   │
│                                      Jim Oswald                   │
│                                      General Foreman              │
│                                      9/24/79                      │
│                                                                   │
└─────────────────────────────────────────────────────────────────┘
```

Figure 13.3

INTEROFFICE MEMO

Dear Dave:

  We've had some fall off in orders this month and this is the time that we normally get a little slow. Checking our order situation, it looks as if it's time to lay off four workers. If normal patterns prevail, we should call them back to work in from six to eight weeks. In the past we've laid off production workers on a seniority basis. The four least senior people are:

Name	Hiring Date
Millie Tompkins	9/1/75
Bryan Wilson	8/15/75
Sandra Jones	7/29/75
Amedeo Garlitos	6/15/75

  Would you please prepare the layoff forms.

9/28/78

Jim Oswald
General Foreman

(Note to the reader: The first three names on this list are black; Garlitos is Puerto Rican.)

Figure 13.4

Staffing is the process that puts flesh onto the bones of the organization structure. Once a structure has been developed to accomplish the organizational goals and objectives, people have to be placed into the structure to make it work. This does not mean that goal setting, organization structure, and staffing take place in a sequential manner, but rather they are linked and are continuing operations (Figure 13.5). In essence, the staffing process involves recruiting employees, placing them in jobs for which they are suited, training employees to meet job demands, organizing and managing the compensation of employees, and managing their movement into, up, over, and out of the organization.

THE STAFFING FUNCTION

The staffing function is the key to the successful operation of any organization because of the important role that human resources play in organizational success. Without the people, organizations would simply be shells. After all, it is people who set goals, develop plans, and create organizations.

As with all of the management functions, the staffing function has become more complex as society and organizations have become more complex. The builders of Stonehenge needed designers, stone cutters, and many strong backs to haul and erect the stones. Although the first two jobs might require special skills, the physical labor portion of the task could be done by almost anyone who wasn't disabled. If one man didn't show up to haul stones one day, he could simply be replaced by another. With the advent of the industrial revolution, and the introduction of the factory system, jobs were differentiated, and individuals learned only the skills needed to carry out a specific operation. This was an attempt to simplify jobs and to increase productivity.

Figure 13.5   Linkage between staffing and other functions.

The attempt was quite successful, and complex jobs began to disappear to be replaced by simple jobs done by "hands." By the turn of the twentieth century, production process and products became more and more complex, and the simple jobs began to increase in complexity. This process was further accelerated as our society moved more and more away from blue-collar work and more toward white-collar and service work. Now, it is not just a matter of attracting factory "hands," but the right types of employees—milling machine operators, accountants, nurses, truck drivers, computer programmers—to fill the many slots in the organization structure.

Thus, although staffing is the job of every manager, most firms have created staff groups and personnel departments to provide expert assistance to managers. Personnel departments, or Human Resources departments as they are sometimes called, manage the staffing process (Figure 13.6). Although the manager has ultimate responsibility for staffing, the complexity of modern business has made it necessary for one group to manage to process to ensure uniformity, legality, and equity in the staffing process.

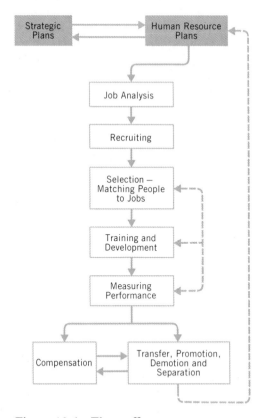

Figure 13.6 The staffing process.

The staffing process is composed of the following steps:

1. Human Resource Planning
2. Job Analysis
3. Recruiting
4. Selection
5. Training and Development
6. Measuring Performance
7. Compensation Management
8. Managing the movement of people up, over, and out of the organization.

Human Resource Planning

Human Resource Planning, as the term implies, is the process of looking toward the future to determine organizational human resource needs and arranging to have the necessary resources available at the right time and in the right place. As with any type of planning process, Human Resource Planning involves a forward look to see what the environment inside and outside the firm might look like. Then, approaches for dealing with any problems that are forecasted must be developed. If the Human Resource Planning process works well, it is hardly noticed, but if it works poorly, there are all kinds of problems as the organization finds itself short of trained people, and always scrambling to fill openings.

For the Human Resource Planning process to work effectively, it must be linked with the corporate strategic planning process. For most organizations, human resources are as important as financial or production resources. Therefore, strategic planners must consider the availability of human resources when they are developing the future direction of the organization. Human Resource Planners must understand the future direction of the organization so that they can develop appropriate plans for providing the needed human resources to accomplish the strategic plan. The ideal situation is to have the strategic and Human Resource planning processes integrated to ensure that both types of plans recognize the needs of the other.

Job Analysis

Job analysis is a method for evaluating jobs and describing them in terms of general characteristics such as level of responsibility, working conditions, and the qualifications required to execute the job. In many ways, job analysis provides the foundation for most of the staffing process. Evaluation of jobs allows for an accurate determination of the numbers and types of employees needed to fill organizational staffing needs. The job analysis process can point out training and development needs for current employees to allow them to fill future openings. The wage and salary system, if it is to be equitable, must be based on accurate analysis of the job structure of the organization. Finally, performance appraisal is based on comparing actual performance with the type of performance described in the job analysis. If we really think about it, how could we begin to recruit new employees if we didn't have a good idea about what kinds of activities we will expect them to perform?

Recruiting

The recruiting process involves attracting potential candidates for positions in the organization. The hope is that a pool of qualified individuals can be assembled from which the manager can select the individual or individuals that seem to be best suited for the available job. Newspaper want ads and college recruiting are just some examples of recruiting activities carried on by firms. The two forms of recruiting just described are examples of recruiting from outside of the organization. But recruiting can also be done inside. Many firms have job posting systems, where job openings are published and the information is made available to current employees either before or at the same time the positions are published outside. This allows current employees who have the needed skills, or who are interested in advancing their careers, to apply. No matter what techniques are used to recruit employees, the idea is to have a good size pool of prospects who have the necessary skills to fill job vacancies. Once the pool exists, the manager must decide how to make a selection.

Selection

In the selection process the organization attempts to choose the right person to fill a job vacancy. To some extent it is a mutual choice process as both the organization and the candidate attempt to determine if there is a proper fit, and if the conditions—wages, working conditions, job responsibilities—are mutually acceptable. A number of techniques, either used singly or in combination, are used to aid in selecting employees who fit the needs of the organization. These techniques include:

1. Just about every prospective employee is asked to fill in an application blank. This provides the organization with basic information about the applicant, such as name, previous work experience, education, but many questions that might lead to discriminatory job practices may not be asked, such as race, religion, and national origin.

2. Screening interviews are held to eliminate obvious "misfits" from the pool of applicants. This interview also gives the organization an opportunity to make its expectations known to the candidate so that the candidate can withdraw if these expectations are not acceptable. The interview also allows the organization to obtain information about the candidate's experience and background and if the individual fits the job requirements.

3. Tests are administered to determine if the potential employee has the necessary knowledge and skills to accomplish the job. Many tests that had been used in the past have been ruled discriminatory, and to be sure that the test does not cause more problems than it solves, the ideal test is one that is clearly job related. For example, a typing test for potential typists or an opportunity to run a milling machine for a milling machine operator candidate would be examples of clearly job related tests. Another type of test that is often used for internal candidates involves the use of assessment centers. In an assessment center the candidates are asked to do a number of joblike tasks and their performance is monitored by trained observers. Assessment centers are probably best suited for screening candidates for managerial positions where leadership, decision making, and interpersonal skills may be the major aspects of the job.

4. Background checks are often made to insure that the information on the application blank is accurate and to determine if there are any problems in the candidate's past which might make him or her a poor employee.

5. In-depth interviews are often the final step in the selection process. After the number of candidates is reduced from one to about six, the finalists are often brought to the work location to be interviewed by the immediate supervisor, other superiors, co-workers, and other significant individuals with whom the person will work. The purpose of the in-depth interview is to allow a fine tuning of the selection process. The expectations of both the individual and the organization are explored to try to reduce misunderstandings when the candidate is finally selected.

Training and Development
In many cases new employees have to be trained before they can begin to work effectively on their new job. Sometimes the newly hired employees have the latent ability to perform the assigned tasks but need additional training to transform latent ability into performance. In other situations the individual simply may need to know how this organization does some things that are done in similar ways in other organizations. Firm A may have different requisition forms than Firm B, and the new employee may have to learn "how it's done here," when entering the employment of Firm A.

Another type of training that takes place in organizations is of an ongoing nature and is designed to keep employees up to date in their jobs. There may be new machines or new ways of doing things that might improve productivity or make the job more satisfying, and this information is transmitted to employees using various training techniques, such as films, newsletters, formal training programs, or informal discussions led by supervisors.

Developmental activities are usually designed to prepare employees to take on new and more challenging responsibilities. Because promotion from within is often a key aspect of the personnel policy in many organizations, providing training and development opportunities helps assure the pool of internal candidates when positions open.

Performance Appraisal

Once individuals begin to work in new positions, the next process that comes into play involves measuring performance. Generally, an individual's performance is measured and compared with some yardstick to see how well he or she is "measuring up." The control process will be discussed in detail in the next chapter, but we should examine the importance of performance appraisal to the staffing process. Although it is important to know how well people are doing in general, performance appraisal systems are often linked directly to compensation and to systems of promotion and other changes in job status.

The two key aspects of any performance appraisal systems are the "yardstick" used to measure against, and the technique used to measure performance. The yardstick issue goes back to the job analysis process where job expectations and demands are determined. In some cases they are simple, such as the production of x number of widgets, but in others they are quite complex. The issue of evaluating managerial performance has always been a problem because the yardstick is covered with fuzzy measures, such as "good interpersonal skills" or "good communicator." Figure 13.7 shows one such yardstick that has been passed from hand to hand and photocopied thousands of times. Its originator is unknown, but this person has contributed greatly to our appreciation of the performance appraisal.

The other issue involves measuring actual performance. This will be discussed in greater detail in the next chapter on Control, but we should keep in mind that there are several issues about measurement which are important. Whom should measure? What should be measured? How should it be measured? And how often should it be measured? Some performances can be measured simply by counting the number of items produced, but as we examine more complex tasks where quality, quantity, and intangibles are involved, measurement is much more difficult. But measure we must, in some cases even if we measure the wrong things, because other aspects of the staffing process require measures of performance.

Job Factor	Performance				
	Far Exceeds Job Requirements	Exceeds Job Requirements	Meets Job Requirements	Needs Some Improvement	Does Not Meet Minimum Requirements
Quality	Leaps tall buildings with single bound	Needs running start to leap tall buildings	Can leap only short buildings	Crashes into buildings	Cannot recognize buildings
Timeliness	Is faster than a speeding bullet	As fast as a speeding bullet	Somewhat slower than a bullet	Can only shoot bullets	Wounds self with bullets
Initiative	Stronger than a locomotive	Stronger than a bull elephant	Stronger than a bull	Shoots the bull	Smells like a bull
Adaptability	Walks on water consistently	Walks on water in emergencies	Washes with water	Drinks water	Passes water in emergencies
Communication	Talks with God	Talks with angels	Talks to himself	Argues with himself	Loses arguments with himself
Career Potential	Belongs in general management	Belongs in executive ranks	Belongs in rank and file	Belongs behind a broom	Belongs with competition
Planning	Too bright to worry	Worries about future	Worries about present	Worries about past	Too dumb to worry

Figure 13.7 Yardstick for managerial job.

Compensation

Individuals in the work force are willing to exchange their time, energy, skills, and abilities for financial compensation, job satisfaction, status, and other things that are important to them. There are some individuals for whom financial compensation is not a factor, for example, volunteers in a hospital. But for most of us, a job is a way of making a living. How an organization manages its wage and salary program will have a great deal to do with how satisfied or how dissatisfied its employees are with their jobs. The key issues for any compensation system are: (1) equity, (2) consistency, (3) comparability. The system must be equitable in that jobs that are harder or require the incumbent to assume more responsibility pay more. Thus, there is usually a distribution of compensation that ranges from the lowest level worker up to the president or Chairman of the Board. Consistency is linked to the issue of equity because it refers to the consistent application of the compensation system. If the system is consistent, two individuals doing the same job should receive approximately the same compensation. There may be a range of salaries for a particular job, but more and more we hear the call for "equal pay for equal work." The problem is to determine what jobs are equal.

Although the compensation system must be equitable and consistent, it also must recognize the reality of the external labor market and provide compensation that is comparable with that provided by other firms competing in the same labor market. If a firm chooses to pay its workers less than the prevailing rates, it stands to lose its mobile workers and will have difficulty in recruiting new workers. It may, on the other hand, decide to pay higher wages than other organizations as a way of increasing its pool of recruits and reducing salary based turnover. Whatever the firm does, it must try to balance equity, consistency, and comparability. There may be cases where one of the three will dominate and upset the other factors, such as situations where there may be a temporary shortage of a certain type of skill. In a case like that, market forces may drive wage rates for that skill completely out of line with the remaining wage rates, but in the short run, the rate must be paid if the jobs are to be filled. There can also be location differences where wages might have to be adjusted because of cost-of-living differences, as in a foreign work assignment. But these are the exceptions and should be treated as such for there is nothing which will upset employees more than a compensation system they think is "unfair."

Up, Down, Over, and Out

The final step in the staffing process is involved with the movement of people up, down, over, and out of the organization. Most people, when they enter an organization, do not expect to be doing the same job for the rest of their lives. Most people expect growth as their careers take them from one assignment to another and from one level of responsibility to another. People expect to move "up the organization ladder." But life is not necessarily all peaks; there may be some valleys, or at least some plateaus. Decisions concerning promotions, demotions, transfers, and even separation are usually based on the results of performance appraisal. If they are not, and the results are discriminatory, the organization is wide open to legal action. But aside from promoting people to increase satisfaction and transferring individuals to satisfy their needs to travel or learn, the organization should have an overall plan in mind. Linking back to the Human Resource Plan, the process of moving people up, down, over, and out of the organization should be designed to ensure that the right people are at the right place at the right time to keep the organization operating effectively and efficiently.

CONSTRAINTS

In making decisions concerning most aspects of the staffing process, management does not have a completely free hand. There are constraints that must be considered in staffing decisions, and in some cases the constraints severely limit management's discretion. The two major constraining forces involved in the staffing process are: (1) government regulation and (2) labor unions.

Legislation and unionization arose from the belief that business organizations had gained excessive power, and as a result were acting in ways that were detrimental to society in general and their employees in particular.

Regulation

Following tax regulations, the relationship between a firm and its human resources is the second most highly regulated area. There are regulations concerning pay and hours of work, working conditions, pensions, discrimination in hiring, firing, and other employment practices, as well as the relationship between a firm and its union. The following are some of the major pieces of federal legislation that affect the staffing process. Please keep in mind that in many cases there are also state and local laws that parallel and enlarge upon the federal statutes.

The *Fair Labor Standards Act* (1938) was originally passed to set a minimum wage of 25 cents an hour and to increase employment during the Depression by requiring employers to pay overtime pay for work over the norm of a 40-hour work week.

In 1963, the *Equal Pay Act* was passed. This act mandates that men and women doing the same jobs must receive equal pay, and strikes a blow against sex discrimination.

The battle against discrimination in employment was given its biggest boost by the passage of the *Civil Rights Act of 1964*. Specifically, Title VII of the act declared that discrimination in employment is illegal, and set up the Equal Employment Opportunity Commission (EEOC) to police that portion of the act. The purpose of the EEOC is to end discrimination based on race, color, religion, sex, or national origin in hiring, promotion, firing, wages, testing, training, apprenticeships, and other conditions of employment; and to promote voluntary action programs by employers, unions, and community organizations to put equal employment into actual operation. The commission was further strengthened by the passage in 1972 of the *Equal Employment Opportunity Act of 1972*.

Discrimination in hiring, firing, promotion, compensation, and other employment conditions on the basis of age was made illegal by the *Age Discrimination in Employment Act of 1967*. As amended in 1978, this act protects employees and prospective employees between the ages of 40 and 69 against discriminatory employment practices.

The *Occupational Safety and Health Act* was passed in 1970 to protect workers against unsafe and unhealthy working conditions.

Even retirement plans have come under regulation as the *Employment Retirement Income Security Act (ERISA)* was passed to protect employee pension rights against firms that might go out of business, and to provide some portability to pension rights that an individual might earn.

Although the bulk of the legislation just mentioned is designed to protect the employee or prospective employee against specific actions that an employer might take, the legislation that concerns union-management relations is of a slightly different nature. Even though there has been a long string of legislation concerning labor-management relations, the major piece of legislation is the *National Labor Relations Act (Wagner Act)* of 1935. The Act made it unlawful for an employer to: (1) refuse to bargain collectively, (2) interfere with the workers rights to collective bargaining, (3) discriminate against union members, and (4) discriminate against any employee who took advantage of their rights. To ensure that the rights of employees were upheld, the National Labor Relations Board (NLRB) was created. The NLRB attempts to ensure democratic processes by holding elections and certifying proper bargaining units. The Board also acts in a quasi-judicial capacity to protect employees against unfair practices.

Unions

Because the firm must bargain with a properly designated representative of its employees, usually a union, agreements that are reached in the collective bargaining agreement act as constraints. Most union contracts, agreed upon by both management and the union, set wage rates; seniority rights that may specify who gets first rights to a job that opens, or who must be laid off first; working conditions; pension plans; fringe benefits; and methods for handling problems that might arise during the time the contract is in force. Thus, we can see that, at least for those employees who are covered under the union contract, management does not have a free hand in determining compensation, training, promotions, transfers, layoffs, and many other conditions of employment. In some cases unions take on some of the staffing functions. There are union-sponsored apprentice training programs and in some cases the union even does recruiting and selection, with management simply telling the union how many of each kind of worker it requires and the union sending over the required number of these workers. But in most cases, the unions and management work together, if for different reasons, in an effort to make the system work.

EMPLOYEE RELATIONS AND UNION ORGANIZING CAMPAIGNS

Union Elections Are Seldom Won or Lost During the Campaign

JAMES H. HOPKINS AND ROBERT D. BINDERUP

The threat of a union organizing drive is a continuing concern that each personnel professional and line manager, operating in a non-union environment, must face. Union elections are seldom won or lost during the campaign prior to election—the outcome is determined by a firm's overall employee relations climate.

This article reviews why labor unions desire to organize and represent employees, why employees may feel a need to support a union and what practices can be followed to create a positive employee relations climate which should minimize those needs. Also outlined is the organizational drive including preliminary signs, National Labor Relations Board (NLRB)[1] procedures for a determination election and what the company can and cannot do during the campaign prior to election.

Many employers feel secure that their employees would never approach a union to request assistance in organizing fellow workers. Those employers are usually shocked to find that generally union organizing efforts are indeed "inside jobs." Most often the union becomes a willing and enthusiastic participant which coordinates and finances the organizational attempt for several reasons.

First, union memberships, while holding stable at about 19.4 million since 1970, are declining as a proportion of the workforce represented from about 25 percent to 20 percent.[2] Unions are businesses and any business which has suffered a marketshare loss of such proportion would jump to regain lost revenue. Increased memberships mean increased dues (revenue).

Second, recent union election statistics reflect a poor showing on a percentage basis. In the fiscal year ended September 30, 1977, the NLRB conducted 9,626 conclusive representation and related elections. Unions won 4,424 of these, or 46 percent. In elections dealing specifically with collective bargaining representation, unions lost 52 percent; they lost 76 percent of decertification elections.[3] Unions need a high volume of elections to gain membership since their winning percentage is low.

Third, unions sometimes target a company or an industry for organization. A non-union company in a heavily unionized area is a likely objective. Certain industries with low wage structures such as retailing, health care and other service industries are attracting increased organizational activity.

Finally, union leadership truly believes that the rank and file worker needs the protection of collective bargaining. Employers who ignore the needs of the modern employee will undoubtedly find that unions can and do provide a countervailing power structure for disenchanted workers.

1. National Labor Relations Board, established by Congress with the National Labor Relations Act of 1935

Source. The Personnel Administrator, March 1980.

2. Labor Relations Yearbook—1978, The Bureau of National Affairs, Inc., Washington, D.C. (1979) . . . 264
3. Ibid., From the Forty-Second Annual Report of the NLRB; Fiscal Year 1977 271

Vulnerability

The needs of the modern employee cannot be conveniently categorized and satisfied. Some employees enjoy hard work, accept reasonable pay and expect a tyrannical boss. Some employees want little or no work, high pay and reject any type of supervision. Fortunately, in most organizations' employees are reasonably satisfied with their jobs, pay and supervision. If this reasonably satisfactory condition deteriorates, workers can withdraw and quit or they can stay and fight, often by turning to a union. It is important to remember that what seems fair and reasonable to management often seems arbitrary and even ridiculous to the workers. To explore some areas of dissatisfaction we present a fairly typical scene:

Time: 9:30 a.m.
Place: Cafeteria
Event: Coffee Break
Participants: Alice, Shipping Department
              Secretary
              Henry, Fork Lift Operator

Henry: Can you believe I paid 25¢ for this dry roll . . . and I hear they're jacking up the coffee prices again!

Alice: Inflation . . . we just can't win.

Henry: Yeah, and our company's jumped on Carter's seven percent bandwagon . . . you didn't see the UAW settle for seven percent. I'm sick of making $6 an hour.

Alice: You're sick? I went to college for two years and graduated from secretarial school and I make $2 an hour less than you do.

Henry: We both should be plumbers . . . they make $14 an hour—but they're in a union.

Alice: You see that Shipping Clerk job posting?

Henry: You mean Mary's job—she's the only one qualified the way they customized the specifications to match hers.

Alice: That really burns me up! But I expected it since the boss is so chummy with her. I should file a grievance—that would end my career here (laughing).

Henry: (Laughing) You're right there! You ever worked for a boss like him?—What a mess. He treats us like kids and he has no idea what's going on.

Alice: Yeah, but he's only following the example upper management sets. If they really cared for us, they'd hire better supervisors. I'd sure like to get a chance at management, but it's not what you know—it's who you know around here.

Henry: Why don't they listen to us anyway? We could show them how to save money and get more profits so they could pay us more!

Alice: Pay us more? I heard there's a big layoff coming. Now that Mary's getting promoted around me, I'd be the first to go.

Henry: I heard that too—I guess we better keep our mouths shut. Let's get back to work—don't want to get chewed out.

Alice: Yeah, managers are the only ones that get away with long breaks around this place.

This conversation dramatizes some main areas of dissatisfaction that cause employees to sign union cards: inequitable pay, favoritism, poor supervision, lack of appreciation, no outlet for gripes or suggestions, job insecurity, unfulfilled leadership aspirations and "we" (the workers) versus "they" (management). Firms failing to address these employee concerns are vulnerable to union organization.

Positive Climate

Employers who feel that remaining non-union is in the best interests of management and the employees eligible for union membership can create an employee relations climate that will prevent unionization. Book after book is written and seminar after seminar is taught concerning methods available to management in its effort to remain non-union. This article does not attempt to provide a detailed analysis of those methods. Rather, we suggest a common-sense approach to positive employee relations, capsulizing those practices essential to running a non-union business. The main areas covered are compensation, policies and practices, supervisory awareness and employee participation.

Companies that hold down wages and benefits to increase profitability will soon share reduced profits with a union bureaucracy. Rates of pay and the total benefit package must fairly and competitively reflect the marketplace for employees. This external equity is not difficult to maintain. Surveys of local, regional, or national wage rates are used depending on the recruiting pattern. Key or "benchmark" jobs provide adequate comparison. Traditional methods of delivery are the automatic progression to job rate in "blue-collar" jobs and merit pay for "white-collar" jobs. Progression systems are much safer to administer than are merit programs due to a reduced perception of favoritism. Keeping updated on benefit improvements is a matter of knowing what your competitors offer and what your employees want. A younger, mobile workforce is probably not as interested in a retirement program as is the typical general manager who often decides new benefits on his/her inaccurate perception of what the "troops" really need (whether they know it or not). Recent inflationary times have created more demand for monetary reward rather than for increased benefit levels.

Once a firm is confident that it is externally competitive, that information should be communicated to the employees. The company need not match every wage in the community, but the overall wage and benefit package must be defendable.

Perceived internal equity problems are nearly impossible to eliminate. Virtually every employee can name at least one other employee who contributes less and makes more. But each company should strive to maintain internal equity among the various job classifications. Whether by ranking, by point/factor, or by other more sophisticated systems, employers should be able to explain why certain jobs pay more than other jobs. Job titles can also cause perceived inequity. In one company, a technician signed some correspondence as "administrator," causing other employees to feel that an under-the-table promotion to an exempt category had transpired. Promotion practices in general are covered in the next section. To

summarize, employers must be aware of the external environment by providing competitive wages and benefits and should strive to minimize internal problems realizing that total elimination of perceived internal inequity is nearly impossible.

Policies and Practices

Once an adequate compensation program and method of updating (usually annual) is established and communicated, the employer should address its policies and practices concerning method of promotion, outlet for grievances and procedure for layoff.

Contrary to most managers' aspirations, many employees most susceptible to unionization have no lofty ambition for promotion. But when an employee does desire promotional opportunity, he/she expects to be treated fairly. The safest method of promotion is to use seniority as the basis. Charges of favoritism are negated, but employees who stay with the firm move up regardless of qualification or performance. No formal system leads to the "who you know" syndrome. A method that provides for notification of available openings, for seniority as the first criterion, for defined minimum qualifications and performance levels will provide equitable promotion paths.

Being passed over for promotion hurts enough, but having no outlet for complaint without fear of reprisal pours salt in the wound. Employers must encourage employees to bring grievances to the attention of someone who has the authority to respond. Formal grievance systems, open-door policies, ombudsmen—all these methods can be effective if employees can use them, get results and fear no adverse effects.

The final area of concern for employees that many managers neglect is the issue of job security. When times are good and overtime is common, no one thinks about layoffs. But let inventories rise and news accounts of impending recession strike— then workers fear the loss of their jobs. Companies should establish a plan to follow when reductions in workforce are necessary. Most plans follow seniority for non-exempt employees and performance for exempt employees. The plan should be referred to when questions surface concerning layoffs.

Formal policies and practices help to alleviate certain employee concerns; however, many needs of the employee can be dealt with only by good common sense supervisory practices. Firstline supervisors undoubtedly get tired of hearing that they are "on the firing line" or the "first line of defense" in an organization's attempt to remain non-union. So we will refrain from saying that (even if it's true). Some brief examples will highlight the key role played by the supervisor:

Employee Question No. 1: Why did Mary get to leave early today when you didn't let me leave early last week?
Supervisor's Answer: Because she had a good reason.
Result: Employee feels that favoritism is present. The supervisor should set parameters so employees will know rationale for decision-making.

Employee Question No. 2: Why don't you discuss my performance when I make standard?
Supervisor's Answer: That's because you're expected to make standard.
Result: Employee feels unappreciated since the only time the supervisor discusses performance is to "chew."

Employee Question No. 3: Why don't we buy this chemical in bulk instead of in individual containers?
Supervisor's Answer: Engineers decide processes; they must have a good reason. Just follow the process. When I get time, maybe I can look into it.
Result: Employee perceives his/her role as being insignificant. The supervisor's lack of concern breeds employee apathy.

Employee Question No. 4: How do you get promoted to supervisor?
Supervisor's Answer: Why would you want a job like this? You've got it made.
Result: Supervisor has created a double put-down of the employee's leadership aspiration and of the role of management.

The supervisor must make time to learn what "turns on" each employee—all are not motivated by the same needs and desires. This supervisory awareness is a critical factor in creating a healthy work climate.

Finally, unions promise employees the opportunity to *participate*. A company that pays little or no attention to the ideas, suggestions and general concerns of their workers will have a difficult job in refuting the union's argument that its employees need a union to be heard. Some traditional methods of participation are the question box, suggestion systems, attitude surveys and general communication meetings. Many companies are setting up systems that allow for employees (often randomly selected) to meet with upper management for more extended communication sessions. Of course, workers must see some results from the input if they are to feel that it is effective.

This listing of positive management practices is surely not exhaustive, but it should provide basic ideas that will assist in strategic planning to provide the type of climate that will prevent a successful unionization drive.

On The Alert

Even if a company follows sound management practices, it may be faced with a union attempting to organize the employees of the company. The best and hopefully the first way management will become aware of any union activity is through the first-line supervisor. A union election is not, for the most part, won or lost at the ballot box, but requires constant vigilance, 365 days a year. First-line supervisors of any company must develop credibility with their employees so every employee will feel comfortable in coming to the supervisor with any concern. In this way, any union activity should be brought to the supervisor's attention. The company's responsibility is to see that all management employees are trained in and develop good human relations skills.

Other ways that management may be alerted to possible union activities are: individuals handing out handbills or leaflets to employees as they enter company premises (these same handbills/leaflets may appear mysteriously on company bulletin boards or cafeteria tables). Generally these are one or two page papers outlining issues that may concern the people and how the union can help rectify them. An obvious way is when authorization cards are being passed out among employees to sign and return to the union. An authorization card is generally a 3″ x 5″ card that may request an election for a particular union or it may be a membership card in a union. With the former, if the union wins the election, it must still obtain members; with the latter, if the union wins the election, the employees who signed are automatically members of the union. Still another way is if employees are acting out of the ordinary; this will best be detected by the first-line supervisor who is sensitive to his/her employees. Some signs to watch for are employees meeting in unusual groupings and employees discontinuing a conversation when a supervisor approaches. These actions are ambiguous at best and should not be taken automatically as a sign of union activity. Finally, union officials may contact a company directly, by telephone, letter, or personal visit.

It is best to combat any feeling of need by employees for representation by a third party before the NLRB becomes involved and orders an election. This is done, as has been outlined above, with a sound employee relations program followed continuously.

The majority of a company's employees in any appropriate bargaining unit may choose a union to represent it in its dealings with the company. To determine an appropriate bargaining unit, the NLRB reviews the similarity of duties, skills, wages and working conditions of the employees; the collective bargaining history of the industry involved; the request of the employees (union); and, the appropriateness of the unit in relation to the organization.[4] If a union gathers what it feels is a sufficient number of authorization cards, it will petition the company. Company officials then have two choices of action: 1) If the company is convinced the union represents a majority of its employees, it may voluntarily recognize the union, or 2) if the company officials have a good faith basis for doubting the union's claim of majority status, they may petition the NLRB for a representation election. A caveat is appropriate at this point: if a company has determined that the union has the support of the majority of the employees, but still refuses to bargain, the NLRB may issue a bargaining order without an election.[5] With this in mind, company officials should not take a private poll of their employees or review any authorization cards presented by the union. Before the NLRB will order an election, they will determine if there is enough interest in the appropriate bargaining unit. This has been defined by the NLRB as 30 percent or more.[6] The biggest issue at this stage will be identifying the appropriate unit. The company and the union are obviously in a numbers game and it will be in the best interest of the company to have a larger unit with any pro-management employees being part of the unit. This will make the required 30 percent more difficult to obtain; remember, the company is better off if an election is never ordered.

If the NLRB directs an election, a simple majority of those employees voting[7] is all that is required to have the union certified as the bargaining agent for the employees. To put this in perspective, if the appropriate unit consists of 10 employees, four may petition for an election. If four vote in the election, three voting for the union can bring about recognition. It is in the company's best interest to have all employees vote. This can be accomplished by the company scheduling section by section the employees' time to vote.

During the organizing campaign, the company may not restrain, coerce or interfere[8] with an employee's right[9] to join or refrain from joining or voting for a union. This does not mean that an employer must keep its opposition to a union quiet.

4. Primer of Labor Relations-Twentieth Edition—BNA Publications (1975) 29

5. Sullivan Electric Co., 199 NLRB 97
6. "LABOR RELATIONS, BNA Policy and Procedure Series" 83:2
7. Ibid. 83:581
8. Labor-Management Relations Act of 1947, Section 8(a)
9. Ibid.—Section 7

An employer has the right to let its employees know it is opposed to unions.[10] But there can be no direct or indirect promise of benefits if an employee doesn't support the union or threats of retaliation if they do.

Restrictions During A Campaign

Some specific items to keep in mind during the campaign are: first, employees may solicit their fellow employees for union support during non-working "free time." This has been defined as lunch time, scheduled coffee breaks, time before or after the start of a regularly scheduled shift and even time standing in line to punch a time clock.[11]

Second, the company can prevent solicitation during work time which is obviously time other than that outlined above. There seems to be a danger here if an employer attempts to keep employees from verbalizing their union feelings during work time when they do not otherwise restrict visiting among employees. This would appear to be a form of prohibited discrimination against union activity.

Third, employees may distribute union handbills or leaflets to other employees in non-working areas, but not in work areas.[12] Examples of non-work areas are an employee lunchroom, lounge, restroom, etc. A company should have a solicitation policy that prohibits the solicitation of employees by non-employees on company premises. The United States Supreme Court has taken the position that a company may withhold permission from a non-employee union organizer to come on company premises to distribute literature.[13] However, this can happen only if the company has refused permission uniformly against all non-employees and is not simply discriminating against the union organizer. Having a no-solicitation rule is part of the 365-days-a-year

program. A company cannot institute such a rule at the outset of a union organizing campaign and expect to be upheld.

Fourth, generally, a company cannot forbid the wearing of union buttons or insignias by its employees.[14] There are exceptions to this, such as when employees have customer contact, etc., but if a company wants to enforce such a ban, it must review circumstances carefully.

Fifth, once a union campaign gets under way, a company cannot unilaterally change wages or benefits.[15] Although there seems to be no clear rule as to when the campaign begins, it would seem to be when the company becomes aware of the union's intent to organize the company's employees. This does not mean that the union can notify the company in an attempt to keep them from making changes with no actual organizing intended. The facts of each situation will be determinative. Once again, there are exceptions to this—the main example being if the change was planned before the campaign began. Before any changes are made, the company should evaluate the circumstances carefully.

Sixth, a company may make predictions as to the possible consequences that may result if they are unionized, provided the results are beyond the company's control.[16] This means a company cannot threaten to close down a plant or move a plant because it is unionized. The company can state that the added financial burden could put the company out of business. The company may indicate whether it prefers one of two competing unions, provided no threats or promises are made.[17]

Seventh, the company can and should discuss the benefits that its employees have enjoyed in the past while being non-union. After all, an employee may not realize the extent of their company's total benefit package. This "selling" of a company's

10. *NLRB v. Scott & Fetzer Co.,* 97 LRRM 2881 (8th Cir. 1978)
11. "LABOR RELATIONS, BNA Policy and Procedure Series" 36:201
12. Ibid. 36:201
13. *NLRB v. Babock & Wilcox Co.,* U. S. Sp. Court, (1956), 38LRRM2001

14. *Republic Aviation Corp. v. NLRB* (1945) 16LLRM620
15. "LABOR RELATIONS, BNA Policy and Procedure Series" 46:421
16. Ibid. 40101
17. Ibid. 40101

benefits to its employees is another part of the 365-days-a-year program.

Eighth, the company may bring to the attention of its employees the union's policies and practices in dealing with members. This can be done by obtaining copies of the union's constitution and highlighting areas like special assessments, discipline procedures, etc. and ensuring that each employee is provided a copy.

Finally, neither the company nor the union can make speeches to the employees during the 24 hour period just prior to the election.[18]

This article is in no way a comprehensive study of the subject and any personnel professional should continually educate himself and his company on the subject of good employee relations. A thought that should be kept in mind: an outside union organizer is like any other vendor—you are not obligated to buy his product, but you owe him the courtesy of treating him professionally.

18. Ibid. 83633

Discussion Questions

1. Why should the climate of the organization affect how the employees feel about a union?
2. Why might employees want to join a union?
3. Why might management not want employees to join a union?
4. Who is right, management or the employees?

FIERY PROVOCATION

Pleasantville, a southeastern city of 100,000 residents, earned the coveted designation of "All-American City" last year as a progressive municipality. Among other notable accomplishments, the city has established human rights councils and has supported affirmative action and equal employment opportunity programs. In fact, the first female firefighter ever to complete training in the city recently has been assigned for duty at Fire Station No. 5. Rookie firefighter Nancy Williams was welcomed for duty as a fully qualified combat firefighter by Fire Chief Dunmore.

The firefighters' work schedule of 24 hours on duty followed by 48 hours off duty required them to eat and sleep at the fire station. Station living facilities, designed for males only, included an open bay with closely spaced single beds, one toilet, a large unpartitioned shower room, and a common kitchen for cooking and eating. The only private bedroom was assigned to and occupied by the shift lieutenant. To accommodate Ms. Williams's presence, a shower schedule was arranged to afford her solitary showering privileges, and most of the men voluntarily began wearing bathrobes over their underwear, in which it was their custom to sleep.

This system worked well and seemed satisfactory until wives of the firefighters began to complain bitterly that they didn't want another woman living with their husbands under the conditions at Fire Station No. 5. It's only a matter of time until some romance blossoms, they argued. Besides that, the wives insisted, under intimate living conditions, the presence of Ms. Williams infringed upon their husbands' right of privacy. These complaints and others became front page news in the local press. Neither the husbands nor Ms. Williams commented publicly on the issue. In rapid succession the wives banded together and hired a prominent lawyer, who implied that legal action was being considered; the city manager (see organization chart, Figure 13.8) stated publicly that the fire chief ran the fire department and was solely responsible for resolving the issue; and the city commissioners declared the problem to be beyond their jurisdiction under the city manager form of government.

Realizing that he had been tossed the ball but not knowing what to do with it, the chief pondered his options, which included but were not limited to: reassigning Ms. Williams to the fire department's Administration and Fire Prevention unit where she would have day shift duty only; moving the shift

Source. John M. Champion and John H. James, *Critical Incidents in Management,* Fourth, Edition. Homewood, Ill. Richard D. Irwin, Inc., Copyright © 1980, pp. 119–127.

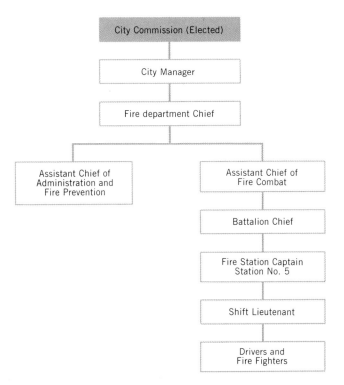

Figure 13.8 Organization of Fire Department.

lieutenant out of his private bedroom and assigning it to the female rookie firefighter; meeting personally with the wives and assuring them their complaints were unfounded; suspending Ms. Williams from duty, with pay, until the furor blew over; seeking a solution through the local firefighter's union; doing nothing; or doing whatever best would protect his position as fire chief.

As several wives of firemen began picketing Fire Station No. 5, Chief Dunmore felt increased pressure for immediate decision and action.

Discussion Questions
1. Identify advantages and disadvantages of each of the optional courses of action that are available to Chief Dunmore.
2. What course of action would you recommend be taken by Chief Dunmore?
3. Justify or challenge the action by the city commission and the city administrator in telling the chief that only he had authority to deal with the issue.

The staffing process gives life to organizations by providing the human resources that are needed to make the organization function. Although staffing decisions are the responsibility of all managers, specialized staff members exist in most organizations to provide technical assistance to line management. The major reasons for the development of specialized personnel staff are the increasing complexity of the staffing process and the constraints that are placed on the manager by outside forces, such as government regulation and unionization.

The staffing process starts with Human Resource Planning to determine the direction that the staffing process will have to follow to support the organization's strategic plans. Job analysis is undertaken to determine what skills and abilities are required of the people who will fill the positions in the organization. Once the kinds of people needed are determined, pools of individuals are recruited and then individuals are selected from the pool to fill the jobs. Training and development activities are undertaken to bring individuals' skills up to the level required to fulfill job demands or to prepare them to meet new challenges. Performance must then be measured and evaluated as an important input to the decisions concerning training and development, compensation, and the movement of people up, down, over, and out of the organization.

Here are some principles:

1. Staffing decisions are among the most important decisions that the manager must make.

2. The proper fit of people to jobs reduces problems by reducing training needs, motivation problems, and productivity problems.

3. The manager's discretion is constrained in staffing decisions by pressures from government regulation and unionized work forces.

CHAPTER FOURTEEN CONTROL

At the conclusion of this chapter you should be able to:

1. Describe the four phases of control.
2. Explain why control is necessary.
3. Describe the relationship between planning and control.
4. Describe the characteristics of an effective control system.

MANAGEMENT CONTROL ROLE PLAY

I. Objectives
    A. To experience some problems in control systems.
    B. To examine ways to improve management control.

II. Premeeting Preparation
    A. Read the instructions and the incident "False Reports."

III. Instructions
    A. Select the teams.
        1. For this exercise, form as many three person teams as needed.
        2. One person will play the role of Max Baxter, the sales manager, another person will play the role of John Fields, president of the Blue Ridge Furniture Manufacturing Company, and the third person will act as an observer.
        3. Select the role players.

> *Time for Step A: 5 minutes*

    B. The Role Play
        1. *Situation:* It is two days after Max Baxter discovered the problem with the false reports. He has been called to Mr. Fields' office to discuss the problem. Max has been trying to anticipate Mr. Fields' questions and thinks that he might be asked to explain what happened, why did it happen, and what he intends to do about it, but is not really sure.
        2. *The Role Play:* Mr. Fields and Mr. Baxter meet to discuss the matter of the false reports. Each of the role players is to act as if he/she was the character of Max Baxter or John Fields, and the observer is to observe the conversation.

> *Time for Step B: 15 minutes*

    C. The role players and observers shall individually complete the Observation Sheet.

> *Time for Step C: 10 minutes*

IV. Discussion
    Your instructor will help you to explore what happened in the exercise and its meaning for management.

> *Time for discussion: 15 minutes*

FALSE REPORTS

Incident

Max Baxter, sales manager of the Blue Ridge Furniture Manufacturing Company, had just completed a two-week trip of auditing customer accounts and prospective accounts in the southeastern states. His primary intention was to do follow-up work on prospective accounts contacted by sales staff members during the past six months. Prospective clients were usually furniture dealers or large department stores with furniture departments.

To his amazement, Baxter discovered that almost all the so-called prospective accounts were fictitious. The people had obviously turned in falsely documented field reports and expense statements. Company salespeople had actually called upon only 3 of 22 reported furniture stores or department stores. Thus Baxter surmised that salespeople had falsely claimed approximately 85 percent of the good-will contacts. Further study showed that all salespeople had followed this general practice and that not one had a clean record.

Mr. Baxter decided that immediate action was mandatory, although the salespeople were experienced senior individuals. Angry as he was he would have preferred firing them. But he was responsible for sales and realized that replacing the staff would seriously cripple the sales program for the coming year.

Source. John M. Champion, and John H. James, *Critical Incidents in Management,* Fourth Edition, Homewood, Ill. Richard D. Irwin, Inc., Copyright © 1980, p. 107.

MANAGEMENT CONTROL ROLE PLAY OBSERVATION SHEET

1. Why did the control system fail?

2. What should Mr. Baxter do now?

3. If Mr. Baxter doesn't fire the salespeople, won't that be an indication to other employees that cheating is condoned?

Planning and control are two interlocking management processes. As we discussed in Chapter 10, planning spells out how an organization can proceed to accomplish its goals or objectives. Control refers to measuring, evaluating, and adjusting activities against established goals or objectives and the planned means to accomplish them. Without control, planning would be limited to an exercise in exploring and expressing intentions in greater or lesser detail. The control system gives the manager the leverage to ensure that the organization is moving in the right direction by allowing systematic checking of actual performance with planned performance. If there is a significant negative gap, that is, performance is not up to standard, then remedial actions can be undertaken to get the organization back onto the right path.

The key steps in the control process are as follows:

1. Develop performance measures.
2. Measure performance against standards (provided by planning).
3. Feedback performance data.
4. Adjust performance.

Standards   Overall, the process is simple to grasp. Machiavelli, for example, once described the means by which a prince might be sure that the mayors of his cities would be fair and just. First, it was necessary to establish fairness and justice as desirable behaviors. Next the prince could find out from citizens of the cities and other subofficials if fairness and justice characterized the mayor's conduct. When the prince had all the feedback he needed, he could judge the mayor. If he was unjust and unfair, Machiavelli suggested that he could be publicly drawn and quartered. That would certainly adjust his performance and underscore the standards expected of his successor.

Obviously, for standards to be meaningful, they must be understood and accepted by the individuals who are being controlled. One standard for performance for a machinist may be that a particular part must be produced to within one ten thousandth of an inch of specifications. This is fine if the part must be produced that accurately, but if it is to be forced into the final assembly with a sledge hammer, who is going to take the specification (standard) seriously? Part of the acceptance of standards is the expectation on the part of the worker that the standard is attainable with a reasonable level of effort. Nothing is more frustrating than trying to meet a standard that is impossible. Before long, the standard is ignored, or the effort to achieve it is stopped. In either case, the organization loses.

MBO

To solve these problems, many organizations have moved participative activities by supervisors and subordinates in setting standards and controlling performance to meet the standards. This type of system is called Management By Objectives (MBO). MBO is one of the most popular innovations in planning and control to be developed in the past 20 years. Its key features are the use of goal-setting and periodic evaluation of performance against goals. It stresses the joint participation of supervisors and subordinates in establishing goals and in reviewing performance. The subordinate exercises more initiative and self-control under MBO than under traditional boss-centered methods.

Professors Stephen J. Carroll, Jr., of the University of Maryland and Henri L. Tosi, Jr., of Michigan State reviewed many studies on the use of MBO and conducted their own study of an MBO program at the Black and Decker Manufacturing Company, a producer of power tools. They reported that MBO makes the following contributions to effective management.

1. Directs work activity toward organizational goals. Because goals are declared, there is less likelihood to drift into unrelated activities.
2. Forces and aids in planning. Regular MBO planning and review sessions induce managers to think in terms of where they are going and how job assignments, time and other resource allocation, and other decisions are related to organizational goals.
3. Provides clear standards for control.
4. Provides improved motivation among managers. MBO sets the stage for achievement-oriented behavior. Managers get involved in committing themselves to goals they have set.
5. Makes better use of human resources. Objectives set by managers are apt to reflect the distinctive style of each manager and to encourage his or her personal growth.
6. Reduces role conflict and ambiguity. MBO clarifies what a manager is supposed to do and how he or she will be judged. This eliminates unclear standards as a source of anxiety.
7. Identifies problems better. The task-oriented discussions held by superiors and subordinates help spot problems to be overcome.

MEASUREMENT

Once the issue of standards is handled, the question of how to measure performance arises. A number of issues concerning measurement must be considered. What to measure? How to measure? When and how often to measure? Who should do the measuring?

What To Measure   What to measure? Quite simply we should measure performance. This may be easy if we are talking about counting the number of pieces produced by a machinest or the dollar sales volume of a salesperson. But for other types of jobs it is not so simple. In modern business firms there are now more and more "knowledge workers"—engineers, staff analysts, coordinators, program managers, research specialists, and others—whose contributions are less susceptible to isolation and measurement. It is also important to be sure that the right things are being measured. It is possible for a manager to make a department appear very profitable in the short run while destroying its ability to survive in the long run. Costs can be held down and profits up in the short run by ignoring maintenance, but in the long run when the machines break down, there may be no production and no profit.

Another possibility is that the recipients of the performance can provide a measurement of the performance. For example, companies of the American Telephone and Telegraph Corporation have, for many years, used a system whereby a staff group, the Service-Observing Group, monitors conversations, on a sampling basis, between service representatives in business offices and customers. In recent years this system has been supplemented with direct surveys of customers who have had contact with a business office concerning service. Rather than infer the quality of service from conversations, the new system records the recipient's direct assessment of the service.

How To Measure   For some jobs, direct quantitative measures are possible. We can count units produced, total sales, or make lists of machines repaired, but for other jobs, such as the knowledge workers or the mayor, contributions to performance, like technical excellence of a product or justice in a city, can only be subjectively defined and measured. Increasingly, many managers believe that a practical way to cope with this problem of developing performance measures is to grant considerable latitude to the performers in providing plans and measures for their own performance.

Who Should Measure?   Once some performance measures are established, however, actual measurements and comparisons of those measurements with standards must be made. In some cases this can also be done by the performers, but in other cases it must be done by managers or by specialized staff groups responsible for control. In the exercise at the beginning of this chapter you saw one of the problems of management not measuring performance. Max Baxter allowed the employees to report on their own performance without any checks to see if the reports were accurate. It shortly became evident to the salespeople that not only were their reports not being checked, but that management probably wasn't using the information. The result was false reports designed to make the employees look good.

In other areas, specific staff groups are created to monitor performance to ensure that performance is adequate. The best example of a group of this type would be a quality control group which is responsible for ensuring the quality of products being produced. In some cases, every item being produced is tested to see if it works properly. This will work well if we are producing television sets, but not if we are making rifle bullets. In the case where testing would destroy the product, statistical sampling is used to select products to be tested. If the sample meets the standards, the entire lot from which the sample is drawn is deemed to be acceptable. But no matter how it is done, the control process cannot prevent every mistake—it tries to keep them from happening again.

When To Measure   The when and how often of measurement is an interesting question. In general it is best to measure and test before starting an expensive operation. If the data going into the computer are wrong, thousands of dollars of computer processing is not going to give accurate information. By the same token, why bother doing $100 worth of machining on a part that is already bad?

In terms of management processes, it is probably best to measure and compare before important decision points. If a sales campaign is not going well, it is important to know that before deciding on funding a follow-up campaign. The opposite of not enough control is too much control. Testing at every step, or reporting every activity, can create a control system that costs $100 to control a process which is worth $25. It may be controlled, but at what cost. As a simple rule of thumb, you don't spend more to control than the part or process is worth.

Actual Versus Desired   Once the measurement is completed, the actual performance must be measured against desired or planned performance. Sales quotas, budgets, tolerances, and quality standards are all examples of the "desired." Measures of actual are then compared with the standards and if the actual meets the level that is desired, that information is fed back and activities are continued (Figure 14.1). If there is a discrepancy between actual and desired performance that is large enough for concern, some type of remedial action is
Feedback   called for. But whether the system is in control, or out of control, there must be feedback to management so that they know what is going on.

Adjust Performance   The most common response to problems shown by controls is that activities must be changed. This might be true, but as we can see from Figure 14.1, this is not the only kind of adjustment that can be made. Once a manager knows that performance is not up to snuff he or she must determine why. If performance is off because the plan was not followed, then making changes in activities may be the proper approach. But, there may be cases where the plan was followed exactly, and there is still a gap between actual and desired performance. Then, maybe the plan itself needs to be changed. Forecasts may have been poor, or unexpected problems may have arisen to make the plan inappropriate to the reality of the situation facing the manager. Finally, the plan might have been good, and the activities appropriate, but the objective might have been unattainable. If an athlete starts out with

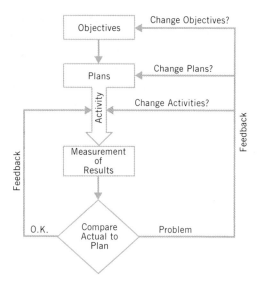

Figure 14.1   The control process.

the objective of high jumping 10 feet, makes a plan to jump ½ inch the first day and increase it by ½ inch per day until reaching 10 feet, then goes out and tries to do that, at some point the athlete will fail. Aside from the physical efforts, and the plan, the objective is unattainable. At least it is today. This doesn't mean that we shouldn't have difficult objectives, for we should. What it means is that in some cases the failure to achieve some desired goal may be caused by the goal being too difficult. Thus, the manager must determine whether activities, plans, objectives, or some combination of the three are causing the problem before meaningful adjustments can be made.

INCONSISTENT CONTROLS

Loss of Control   The central problem with controls is that they are no guarantee of control. That is, taking measurements and comparing them with standards may be controlling, but there is no assurance that it leads to improved guidance and direction of the enterprise. In fact, the controls can lead to loss of control.

For example, the Service-Observation Group at AT&T which we mentioned earlier, has an elaborate and comprehensive set of measurements it takes on service representatives as they converse with customers. The goal of this controlling activity is to provide good service. The measurements taken include such items as providing correct information, completing arrangements in one conversation, and avoiding delays for the customer. As the system works in practice, however, the service representatives come to believe that it is important to avoid being caught in an error. Some of them have come to believe that these measurements are so important that they actually provide misinformation or otherwise try to fool the customer or the service observer to avoid "being scored." Making the numbers look good proves to be more important than providing good service.

Thus, control practices can introduce inconsistencies among goals, plans, and control. What superiors count seems to specify what they regard as really important in the job. Measurements and feedback, therefore, must be well chosen, well taken and well handled if they are not to subvert desired performance.

CHARACTERISTICS OF EFFECTIVE CONTROL SYSTEMS

Various authors present lists of what a control system must have to be effective, but there is general consensus on the following aspects of effective control systems:

1. Controls must lead to action. If the control system shows significant deviations, actions to change the situations must follow.
2. Controls must be timely. If actions are going to be taken, the control system must give indications of problems at a time when remedial action can be taken.
3. Controls must be economical. Control should not cost more than the process itself is worth.
4. Controls must be flexible. As the environment in which the firm operates changes, the control system must be flexible enough to change with it.
5. Controls must exist at strategic points. Controls should exist at points where proceeding could be quite costly if there is a problem. The problem should be identified before additional costly activities are undertaken.
6. Controls must measure accurately. If the information provided to management by the control system is inaccurate, a good decision would be a matter of chance. It is simply a case of "garbage in, garbage out."
7. Controls must be understood and accepted by subordinates. Control systems that are not understood will not be taken seriously and those that are not accepted will be evaded, cheated or manipulated to show management what "they" want to see.

NEW PATTERNS IN CONTROL

Professor Rensis Likert of the Institute of Social Research at the University of Michigan offers a new perspective on control. Likert pictures a business organization as having three sets of factors: causal, intervening and end result. They include the following:

Causal
  Controls
  Policies
  Organization Structure
  Leadership
Intervening
  Attitudes
  Motivations
  Perceptions
End Result
  Productivity
  Costs
  Earnings

Virtually every company measures its end results. But most controls pay little heed to intervening factors. Consequently, managers manipulate causal factors in response to end results only, not on the intervening factors that influence those results.

Because of this control information gap, Likert believes that managers take actions that harm their organizations. They cut costs in response to a drop in earnings, for example. This shows a short-run improvement in earnings. But the long-run damage to attitudes and motivation is never measured, nor can the long-term negative impact on earnings be measured due to intervening factors by cost cutting.

To remedy this neglect, Likert has created a new set of measurements that cover both the causal and intervening variables. The questionnaire data depict what Likert calls the "management system"—the cluster of factors including structure, controls, policies, and leadership, plus the attitudes, motivations, and perceptions of organization members. End results are also measured.

Under Likert's direction, the Institute for Social Research has investigated a large number of organizations. His findings reveal that end results tend to be weaker in companies whose management systems are more authoritative and tightly controlled and better in cases where the management systems are more participative and emphasize self-control.

Another of Likert's ideas is that in measuring the end results of a company, such hitherto uncounted assets as the firm's human organization, its customer loyalty, its shareholder loyalty, its supplier loyalty, its reputation among the financial community, and its reputation in the communities in which it has plants should be considered. Some rough methods are being used to estimate the value of a firm's human organization; they usually yield a value of three to five times payroll. The point of these measurements is that they give a more complete picture than figures currently used. When human resources are ignored in an accounting report, as is done in most firms, stated earnings can show a favorable picture for years when assets are actually decreasing. The result may be a management control system that is at best inaccurate and at worst misleading.

SUMMARY

We have seen that the control process consists of a number of subprocesses including such activities as setting standards, measuring performance, feedback, and corrective action. Each of the subprocesses is linked and must be present and properly used if the organization is to keep moving in the right direction. Effective controls keep the organization on the "straight and narrow." Ineffective controls cause the organization to drift, and there are many dangerous rocks onto which the organization can drift.

MORALITY OR ETHICS? TWO APPROACHES TO ORGANIZATIONAL CONTROL

DAVID K. BERLO

Organizational control is often attempted through either of two stylistic approaches—morality or ethics. Let me clarify how I am using these three terms: control, morality, and ethics. To me, *control* is the maintenance of predictability of relationship, some regularity of the system for whatever purpose it is intended. When we say a system is under control, it is regulated, that is, the rhythms of the system are regular, patterned, consistent. Events are predictable. As that rhythm is disrupted, control is lessened; when there are no predictable patterns, we say the system is out of control.

Questions of *morality* focus on the quality of individual existence, the goodness of one's actions, the referencing of one's behaviors and beliefs against some criterion of personal taste, personal correctness. It is a question of private behavior, personal values, and personal guidance.

Questions of *ethics* focus on the quality of human relationships, on fairness, rather than goodness, on equity more than virtue, and so on. It is a question of social behavior, of relationships between people, concerned more with what is just and honorable than with what is virtuous and good.

As managers, we have a responsibility for facilitating organizational control in an optimal fashion. We also have a responsibility and concern ?? questions of morality and ethics, for helping organizations behave in ways that will contribute to both goodness and fairness for all involved, whenever possible. How do questions of morality and ethics impinge on our decisions as to organization and control?

I know of only four basic control systems for human organization: *chance, force, trust,* and *contract.* Any existing system can be described in terms of some amalgam of these four.

There are those who abdicate from any personal responsibility for the management of their organization, leaving it either to the will of God or the laws of chance. Neither is acceptable to those of us who believe in human intervention in managing the system. As I observe the actual control systems within corporate structures, I sometimes find no control other than what appears to be chance; however, I am always assured it isn't intentional.

Control by Authority (Force)

The traditional control system, of course, is force and authority based on the potential use of force. Communication is a tool of authority, and the two major communication processes in a force- or authority-based control system are instructions and appraisal, followed by the appropriate judicial awarding of rewards and punishments. Such a system preaches the morality of hard work and submissive compliance and defends the justice of a class system in which some are instructors and some are instructees; however, the on-going management system doesn't invoke concepts of either morality or ethics as part of the daily routine.

The direct use of force and force-based authority are, for the most part, obsolete because:

Source. Reproduced here by permission from *The Personnel Administrator* (April 1975), Copyright © 1975 by The American Society for Personnel Administration.

Counterforce is more readily available to those to whom force might be applied.

Force is not easy to apply to knowledgeable workers since it is harder to detect the withholding of work and poor quality.

Conscience makes force an unacceptable means.

Information crucial to production is "owned" by subordinates, increasing the interdependency between supervisor and subordinate.

Control by Persuasion (Force)

The rejection of the use of force led to the greater use of and concern with persuasion. Persuasion makes a tacit recognition of voluntary compliance, but uses language to lead people to positions predetermined by the persuader as in *his* or *her* best interest. It is a form of external control, often having the appearance of cooperation and voluntariness, but, in fact, being a surrogate for force-power.

Techniques of persuasion use principles of conditioned learning, principles through which an individual is controlled by his environment, by external agents. There are two basic principles of persuasion: reinforcement and contiguity. In practical terms, these can be translated as (1) one thing leads to another and (2) birds that are flocked together become of a feather.

The principle of reinforcement simply says that behaviors that are reinforced (that is, rewarded) will get stronger and behaviors that are ignored will get weaker. It is the symbolic form of the "carrot and stick" routine familiar to us all.

Persuasion through reinforcement still is a management technique of control; however, its effectiveness is diminishing and will continue to do so. Why? People are becoming less and less naive, the reinforcements at the manager's disposal are less alluring, there is reduced trust in the competence-trustworthiness and ability-to-deliver of the manager and, maybe most importantly, there is a rising aversion to external control, to manipulation by the environment. Also, the commitment to self-determinism is continuing to rise and youthful managers share the belief of workers that manipulation, the preaching of

morality by telling people what's good for them, is unacceptable—both to the persuadee and the persuader.

Control by Personal Trust

Recognition of a growing interdependence among employees at all levels led to another basic form of control: personal trust. The field of human relations training—behavioral techniques—was founded on the assumption that the more open, honest and interested a manager is—or appears to be—to his employees, the more he will be trusted. A work group can be viewed as a team, striving for the same goals, the same ideological outcome, with the manager as a coach or even as a player-coach. Work decisions can be shared among the team.

Although there are situations in which personal trust is a useful and satisfying and adequate control system, I feel that those situations are quite limited in number and seldom include the typical managerial role in large and complex organizations.

If we analyze the use of personal trust as a management style, we find that either it does represent a sharing of control (which seldom is practical) or it represents an extremely subtle form of persuasion embodying the second principle of conditioning learning—contiguity. This principle suggests that we can manipulate how people see things by controlling how things are presented to them. We need not get involved in the reinforcement techniques of manipulation at all. Rather, if we arrange the environment so that things we wish to be seen as favorable are always associated in time or space with things that are already accepted as favorable by the individual we are attempting to influence, that person will unconsciously do as we wish.

Behavioral techniques leading to perceptions of trust do not suffice over time in complex organizations because they are a morality-based control system. Subtly, often insidiously, they are based on the assumption that one person knows what is good for the other and can help lead the other to the promised land. The management process still involves a morality play, couched in sophisticated social scientific language and principles. And, over time, it doesn't work.

But, what do we do? I suggest that we abandon principles that are based on telling people what's good for them and that we recognize that only the individual can know what is good for himself: Morality is a matter of personal choice and personal style and personal taste, and the internal development of the individual is the individual's business, subject only to whatever *social contract* he has negotiated with his manager. Why the concept of social contract? Because it provides a basis for trust. A social contract need not be on paper; however, it must be thoroughly understood by both parties. And that is important. Some basis for trust is necessary to maintenance of our organizations and social systems. We must be able to believe that something is reliable, consistent, predictable, and so forth.

I would suggest that we need to place trust in the rules of fairness, the rules governing social relationships, that is, on *ethics*. I would further suggest that those rules are under relatively continual negotiation, must be agreed upon by both parties, and must be followed scrupulously.

The underlying role of an ethics-based control system is that I won't tell you what's good for you, and you won't tell me what's good for me. Rather, let's tell each other what we consider to be fair treatment: Let's negotiate an agreement on fair treatment and let's both follow the contract, renegotiating as needed.

What can be negotiated between the manager and his subordinate? Anything affecting how they will treat each other. For one thing, the job itself: How complex or "enriched" shall it be? We often err by assuming that everyone wants more enrichment. Not so: Some people don't see their jobs as the focus of life, and they want to negotiate a contract in which they'll do what's expected of them, collect the "bread" they need, and go off on their own to enrich their own lives. The quality of the job can be negotiated in terms of what is fair to both parties.

Certainly we can negotiate how open we shall be with one another—and that too is a variable. The assumption that "the more open the better" is not held by all; it can be negotiated. We also can— and should—make a contract to try to tell it like it is, to report to each other under a simple rubric, tell the truth—regardless. That single rule, if followed and trusted, would do much to end our current malaise. We should negotiate what is expected, trying to be operational, so that appraisal is based on contact. We can call that "management by objectives." We often call it "contract learning." What we call it is not as important as whether we do it.

In short, we can negotiate anything affecting our relationship. In so doing, the manager's job begins to change from a task of managing a team to the task of managing the game itself. He is becoming less a coach and more a referee. The referee is in charge of the game, responsible for insuring that the rules of fair play are followed. To him indeed, winning *is* how you play the game.

Discussion Questions

1. How do control by chance, force, trust, and contract differ?
2. How are Berlo's ideas about control different from traditional concepts of the control process?
3. Does Berlo argue for the use of morality or ethics for control purposes? Is his argument valid and supportable?

A CASE

QUALITY CONTROL

"Jim, I don't know what to do with you," Al Barker, the production manager, said. Jim was his young purchasing agent, and they were wandering down their assembly line, watching the rollered platforms being assembled. The platforms were used by equipment makers for small computers.

"What did I do wrong this time?" Jim asked.

"Those bearings, Jim. How could you? All used materials!" Barker picked up a bearing. "Look at this—all full of grease and rust. You know that our directive is not to use anything but the best, and here you come up with these things!"

"They're not rusty," Jim said. He wiped off some grease. "Look—brand new. These bearings are four times as good as the specs call for, and they cost only a fraction as much."

"But they're used. Air Force surplus. For heaven's sake, Jim!"

"You told me to buy the best bearings I could find, 15,000 of them, as cheaply as I could. So I found some Air Force surplus stocks. If you bought these from our usual suppliers, they would cost $1.57 each, and they barely would match specs. These were originally in B-47s and F-84s—they cost $26.50 each back in 1951. I got 20,000 of them for 18 cents each. So what if they've been used a bit? I checked that, too, and found out that none of the parts they were in ever got out of the Air Force warehouse. All the seller had to do was to disassemble the flap mechanisms, and we have ended up with some very good, cheap bearings. Those computers will be 100 years old before these things wear out."

Barker sighed. "I have a letter from Mr. Paxton, the vice-president. Apparently, someone heard about your deal and asked him why we use junk in our products. The buyer was very upset. Now I have to explain to him what we're doing, and I don't really think that I know. I keep telling you to buy wisely, and you keep coming up with wild deals like this."

"Look, Mr. Barker, all I'm trying to do is to save the company money. You want me to save money, and I've saved it. Boy, I made my salary back twice this year on this one deal alone, and now you're mad. I should get a bonus."

Source. Richard N. Farmer, Barry M. Richman, and William G. Ryan, *Incidents for Studying Management and Organization* (Belmont, Calif.: Wadsworth Publishing Company, 1970), pp. 103–104.

Discussion Questions
1. What should Mr. Barker say in his letter to the irate customer?
2. What are the control questions here?
3. Was Jim right in buying these bearings? Why or why not?

Control can be thought of as the enforcer of plans. It consists of developing performance measures, measuring performance against the standards provided by planning, feeding back data, and adjusting performance. Improperly designed or improperly applied controls can introduce inconsistencies between goals, plans, and controls and create misdirection. How planning and control actually work is a function of the climate or spirit in which these management processes are carried out.

Here are some principles:

1. Without controls organizations will simply drift.

2. Controls must be understood and make sense if they are to be effective.

3. Measurements of performance have motivational power and must be consistent with goals or they too can misdirect employees.

The climate of control can be critical. Fear and mistrust can stimulate anxious numerical compliance. Support and trust coupled with serious standards can foster reasoned venturesomeness.

IV.
THE FUTURE

Having now come to the end, we are at the beginning again. As Albert Einstein pointed out, time and space are curved. If you could theoretically travel long enough and far enough you would return to the beginning again. So it is with *Management Today*. Here we are at the end, but it is really only the start—the start of looking down the road towards your tomorrow. In the next chapter we focus very specifically on you and your future career. Just as organizations and groups have objectives, so do individuals. The following chapter provides you the opportunity to think through some of your objectives in a systematic way so that you can more realistically prepare yourself for that bigger and better tomorrow just around the bend.

In the past fourteen chapters we have tried to spell out and help you experience some of the activities that comprise management today. Thus armed, we hope you can be more equipped to deal with management activities when you encounter them. Until the dawning of that better tomorrow you will help plan in this chapter—we wish you the joys of *Management Today*.

ORGANIZATIONS IN THE FUTURE

LEARNING OBJECTIVES

At the end of this chapter you should be able to:

1. State the circumstances under which the future may be an extension of the present and when it may not.
2. Describe several changes in the nature and character of those who will work in 1995.
3. Describe at least two changes in the nature of the work performed that will occur by 1995.
4. Describe at least two changes that will occur in the way people and work will be organized by 1995.

LIFE PLANNING

I. Objectives
   A. To assist you in planning your future career both on and off the job.
   B. To experience some of the difficulties in anticipating and planning for the future.

II. Premeeting Preparations
   A. Complete the sheet entitled My Skill Inventory contained on page 425.
   B. Prepare a one-page visualize in the Future Life on pages 427–428.
   C. Prepare the Preparation for Goal Setting on page 429.

III. Instructions
   A. For the exercise the class should be divided into groups of three. If this does not work out evenly, one or two groups of four should be formed.

   > *Time for Step A: 5 minutes*

   B. The trios should discuss the Future Life Fantasy, Skill Inventory, and Preparation for Goal Setting with each member. Three questions should form the basis for this discussion:
      1. What is the person's top priority goal?
      2. How realistic is the goal, given the individual's abilities and resources?
      3. What are the key subgoals required to achieve the long-term goals (e.g., completing law school to become a lawyer)?

   > *Time for Step B: 30 minutes*

   C. At the end of this exercise, each member of the trio should have in mind a specific goal she or he wants to achieve. This goal is the focus of goal achievement plan in the next part.
   D. Students are to complete the Goal Planning sheet after class.

IV. Discussion
   Your instructor will discuss with you the significance of the exercise and its meaning for management.

   > *Time for discussion: 15 minutes*

MY SKILL INVENTORY

I. Those things I DO WELL are . . .
—those qualities or skills that you know you do well that you see as your strong points. (Include both job and personal activities.)

II. Those things I PARTICULARLY ENJOY are . . .
—those events and conditions that give life purpose and meaning, making it fun, and/or are seen as highpoints. (Include both job and personal activities.)

VISUALIZE LIFE IN THE FUTURE

It is often difficult to achieve life goals because we have so many goals and we are not quite certain which ones deserve priority. The first task is to select one goal that you wish to accomplish in the next 10 years. One way to do this is to have you develop a fantasy about your future life and share this with the other members of the group. The others can then give their impressions about what seem to be the most important goals realized in your fantasy.

Describe a typical day that will occur in your life 10 years from now. Describe in *as great a detail as possible* what you do (your job title, responsibilities, duties, etc.), the people with whom you do work, the kind of office (right down to the color of the carpet), your home, how you get to work, where you live, what you do on/off job hours. *Be as specific and complete as possible—and realistic.*

Please write your visualization in the space below.

PREPARATION FOR GOAL SETTING

To be completed by you before the exercise.

A. Scan the inventory and visualization for possible connections. Consider the following questions:
1. In comparing your visualization about your future life and your current skills, what needs to be changed (added, dropped) in order to make your visualization become reality? In other words, how and in what specific ways will you have to change, and what will you have to accomplish to realize your visualization?
2. What can you change to build more fun and meaning into life?
3. What can you do to get the best mileage out of your strengths?
4. What things can you stop doing that would allow you to start doing other things—that can make a difference in your usefulness to yourself and to others?

B. Based upon these answers, identify one or two long-term goals and one or two short-term goals. These should be steps along the way to help you realize your visualization.

Long-Term Goal (5 to 10 years)
1.

2.

Short-Term Goal (6 months to 5 years)
1.

2.

GOAL PLANNING

To be completed by you after the exercise.

A. Sharpen the goal statement into something bite size and do-able as well as measurable. Rather than "Improve performance," consider, "Be promoted to _____ by _____ (time)." Rather than, "Play the guitar," try, "Be able to play 'With A Little Help From My Friends' on the guitar by _____ (date)."

B. What specific steps do you plan to take to achieve this goal?

C. Go back and put a time line on each step.

D. What blocks in yourself will you have to overcome to achieve this goal?

E. What blocks in your circumstances will you have to overcome to achieve this goal?

Now that we have completed a tour of the current management scene, you should have some idea concerning the current practice of management. But, no sooner is the ink dry on this page than something new has emerged which renders obsolete the words that have just been written. In this management business, as in most other aspects of our current life, the only constant we can count on is that things will be different tomorrow. Unlike previous times when stability was the order of the day, the only stable expectation we can have is that there will be change. With that in mind, and as the Greek philosopher cautioned us, "The wise person looks to the future," let us be wise and look to the future.

One word of warning before we look into the fantasy world of tomorrow, however. The crystal ball is cloudy, and whether you believe in astrology, ouiji boards, or ESP, when it comes to predicting the future, beware the "merchants of certainty." In the future, as in the present, we talk in terms of probability, and the further into the future we project the more uncertain we must be. With this caution in mind, let us all join hands, gaze intensely into the lighted crystal ball, and attempt to predict what will occur in 1995.

THE FUTURE

An Extension of the Present?

Before we begin, however, we must answer the question, "Will the future be an extension of the present?" That is, can we look at the trends that are currently developing and simply extend them into the future? For example, there is a growing number of female managers and executives. Can we assume that the number of female managers will continue to grow in the future at the same rate that it has in the recent past? As another example, the number of openings for computer programmers has doubled over the past five years. Can we assume that the programmer jobs will double again over the next five years? The answers to both questions are interesting examples of the hazards of projecting the present into the future. In the case of female executives, the prospect is that there will be many more in the coming years than there are today. In fact, given the large number of female MBA students (as many as 40 percent of current enrollments), the trend will likely accelerate.

Similarly, the need for computer programmers is limited by the number of computer installations. Although these have grown recently, there are signs that the number of new computer installations (as opposed to replacement of current on-line facilities with new equipment) will tail off—thus limiting the need for additional programming personnel. But, the growth in the minicomputer field has generated whole new opportunities for programmers in software development firms who produce prepackaged programs for the "minis."

The Immediate Future Is—

It must be obvious to you that to some extent the future, particularly the immediate future, is an extension of the present. Events and trends developing today have a certain inertia that will make them continue into the future. But new factors will come into play that modify and may even reverse the trend. So, the future may be an extension of the present—sometimes!

CHANGES IN WHO WORKS

More Female and Minority Managers

The first observation we can make about 1995 is that the people who work and the kind of jobs they hold will likely be very different. Trends that began in the 1970s will have probably accelerated by the late 1980s and 1990s. For instance, there will be many more minority and women managers—and the attitude toward working women will have changed considerably. Although the executive washroom may still have separate (but equal) facilities, in most other ways discrimination barriers will be a thing of the past. Under the urging of government equal opportunity regulations, and a shortage of white males in the executive age bracket, industry of all types will probably increasingly employ women and minorities to fill managerial positions at all levels of the hierarchy.

More White-Collar Specialists

Not only will there be more minority managers, but there will be a lot more white-collar employees. The day of the blue-collar worker will be largely over. Specialists of all types abound in the 1995 organization—including many whose names we cannot know here in the early 1980s. The information explosion, automation, and larger markets to draw from will combine to shift the emphasis in the modern 1995 organization to distribution and control office types, but who are rated higher in skill and salary than the traditional production worker. There will be a large number of technician-type persons who perform a wide range of semitechnical, semimanagerial jobs. These will be the quasi-white collars, and there will be almost as many of them as there are white collars.

More Educated Employees

And, these white-collar and quasi-white collar employees will generally be more educated. College degrees will be common, with virtually no one in the management ranks having less than a bachelor's degree. Even among the nonmanagement personnel, virtually all will have finished high school, and some will have two years of some technical training.

More Service Organizations

Finally, there will also be a relatively small number of manufacturing and processing organizations as compared with the larger number of service-type organizations. These service organizations range all the way from the corner convenience store and barber shop to large governmental agencies, universities, and computer service bureaus. The trend that began in the 1970s is expected to grow more rapidly in the 1980s and early 1990s, until by 1995 the economy will likely be dominated by large service organizations. Thus by 1995, the nature of the people who live in organizations will change. Basically, they will be better educated, more white collarish, with more female and minority managers, and most likely, employed in a service rather than a manufacturing industry.

CHANGES IN WHAT WORK IS PERFORMED

Less Mechanical and Larger Jobs

As the people will have changed by 1995, so will the jobs they do. It will be hard to find a traditional assembly line job in 1995. To be sure, there still will be some around (we could not produce much of our mass produced hard goods—autos, freezers, etc. without them), but machines will probably perform many of the multiple routine tasks, and there will be fewer people who will work individually. Rather, much of the work will be done as part of the team, where the team is responsible for entire subassemblies or maybe even assembling the entire unit. The process of job enrichment and autonomous work groups was begun in earnest by concerns such as Volvo and Saab in the 1970s and is expected to grow until it becomes the dominant method of job organization. Thus, teams of blue collar and semi-white collar technicians will work together using very sophisticated equipment. This team concept will also be apparent among the white-collar groups. Clusters of technical and administrative personnel will dot the organizational scene—teams from several different backgrounds working together in the solution of common organizational problems.

More Responsibility for Decisions

Second, there will probably be an absence of close supervision; that is, many decisions will be made at low levels in the organization. Combined with this increased responsibility on lower organization levels will be a well-developed information reporting and control system that will be tied into a central computer. In this manner, by using the exception principle (looking only at actions that vary from established principle) top management will be able to adequately control all of the organization's operations. Thus, through the use of computerized controls, budgeting and management information systems, more operating flexibility will be provided at the lower levels of the organization, while still maintaining a strong sense of central direction from the top.

In summary, mechanical jobs will be more mechanized, and finely developed assembly line jobs will have mainly disappeared, being replaced by team efforts, with more decision-making responsibility being permitted at lower levels in the organization, combined with "Big Bertha," the computer that provides an elaborate control and reporting system.

CHANGES IN HOW PEOPLE ARE ORGANIZED

As jobs and people will have changed, so will organizational philosophies. The traditional line-staff organization will have largely disappeared from view by 1995. In its place will be the matrix organization or team concept, where individuals have at least two organization homes—one in a typical discipline department such as mechanical engineering or quality control, and the other as part of a project team. A typical organization chart for a 1995 firm is reproduced in Figure 15.1.

The Matrix or Team Organization—More Specialists

Populating this matrix organization will be a large group of specialists. Specialists of all kinds will swarm over the organizational beehive. Operation research specialists, market research analysts, management information systems programmers, employee motivation planners, and many specialists who were not even known in 1980 will constitute the majority of employees in most organizations of the future. These specialists will organize, analyze, and control operations. In carrying out their jobs they will work in teams composed of specialists from other disciplines and management personnel.

CHANGES IN MANAGEMENT

All of these changes—the more independent, more educated work force, performing larger team-type jobs with more specialists—indicate that the

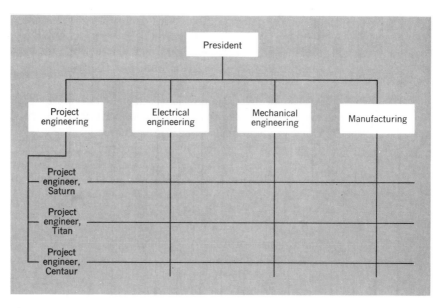

Figure 15.1

manager of 1995 will have fundamentally changed in several important ways. First, the manager in 1995 will have to be much the generalist, more of a generalist than a specialist. The manager must have an overall grasp of the business and the ability to integrate and synthesize the activities and viewpoints of many diverse specialists—specialists who will probably know more about the specialty than the manager.

Consider, for instance, the manager of 1980 supervising 15 persons performing a similar task where the primary concern is information transfer, and the integration of product output with several similar other outputs. The manager probably reports to another manager, who reports to yet another manager, who may, in turn, report to the top-level management official. In all probability, the manager rarely deals directly with outside individuals or groups, such as customers, community action persons, and so on. In such a setup, the manager could literally perform any job in the unit as well as the average employee. By 1995, much of this will have changed. The manager will be responsible for 25 to 30 persons, performing several different kinds of tasks. Because the tasks will be more varied, it is more likely that the manager will not be competent to perform them all as well as the current employee staff. Information transfer will be largely handled by the electronic wizard. The manager, because of the more integrated nature of work, will deal with top management personnel more regularly, together with many specialists, customers, and other outside persons. This means that the manager must understand the basic operations of the entire business, not just the little unit, and take into account the "ripple" effect of action on the entire organization. By 1995, each manager will be more like the president of a separate company—at least in terms of outlook, perspective, and knowledge of overall organization operations.

Second, these changes in the management job will change the fundamental relationship between managers and employees. In the 1970s, managers could rely on expertness, information control, or even raw power. By 1995, these bases for influence will be eroded. The manager no longer will have expertness as a base. In many important ways, the manager will be dependent upon the specialists in the unit for their specialized knowledge. Managers will likely be knowledge consumers instead of knowledge dispensers. In addition, the implementation of computerized information systems means that the manager will no longer be able to control the flow of information to and from employees. Compounding this trend will be the increased independence of employees in general. All of this means that the manager must rely more extensively on interpersonal influence skills rather than on formal organizational power.

More Interpersonal Skills

The manager of 1995 will be a motivator—a constructor of situations in which people can satisfy their needs through the accomplishment of the unit's work. The manager must be able to analyze individual needs, understand people, and be skillful in leadership and communication techniques. More than anything, the 1995 manager will be a people manager, not a thing manager—a people grower and producer rather than a product or service producer.

Able to Function in Ambiguous Situations

Third, the single most outstanding trait of the 1995 manager will be the ability to work effectively in ambiguous and uncertain situations. This uncertainty will stem from several sources. First, there will be the constantly shifting employee population. Given the team project approach, individual employees will work with given managers only for the life of a project, which may last several weeks or months. Each change will force the manager to build up relationships with a new and different group of employees. Second, dealings with customers and other outside groups always pose uncertainties, and the manager will spend some time in those pursuits. Third, the constantly changing nature of the technology will introduce additional uncertainty. In short, the only constant is that tomorrow will be different from today.

All of this will mean that the manager's career of 1995 will probably be very different from the 1980 counterpart in at least two ways. First, there will likely be an increasing tendency for several management careers, for managers to rotate through various specialist and management jobs, working for short (two to three years) periods of time on each assignment. Thus, a manager might start as an Operations Research specialist, move in three years to be an accounting supervisor, move again to be a manufacturing planner, and again to a manufacturing superintendent. Thus, rather than one career, management personnel will probably experience several different "mini-careers."

Continuing Management Education For each "mini-career," the manager will go through a new educational preparation. This might be likened to the engineer who graduates with a degree in Electrical Engineering, becomes a manager and acquires an M.B.A., then becomes an executive who acquires a Harvard Certificate in Executive Management. Continuing education will play an important part in 1995 managerial life.

SUMMARY

In short, the manager of 1995 will probably be a generalist rather than a specialist, rely on interpersonal skills, be comfortable in uncertain situations, and experience several different mini-careers. These differences may be traceable to the changing nature of the employee group, the changing nature of the work they perform, and the changing nature in the way in which people and work are organized.

As the crystal ball grows dim, we must be impressed by the improved quality of managerial life in 1995: more independence and freedom to be creative, more responsibility for our own results, more challenging and growthful work. Yet, the constant change, the uncertainty, and the often lonely and difficult path the 1995 manager will walk are sometimes frightening. Is it better? We do not know. Nor is the question really important. For people who do not seek the risks of responsibility and the challenges of growth, there will be many specialist jobs that require a security oriented person. Regardless, the wise person looks to the future—and we urge you to look to your future. Whatever you do choose, the heat of the kitchen or the comfort of the living room, probably the single most important step you can take toward the future is to follow Socrates' injunction to "Know thyself," or in popular terms, "Get your act together."

WHAT THE "EXPERTS" SAY ABOUT THE FUTURE

Having read what we say, let's look at the experts opinions. Although "research" on the future is scarce, the volume of written material is not. Futurologists are multiplying by the score. Such organizations as the Institute for the Future, The Commission on the Year 2000, Europe 2000, Mankind 2000, and the World Future Society have sprung up. Futurist centers of study have been founded in London, Rome, Moscow, and Caracas. Many have speculated on the future—and many views of the crystal ball have been pessimistic indeed. A group of scholars at one of these futurist centers, for instance, utilizing a computer-based program, has predicted by the year 2000 that:

1. The world population will have grown to the point that the entire globe will have a population density of current downtown Tokyo, where people are literally on top on one another.
2. The world's population will have outstripped food production to the point that serious famine will plague the land.
3. We shall have outgrown our capacity to generate energy—even given newer energy forms such as nuclear and thermonuclear energy—to the point where brownouts and energy rationing are common.
4. Pollution will have become so bad that the air will not be fit to breathe, the water not fit to drink, or plant food fit to eat.
5. Close living quarters, shortages, and other hardships will lead to increasing conflicts between persons and nations. Wars shall be a regular occurrence.

Not a very pleasant world—the year 2000—if these predictions are even partially true!

Alvin Toffler, and other futureologists, have an equally dim view of the future.[1] Toffler argues:

1. The pace of change will quicken with dramatic new developments occurring every few years.
2. These dramatic changes will completely revolutionize our life-style, causing it to change radically every few years.
3. The pace of change will become so furious that more and more individuals will suffer from "change neuroses," a severe form of emotional disability.

So, if we survive to the year 2000, we may all be out of our heads!

Challenging these pessimistic views, several other researchers using similar computer programs draw some very different conclusions. By slightly varying the assumptions built into the model, they have concluded that:

---

[1]A. Toffler, *Future Shock*. Random House, 1970; D. Bell, (ed.), *Toward the Year 2000*. Houghton Mifflin, 1968 (This is the book version of the special issue of *Deadalus*, Summer, 1967, based on the work of the commission on the year 2000); P. Drucker, *The Age of Discontinuity*. Harper, 1968; H. Kahn, and A. Weiner, *The Year 2000*. MacMillan, 1967; O. Helmer, *Social Technology*. Basic Books, 1966; T. Gordon, and O. Helmer, *Report on a Long Range Forecasting Study*, Rand Corporation, 1964.

1. Population growth will level off, though population centers will shift, and more larger cities will emerge.
2. Food supply will not be outstripped by population growth, though there will continue to be food shortages in some parts of the world.
3. Serious pollution problems will persist with some areas becoming virtually uninhabitable.

What a difference a little change in assumption makes! One organization, The Institute for the Future in Middletown, Connecticut has developed a new technique for forecasting the future. This technique, the Delphi method, utilizes the combined "guessmates" of a large number of experts. Another technique, the Cross Impact Matrix Analysis traces the effects of innovation on society. These advanced techniques still leave much room for judgement. So, choose your own view of the future, regardless of the "research."

CAPITALIZING ON SOCIAL CHANGE

When it comes to predicting the future, most managers have long been preoccupied with financial plans and economic forecasts, nearly to the exclusion of any attempts to foresee many long-term social and political changes that can affect their operations dramatically. Yet many have found that such social shortsightedness—particularly in an age of consumer activism and societal protest can be just as costly as laxity in tracking economic trends.

General Motors Corp. and other auto makers paid dearly for failing to recognize early enough that Ralph Nader's objection to the Corvair model was a forerunner of a broad-based consumer movement for safer products and tougher liability standards. Similarly, by ignoring early warnings from environmentalists, hundreds of manufacturers were forced to retrofit plants with pollution-control gear that could have been incorporated more cheaply in the original plant design. More recently, Nestlé Co. faced a worldwide boycott of its products after it seemingly ignored the public outcry against its marketing of infant formula in underdeveloped countries where it was a far too expensive substitute for mother's milk.

Such costly mistakes, however, may at last be driving home the importance of watching social trends, and recently a number of companies have begun expanding their forecasts well beyond the realm of economics. Some have set up internal departments to predict the future social and political environment in which they will operate, while others are relying on a growing number of consultants who specialize in such crystal-ball gazing. Social predictions even are trickling into strategic plans, and line managers increasingly are called to task for not following them as closely as technical or pricing trends. The ultimate goal is to prevent unexpected social changes from wreaking havoc with profitability. As Robert L. Thaler, a senior vice-president at Security Pacific National Bank, puts it: "If we don't manage social change, change will manage us."

Cooperative Effort

While this new interest in assessing the business impact of future social changes often goes no further than informal discussions among managers, some formal forecasting programs do exist, and occasionally, they even transcend traditional corporate rivalries. For example, executives from such companies as AT&T, IBM, and Sperry—all fierce competitors—are sharing their techniques under the auspices of the Diebold Corporate Issues Program (DCIP), sponsored by Diebold Group Inc., New York-based management consultants. For nearly three years, the 20-member corporate group has been meeting periodically to discuss such questions as whether communications breakthroughs will push more employees into working at home, or how companies should change their product development techniques to anticipate any future environmental or consumer concerns.

The executives also explore changing demographics and value systems and, most important, tell each other about structures—new research departments, shifting lines of authority, and the like—they have set up within their organizations to forecast and react to social change. The group's main concern, says Robert F. Kamm, DCIP's director, is that "more and more traditionally non-P&L items are affecting profit and loss."

Corporations within and outside the DCIP are experimenting on their own with ways to keep that effect positive by focusing more closely on social trends. One popular method is "environmental scanning," which involves extensive reading of publications to identify various social and political factors that will help shape the future business environment. For example, PPG Industries Inc.

Source. Business Week, October 29, 1979.

recently hired Cynthia S. Angrist, a Carnegie-Mellon University sociologist, to fill the newly created post of manager of public policy research. She scans the publications of government agencies, public interest groups, research institutes, and other periodicals. She pays particular attention to politically extreme publications or to futurist journals, such as *Alternative Future,* all of which usually run counter to the way corporate America thinks. At management's request, Angrist also researches specific issues, such as a proposed law or an apparent cultural trend, and prepares reports on the issue's long-term ramifications for the company. Although Angrist admits that PPG has not yet managed the formal integration of social, political, and economic trends into its strategic plans, she says her weekly briefings with the company's chairman are evidence that there is "interest at the highest level."

Scanners

Still other corporations are increasingly employing outside research services and consultants specializing in the kind of scanning work that Angrist does. For example, IU International Corp. retains consultant Kurt Lewin, a New York-based economist and specialist on social and political developments abroad, and IU Vice-Chairman Robert F. Calman says Lewin has helped his company ascertain the "mood" of foreign countries. IU also uses Williams Inference Service, a private environmental scanning group, which monitors and analyzes 150 publications each week.

Calman believes that nearly every social trend that will affect business 20 years from now is being "previewed" today somewhere, and he says he employs scanners out of "fear of missing a big opportunity or stepping into a crack." Apparently, Calman's concerns are shared. Although Williams Inference has been around for 15 years, it shuffled along with about six clients for the first 11 years, then signed on nearly 60 more in the last four years alone.

Ironically, even founder James S. Williams admits that scanning reports are often read for entertainment. Nevertheless, some companies are now making organizational changes to make sure

that these reports and other social indicators are heeded by managers.

A prime example is Mead Corp.'s Human & Environmental Protection Dept. In just six years, the group has evolved from a run-of-the-mill environmental watchdog staff, sequestered in the research department, to a major part of the company's planning function. Russell E. Kross, the department's director, says it now reviews each of Mead's one- and five-year plans to make sure that they meet regulatory requirements. But in Mead's site-selection process for new plants, the company goes beyond legal issues to include such things as community sentiment. "In the past, we would say 'We've got to build here,'" Kross recalls, noting that the decision to zero in on one site was often based solely on conventional economic factors. Now, he says, Mead routinely selects three or four potential sites for new plants and evaluates each one for impact on local schools, traffic patterns, and the like before committing itself to a single site.

Hiring Its Critics

A few corporations are even eliciting the help of their critics in identifying future trouble spots. Velsicol Chemical Corp., apparently tired of its costly fights with the Environmental Protection Agency and various environmentalists, recently hired two former EPA officials and gave one of them line responsibility—complete with a full budget—to make sure that Velsicol's plants and products meet current safety standards. But a major part of their job is preventing any future problems as well. For example, Velsicol recently trucked fresh water at a cost of $1,200 a week for five months to homes in Tennessee when a preliminary report showed a possible chance that the company's landfill could contaminate wells.

A handful of companies have become downright formal about factoring social and political concerns into strategic plans. Every Wednesday, for example, 13 top vice-presidents at Security Pacific National Bank check all plans against a rundown of relevant external factors provided regularly by the 16-person in-house staff that handles the company's environmental scanning.

When that staff projected that 75% of married women will be working by 1990, the committee decided that the trend calls for more automatic teller machines, pay-by-phone setups, and automatic payroll deposits to speed up banking for busy women. Concurrently, it is looking carefully at its original plan to build more suburban branches.

All of these companies, however, still face a major hurdle in getting operating managers to think beyond the next quarter. "Managers with profit-and-loss responsibility only look at larger issues when they are dragged in kicking and screaming," admits Richard R. Mac, vice-president of corporate and government relations for Sperry Corp. Thus, Sperry, Allied Chemical Corp., and others are tinkering with traditional employee education, appraisal, and incentive plans to spur line managers to grapple with social developments.

Measuring Success

Allied has perhaps the most ambitious program. Since 1974 it has been sending high-level managers through three-day corporate ethics seminars, which deal with situations ranging from questionable gifts and payments to handling employees during a plant closing. Charles J. Bischoff, Allied's director of management resources, says the seminars will eventually include middle managers. Moreover, since 1976, Allied has included a manager's contribution to the community in evaluations for incentive bonuses. "We felt the pocketbook was a good place to attract people's attention," Bischoff says.

Measuring the results of a company's increased awareness to social trends is anything but an exact science. "We measure success by the lack of negative results," concedes DCIP's Kamm.

Still, DCIP members seem to feel they get their money's worth. J. Paul Lyet, Sperry chairman, claims that once a company indicates to its own employees that it is a positive force in the communities in which it operates, the bottom-line payout comes in lowered turnover and improved morale. But Lyet, too, stresses that concentrating on social and political factors is as important as preventive medicine. "It dawned on me," he says, "that it was external factors over which we have no control that influence the stock." As he sums it up, "I realized that many little seeds could flower into bushes of poison ivy."

Discussion Questions
1. Why is it important for firms to try to forecast the future?
2. What single issue do you feel will have the biggest impact on American corporations over the next 10 years? Why?

Mr. Frank Telson, president of the 21st Century Electronics Company, was explaining his firm's organization. "I founded this firm in 1958, when I was a professor of physics at the state university," he said. "By 1962, we were doing $20 million in business, mainly with the federal government in advanced control devices. It's still our major customer, although our control systems are used by some advanced major firms. Now we gross over $85 million per year.

"I realize that our organization may seem a bit disorganized to some," Mr. Telson states (see Figure 15.2), "but it works well for us. I have read that spans of control shouldn't be much over five or six for key executives. However, my key people are very highly skilled, and they know what they are doing. Most of them are old personal friends of mine. We've worked together for years, and I rarely have to tell them what to do. As a result, we have a few coordination problems, but generally speaking, we do all right."

The president of Advanced Systems, Inc., Mr. Walls, had a different view of this organizational problem. "We compete with 21st Century, and we feel that they have real organization problems. Our organizations are about the same size, and we sell competing hardware and systems. Our organization believes that it is critical to have just a few persons report to the president. The highly complex nature of our business means that there will be frequent consultations among key people, and I can't expect to have 15 or 20 people to coordinate at once. Our organization is thus quite narrow (see Figure 15.3); only five executives report to me. We can easily work out very complex problems this way. It is impossible to have a broad span of control at the top of a high technology, complex firm such as ours. I respect Frank Telson, but he's dead wrong on this point."

In 1969, 21st Century Electronics grossed $85 million and netted $6.5 million. Advanced Systems, Inc., grossed $94.2 million and netted $2.1 million. The former has consistently shown better profits and growth than Advanced Systems, although both companies have worked in many of the same fields and have competed closely for over a decade.

Discussion Questions
1. What are some of the differences likely to be between 21st Century and Advanced Systems in terms of type of people employed? How work is arranged?
2. Describe the probable problems faced by a manager in 21st Century.
3. Which company would you rather work in—21st Century or Advanced Systems? Why?
4. If you were king, would you order all companies to be organized the way 21st Century is? Why?

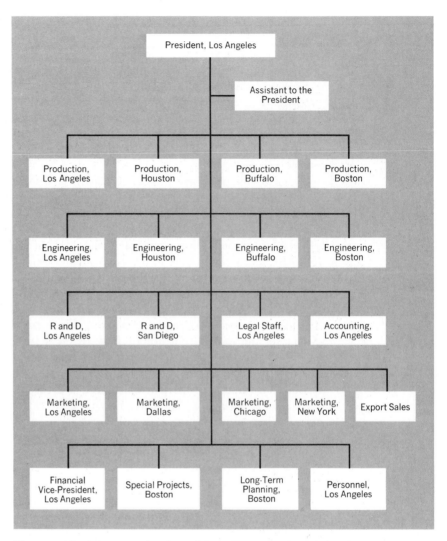

Figure 15.2 The organization of 21st Century Electronics Company.

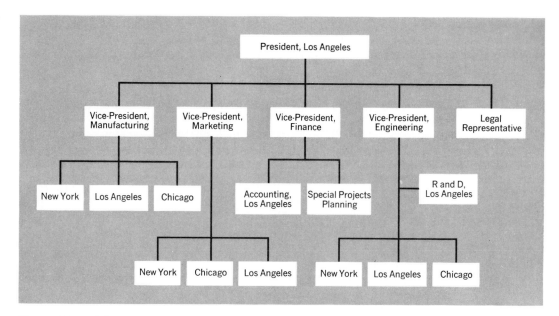

Figure 15.3 The organization of Advanced Systems, Inc.

This chapter has focused on looking 15 years ahead, what the world will be like in 1995. None of us really know, and the "experts" disagree. But with some degree of certainty, we can predict that there will be more minority and female managers, more educated employees, and more white-collar specialist-type employees. In general, most of us who work will be employed in less mechanized and in large jobs with more responsibility in decision making. We are also likely to be employed in a matrix or team-oriented organization. Those of us in management positions are likely to be more generalists rather than specialists, possess more interpersonal skills, and move through several different management careers.

Here are some principles:

1. As you move further into the future, it becomes increasingly difficult to predict that future based on an extension of the present and past.

2. As more educated specialists enter the labor force, there is a tendency toward the enlargement of jobs and the concurrent reduction in their mechanical aspects, the decentralization of decision making, and the utilization of project and matrix organization schemes.

3. As organization structure becomes more decentralized and employees more educated staff specialists, managerial positions become more generalist in orientation and stress interpersonal skills.

4. As organizations grow more complex with matrix and team concepts, managerial careers become more varied. Many careers will likely emerge requiring educational retooling.

NAME INDEX

SUBJECT INDEX